INTERNATIONAL LAW AS BEHAVIOR

This volume includes chapters from an exciting group of scholars at the cutting edge of their fields to present a multi-disciplinary look at how international law shapes behavior. Contributors present overviews of the progress established fields have made in analyzing questions of interest, as well as speculations on the questions or insights that emerging methods might raise. In some chapters, there is a focus on how a particular method might raise or help answer questions, while others focus on a particular international law topic by drawing from a variety of fields through a multi-method approach to highlight how these fields may come together in a single project. Still others use behavioral insights as a form of critique to highlight the blind spots and related mistakes in more traditional analyses of the law. Throughout this volume, authors present creative, insightful, challenges to traditional international law scholarship.

Harlan Grant Cohen is Gabriel M. Wilner/UGA Foundation Professor in International Law and Faculty Co-Director at Dean Rusk International Law Center, University of Georgia. He is an expert in international legal theory, global governance, and U.S. foreign relations law, as well as an elected member of the Board of Editors of the *American Journal of International Law* and the American Law Institute. He is co-editor of *Legitimacy and International Courts* (2018, with Grossman, Follesdal, and Ulfstein).

Timothy Meyer is Professor of Law and Director of the International Legal Studies Program at Vanderbilt University Law School. A former U.S. State Department lawyer, he is an expert in public international law. His research has appeared in the *Columbia Law Review*, the *University of Pennsylvania Law Review*, the *California Law Review*, the *Vanderbilt Law Review*, the *Journal of Legal Analysis*, and the *European Journal of International Law*.

ASIL STUDIES IN INTERNATIONAL LEGAL THEORY

Series Editors

Mark Agrast, ASIL
Mortimer Sellers, University of Baltimore

Editorial Board

The purpose of the ASIL Studies in International Legal Theory series is to clarify and improve the theoretical foundations of international law. Too often the progressive development and implementation of international law has foundered on confusion about first principles. This series raises the level of public and scholarly discussion about the structure and purposes of the world legal order and how best to achieve global justice through law. This series grows out of the International Legal Theory project of the American Society of International Law. The ASIL Studies in International Legal Theory series deepens this conversation by publishing scholarly monographs and edited volumes of essays considering subjects in international legal theory.

Books in the series

International Law As Behavior
Edited by Harlan Grant Cohen and Timothy Meyer

Space and Fates of International Law: Between Leibniz and Hobbes
Ekaterina Yahyaoui Krivenko

Why Punish Perpetrators of Mass Atrocities?: Purposes of Punishment in International Criminal Law
Edited by Florian Jeßberger and Julia Geneuss

The Challenge of Inter-legality
Edited by Jan Klabbers and Gianluigi Palombella

The Nature of International Law Miodrag A. Jovanović

Reexamining Customary International Law
Edited by Brian D. Lepard

Theoretical Boundaries of Armed Conflict and Human Rights
Edited by Jens David Ohlin

International Law As Behavior

Edited by

HARLAN GRANT COHEN
University of Georgia

TIMOTHY MEYER
Vanderbilt University

CAMBRIDGE
UNIVERSITY PRESS

University Printing House, Cambridge CB2 8BS, United Kingdom

One Liberty Plaza, 20th Floor, New York, NY 10006, USA

477 Williamstown Road, Port Melbourne, VIC 3207, Australia

314–321, 3rd Floor, Plot 3, Splendor Forum, Jasola District Centre, New Delhi – 110025, India

79 Anson Road, #06–04/06, Singapore 079906

Cambridge University Press is part of the University of Cambridge.

It furthers the University's mission by disseminating knowledge in the pursuit of education, learning, and research at the highest international levels of excellence.

www.cambridge.org
Information on this title: www.cambridge.org/9781107188433
DOI: 10.1017/9781316979792

© Cambridge University Press 2021

First published 2021

A catalogue record for this publication is available from the British Library.

Library of Congress Cataloging-in-Publication Data
NAMES: Cohen, Harlan Grant, editor. | Meyer, Timothy, 1981– editor.
TITLE: International law as behavior / edited by Harlan Grant Cohen, University of Georgia; Timothy Meyer, Vanderbilt University, Tennessee.
DESCRIPTION: Cambridge, United Kingdom ; New York : Cambridge University Press, 2020. | Series: ASIL studies in international legal theory | Includes index.
IDENTIFIERS: LCCN 2020031027 (print) | LCCN 2020031028 (ebook) | ISBN 9781107188433 (hardback) | ISBN 9781316979792 (ebook)
SUBJECTS: LCSH: International law.
CLASSIFICATION: LCC KZ3410 .I57533 2020 (print) | LCC KZ3410 (ebook) | DDC 341–dc23
LC record available at https://lccn.loc.gov/2020031027
LC ebook record available at https://lccn.loc.gov/2020031028

ISBN 978-1-107-18843-3 Hardback

For Shirlee, Bram, and Maddy.
  - HGC
For Wyatt and Cash, who have very different ways of looking at things.
  - TM

Contents

Tables

Contributors

ELENA BAYLIS, Professor of Law, University of Pittsburgh School of Law.

ANNA SPAIN BRADLEY, Professor of Law, University of Colorado School of Law.

TOMER BROUDE, Bessie & Michael Greenblatt, Q.C., Chair in Public and International Law, Faculty of Law and Department of International Relations, Hebrew University of Jerusalem; Academic Director, Minerva Center for Human Rights, Jerusalem.

HARLAN GRANT COHEN, Gabriel M. Wilner/UGA Foundation Professor in International Law and Faculty Co-Director of the Dean Rusk International Law Center, University of Georgia School of Law.

JEAN GALBRAITH, Professor of Law, University of Pennsylvania Law School.

TAMAR MEGIDDO, Post-Doctoral Fellow, Minerva Center for the Rule of Law under Extreme Conditions, University of Haifa.

TIMOTHY MEYER, FedEx Research Professor of Law and International Legal Studies Program Director, Vanderbilt University Law School.

GALIT A. SARFATY, Associate Professor and Canada Research Chair in Global Economic Governance, University of British Columbia School of Law.

RYAN M. SCOVILLE, Associate Professor of Law, Marquette University Law School.

YAHLI SHERESHEVSKY, Post-Doctoral Fellow, The Federmann Cyber Security Center, Hebrew University of Jerusalem.

ANDREW KEANE WOODS, Professor of Law, University of Arizona College of Law.

Acknowledgments

This volume grew out of a workshop held at Tillar House, the Washington DC headquarters of the American Society of International Law (ASIL), in November 2015. That workshop would not have been possible without the support of its cosponsors, the ASIL International Legal Theory Interest Group and the University of Georgia School of Law, whose financial contribution was essential. Thank you to Georgia Law Deans Rebecca White and Peter Bowman "Bo" Rutledge for greenlighting the project and for continuing to support it. Along with authors featured in this volume, that workshop benefited enormously from the involvement of Anne Van Aaken, Adam Chilton, Sungjoon Cho, Evan Criddle, Ron Levi, and Kathryn Sikkink, and their insights are reflected in various chapters of this book. We also very much appreciate the support of Mortimer Sellers, editor of the ASIL Studies in International Legal Theory Series. Finally, thanks to Vanderbilt Law School for financial support in completing the project.

This project was also featured prominently on *Opinio Juris*, and we are grateful to its contributors, in particular Chris Borgen, for sharing their platform.

Finally, we are also grateful for the assistance of Victoria Barker, Lauren Brown, Sarah Burns, Stephen Morrison, Erin Parr-Carranza, Shaniqua Singleton, and Lawrence Winsor in rounding this volume into form. Their insights and attention to detail were invaluable.

1

International Law As Behavior

An Agenda

Harlan Grant Cohen and Timothy Meyer

What does it mean to study international law as behavior? Over the past few decades, scholars in a variety of fields – economics, psychology, sociology, anthropology, and international relations, among others – have made enormous strides studying the behavioral roots of international law. Seeking a deeper understanding of international law and international relations, they have explored individual motivations, described organizational cultures, and mapped communities of practice. Taken together, the work of these scholars presents a complex, nuanced understanding of how international law works – why it succeeds and why it fails.

But these projects are rarely taken together. Separated by academic enclosures and often focused on different subfields within international law – international economic law or international criminal law, international environmental law or human rights – scholars using these different methodologies rarely talk to each other. And the impact of interdisciplinary scholarship on the practice of international law or international law doctrine, both of which continue on much as they always have, has been muted compared to domestic law.

This book's goal is to break down some of these barriers and provide a glimpse of what an international law more focused on behavior and more engaged with these other fields might look like. Section 1.1 of this chapter sets the scene, describing international law's long interest in behavior and past attempts to explore that relationship. Sections 1.2 and 1.3 describe the book's approach and lay out the contributions in each chapter. Section 1.4 starts the process of bringing these insights together, outlining a series of takeaways for future studies of international law as behavior.

1.1 THE LONG COURTSHIP

Behave. Behave! The exclamation point has a dramatic effect on that simple word, turning a neutral synonym for "act" into a command to act in a particular way, specifically, in accordance with a particular group's accepted rules. The word's double meaning instantiated in that exclamation point highlights the complex dance between law and behavior. On the one hand, law purports to control behavior; on the other hand, international law – more than most forms of domestic law – changes in response to the behavior of the governed.

Behavior is a core concern of the law. Laws are designed to shape behavior, to encourage certain actions and discourage others. As such, beliefs about behavior, whether based on folk theories and anecdotal evidence, history, big data empirical studies, psychology, sociology, or other social scientific tools, are central to thinking about the law. Lawyers, legislators, judges, and the public cannot assess the value of existing laws or the desirability of new ones without some theory, implicit or explicit, well-informed or ill-informed, of what regulated actors do and why.

This is no less true of international law, where the behavior of international actors has long been a central concern. When and why do states enter into agreements, whether legal or nonlegal? When and why will states comply with agreements, the decisions of international tribunals, or rules derived from customary practice? What constrains the behavior of international judges? What motivates military commanders and soldiers? Do investors care what international investment rules are in place when making investments in foreign countries? Spoken or unspoken theories of international behavior underpin every international regime.

International law's connection to behavior runs deeper, however, than merely asking how states and other international actors respond to a particular set of rules. International law often grants legal significance to behavioral regularities among states. Indeed, early-modern framers of international law often started with behavioral regularities. If nations seemed to follow patterns of behavior toward one another, refraining from or condemning certain acts, while engaging or encouraging others, what might explain such decisions? For many of these thinkers, empirical studies of international practice and theories of international behavior merged. Empirical studies of international practice, derived from history and current events, supported theories about how and why international actors behave. Theories of international behavior, whether derived from religion (Vitoria and Suarez),[1] morality (Grotius),[2] right-reason (Gentili),[3] or imagined natural histories (Hobbes)[4] gave meaning to the patterns visible in extant stories of the past. Eventually, versions of these accounts of international behavior became codified in international law doctrine, most notably in the customary international law's basis in general practice (requiring an empirical assessment of how states behave) and *opinio juris* (requiring a subjective assessment of why they behave that way).

Even as questions about behavior were incorporated into international law doctrine, international lawyers continued to ask questions about when, how, and why international actors act the way they do. In the period since World War II alone, scholars have developed a wide range of approaches to these questions. In the United States, building on the insights of the American Legal Realists, Myres McDougal and Harold Lasswell developed an empirically tinged sociological jurisprudence.[5] Together with Michael Reisman, they inaugurated a New Haven School of international law that emphasized how international actors actually make decisions over reading the formal rules.[6] A similar focus on empiricism emerged from the Law and Society movement.[7] Acolytes like Gregory Shaffer have developed a "New Legal Realism" for international law that emphasizes pragmatic approaches to law and governance built on sophisticated empirical study of how international actors actually behave.[8] This approach has drawn from developments in social science that use sophisticated qualitative and quantitative methods to collect and analyze data.[9]

---

[1] Francisco de Vitoria, *On the Laws of War, in* POLITICAL WRITINGS 293 (Anthony Pagden & Jeremy Lawrance eds., 1991); Francisco Suarez, *On War, in* SELECTIONS FROM THREE WORKS 800 (Gladys L. Williams et al. eds., 1995). *See also, e.g.,* Geoffrey R. Watson, *The Death of Treaty,* 55 OHIO ST. L.J. 781, 786 (1994); Cornelius F. Murphy, Jr., *The Grotian Vision of World Order,* 76 AM. J. INT'L L. 477, 482 (1982).

[2] HUGO GROTIUS, DE JURE BELLI AC PACIS LIBRI TRES (James Brown Scott ed., Francis W. Kelsey et al. trans., 1925) (1625). *See also* Benedict Kingsbury, *A Grotian Tradition of Theory and Practice? Grotius, Law, and Moral Skepticism in the Thought of Hedley Bull,* 17 QUINNIPIAC L. REV. 3, 22–23 (1997).

[3] ALBERICO GENTILI, DE IURE BELLI LIBRI TRES (John C. Rolfe trans., 1933) (1612).

[4] THOMAS HOBBES, LEVIATHAN 104 (1950) (1651).

[5] *See, e.g.,* MYRES MCDOUGAL, INTERNATIONAL LAW, POWER, AND POLICY: A CONTEMPORARY CONCEPTION (1954).

[6] W. MICHAEL REISMAN, FOLDED LIES: BRIBERY, CRUSADES, AND REFORMS 15–36 (1979). *See also* Harold Hongju Koh, *Why Do Nations Obey International Law?,* 106 YALE L.J. 2599, 2618 (1996).

[7] *See, e.g.,* Gregory Shaffer, *The New Legal Realist Approach to International Law,* 28 LEIDEN J. INT'L L. 189 (2015).

[8] *Id.; see also* Victoria Nourse & Gregory Shaffer, *Varieties of New Legal Realism: Can a New World Order Prompt a New Legal Theory?,* 95 CORNELL L. REV. 61 (2009).

[9] *See, e.g.,* Gregory Shaffer & Tom Ginsburg, *The Empirical Turn in International Legal Scholarship,* 106 AM. J. INT'L L. 1 (2012).

A more normatively tinged set of theories sought to understand international behavior as a function of legitimacy. Thomas Franck, for example, suggested that laws bearing certain indicia of legitimacy – determinacy, cohesion, adhesion, and pedigree – exerted greater "legitimacy pull" on actors and with it, compliance.[10] Jutta Brunnée and Stephen Toope drew instead on Lon Fuller's principles of legality to explain international law's normative pull on behavior.[11]

Others, including Andrew Guzman,[12] Joel Trachtman,[13] Alan Sykes,[14] and Eric Posner,[15] have drawn from economics to develop rationalist approaches that model states' behavior by imagining them as rational actors maximizing state welfare. Some in political science followed similar assumptions to develop realist or rationalist approaches to state behavior.[16] Others, like Andrew Moravcsik, developed liberal approaches focused less on the behavior of states than on the behavior of the domestic political actors fighting with each other to develop state policy.[17] For these scholars, international behavior was best understood as the product of domestic political interests. Kathryn Sikkink,[18] Martha Finnemore,[19] John Ruggie,[20] Emmanuel Adler,[21] Peter Haas,[22] and others also focused on substate actors, including those acting across, rather than within, particular states. These scholars have focused on the behavior of transnational advocacy groups, epistemic communities, and

---

[10] Thomas M. Franck, *Legitimacy in the International System*, 82 AM. J. INT'L L. 705 (1988).
[11] JUTTA BRUNNÉE & STEPHEN J. TOOPE, LEGITIMACY AND LEGALITY IN INTERNATIONAL LAW: AN INTERACTIONAL ACCOUNT (2010).
[12] *See, e.g.*, ANDREW T. GUZMAN, HOW INTERNATIONAL LAW WORKS: A RATIONAL CHOICE THEORY (2007).
[13] *See, e.g.*, JOEL P. TRACHTMAN, THE ECONOMIC STRUCTURE OF INTERNATIONAL LAW (2008).
[14] *See, e.g.*, Alan O. Sykes, *The Economic Structure of International Investment Agreements with Implications for Treaty Interpretation and Design*, 113 AM. J. INT'L L. 482 (2019).
[15] *See, e.g.*, ALAN O. SYKES & ERIC A. POSNER, ECONOMIC FOUNDATIONS OF INTERNATIONAL LAW (2013).
[16] *See, e.g.*, Barbara Koremenos, Charles Lipson & Duncan Snidal, *The Rational Design of International Institutions*, 55 INT'L ORG. 761 (2001).
[17] Andrew Moravcsik, *The Origins of Human Rights Regimes: Democratic Delegation in Postwar Europe*, 54 INT'L ORG. 217 (2000).
[18] MARGARET E. KECK & KATHRYN SIKKINK, ACTIVISTS BEYOND BORDERS: ADVOCACY NETWORKS IN INTERNATIONAL POLITICS (1998).
[19] Martha Finnemore & Kathryn Sikkink, *International Norm Dynamics and Political Change*, 52 INT'L ORG. 887, 896 (1998).
[20] John Gerard Ruggie, *The New Institutionalism in International Relations*, in CONSTRUCTING THE WORLD POLITY 45, 55 (1998).
[21] EMANUEL ADLER, COMMUNITARIAN INTERNATIONAL RELATIONS: THE EPISTEMIC FOUNDATIONS OF INTERNATIONAL RELATIONS (2005).
[22] Peter M. Haas, *Introduction: Epistemic Communities and International Policy Coordination*, 46 INT'L ORG. 1 (1992).

communities of practice[23] in bringing ideas about international law or justice from one state to another.

A series of sociological approaches developed in parallel (and sometimes in conversation) with these approaches,[24] particularly in Europe. Such sociological approaches drew on Max Weber,[25] Emile Durkheim,[26] Pierre Bourdieu,[27] and Niklas Luhmann[28] to develop accounts of international behavior focused on hermeneutics and competitions for social and political capital in legal fields. Much of the work in these veins has focused on specific areas of international practice, whether international commercial arbitration,[29] regional human rights courts,[30] or international trade negotiations.[31] Work on legal pluralism[32] in the wake of colonialism drew anthropologists like Sally Engle Merry[33] into international law and with them ethnographic methods for studying the impact of international norms on the behavior of different communities. As outlined by Galit Sarfaty, such methods have also been used to understand the workings of international organizations.[34]

---

[23] For applications to international law, see Harlan Grant Cohen, *Theorizing Precedent in International Law, in* INTERPRETATION IN INTERNATIONAL LAW (Andrea Bianchi, Daniel Peat & Matthew Windsor eds., 2015) [hereinafter Cohen, *Theorizing Precedent*]; Harlan Grant Cohen, *Finding International Law, Part II: Our Fragmenting Legal Community*, 44 N.Y.U. J. INT'L L. & POL. 1049 (2012).

[24] *See, e.g.*, MOSHE HIRSCH, THE SOCIOLOGY OF INTERNATIONAL LAW (2015).

[25] *See, e.g.*, Max Weber, *Politics as a Vocation, in* FROM MAX WEBER: ESSAYS IN SOCIOLOGY 77, 78 (H. H. Gerth & C. Wright Mills eds., 2001).

[26] *See, e.g.*, EMILE DURKHEIM, THE DIVISION OF LABOR IN SOCIETY (1933).

[27] Pierre Bourdieu, *The Force of Law: Toward a Sociology of the Juridical Field*, 38 HASTINGS L.J. 805 (1987). *See also* Yves Dezalay & Mikael Rask Madsen, *The Force of Law and Lawyers: Pierre Bourdieu and the Reflexive Sociology of Law*, 8 ANN. REV. L. & SOC. SCI. 433 (2012).

[28] NIKLAS LUHMANN, LAW AS A SOCIAL SYSTEM 213 (2004). *See also* SUNGJOON CHO, THE SOCIAL FOUNDATIONS OF WORLD TRADE: NORMS, COMMUNITY, AND CONSTITUTION (2015); GUNTHER TEUBNER, LAW AS AN AUTOPOIETIC SYSTEM (1993).

[29] BRYANT GARTH & YVES DEZALAY, DEALING IN VIRTUE: INTERNATIONAL COMMERCIAL ARBITRATION AND THE CONSTRUCTION OF A TRANSNATIONAL LEGAL ORDER (1996).

[30] *See, e.g.*, Mikail Rask Madsen, *The Challenging Authority of the European Court of Human Rights*, 79 LAW & CONTEMP. PROBS. 141 (2016).

[31] Sungjoon Cho, *Beyond Rationality: Toward a Sociological Construction of the World Trade Organization*, 52 VA. J. INT'L L. 321 (2012).

[32] *See, e.g.*, PAUL SCHIFF BERMAN, GLOBAL LEGAL PLURALISM: A JURISPRUDENCE OF LAW WITHOUT BORDERS (2012); Ralf Michaels, *Global Legal Pluralism*, 5 ANN. REV. L. & SOC. SCI. 243 (2009).

[33] *See, e.g.*, Sally Engle Merry, *Anthropology and Activism: Researching Human Rights Across Porous Boundaries*, 28 POL. & LEGAL ANTHRO. REV. 240 (2005); MARK GOODALE & SALLY ENGLE MERRY, THE PRACTICE OF HUMAN RIGHTS: TRACKING LAW BETWEEN THE GLOBAL AND THE LOCAL (2007).

[34] Galit A. Sarfaty, *Toward an Anthropology of International Law, infra* pp. 132–135 (Chapter 6 of this volume). *See also* GALIT A. SARFATY, VALUES IN TRANSLATION: HUMAN RIGHTS AND THE CULTURE OF THE WORLD BANK (2012).

Most recently, behavioral economics has brought psychology to international law, using experimental findings about cognitive biases and heuristics to try to develop more refined models of international behavior.[35]

Each of these veins of study is rich, but as each has branched off from the others, these fields of inquiry have grown farther apart, often unaware of parallel developments in the others. Moreover, few make their way to the heart of international law practice or scholarship, both of which remain dominated by doctrinal analysis. International law's engagement with these scholarly developments has been sporadic at best, an insight borrowed here or there. For various reasons, as international law has developed, deep engagement with how international actors behave has been shunted off to the corners of the field.

The decline of behavior's importance to international practice and doctrine is apparent when one compares the relatively weak influence of contemporary, behaviorally informed scholarship with the profound impact of early scholars such as Grotius, Gentili, or Hobbes. Paradoxically, it may be behavior's influence on international law doctrine – so central to the success of early theorists – that has led to the marginalization of behavioral insights today. As behavioral studies have become more varied and technical, they often require expertise that formally trained lawyers may lack. International lawyers have often responded by transforming empirical and psychological questions about international behavior into stylized matters of legal technique, bounded by legal rules and norms, and guarded by international lawyers themselves.[36] International lawyers become increasingly occupied with doctrinal debates over the relative value of this military manual or that domestic court decision, these states' actions or those states' silence as evidence of state practice and/or *opinio juris*. Engaging in those debates requires expertise in law, legal doctrine, and legal argument, rather than the science of behavior. Extralegal studies of legal questions are rendered beside-the-point doctrinally, precisely because they threaten to replace lawyers with social scientists and, in turn, law with policy.[37]

---

[35] *See, e.g.*, Anne van Aaken, *Behavioral International Law and Economics*, 55 Harv. Int'l L.J. 421 (2014); Tomer Broude, *Behavioral International Law*, 163 U. Pa. L. Rev. 4 (2015); Jean Galbraith, *Treaty Options: Towards a Behavioral Understanding of Treaty Design*, 53 Va. J. Int'l L. 309 (2013); Ganesh Sitaraman & David Zionts, *Behavioral War Power*, 90 N.Y.U. L. Rev. 516 (2015).

[36] For an effort to bring behavioral insights to bear on that stylized process, see Ryan M. Scoville, *Egocentric Bias in Perceptions of Customary International Law*, *infra* pp. 91–97 (Chapter 4 of this volume).

[37] For an interesting twist on this insight, see Sarfaty, *supra* note 34, in which she recounts how lawyers at the World Bank jealously protected legal opinions from non-Legal Department

But the stylized versions of empirics and theory embedded in modern doctrine also allow international lawyers to wave their hands at the ever-increasing complexity of each. On the empirical side, studying the behavior of international actors requires choices about whose behavior to study. Orthodox doctrine tells us to focus on the behavior of states and those who act or speak on their behalf. But practically, those may or may not be the actors whose behavior matters most in achieving international law's goals or in assessing international law's effectiveness.[38] International law covers vast swathes of policy territory from investment protection to tariffs, freedom of speech to labor standards, armed attacks to human shields, financial regulation to piracy. Depending on the topic, the most relevant actor might be a municipality or a bureaucrat, a judge or a corporate board, a general or a soldier, a banker or a fisherman. Any or all of their actions might matter. Each may be motivated in different ways. Even where our primary concern is the action of the state, those actions may be the product themselves of different actors, whether collective bodies of elected officials, military leaders, trade negotiators, or judges, each with different motivations and decision-making processes.

On the theoretical side, the methodological tools, norms, and languages of sociology, psychology, anthropology, economics, and empirics have developed to a point where rigorous study requires significant expertise. Even borrowing insights from these various fields requires enough familiarity with a methodology's specific beats to allow translation out of the field's language and into that of international law. Nor is translation across these fields any easier. The same terms may have subtly or starkly different meanings in each, and each may operate against very different assumptions.

1.2 A CONTEMPORARY PROJECT

The project of this volume is to bridge the gaps both between diverse fields engaged with the study of behavior and international law, and between these fields and more traditional international law, to imagine a study of international law behavior that looks far and wide for the tools best suited to answering the diverse set of questions contemporary practitioners and scholars face.

World Bank employees in an effort to guard their interpretative control. For a related argument that lawyers have sought to expand the sources of international law in order to enhance their control over international relations, see Jean d'Aspremont, *Softness in International Law: A Self-Serving Quest for New Legal Materials*, 19 EUR. J. INT'L L. 1075 (2008).

[38] *See* Tamar Megiddo, *The Missing Persons of International Law Scholarship*, *infra* pp. 245–255 (Chapter 9 of this volume).

What would such a unified project look like? What would be the challenges to bridging these gaps? What would be the opportunities?

Two decades ago, a number of prominent scholars[39] issued a call for a renewed dialogue between international law and international relations. Since that time, scholars in both fields have made significant progress in understanding the functioning of international law and the international system. Studies of the rational design have yielded significant insights into the shape of international agreements[40] and international organizations[41] and the choice between hard and soft law.[42] Economic analysis has helped explain cooperation[43] and compliance.[44] But while rationalist and economic analyses of international law have thrived, insights and methods from other areas of the social sciences have often been neglected, underappreciated, or at the very least siloed.

This project's goal is to expand the previous call to include the broad range of scholars studying international legal behavior. We increasingly understand how and why rational actors might develop international law and international regimes. What we need now are tools to complicate that picture by exploring how international actors actually behave, how their rationality is bounded by psychology, how they operate as members of groups and recipients of culture, and how they write and follow organizational scripts. Dialogue between these approaches should only help to enrich all of them, suggesting new paths, blind spots, and even wrong turns for each. Some of these methods will fit together well; others, whether because of initial assumptions or research styles and demands, may not. Additionally, different approaches may have an advantage depending on the specific questions about international behavior being asked. These are all questions that we explore in this volume.

[39] Kenneth W. Abbott, *Modern International Relations Theory: A Prospectus for International Lawyers*, 14 YALE J. INT'L L. 335, 337–38 (1989); Anne-Marie Slaughter, *International Law and International Relations Theory: A Dual Agenda*, 87 AM J. INT'L L. 205 (1993).

[40] Koremenos, Lipson & Snidal, *supra* note 16; Laurence Helfer, *Exiting Treaties*, 91 VA. L. REV. 1579 (2005); Timothy L. Meyer, *Power, Exit Costs, and Renegotiation in International Law*, 51 HARV. INT'L L.J. 379 (2010); Timothy L. Meyer, *From Contract to Legislation: The Logic of Modern International Lawmaking*, 14 CHI. J. INT'L L. 559 (2014).

[41] Andrew Guzman, *International Organizations and the Frankenstein Problem*, 24 EUR. J. INT'L L. 999 (2013).

[42] Kenneth W. Abbott & Duncan Snidal, *Hard and Soft Law in International Governance*, 54 INT'L ORG. 421 (2000); Andrew Guzman & Timothy L. Meyer, *International Soft Law*, 2 J.L. ANALYSIS 171 (2010).

[43] ROBERT KEOHANE, AFTER HEGEMONY (1984).

[44] GUZMAN, *supra* note 12.

Over time, this project has benefited from the insights of a broad range of senior and junior scholars taking a number of approaches to the study of international law, including: law and economics, constructivist international relations theory, the New Haven School, behavioral law and economics, sociology, psychology, anthropology, empirical methods, and neuroscience. The scholars involved have also brought insights from across international law's subfields, including trade, arms control, human rights, international humanitarian law, international criminal law, international environmental law, and international courts and tribunals. They have written on a range of international law issues, including regime design, negotiation theory, customary international law formation, soft law, and compliance. This book includes a representative subset of those scholars and topics. Others who participated in the initial project workshop included Kathryn Sikkink, Ron Levi, Sungjoon Cho, Adam Chilton, and Anne van Aaken. Their contributions to the project were invaluable and their insights appear both in this introduction and in the chapters that follow.

1.3 PLAN OF THE BOOK

This volume includes chapters from an exciting group of scholars at the cutting edge of their fields. Some chapters provide incisive overviews of the progress more established fields like anthropology have made in analyzing questions of interest to international law. Others are more speculative, suggesting the sorts of questions or insights that newer fields like neuroscience might offer. Some focus on a particular method, like behavioral psychology, the questions it might raise or help answer, and the insights it might provide. Others focus on a particular international law topic like hybrid criminal tribunals, drawing from a variety of fields through a multi-method approach to highlight how these fields might be drawn together into a single project. Still others use behavioral insights as a form of critique to highlight the blind spots in more traditional analyses of the law. All of the chapters present creative, insightful additions, and in some cases, challenges to traditional international law scholarship.

The first two chapters consider the role behavioral insights can play in the design of international institutions.

In Chapter 2, "Deadlines As Behavior in Diplomacy and International Law," Jean Galbraith explores an underappreciated phenomenon in international law: deadlines. As Galbraith explains, deadlines are ubiquitous in international law; they discipline negotiations, frame ratification decisions,

and structure compliance. And yet, they are understudied and poorly theorized. Drawing on insights on deadlines from behavioral psychology, and
using the example of the Chemical Weapons Convention, Galbraith demonstrates how such insights might reshape both treaty negotiations and treaty
substance. Importantly, Galbraith also uses the opportunity to survey some of
the challenges posed in translating insights gleaned from individuals in the
laboratory to state actors in the real world. The specific case study thus
provides a framework for future work applying behavioral psychology insights
to international law.

In Chapter 3, "Cooperating without Sanctions," Timothy Meyer explores
the role of information production in promoting international cooperation.
Surveying developments in international health and environmental law,
among other areas, Meyer notes a new trend, what he terms "epistemic
regimes." Unlike traditional compliance regimes, in which information is
used to help monitor and enforce obligations, epistemic regimes produce
shared scientific information that helps states better understand their interests
and options. Using rationalist tools, Meyer develops a series of theses about
when such information producing regimes should be desirable alternatives to
more traditional credible commitment regimes.

The next two chapters use behavioral insights to solve doctrinal puzzles
within international law.

In Chapter 4, "Egocentric Bias in Perceptions of International Law," Ryan
M. Scoville explores how insights from behavioral psychology might complicate traditional doctrinal practices within international law. Scoville focuses
on two specific cognitive biases that have been identified, the "False
Consensus Effect" (FCE) and the "False Uniqueness Effect" (FUE). Both
biases lead individuals to miscalculate how common certain views or traits are,
and Scoville posits that they may disrupt the seemingly neutral practices of
identifying customary international law from evidence of state practice and
opinio juris. Carefully considering the applicability of these biases to these
circumstances, Scoville makes a compelling case for adding such methods to
the international lawyer's toolbox. The chapter demonstrates the ways behavioral psychology can disrupt current practices and provide pathways to
doctrinal reform.

In Chapter 5, "Explaining the Practical Purchase of Soft Law," Tomer
Broude and Yahli Shereshevsky challenge existing explanations for why soft
law, despite not being binding, carries force. Focusing specifically on
references to soft law in judicial opinions, and finding rationalist explanations unsatisfying, they test the purchase of a variety of insights from
behavioral psychology, including with regard to status quo biases, pressure

to conform, and difficulties discounting information. The insights into why soft law matters have the potential to help not only understand the actions of international actors, but also to help refine the production and invocation of soft law as well.

The three chapters that follow consider insights behavioral methods can provide into the implementation and effectiveness of international regimes.

In Chapter 6, "Toward an Anthropology of International Law," Galit A. Sarfaty describes the methods of ethnographic research, the types of questions those methods are well-situated to answer, and the contributions of those methods to the study of international law. Studying culture and focused on fieldwork and interviews, ethnographic research provides insights into the behind-the-scene dynamics that help explain the place of international law within organizations and tribunals, as well as the ways in which international law norms are (or are not) transferred, translated, and internalized. These research methods emphasize complexity, deep description, and understanding. Sarfaty then provides a nuanced, illustrative case study from the World Bank, one that focuses on individuals interacting within an organizational culture with its own professional hierarchies and incentives. The study provides a stark, compelling challenge to the statist orientation of traditional international law.

In Chapter 7, "Transnational Collaborations in Transitional Justice," Elena Baylis seeks a deeper understanding of the challenges faced by hybrid criminal tribunals – tribunals that combine international and national elements. Looking beyond the norms applied or the institutional structures chosen, Baylis explores the key relationship at the heart of the hybrid tribunal model, that between the professionals from abroad, "the internationals," and the domestic professionals, "the nationals," who together staff these justice mechanisms. The success of these tribunals is contingent in many ways on the success of those relationships. Baylis combines a theoretical framework for that relationship based on theories of communities of practice with her own interviews of internationals. A sophisticated and nuanced dissection of both the types of interactions between internationals and nationals and the challenges inherent in them results in a set of positive lessons in how to make hybrid tribunals more effective.

In Chapter 8, "Advancing Neuroscience in International Law," Anna Spain Bradley explores an emerging field of behavioral study: neuroscience. Bradley explains how new technologies have provided scientists with windows on brain function that reveal mental processes different from what we had previously imagined. The newly discovered pathways and linkages challenge traditional assumptions, embedded in international law, about how a range of international actors, including international judges and diplomats, make decisions. As such, the chapter suggests new hypotheses to test about the ultimate motivators of international legal behaviors.

Finally, the last two chapters look to behavioral methods as sources of critique, providing reasons to re-center the focus of international law scholarship more generally.

In Chapter 9, "The Missing Persons of International Law Scholarship," Tamar Megiddo uses the behavioral frame as a tool of critique. Megiddo demonstrates the disconnect between law's behavioral focus on individuals, highlighted by the methodologies profiled in this volume, and the doctrinal and theoretical focus of international law on states. The pervasive statist focus on international law scholarship, she argues, obscures the ways international law actually has its influence. The result is a call for re-centering international law, not around individuals nested within states, but individuals interacting with each other within and across borders.

In Chapter 10, "The Wrong Way to Weigh Rights," Andrew Keane Woods also adopts a critical stance. For Woods, a deeper focus on international law behavior reveals the limits of current empirical work on human rights. Focused too much on measuring state action, on more easily measured rights, and on binary questions of compliance or noncompliance, many contemporary studies fail to capture both how human rights do their work and what they seek to achieve. A study of human rights based in the more diverse methodologies, including psychology and sociology, would paint a much richer, more complex picture of human rights' relative successes and challenges.

1.4 FRAMEWORKS FOR FUTURE STUDY

The chapters in this volume are varied, intriguing, and challenging, but what, if anything, binds all these disparate accounts together? Are there lessons to be learned about how these projects and methods can fit together into some greater whole?

It can be tempting to see these behavioral projects as puzzle pieces, which when assembled in the correct order, reveal a larger picture of the international order. Each brings its own insights: rational choice sets up testable, generalizable hypotheses about how states might interact given express assumptions about state behavior. Neuroscience and behavioral psychology can complicate or refine those hypotheses, while sociology and anthropology can test them against real-world scenarios, explaining why specific situations diverge from those expectations, whether as a result of social structures, culture, or human psychology. Experimental methods can help identify the actual preferences of international actors. Constructivist accounts can build upon sociology, anthropology, and psychology to explain where state preferences come from and how they change. Focused primarily on different, overlapping units of analysis – individual actors, the communities in which they practice, the culture in which they are embedded, the states on behalf of whom they act, and the larger structures in which those states are embedded – these approaches might seem like natural complements, snapshots taken from one angle, which when spliced together might provide a panoramic view of the international system. Together, these studies might provide a more complex account of the different processes, preferences, beliefs, and incentives that might drive the vast array of actors who operate in international law, whether grassroot activists, transnational norm advocates, technocratic experts, politicians, bureaucratic careerists, or diplomats.

But imagining all of these accounts as different harmonies converging in one glorious tune is too simplistic and overly optimistic; a grand theory of international legal behavior is an unrealistic goal. For one thing, these methodologies overlap considerably more than the generalizations above might suggest, sometimes offering competing answers to the same questions. But even where they are complementary, any attempt to eliminate the boundaries between methodologies faces significant hurdles.

Some of these may be discursive hurdles: different methodologies are steeped in their own languages and terminologies that structure quality work in those fields, but that might seem impenetrable to those outside it, like discussions of "field" and "practice" within sociology.[45] For Bourdieu, for example, the "field" is not just a space in which actions take place or a "particular branch of study or sphere of activity or interest,"[46] but a specific concept meant to describe a network or system of relationships between individuals who compete for specific forms of social and political capital.[47] Terms of art may also sound similar but mean different things in different methodologies, creating confusion. As Martha Finnemore noted, "sociologists use the term 'institution' in very different ways than do rational-choice scholars or historical institutionalists, emphasizing the social and

---

[45] *See generally* Jen Meierhenrich, *The Practice of International Law: A Theoretical Analysis*, 76 LAW & CONTEMP. PROBS. 1 (2014) (on definitions of practice).

[46] *See Definition of Field in English*, LEXICO, https://www.lexico.com/en/definition/field (last visited May 1, 2020).

[47] *See, e.g.*, Dezalay & Madsen, *supra* note 27, at 439; Kim Lane Scheppele, *Judges as Architects*, 24 YALE J.L. & HUMAN. 345, 350–56 (2012).

cognitive features of institutions rather than structural and constraining features."[48]

Other hurdles may be set by conflicting methodological commitments: rational choice favors parsimony, prediction, and generalizability; anthropology and sociology favor deep description. Anthropological research, Galit Sarfaty explains, "is not based on prior assumptions or models. Rather, hypotheses and theories emerge from the data, and are constantly evaluated and adjusted as the research progresses."[49] This contrasts it and methods like it with others designed specifically to test hypotheses. Beginning from such different starting points may make such contrasting approaches difficult to pursue in tandem. For example, "interviews [in anthropology] are usually unstructured or semi-structured with open-ended questions developed in response to observations and ongoing analysis,"[50] a stark contrast to the structured, carefully worded questions used in some experiments inspired by other methodologies.

Training in any of these methodologies can also create blinders, framing international law questions for researchers as ones their expertise can answer and obscuring the need for other tools. As both Andrew Woods and Tamar Megiddo argue, traditional international law and the fields closely associated with it have a statist bias and tend to focus on testable questions like compliance. Lost are different types of international law behavior that do not invoke state power and that operate in less binary ways by shifting discourse, reforming culture, or triggering advocacy.

Finally, different approaches may also create research hurdles; they may involve methods difficult to pursue at the same time or by the same scholars. Applying insights from neuroscience to the law requires expertise in brain science and emergent medical technologies. Rationalist and experimental methods may require mathematical expertise not widely shared outside of certain fields. "Ethnographic research involves case-oriented study, including long-term fieldwork and in-depth interviews," as Galit Sarfaty explains.[51] The burdens of doing such work well may make it difficult for all but the most committed to undertake.

What might be more fruitful is to think about ways different methods might relate to one another in a study of international law as behavior. The chapters in this book and prior discussion at the workshop suggest four basic models of

---

[48] Martha Finnemore, *Norms, Culture, and World Politics: Insights from Sociology's Institutionalism*, 50 INT'L ORG. 325, 326 (1996).
[49] Sarfaty, *supra* note 34.
[50] *Id.*
[51] *Id.* at p. 129.

interaction: *Collaboration, Reflective Dialogue, Burden Sharing,* and *Competition.*

1.4.1 *Collaboration*

In a model of collaboration, multiple methods might be used as part of a single effort (either by a single researcher or by collaborators with different expertise) to answer a specific question. Such multi-method approaches may be fruitful ways to answer or explore certain international law questions or phenomena. A particularly good example of such a project would be Katerina Linos' *The Democratic Foundations of Policy Diffusion*,[52] which uses public opinion experiments, cross-national statistical analysis, and specific country case studies to explore where state health and family policies come from. In this book, Elena Baylis's chapter on hybrid international tribunals comes closest to this ideal,[53] marrying theoretical insights from sociology and constructivist international relations theory with anthropologically inspired interviews of those actually staffing the tribunals. When a multi-method approach works, as it does in both those places, the whole ends up greater than the sum of its parties, with the convergence between methods itself acting as a powerful argument in favor of the thesis. Some projects, particularly ones that require understanding the actions of multiple actors facing a range of different incentives (like the emergence of precedent within international law),[54] or those where the unit of focus overlaps, may lend themselves to this kind of study.

1.4.2 *Reflective Dialogue*

A different model might be reflective dialogue. In this model, the results of parallel studies by different scholars following different approaches are used to inform or tweak each other in an effort to improve their respective results. As Jean Galbraith,[55] Ryan Scoville,[56] Tomer Broude and Yahli Shereshevsky[57] suggest, insights from behavioral psychology might be used to revise rationalist

---

[52] Katerina Linos, The Democratic Foundations of Policy Diffusion: How Health, Family, and Employment Laws Spread Across Countries (2013).

[53] Elena Baylis, *Transnational Collaborations in Transitional Justice, infra* pp. 158–190 (Chapter 7 of this volume).

[54] *See* Cohen, *Theorizing Precedent, supra* note 23.

[55] Jean Galbraith, *Deadlines as Behavior in Diplomacy and International Law, infra* pp. 19–44 (Chapter 2 of this volume).

[56] Scoville, *supra* note 36.

[57] Tomer Broude & Yahli Shereshevsky, *Explaining the Practical Purchase of Soft Law, infra* pp. 98–127 (Chapter 5 of this volume).

assumptions about doctrine, compliance, or rational treaty design. Timothy Meyer's chapter arguably represents just such an endeavor, drawing inspiration for psychological work on the use of information and "nudges" to develop a more sophisticated rationalism.[58] Insights from rational design, in turn, might provide starting points for sociological or anthropological research, to study as Galit Sarfaty suggests, "disjunctures between how laws are written and how they are implemented on the ground."[59] Insights from anthropology, sociology, or neuroscience might inform the design of experiments. Ethnographic and historical case studies may help refine constructivist theories of norm diffusion and normative change.

1.4.3 *Burden-Sharing*

A third model might be burden-sharing. Some methodological approaches are better equipped to answer some international law questions than others. Rationalist accounts may be better equipped to make general predictions about "states" than to explain specific individual decisions.[60] Anthropology, on the other hand, may be able to explain those individual decisions, but with its emphasis on deep description, may not yield many generalizable hypotheses. Controlled experiments will be easier to carry out in some contexts than others: it is easier, for example, to test the opinions of the general public than that of experts in negotiation or on the battlefield. Public opinion, though, may not readily answer the questions that concern us; public opinion might or might not have any bearing on the behavior of diplomats, or politicians, or soldiers. Different approaches may be necessary to explain the relationship between public opinion and official action and the mechanisms – elections, training, culture, the market – that might relate one to the other. As Tomer Broude has explained elsewhere, behavioral psychology may be on firmer ground describing areas of international law where individual decision-making dominates, for example, individual targeting decisions in international humanitarian law or judicial decisions.[61] But as Jean Galbraith suggests, it may need to be more tentative in describing group decisions, where individual psychological biases might be muted, or the decision-making of agents, like diplomats, who may negotiate at some remove from those directly affected by the treaties they might produce.[62]

[58] Timothy L. Meyer, *Cooperating without Sanctions*, *infra* pp. 55–72 (Chapter 3 of this volume).
[59] Sarfaty, *supra* note 34, at p. 129.
[60] *See* Andrew Keane Woods, *The Wrong Way to Weigh Rights*, *infra* pp. 271–274 (Chapter 10 of this volume).
[61] Broude, *supra* note 35.
[62] Galbraith, *supra* note 55.

We might thus ask scholars using different methods to focus on specific areas where their methods might be most powerful and suggestive. Studying international courts and tribunals, for example, we might look to rational choice to explain their design, sociology to study the practice that emerges around them (as Elena Baylis suggests here,[63] and Harlan Cohen has suggested elsewhere[64]), and behavioral psychology or neuroscience to better understand judicial votes[65] and justifications.[66] We could then daisy-chain these explanations together to explain how courts evolve from their original mandate to their current practice

1.4.4 *Competition*

Finally, we might simply encourage competition. With regard to some questions, the assumptions or biases of different methodologies may simply be too hard to reconcile. We might instead encourage the strongest, most methodologically pure responses to those research questions, allowing their possibly contradictory explanations or predictions to live side-by-side. The ideal here might be something along the lines of the classic Kurosawa film *Rashomon*,[67] which, depicting the conflicting testimony of multiple characters without commentary, forces the viewer to reconcile the stories for herself. Ideally, the viewer gains greater insight into the actual events from the overlapping accounts than might be possible from one supposedly neutral version. Taking the example of the Chemical Weapons Convention suggested by Jean Galbraith,[68] we might encourage a rationalist account of broader state actions and choices during negotiations and implementation,[69] a behavioral economics approach focused on the specific, micro-effects on negotiators and policymakers of particular psychological biases,[70] a sociological or anthropological account focused on the epistemic communities to which negotiators and policymakers belong,[71] and a constructivist approach focused on the discursive effects of the Chemical Weapons Convention on transnational advocacy and

[63] Baylis, *supra* note 53.
[64] Cohen, *Theorizing Precedent, supra* note 23.
[65] *See* Anna Spain Bradley, *Advancing Neuroscience in International Law, infra* pp. 217–220 (Chapter 8 of this volume).
[66] *See* Scoville, *supra* note 36; Broude & Shereshevsky, *supra* note 57.
[67] RASHOMON (Daiei Film 1951).
[68] *See* Galbraith, *supra* note 55.
[69] *See* Meyer, *supra* note 58 (noting the distinct games of negotiation and compliance).
[70] *See* Galbraith, *supra* note 55.
[71] *Cf.* Sarfaty, *supra* note 34; Baylis, *supra* note 53.

perceptions of the acceptable and unacceptable in international relations.[72] Placed side-by-side, the accounts may in part overlap, and may in part be inconsistent; rather than be reconciled, they may provide a deeper understanding of the complexity of international law suspended in their contradictions.

Key in considering these models is shifting away from thinking about what these methods can do and toward what particular international law question might require. These different bridging mechanisms will be better or worse suited to different international law projects and questions. What the conversation reflected in this book suggests is that figuring out how to relate these projects is something best achieved through active dialogue between the scholars pursuing them. Hopefully, this volume, showcasing the contribution each of these behavioral fields can make to the others, will be a spur to many further such collaborations.

[72] *Cf.* Megiddo, *supra* note 38; Woods, *supra* note 60.

2

Deadlines As Behavior in Diplomacy and International Law

Jean Galbraith*

In the last fifty years, empirical work in economics, psychology, sociology, and other fields has produced increasingly powerful accounts of human behavior. This work is clearly important at the individual level and often at the group level, but what does it offer for international affairs? Scholars grappling with this question must consider two issues: relevance and proof. Relevance goes to the ways in which insights developed in other settings are applicable to the conduct of international affairs and to the magnitude of their applicability. The issue of proof requires us to determine how confident we are about relevance or irrelevance. How much weight do we assign to the strength of the underlying research, to deduction, to analogy, or to other evidence of connections?

Different fields dealing with international affairs have taken different approaches. Diplomatic studies lie at one end of the spectrum. As a skim through the classic texts demonstrates, this field presumes that individual behavior matters to international affairs and has further embraced the relevance of research on individual and group behavior based on fairly low levels of proof. Fred Iklé's 1964 classic on *How Nations Negotiate*, for example, contained an entire chapter on "Personalities" and took into account existing psychological research on the bargaining process.[1] Subsequent scholars of diplomacy have similarly drawn on insights from empirical research

* I thank Anne van Aaken, Tomer Broude, Harlan Cohen, Kristina Daugirdas, Meg deGuzman, Craig Konnoth, Tim Meyer, Chuck Mooney, Jaya Ramji-Nogales, Tess Wilkinson-Ryan and participants at the ASIL Legal Theory workshop on International Law as Behavior, the Penn Law faculty workshop, and the Philadelphia JILSA summer workshop. I also thank the Penn Law library staff, especially Gabriela Femenia and Benjamin Meltzer, for terrific support on this project.
1 FRED CHARLES IKLÉ, HOW NATIONS NEGOTIATE 143–163 (1964); *see also id.* at 262–264 (devoting a third of his bibliography to work on game theory, psychological research on bargaining and expectations, and studies on labor negotiations).

conducted in other contexts.[2] They acknowledge uncertainty about relevance, but nonetheless think it worthy of inclusion among the many lenses applied to the field. As William Zartman and Maureen Berman put it, "one might well wonder about the value or applicability of this new type of evidence, and yet the proper conclusion is that much of it needs to be translated rather dismissed."[3]

International legal scholarship traditionally was less welcoming of empirically grounded research on individual and group behavior. Although scholars engaged deeply with the question of how states behave in relation to international law, they did little to connect their theories with this empirical research. Instead, they grounded their theories on observations drawn from legal practice[4] or on assumptions of instrumental rationality.[5] But over the last decade, this has changed. There is now a substantial – and rapidly growing – body of work that expressly approaches international law using insights on human behavior drawn from empirical research on individuals and groups, with special attention paid to developments in behavioral economics and cognitive psychology.[6] This new wave of international legal scholarship posits the relevance of certain of these insights and seeks to demonstrate it through a variety of methods of proof.

---

[2] For example, I. WILLIAM ZARTMAN & MAUREEN R. BERMAN, THE PRACTICAL NEGOTIATOR 4–6 (1982) (describing social scientific research on the bargaining process as an important strand of evidence for diplomacy); Jeffrey Z. Rubin, *Psychological Approach, in* INTERNATIONAL NEGOTIATION: ANALYSIS, APPROACHES, ISSUES 256–287 (Victor A. Kremenyuk ed., 2d ed. 2001) [hereinafter INTERNATIONAL NEGOTIATION]; Christer Jönsson, *Cognitive Theory, in* INTERNATIONAL NEGOTIATION, *supra.*

[3] ZARTMAN & BERMAN, *supra* note 2, at 5 (discussing several types of evidence, including empirical work from other contexts). Some scholars working more generally in international relations also draw on insights from empirical work in domestic contexts. For example, Jack S. Levy, *Loss Aversion, Framing, and Bargaining: The Implications of Prospect Theory for International Conflict*, 17 INT'L POL. SCI. REV. 179 (1996).

[4] For example, ABRAM CHAYES & ANTONIA HANDLER CHAYES, THE NEW SOVEREIGNTY (1995); Harold Hongju Koh, *Why Do Nations Obey International Law*, 106 YALE L.J. 2599 (1997); ANNE-MARIE SLAUGHTER, A NEW WORLD ORDER (2004).

[5] For example, JACK L. GOLDSMITH & ERIC A. POSNER, THE LIMITS OF INTERNATIONAL LAW (2005); ANDREW T. GUZMAN, HOW INTERNATIONAL LAW WORKS (2008).

[6] For example, Anne van Aaken, *Behavioral International Law and Economics*, 55 HARV. INT'L L.J. 421 (2014); Tomer Broude, *Behavioral International Law*, 163 U. PA. L. REV. 4 (2015); Jean Galbraith, *Treaty Options: Towards a Behavioral Understanding of Treaty Design*, 53 VA. J. INT'L L. 309 (2013); Andrew K. Woods, *A Behavioral Approach to Human Rights*, 51 HARV. J. INT'L L. 51 (2010); *see also* Ryan Goodman & Derek Jinks, *How to Influence States: Socialization and International Human Rights Law*, 54 DUKE L.J. 621 (2004); UNDERSTANDING SOCIAL ACTION, PROMOTING HUMAN RIGHTS (Ryan Goodman, Derek Jinks & Andrew K. Woods eds., 2012).

This chapter explores the potential for connections between empirical social science research on behavior in domestic contexts on the one hand, and international affairs on the other hand, by focusing on a procedural mechanism used at all levels of human society. This mechanism is deadlines. Deadlines – predetermined points in time by which actions are due to be completed – feature in almost every kind of human interaction. Indeed, the preparation of this book chapter has involved four deadlines set by the editors (all scrupulously met) and numerous self-imposed ones (none successfully met). They are essential to individual achievement, social interaction, the conduct of business, and governmental operation. In the international sphere, unfriendly deadlines were used at least as far back as the Peloponnesian War.[7] Today deadlines are an inescapable part both of the negotiation and operation of international legal regimes, as I illustrate in Section 2.1 through a case study of the Chemical Weapons Convention. There are deadlines related to the negotiation of treaties, deadlines related to the subsequent decisions of states as to whether or not to sign or ratify treaties, deadlines written into treaties that establish the boundary between compliance and noncompliance with the treaties' obligations, and other kinds of deadlines that arise in the operation of the treaty regime.

Empirical research on deadlines in other contexts has the potential to be very useful for understanding how deadlines function in international legal practice. For one thing, there is a great deal of research on deadlines in other contexts, but almost none on deadlines in international legal practice.[8] Moreover, this research in other contexts deals with different kinds of deadlines – such as negotiating deadlines, deadlines related to decisions about whether to exercise options, deadlines for project completion, and deadlines in administrative regulatory contexts – and therefore allows for fine-tuned insights with regard to specific kinds of deadlines. For another thing, as I discuss further in Section 2.2.1, aspects of this research suggest results that are not necessarily intuitive and have direct practical implications. These results come largely from experiments conducted in laboratory settings, which allow researchers to answer very precise questions with a high degree

---

[7]   Thucydides, The History of the Peloponnesian War 482–483 (Richard Crawley trans., Penguin Classics rev. ed. 1976) (describing how a Spartan leader "sent a herald to tell [the Athenians] that, if they would evacuate Sicily with bag and baggage within five days' time, he was willing to make a truce accordingly"); *see also, e.g.,* 1 *Samuel* 11:3 ("Give us seven days so we can send messengers throughout Israel; if no one comes to rescue us, we will surrender to you.").

[8]   Deadlines have received a bit more attention in diplomatic studies. *See infra* notes 84–85 and accompanying text.

of causal certainty. In these settings, psychologists have shown that deadlines can increase behavioral biases. For example, people tend to approach negotiations in more closed-minded ways once deadlines are set and be more susceptible when making decisions under deadlines as to whether choices are framed as losses or gains.

To the extent that this research has relevance for international affairs, then it could prove quite helpful for diplomats, negotiators, executive figures in international organizations, and other international actors. First, awareness of this research would make international actors more conscious of when they may be acting subject to behavioral biases and thus more capable of attempting "debiasing" strategies.[9] Second, international actors could harness insights from this research in pursuit of their substantive goals, such as drawing on insights from the domestic negotiations context in setting international negotiating deadlines or drawing on insights from domestic research on how actors respond to deadlines in determining what substantive deadlines to write into a treaty. By way of example, this research suggests that negotiators confronting complex issues should be wary of setting negotiating deadlines too early, that deadlines related to signature or ratification of a treaty can have strategic values that go beyond what a rational choice model might predict, and that international actors seeking to encourage compliance on the part of others should take into account phenomena like the planning fallacy.

Yet these practical payoffs all depend on the relevance of this research for international affairs. In Section 2.2.2, I take up the twin issues of relevance and of proof to date. I begin by drawing analogies between findings from this research and the way in which deadlines have worked or failed to work in the context of the Chemical Weapons Convention. These analogies suggest how insights from domestic social science research, if relevant, might explain aspects of the Convention and ways which it could have been improved. I then consider the issue of proof for and against relevance. This is an immensely complex question. In my view, the evidence suggests that many of the empirical findings discussed here have at least modest relevance to uses of deadlines in international affairs. But considerable uncertainty remains – and while this uncertainty could be reduced by future research, it can never be fully eradicated. Accordingly, as I turn to in Section 2.2.3, the most important question may be whether and when international actors should assume

---

[9] For a general discussion of debiasing and its potential for effectiveness, see Jack B. Soll et al., *A User's Guide to Debiasing, in* 2 WILEY-BLACKWELL HANDBOOK OF JUDGMENT AND DECISION MAKING (Gideon Keren & George Wu eds., 2016), http://papers.ssrn.com/sol3/papers.cfm?abstract_id=2455986.

relevance in the face of uncertainty. I suggest that more awareness of these issues and preliminary acceptance of their relevance would be valuable both in treaty negotiations and in practice once a treaty has been established, despite certain differences between these two contexts.

2.1 DEADLINES IN INTERNATIONAL LEGAL PRACTICE: THE EXAMPLE OF THE CHEMICAL WEAPONS CONVENTION

Deadlines are central to international legal practice. They can be found almost anywhere one looks: in the creation and entry into force of international agreements, in the terms set by international agreements, in the communications among nations and other international actors in relation to international legal obligations, in the operation of international organizations, and in the practice of international tribunals. These deadlines arise in quite different contexts and vary substantially as to their purposes and their practical pliability. In addition, these deadlines can have different kinds of legal effects. Some have no legal effect at all, such as many negotiating deadlines. Others mark a legal boundary of opportunity, such as the last date on which a particular treaty can be signed or a legal filing submitted to an international court. Still other deadlines serve as a legal line between compliance and noncompliance with international obligations, such as ultimatums given by the Security Council or reporting deadlines set out in treaties.

To illustrate these points, this section briefly highlights some uses of deadlines in relation to an important multilateral treaty: the Chemical Weapons Convention.[10] This description illustrates how actors engaged in international legal matters inevitably find themselves in the business of setting deadlines (or not setting them), working to meet deadlines (or sometimes failing to do so), and deciding what to do when they or others miss deadlines. The discussion here does not exhaust the roles that deadlines can play in international legal practice.[11] But since the Convention relies more heavily on deadlines than do

---

[10]   Convention on the Prohibition of the Development, Production, Stockpiling and use of Chemical Weapons and on their Destruction, *opened for signature* Jan. 13, 1993, 1975 U.N. T.S. 45, 32 I.L.M. 800 (entered into force Apr. 29, 1997) [hereinafter Chemical Weapons Convention].

[11]   In addition, there are other kinds of timing rules that I do not further discuss in this chapter, such as ones that operate like reverse deadlines. For example, the deal reached in 2015 between major powers and Iran regarding nuclear weapons and sanctions includes some dates by which Iran can begin to undertake certain activities (such as increasing its research and development regarding uranium enrichment after eight years have passed). *See* Joint Comprehensive Plan of Action Between the EU/E3+3 and Iran, July 14, 2015, https://www.europarl.europa.eu/cms data/122460/full-text-of-the-iran-nuclear-deal.pdf.

many other international regimes, this discussion does showcase a variety of ways in which deadlines can be used.

2.1.1 *Negotiation of the Convention*

Negotiations for the Chemical Weapons Convention occurred over many years,[12] and, strikingly, there seems to have been little emphasis on negotiating deadlines until near the end of the process. Discussions began during the late 1960s, when the Cold War superpowers signaled their openness to conversations about disarmament of biological and chemical weapons. A 1925 treaty already prohibited the use of such weapons in war, but it did not address disarmament and in any event had not attracted comprehensive ratification.[13] Under the auspices of a UN disarmament group that included both the United States and the Soviet Union, the Biological Weapons Convention was negotiated by 1971. The text of this treaty contained substantive obligations only with respect to biological (rather than chemical) weapons, but it did require state parties to "continue negotiations in good faith" with regard to chemical weapons.[14] These negotiations did continue, but for a long time did so without any emphasis on reaching conclusion. In the mid to late 1980s, the negotiating process picked up, and the General Assembly began to pass resolutions urging the "final elaboration of a convention at the earliest possible date."[15] Finally, in May 1991, President George H. W. Bush announced the intention of the United States to "call for setting a target date to conclude the convention and recommend the Conference [on

---

[12] For a detailed history of the negotiations up to 1990, see THOMAS BERNAUER, THE PROJECTED CHEMICAL WEAPONS CONVENTION: A GUIDE TO THE NEGOTIATIONS IN THE CONFERENCE ON DISARMAMENT (1990). *See also* Julian Perry Robinson, *The Negotiations on the Chemical Weapons Convention: A Historical Overview*, in THE NEW CHEMICAL WEAPONS CONVENTION: IMPLEMENTATION AND PROSPECTS 17, 17–36 (M. Bothe et al. eds., 1998) [hereinafter NEW CHEMICAL WEAPONS CONVENTION].

[13] The treaty mentioned is the Protocol for the Prohibition of the Use in War of Asphyxiating, Poisonous or Other Gases, and of Bacteriological Methods of Warfare, June 17, 1925, 26 U.S.T. 571, 94 L.N.T.S. 65. Many states had attached reservations reserving the right to retaliate in kind if they were the victims of chemical or biological warfare and the United States did not even become a party until 1975, after the Vietnam War. BERNAUER, *supra* note 12, at 12, 15.

[14] Convention on the Prohibition of the Development, Production and Stockpiling of Bacteriological (Biological) and Toxin Weapons and on Their Destruction art. IX, Apr. 10, 1972, 1015 U.N.T.S. 163.

[15] G.A. Res 41/58, ¶ D.3 (Dec. 3, 1986) (further urging the negotiators to submit a draft convention by the next General Assembly session); *see also* G.A. Res 42/37 (Nov. 30, 1987); G.A. Res. 45/57 (Dec. 4, 1990).

Disarmament] stay in continuous session if necessary to meet the target."[16] The negotiators then embraced a target deadline of one last year of negotiations. This was not a deadline with legal effect, but after this point the negotiations sped along. The final version of the treaty was sent to the General Assembly in September 1992.[17]

2.1.2 *Entry into Force of the Convention*

The Convention provided that it would enter into force 180 days after it received its sixty-fifth ratification.[18] The date the Convention entered into force – ultimately April 29, 1997 – served as a deadline for several kinds of legal opportunities. For example, it marked the end of the Convention's availability for signature.[19] This was mostly a matter of symbolism, as accession remained an option after the Convention entered into force.[20] Nonetheless, it triggered action: while the overwhelming majority of signatories signed in 1993, which was the year the Convention opened for signature, four out of the eleven subsequent signatures were added in the single month of April 1997.[21]

The entry-into-force date also served as a deadline in more important ways. In the United States, it galvanized the Convention's supporters from President Clinton on down to strive for the advice and consent of two-thirds of the Senate, which is a prerequisite to ratifying treaties made through the process set out in Article II of the US Constitution.[22] In testimony before the Senate Foreign Relations Committee on April 8, 1997, Secretary of State Madeline

---

[16]   President George H.W. Bush, Statement on Chemical Weapons, *in* 1 PUBLIC PAPERS OF THE PRESIDENTS OF THE UNITED STATES: GEORGE H.W. BUSH 503 (1991).

[17]   Robinson, *supra* note 12, at 29–30.

[18]   Chemical Weapons Convention, *supra* note 10, at art. XXI, ¶ 1 (further providing a two-year minimum between its opening for signature and its entry into force).

[19]   *Id.* at art. XVIII.

[20]   *Id.* at art. XX.

[21]   Author's calculations from *Chapter XXVI: Disarmament*, UNITED NATIONS TREATY COLLECTION, https://treaties.un.org/pages/ViewDetails.aspx?src=TREATY&mtdsg_no=XXVI-3&chapter=26&lang=en (a record of the signatures on the Chemical Weapons Convention, which lists a total of 165 signatories, 154 of whom signed in 1993).

[22]   U.S. CONST. art. II, § 2, cl. 2. For a description of how "with its back against the wall" the Clinton Administration collected endorsements from leading Republicans, cut side-deals with key Republican Senate leaders, and pushed the treaty through the Senate, see John V. Parachini, *U.S. Senate Ratification of the CWC: Lessons for the CTBT*, 5 NONPROLIF. REV. 62, 65–68 (1997). *See also, e.g.*, Steven Lee Myers, *Clinton Mobilizes Bipartisan Effort on Chemical Arms*, N.Y. TIMES (Apr. 5, 1997), http://www.nytimes.com/1997/04/05/world/clinton-mobilizes-bipartisan-effort-on-chemical-arms.html (describing how "[t]he deadline of April 29 has given the issue a sense of urgency").

Albright powerfully described this date as a deadline which had legal and practical effects that should inspire the Senate into action:

> The CWC will enter into force on April 29. Our goal is to ratify the agreement before then so that America will be an original party. . . .
> [I]f we fail to ratify the agreement by the end of April:
>
> - we would forfeit our seat on the treaty's Executive Council for at last one year, thereby costing us the chance to help draft the rules by which the Council will be enforced;
> - we would not be able to participate in the critical first sessions of the Organization for the Prohibition of Chemical Weapons, which monitors compliance;
> - we would lose the right to help administer and conduct inspections; and
> - because of the trade restrictions imposed on non-member states, our chemical manufacturers are concerned that they would risk serious economic loss.[23]

This rhetorical use of the entry-into-force date as a deadline exaggerated its actual importance. Albright's first concern was legitimate, although in practice the real deadline for it was likely a week or so later than the entry-into-force date.[24] The second and third concerns were not consequences of missing the entry-into-force date, but rather were more general consequences of not being party to the treaty. Finally, as for the trade concerns alluded to, these would at first have applied only to chemicals used almost exclusively for chemical warfare and presumably thus not for the kinds of chemicals that US manufacturers were exporting in practice.[25]

---

[23] Secretary of State Madeleine K. Albright, Statement before the Senate Foreign Relations Committee on Chemical Weapons Convention (Apr. 8, 1997), http://1997-2001.state.gov/www/statements/970408.html (further adding "I have heard the argument that the Senate really need not act before April 29. But as I have said, there are real costs attached to any such delay.").

[24] The Conference of State Parties met for its first session on May 6, 1997 and selected its Executive Council not long after that. *See Report of the Organisation on the Implementation of the Convention* 1, 3 ORG. PROHIBITION CHEM. WEAPONS (OPCW) (1998), https://www.opcw.org/sites/default/files/documents/CSP/C-III/en/C-III_3-EN.pdf [hereinafter OPCW 1998 Report].

[25] Chemical Weapons Convention, *supra* note 10, at Annex on Implementation and Verification art. VI. *See also* Thilo Marauhn, *National Regulations on Export Controls, in* NEW CHEMICAL WEAPONS CONVENTION, *supra* note 12, at 487, 490–492 (explaining how these restrictions at first applied only to Schedule 1 chemicals, with restrictions on transfers of Schedule 2 and potentially Schedule 3 chemicals to be phased in later).

Yet the impetus of the deadline proved "critical to moving the US process of ratification"[26] at a time when the Senate declined to act on other major but somewhat controversial multilateral treaties. The Senate advised and consented to the treaty 74–26 on April 24, 1997.[27] The United States ratified the Convention the next day, becoming one of fourteen countries to ratify in the week leading up to the Convention's entry into force.[28]

2.1.3 *Deadlines in the Text of the Convention*

The Convention was designed to achieve not only state commitment, but also state compliance. Its text is permeated with deadlines – indeed, it is impossible to imagine how the Convention could function without them. There are deadlines by which nations are to take certain actions, most notably for completing the destruction of their chemical weapons and of their production facilities for these weapons.[29] There are deadlines related to the inspection process.[30] There are reporting deadlines for state parties.[31] There are procedural deadlines related to how the international organization established by the Convention will operate.[32] And there are other kinds of deadlines as well.[33]

Unlike the negotiating deadlines and the entry-into-force deadline, most of these deadlines mark the legal line between compliance and noncompliance. Those countries that have failed to meet these deadlines are in violation of

---

[26]   Parachini, *supra* note 22, at 62.

[27]   Adam Clymer, *Senate Approves Pact on Chemical Weapons After Lott Opens the Way*, N.Y. TIMES (Apr. 25, 1997), http://www.nytimes.com/1997/04/25/world/senate-approves-pact-on-chemical-weapons-after-lott-opens-way.html.

[28]   Author's calculations from *Chapter XXVI: Disarmament*, *supra* note 21 (including Cuba, which ratified on the entry-into-force date).

[29]   Chemical Weapons Convention, *supra* note 10, at art. IV(6) (providing that destruction is to be completed within ten years of the Convention's entry into force for countries that are parties to the convention during that period); *id.* at art. V(8) (providing similar deadlines for the destruction of production facilities); *see also id.* Annex on Implementation and Verification IV(A).C.24–26 (allowing the deadlines for destruction to be extended to up to five more years under certain conditions).

[30]   *Id.* at art. IX (providing very detailed deadlines that are triggered when state parties raise certain concerns or request inspections with regard to other state parties).

[31]   For example, *id.* at art. III(1) (initial declarations due within thirty days of the Convention's entry into force); *id.* at art. IV(7) (specifying various other reporting deadlines); *id.* at art. V(9) (more reporting deadlines).

[32]   *Id.* at art. VIII(B) (providing deadlines by which certain sessions must occur and by which certain reviews of the Convention must happen); *id.* at art. VIII(D) (39) (providing a deadline for the Technical Secretariat to undertake certain steps).

[33]   For example, *id.* at art. X(8)–(9) (identifying the deadline-laden process that a state party can invoke if it believes chemical weapons have been used against it); *id.* at art. XV (identifying deadlines in relation to the amendment process).

international law. In particular, the United States and Russia have violated the
Convention's deadlines for the destruction of chemical stockpiles.[34] The
Convention requires state parties to destroy their chemical weapons, beginning "no later than two years after this Convention enters into force" for the
parties and "finish[ing] not later than 10 years after entry into force of this
Convention," with certain intermediate deadlines as well.[35] There was also
a possible further extension of up to five years.[36] These deadlines were, in the
later words of one US official:

> inserted into the text with the vigorous support of the United States. With the
> information then available to us and the program projections then being
> used, the deadlines offered what we judged as a very safe margin [for the
> United States] while not allowing other states to procrastinate indefinitely in
> their own destruction programs.[37]

But long before April 2012, the United States knew that it was not going to meet
these deadlines, apparently due to a combination of environmental issues, not-
in-my-backyard community concerns, and funding limitations.[38] It made
a deliberate choice to be noncompliant rather than to ramp up its efforts to
ensure compliance or to seek amendment of the Convention.[39] In essence, US
officials appear to have calculated that as long as the United States continued
making genuine, good-faith progress toward the destruction of chemical
weapons, it could absorb the normative and reputational consequences of an
international legal violation.[40] By about 2014, The United States had destroyed

[34] *See generally* David A. Koplow, *Train Wreck: The U.S. Violation of the Chemical Weapons
Convention*, 6 J. NAT'L SEC. L. & POL'Y 319 (2013) (providing an excellent account of the US
noncompliance and also describing the noncompliance of Russia and certain other parties).
[35] Chemical Weapons Convention, *supra* note 10, at art. IV(6) (adding that "A State Party is not
precluded from destroying such chemical weapons at a faster rate."); *id.* at Annex on
Implementation and Verification IV(A).C.17–26. The annex also includes intermediate deadlines; thus, each country is to destroy at least 1 percent of Category 1 chemical weapons within
three years of the entry into force, 20 percent within five years, and 45 percent within seven
years. *Id.* at Annex on Implementation and Verification IV(A).C.17.
[36] *See id.* at Annex on Implementation and Verification IV(A).C.17–26.
[37] Donald A. Mahley, Deputy Assis. Sec'y for Arms Control Implementation, Statement on
Chemical Weapons Demilitarization Before the Senate Armed Services Committee's
Subcommittee on Emerging Threats and Capabilities (Apr. 11, 2005), http://2001-2009
.state.gov/t/ac/rls/rm/44633.htm [hereinafter Mahley Statement]; *see also* Koplow, *supra*
note 34, at 328 n.58, 333 n.84 (providing additional evidence of U.S. confidence at the time
of ratification in its ability to meet the deadlines).
[38] Koplow, *supra* note 34, at 334–338.
[39] Mahley Statement, *supra* note 37.
[40] *Id.* (stating that "I do not believe that we will damage our international influence fatally, if we
have not completed our destruction by the deadline, so long as we are continuing to devote
obvious and extensive efforts and resources to the program and so inform the other parties.");

around 90 percent of the stockpile it declared in the 1990s, and Russia had destroyed around 60 percent of its declared stockpile.[41]

2.1.4 *Supplemental Deadlines*

In addition to the deadlines written into the Convention itself, practice under the Convention can give rise to other deadlines. Events regarding Syria provide an especially prominent example. After the use of chemical weapons in Syria in 2013, a diplomatic resolution was reached whereby Syria acceded to the Convention and committed to destroying its chemical weapons. The time frame developed for destruction involved a series of distinct deadlines: mustard gas was to be removed from Syria by December 31, 2013 and destroyed elsewhere by March 31, 2014; other declared chemicals were to be removed from Syria by February 5, 2014 and destroyed by June 30, 2014; and other deadlines were provided for containers and production facilities.[42] Syria did not fully comply with these deadlines, did not declare all its chemical weapons, and continues to carry out egregious attacks using chemical weapons.[43] Nonetheless, these deadlines proved important in measuring and drawing salience to Syria's degree of compliance with respect to its declared chemical weapons[44] – and thus likely improved the effectiveness of the process. By August 28, 2014, 94 percent of Syria's declared chemical weapons stockpile had been destroyed.[45]

    see generally Koplow, *supra* note 34 (describing and analyzing the approach taken by the United States).

[41] *See* Guy Taylor, *Foot-Draggers: U.S. and Russia Slow to Destroy Own Chemical Weapons amid Syria Smackdown*, WASH. TIMES (Sept. 22, 2013), http://www.washingtontimes.com/news/2013/sep/22/us-and-russia-press-syria-but-are-slow-to-destroy-/?page=all#pagebreak. The United States and Russia are not the only nations having difficulty with the timely destruction of chemical weapons – for example, under the Convention Japan has an obligation to destroy chemical weapons that it left in China during World War II, and this destruction is moving slowly. *See* Koplow, *supra* note 34, at 352.

[42] *Decision on Detailed Requirements for the Destruction of Syrian Chemical Weapons and Syrian Chemical Weapons Production Facilities* 3, OPCW (Nov. 15, 2013), http://www.opcw.org/fileadmin/OPCW/EC/M-34/ecm34deco1_e_.pdf.

[43] *See* Anne Barnard & Michael R. Gordon, *Worst Chemical Attack in Years in Syria; U.S. Blames Assad*, N.Y. TIMES (Apr. 4, 2017), https://www.nytimes.com/2017/04/04/world/middleeast/syria-gas-attack.html.

[44] For example, news coverage of Syria's compliance with its agreement tended to be more intense around the time of deadlines and focused heavily on the deadlines. For example, Rick Gladstone, *Syria to Miss Deadline on Weapons, Official Says*, N.Y. TIMES (May 28, 2014), http://www.nytimes.com/2014/05/29/world/middleeast/chemical-weapons-syria.html.

[45] Press Release, OPCW, All Category 1 Chemicals Declared by Syria Now Destroyed (Aug. 28, 2014), http://www.opcw.org/news/article/opcw-all-category-1-chemicals-declared-by-syria-now-destroyed/.

2.2 DEADLINES AND BEHAVIOR: RESEARCH AND CONUNDRUMS

Deadlines abound in domestic affairs, just as they do in international ones. Indeed, they are probably even more pervasive – and they are certainly much more studied. There is an impressive body of empirical research on deadlines in various domestic contexts involving individual and group decision-making, including deadlines for negotiations, deadlines for deciding whether to take specific actions, deadlines by which projects are due to be completed, and deadlines in the administrative law context. Interestingly, this research suggests that people tend to set and respond to deadlines in ways that reveal behavioral biases rather than perfect rationality. As one literature review bluntly puts it, "[g]iven the value of deadlines and how frequently people encounter them, it is surprising that people are poor at setting optimal deadlines for themselves."[46]

This section first engages with some of this social scientific research on deadlines, describing empirical work on deadlines in relation to negotiations, to choosing to take specific actions, to project completion, and to governmental regulation. It then considers what relevance this research might have for similar types of deadlines in international affairs by returning to the example of the Chemical Weapons Convention. It next takes up the question of how much proof we have of relevance or irrelevance. Finally, it considers the extent to which, in the absence of strong proof, practitioners in diplomacy and international law should care about domestic social science research on deadlines.

2.2.1 *Empirical Research on Deadlines in Domestic Settings*

Deadlines are essential to human activity. They set priorities among different projects, coordinate activity among multiple actors, measure and incentivize compliance, and generally further action where delay is costly. Yet deadlines are a double-edged sword, as the values of avoiding delay are paired with the costs that come with haste. Moreover, both the gains and the costs depend on human behavior in relation to deadlines – and especially on how rational people are in setting deadlines and in responding to them.

In what follows, I briefly describe some empirical research on deadlines in four distinct contexts – negotiation, deciding whether to take action, project

---

[46] Don A. Moore & Elizabeth R. Tenney, *Time Pressure, Performance, and Productivity, in* LOOKING BACK, MOVING FORWARD: A REVIEW OF GROUP AND TEAM-BASED RESEARCH 305, 316–317 (Margaret Neal & Elizabeth Mannix eds., 2012).

completion, and administrative law. More particularly, I focus on work which suggests that deadlines can trigger or exacerbate the cognitive biases that broader research in psychology and behavioral economics has shown to exist. I thus do not address the pros and cons of deadlines under a theoretical framework grounded in rational choice. I also omit considerable bodies of research (such as work in cultural studies), and even with respect to work on deadlines in psychology and behavioral economics, my discussion is far from comprehensive.

2.2.1.1 Negotiation

Perhaps the area in which deadlines have received the most study has been negotiations between individuals. Lab experiments have studied many aspects of time pressure of negotiations, including how it affects strategy,[47] how it affects concessions and perceptions of concessions,[48] and how it affects the quality of agreements. One important and well-substantiated result is that time constraints lead to less innovative negotiations – that is, to negotiations that focus on dividing the pie rather than identifying ways to increase its size.[49] More focused work suggests that this result does not simply reflect the fact that less time provides less opportunity for thinking of creative solutions. Instead, it stems at least partly from a cognitive shift: when people feel themselves under time pressure, they are more likely to close off their minds and rely on preexisting assumptions.[50]

---

[47] For example, Uri Gneezy et al., *Bargaining under a Deadline: Evidence from the Reverse Ultimatum Game*, 45 GAMES & ECON. BEHAV. 347 (2003) (finding in lab experiments that individuals take advantage of strategic possibilities presented by deadlines – such as by trying to make offers close enough to deadlines that they force binary options upon their negotiating partners – but don't do so as much as rational choice predictions would suggest).

[48] For example, Igor Mosterd & Christel G. Rutte, *Effects of Time Pressure and Accountability to Constituents on Negotiation*, 22 INT'L J. CONFLICT MGMT. 227 (2000) (finding in lab experiments that when acting under time pressure negotiators are more likely to make concessions on their own behalf but less likely to make them on behalf of their principals); Don. A Moore, *Myopic Biases in Strategic Social Prediction: Why Deadlines Put Everyone Under More Pressure Than Everyone Else*, 31 PERSON. & SOC. PSYCHOL. BULL. 668 (2005) (finding in lab experiments that people tend to overestimate the degree to which their own deadlines will harm them in the negotiating process).

[49] *See* Carsten K. W. De Dreu, *Time Pressure and Closing of the Mind in Negotiation*, 91 ORG. BEHAV. & HUM. DECISION PROCESSES 280, 280–282 (2003) (reviewing the literature on this issue).

[50] *Id.* at 286–290. This experiment gave two groups of subjects exactly the same amount of time for a negotiation, but told one group that this time was more than enough to complete the negotiation and told the other group that this time limit would make things tight. Negotiating

2.2.1.2 Deciding Whether to Take Action

In the individual decision-making context, research suggests that deadlines encourage people to take action.[51] Research also suggests that deadlines magnify the power of heuristics. As one literature review puts it, "Decision makers under time pressure . . . are less likely to revise their initial impressions, are less likely to deviate from habitual modes of attribution, are more likely to rely on cognitive heuristics, are less accurate, and are less confident in the accuracy of their decisions."[52] Where a deadline prevents an individual from gathering and absorbing all the information she would ideally like to have in order to make a decision, then reliance on heuristics may sometimes be a rational strategy.

But research suggests that deadlines may also increase the power of irrational biases as well. One of the core insights in behavioral economics is that people can be responsive to framing effects. For example, they may respond differently to the same event depending on whether this event is characterized as a gain or a loss, because their aversion to perceived losses is greater than their pleasure at perceived gains.[53] Time pressure appears to magnify framing effects in relation to loss aversion. In one lab experiment, each subject was asked how likely it was that he/she would tell a potential buyer of a stereo that another offer had also been received, when in fact there was no such other offer.[54] For some subjects, the instructions framed the transaction as a gain (they had a "25 percent chance of gaining" a sale) while for other subjects the instructions framed the transaction as a way to avoid a loss (they had a "75 percent chance of losing out on" a sale).[55] Where the subjects were encouraged to respond as quickly as possible, they showed high susceptibility to the framing effects. Those for whom the transaction was framed as a loss were significantly more likely to answer that they would claim another offer had been received.[56]

---

pairs from the group told that that time limit would make things tight proved significantly less likely to come to innovative agreements that grew the pie.

[51] *See* Eyal Zamir et al., *It's Now or Never! Using Deadlines as Nudges*, 42 Law & Soc. Inquiry 769 (2017) (finding that individuals are more likely to take action when asked to do so under a deadline in contexts such as providing optional feedback).

[52] Moore & Tenney, *supra* note 46, at 307–308 (citations omitted).

[53] For example, Daniel Kahneman & Amos Tversky, *Choices, Values, and Frames*, 39 Am. Psychol. 341, 343–344 (1984); William Samuelson & Richard Zeckhauser, *Status Quo Bias in Decision Making*, 1 J. Risk & Uncertainty 7, 35–36 (1988).

[54] Mary C. Kern & Dolly Chugh, *Bounded Ethicality: The Perils of Loss Framing*, 20 Psychol. Sci. 378, 381 (2009).

[55] *Id.*

[56] *Id.* By contrast, the frames in this experiment had basically no effect for subjects who were told to take their time in answering.

2.2.1.3 Project Completion

Research from a variety of contexts suggests that individuals and groups suffer from a "planning fallacy" of overoptimism about how long it takes to get things done.[57] Deadlines are often essential to generating action, even though people do not always meet them. Yet deadlines do not always work quite in the ways we might rationally predict. Although one might think that individuals do better with maximum flexibility (since then they have the most options for how to rationally allocate their time), the existence of intermediate deadlines can noticeably improve performance. One field experiment by Dan Ariely and Klaus Wertenbroch gave proofreaders three error-laden texts to read and randomly assigned them to one of three conditions: first, where all three texts were due back at the end of three weeks, second, where one text was due back a week for three weeks; and third, where the proofreaders set their own deadlines (with an outer limit of three weeks).[58] The proofreaders with the assigned weekly deadlines caught the most errors, the proofreaders with the single deadline after three weeks caught the least errors, and the group with self-imposed deadlines performed in the middle.[59]

Other research suggests that the first intermediate deadline can play an outsized role in setting the pace on a project. In one laboratory experiment, small groups were given the same total amount of time to complete a project, but were randomly assigned to different sets of intermediate deadlines.[60] Thus, one set of groups had first five minutes, then ten minutes, then twenty minutes for an anagram-solving project, while the other set of groups had first twenty minutes, then ten minutes, then five minutes for the same project. The first set of groups – the ones given shorter initial deadlines – were more substantially productive than

---

[57] DANIEL KAHNEMAN & AMOS TVERSKY, INTUITIVE PREDICTION: BIASES AND CORRECTIVE PROCEDURES 2 (1977); Roger Buehler et al., *Collaborative Planning and Prediction: Does Group Discussion Affect Optimistic Biases in Time Estimation*, 97 ORG. BEHAV. & HUM. DECISION PROCESSES 47 (2005) (finding the planning fallacy to exist in group predictions in both laboratory and real-world projects and to be even stronger than with regard to individual predictions).

[58] Dan Ariely & Klaus Wertenbroch, *Procrastination, Deadlines, and Performance: Self-Control by Precommitment*, 13 PSYCHOL. SCI. 219 (2002) (also conducting a similar experiment with term papers by executive-education students).

[59] *Id.* at 222–223.

[60] Joseph E. McGrath et al., *The Social Psychology of Time: Entrainment of Behavior in Social and Organizational Settings*, 5 APPLIED SOC. PSYCHOL. MANUAL 21, 30–31 (1984).

the second set of groups.[61] Several other laboratory experiments have found similar "rate persistence."[62]

2.2.1.4 Regulatory/Legal Deadlines

The deadlines discussed so far in this section have mostly been small-stakes affairs and it is hard to know the extent to which they scale-up to matters of great importance. In addition, these deadlines have also not carried the force of law, and it may be that the normative or practical risks of legal violations trigger different behavioral instincts (or at least different magnitudes). Although research on legal deadlines is more limited, there is some observational work on their role, particularly in US regulatory law. In keeping with the other findings on deadlines, this research suggests that deadlines are often not used to best effect. Regulatory deadlines set in statutes are frequently far too overoptimistic. Agencies often miss legal deadlines, and even when they make the deadlines it is sometimes at the expense of other tasks that lack deadlines but that may in fact have more substantive importance.[63] In one case study of EPA decision-making under deadlines, Philip Bromily and Alfred Marcus found that time pressure imposed by deadlines combined with agency habits of routine in ways that minimized innovation.[64] Their account bears considerable resemblance to the findings described above in the individual context regarding how deadlines can close minds and overly increase reliance on preexisting heuristics.

2.2.2 *Behavioral Research and International Legal Practice*

What if anything does this behavioral research on deadlines tell us about international legal practice? This section takes up this question – first in an

---

[61] *Id.*

[62] Moore & Tenney, *supra* note 46, at 315–316.

[63] Alden F. Abbot, *The Case Against Federal Statutory and Judicial Deadlines: A Cost-Benefit Appraisal*, 39 ADMIN. L. REV. 171, 181–183 (1987); *see also* Jacob E. Gersen & Anne Joseph O'Connell, *Deadlines in Administrative Law*, 156 U. PA. L. REV. 923, 973–975 (2008) (considering how deadlines may distort agency priorities in undesirable ways); Daniel Carpenter et al., *The Complications of Controlling Agency Time Discretion: FDA Review Deadlines and Postmarket Drug Safety*, 56 AM. J. POL. SCI. 98 (2012) (finding that drugs approved right before FDA statutory deadlines tend to have more safety problems than drugs approved at other times, and concluding that this is likely due to differences in time pressure).

[64] Philip Bromiley & Alfred Marcus, *Deadlines, Routine, and Change*, 20 POL'Y SCI. 85, 87–93 (1987). *But see id.* at 93–98 (finding that deadlines helped trigger more substantial changes where there was a preexisting period of turmoil).

indirect manner, and then in a more direct one. I begin indirectly by assuming the relevance of this research and considering what it might suggest about the use of deadlines in the Chemical Weapons Convention. This discussion is meant as an example of how insights from this research, if relevant, could be useful in international legal design. I then turn directly to the question of how much proof we have of the relevance of these insights.

2.2.2.1 The Chemical Weapons Convention's Deadlines in Light of Behavioral Research on Deadlines

As discussed earlier, the Chemical Weapons Convention has involved many different kinds of deadlines – including negotiating deadlines, deadlines for exercising legal options, and legally binding deadlines for project completion. There are interesting parallels between the roles played by these various deadlines and the research described above – which, as noted, has different implications for different types of deadlines.

First, returning to the negotiation of the Convention, it is notable how little emphasis there was on deadlines until near the end of the process. If we assume the relevance of the behavioral research discussed above, we would expect that this furthered the likelihood that the negotiations would produce an innovative, surplus-producing agreement. Because of the absence of deadlines in the formative years of the negotiations, time pressure is unlikely to have served either as an objective constraint or as a subjective constraint that caused the closing of minds. And, indeed, in the Chemical Weapons Convention we see a remarkably creative agreement by international legal standards. It is "unprecedented in its scope"[65] and contains a robust and unusual compliance scheme.[66]

Second, considering the ratification of the Convention by the United States, it is striking how significant the entry-into-force date proved to this decision-making process. As discussed earlier, the practical importance of meeting this deadline was modest at best, but its power as a rallying force

---

[65] William J. Clinton, Message to the Congress Transmitting the Chemical Weapons Convention, *in* 2 Public Papers of the Presidents of the United States: William J. Clinton 2061, 2062 (1993).

[66] *See* Bothe et al., *Conclusions, in* New Chemical Weapons Convention, *supra* note 12, at 591 (discussing how the Convention is "an unprecedented instrument if compared with the provisions of other international disarmament agreements"). The path-breaking elements of the Convention, including its compliance scheme, were developed during negotiations in the 1970s and 1980s, although they were refined during the final year of negotiation. *See* Walter Krutzsch & Ralf Trapp, A Commentary on the Chemical Weapons Convention 3–4 (1994).

was immense. Conveniently, the deadline came toward the beginning of the legislative session, rather than at the packed end of a term.[67] The deadline made it easier for the treaty's supporters to frame timely ratification in a way that would trigger loss aversion – that is, that failure to ratify by the entry-into-force date would be an opportunity that would be lost forever if not exercised. Madeline Albright's testimony emphasized the losses that would follow from nonratification by the deadline: the United States would "forfeit" its Executive Council seat, "lose the right" to set inspections in motion, and "risk serious economic loss" for US industry.[68]

Third, regarding how the Convention's deadlines are working in practice, it is clear that many of these deadlines have not been met. Research on deadlines in the domestic context, if relevant, may shed some light on how these deadlines have and have not worked. Research on the planning fallacy would predict that the Convention's deadlines would be overoptimistic, and indeed this has proved to be the case. Some of the Convention's deadlines were probably known to be aspirational when put into place.[69] Yet the fact that the United States has missed the final deadline for destruction of chemical weapons is one that may not have been predicted at the beginning. As discussed earlier, the United States thought that the deadlines would allow it plenty of time. It was too sanguine about the technical ease of the destruction process and also failed to take adequately into account environmental issues and not-in-my-backyard resistance. In consequence, we have what David Koplow describes as an "international law train wreck" – despite being a "prime mover in negotiating and implementing" the Chemical Weapons Convention, the United States has "fall[en] into [a] conspicuous violation."[70] The deadlines presumably helped spur some action – and thus to generate some effectiveness on the part of the Convention – but they ultimately also have come to serve as the markers of international legal violations.

Perhaps the Convention's negotiators could have made better initial choices with regard to the destruction deadlines. If phenomena like the planning fallacy and rate persistence are applicable at the international law

---

[67] By way of contrast, the Law of the Sea Convention entered into force in mid-November 1994, very soon after a round of congressional elections (and thus a poor time for congressional action). It got no traction at that time and, despite powerful supporters, has still not received US ratification. *See* Jean Galbraith, *Prospective Advice and Consent*, 37 YALE J. INT'L L. 247, 302 (2012).

[68] Albright, *supra* note 23.

[69] For example, the requirement that nations submit initial declarations within thirty days of the Convention's entry into force had an initial compliance rate of around a third. OPCW 1998 Report, *supra* note 24, at 3–4 (noting that another third came in over the next five months).

[70] Koplow, *supra* note 34, at 319.

level and negotiators are aware that this is the case, then negotiators might factor these issues into compliance design. If they factored in concerns about the planning fallacy, for example, negotiators might have structured the compliance regime differently to make more provision for reasonable but unsuccessful efforts to meet the deadlines. Relatedly, the design of intermediate deadlines in the Convention seem problematic if one is conscious of rate persistence. These deadlines – 1 percent destruction by three years, 20 percent within five years, and 45 percent within seven years[71] – assumed that destruction would ramp up sharply over time (presumably based on technological assumptions). But if rate persistence is indeed a concern, then this uphill design is problematic. It might have been better to set higher targets earlier, even though the risk of missing these targets would also be higher. An approach like this was in fact taken with respect to Syria. The initial deadlines were quite ambitious and were not met. Yet they proved quite effective in furthering the prompt destruction of most of Syria's declared chemical weapons.[72]

As this discussion suggests, if domestic social science research on deadlines is relevant, then it could be quite useful to diplomats and other international actors. Quite unintentionally, the Chemical Weapons Convention may have harnessed some behavioral mechanisms that benefitted it – though unfortunately not all of them. Although the absence of initial negotiating deadlines stemmed from Cold War realities, it may have proved valuable in enabling the development of a far-reaching and creative agreement. And although the triggers attached to the entry-into-force provisions had other purposes, they ended up helping the Convention's US supporters rally around the entry-into-force date and to frame nonratification by that date as a loss for the United States. In the future, diplomats could use these mechanisms more strategically. Similarly, if the domestic research social science on deadlines is relevant to international regime design, then it has important implications for how deadlines can most effectively further compliance on the part of states and other international actors.

2.2.2.2 The Challenge of Proving Relevance or Irrelevance

This section considers how relevant the domestic social science research on deadlines discussed here is to international legal practice. Broadly speaking,

---

[71] Chemical Weapons Convention, *supra* note 10, at Annex on Implementation and Verification IV(A).C.17 (containing the deadlines for Category 1 substances).

[72] As noted *supra* note 43 and accompanying text, Syria has nonetheless continued to engage in chemical weapons attacks using chemicals that were not declared or were not subject to the declaration process.

I ask how much proof we have of this relevance by looking at two types of evidence: first, evidence addressing the broader relevance of behavioral principles to international legal practice; and, second, evidence specific to the use of deadlines. Taken together, I think the evidence suggests that this domestic social science research is relevant (and more than trivially so), but also that this evidence is not conclusive.

2.2.2.2.1 BEHAVIORAL PRINCIPLES There is an increasing body of work linking behavioral research to international legal practice. A core insight in favor of this connection is deductive: evidence strongly suggests that aspects of this research demonstrate general human traits and, after all, international legal practice is ultimately the work product of humans. Against this is doubt about whether international actors partake of behavioral traits in ways predictable enough to be helpful in understanding international legal practice. This doubt has many possible bases, including the potential differences between domestic experimental subjects and international decision-makers, the group-based nature of international decision-making, and the complexity of international issues and processes. Empirical work is increasingly bridging this gap and showing that, at least in some contexts, the connections hold. This work includes research showing that groups also display heuristic biases (though with somewhat different emphases)[73] and work providing evidence of such biases on the part of international actors in certain contexts. In prior work on treaty clauses allowing states to either opt in or to opt out of International Court of Justice jurisdiction, for example, I have shown that states' behavior does not follow the predictions of a rational choice model but rather parallels findings from domestic behavioral research.[74]

The more that behavioral principles are shown to be at work in international legal practice in certain contexts, the stronger the case is for concluding that behavioral principles are at work as well in other contexts. Even so, however, caution and care must be brought to bear. The relationship between behavioral principles and outcomes is heavily context dependent and requires

---

[73] van Aaken, *supra* note 6, at 446–449 (Part II) (describing some of this work).

[74] *See generally* Galbraith, *supra* note 6; *see also* Lauge N. Skovgaard Poulson & Emma Aisbett, *When the Claim Hits: Bilateral Investment Treaties and Bounded Rational Learning*, 65 WORLD POL. 273 (2013) (demonstrating through interviews of international decision-makers that bounded rather than ideal rationality drove certain decision-making in relation to bilateral investment treaties and complementing this with quantitative work suggesting a similar conclusion).

"due regard for the relevant decision-making capabilities of the actors in [their] specific setting."[75]

2.2.2.2.2 DEADLINE-SPECIFIC EVIDENCE With regard to the use of deadlines, I think the evidence supports a connection between at least some of the empirical findings in domestic contexts discussed above and international legal practice. The broader principles developed from this research – that low time pressure fosters more creative agreements, that framing matters, and that the planning fallacy is common – have evidentiary support from a variety of contexts. Observational findings in the domestic regulatory context, as discussed in Section 2.2.1, appear consistent with these principles. The prevalence of these findings suggests that they will likely prove true in international legal contexts. Moreover, some matters of international legal practice are largely domestic in practice, including ratification and aspects of implementation. Here, the parallels to the domestic regulatory context are even stronger.

We also have some initial work connecting behavioral patterns from domestic contexts to the international context. I offered the case study of the Chemical Weapons Convention above primarily to show how empirical findings in domestic contexts, if relevant, could help with good regime design, but I think this case study is also suggestive of relevance. Far more extensively, Marco Pinfari has explored the role of deadlines in peace negotiations, using four case studies and data drawn from sixty-eight negotiations.[76] While, as noted earlier, work in diplomatic studies has historically been quite open to drawing inferences from domestic social science research, Pinfari's work is the most up-to-date exploration of how such research on negotiating deadlines might relate to their use internationally.[77] Pinfari finds a negative correlation between peace negotiations undertaken under conditions of time pressure and the ultimate durability of resulting agreements.[78] Pinfari concludes that "this analysis goes some way to confirming the argument that emerges from a variety of works in experimental psychology according to which the absence or low levels of time pressure can be associated with positive negotiation results

---

[75] Russell B. Korobkin & Thomas S. Ulen, *Law and Behavioral Sciences: Removing the Rationality Assumption from Law and Economics*, 88 Calif. L. Rev. 1051, 1058 (2000).

[76] Marco Pinfari, Peace Negotiations and Time: Deadline Diplomacy in Territorial Disputes (2013).

[77] *See id.* at 1–10 (discussing prior work in diplomatic studies in relation to deadlines).

[78] *Id.* at 57–61, 138–139. He does not have sufficient power to apply regression analyses and look for statistical significance, and instead uses a fuzzy set methodology.

in the presence of elements of complexity."[79] Based on his findings, Pinfari suggests that "[d]iplomats, mediators and any actor involved in conflict resolution efforts should thus be aware of the fact that little evidence exists to suggest that [artificially imposed] pressure results in durable agreements in complex negotiations."[80] His conclusions are in line with what a French diplomat tweeted in relation to negotiations with Iran in the spring of 2015: "Instead of dramatizing a so-called 'deadline,' let's get the substance of a possible agreement right. Much more important."[81]

Although supportive of the relevance of behavioral principles to the international use of deadlines, there is nonetheless considerable grounds for doubt. Case studies may be the creatures of selection effects and in any event may support alternative causal hypotheses. Perhaps deadlines have played an entirely rational role in the Chemical Weapons Convention. The innovative agreement could stem not from open minds occasioned by the absence of deadlines, but rather by good negotiators taking sensible advantage of additional time; the entry-into-force date may have served as a rational focal point for President Clinton and the Senate; and the US failure to destroy its chemical weapons by the compliance deadline may have been due not to an initial planning fallacy, but rather to strategic noncompliance or a rational change in priorities. I read the evidence as solidly supporting a behavioral account in relation to the second and third issue (and unclear on the first issue), but I cannot conclusively rule out these alternatives. Pinfari's results are similarly vulnerable to alternative explanations. For example, low time pressure could correlate to better outcomes in peace negotiations because better negotiators and mediators happen to prefer patient approaches. Alternatively, the correlation could be explained simply by the objective benefits that come with more time for deliberation.

Much more research is needed to fine-tune our understanding of how deadlines operate in the international legal context and the ways in which behavioral principles are applicable. The particulars matter, and the evidence on the particulars is less than ideal. For example, it is hard to know how strongly the laboratory-grounded finding that deadlines subjectively close minds translates to actors working with long-term rather than immediate deadlines. Similarly, while the planning fallacy is well-supported, there is

---

[79] *Id.* at 138, 143–144. Pinfari cautions wariness, however, about uncritical application of lab-based insights to international negotiations.

[80] *Id.* at 150.

[81] Gérard Araud (@GerardAraud), TWITTER (Mar. 29, 2015, 4:54 PM), https://twitter.com/GerardAraud/status/582330027053809664?lang=en.

less strong evidence about how best to overcome it or harness it. The increased use of well-structured intermediate deadlines seems like a mechanism with promise, but more work would be useful in assessing this. As another example, some international legal deadlines may trigger salience biases and draw out-sized attention to issues (relative to what we would rationally expect) by states and nonstate actors as well.[82] Case studies, quantitative observational work, and perhaps some elite-focused experiments would help elucidate these issues. Especially in the absence of field experiments – and these are function-ally impossible in most real-world international legal contexts[83] – we must operate against a backdrop of uncertainty about causal mechanisms and continually update our best understandings in light of additional evidence.

2.2.3 *Deadlines, Diplomacy, International Law*

Proof of the degree and manner of relevance of domestic social science research on deadlines to international legal practice remains modest. Yet the question of relevance is one of immediate practical importance. If deadlines tend to trigger a subjective closing of the minds of international negotiators, for example, then perhaps negotiators should undertake extra efforts to avoid setting deadlines early on (even at the cost of shorter ones down the road). If deadlines make the costs of not ratifying a treaty unusually salient, then perhaps important treaties should tie more consequences to ratification by particular dates. If the planning fallacy holds for international actors, then we should predict considerable noncompliance with international legal dead-lines despite good faith intentions. If states are susceptible to rate persistence, then negotiators, executive actors in international organizations, and nonstate actors might want to strive to structure compliance regimes to take advantage of this susceptibility. The more international actors exhibit behavioral ten-dencies, the more these tendencies should matter for the design and imple-mentation of timing mechanisms.

---

[82] *Cf.* Galbraith, *supra* note 6, at 353–355 (explaining how the greater ratification rates of optional protocols, as opposed to legally equivalent opt-in clauses, might be explained by salience biases on the part of states or of advocacy groups).

[83] Some forms of field experiments may be plausible in international law. *See* Adam Chilton & Dustin Tingley, *Why the Study of International Law Needs Experiments*, 52 Colum. J. Transnat'l L. 173, 233–238 (2013) (giving examples of a field experiment using random assignment of electoral monitors and another email-based audit study of firms providing transnational incorporation services). But the challenges of running power-generating experi-ments on actual diplomatic negotiations, the entry into force of treaties, or many forms of international legal implementation seem effectively insurmountable.

Given uncertainty, what should practitioners take into account in setting deadlines? The fields of law and diplomacy have traditionally taken different approaches to these questions. Work in international law says very little about deadline design generally. By contrast, scholarship in diplomatic studies, including scholarship aimed at practitioners, has historically included considerable discussion of negotiating deadlines. This discussion tends to identify all kinds of considerations, including empirical research in other contexts,[84] but to avoid drawing strong conclusions.[85] Importantly, even where this work does offer specific suggestions based on behavioral research, as with Pinfari's work, the focus is exclusively on *negotiating* deadlines, rather than on the kind of deadlines that negotiators might put into agreements.

More awareness about empirically grounded insights from other contexts on deadlines would be valuable to international practitioners, even though considerable uncertainty remains about the applicability of these insights. Negotiators can potentially benefit not only from insights related to negotiating deadlines, but also from insights related to other kinds of deadlines that are akin to the deadlines that they write into a treaty. After all, in the international legal context it is negotiators who identify how a treaty can be joined by state parties, who set the entry-into-force deadlines, and who set the compliance deadlines (or decide to delegate this authority to an international organization). Conversely, international actors involved in meeting deadlines – whether diplomats, international lawyers, or others – could benefit from awareness of how behavioral biases might have affected the choices of negotiators in setting the deadlines as well as in thinking about how such biases might affect choices related to compliance with these deadlines.

In making this call for awareness, I do not mean to equate international diplomacy and international law. As discussed earlier, the behavioral implications for negotiating deadlines are distinct from the behavioral implications for other kinds of deadlines. Moreover, there is an important normative difference between deadlines for political decision-making and deadlines for

---

[84] *E.g.*, IKLÉ, *supra* note 1, at 72–80 (posing a number of considerations in relation to deadlines, although relying heavily on examples from past international negotiations); ZARTMAN & BERMAN, *supra* note 2, at 191–199 (drawing on a variety of sources in discussing deadlines); Dean Pruitt, *Strategy in Negotiation, in* INTERNATIONAL NEGOTIATION, *supra* note 2, at 89; *cf.* ROGER FISHER & WILLIAM URY, GETTING TO YES 141 (1991) (approaching negotiations as a unitary field across domestic and international contexts and discussing practices on deadlines in labor negotiations).

[85] *E.g.*, ZARTMAN & BERMAN, *supra* note 2, at 195 (concluding rather unhelpfully that "[d]eadlines tend to facilitate agreement, lower expectations, call bluffs, and produce final proposals, but also lead negotiators to adopt a tough position that will make them look good if – and therefore when – negotiations fail.").

legal compliance, as missing the latter kind of deadline puts a country in violation of its international legal obligations. Yet to the extent that behavioral tendencies cut across these differences, practitioners on both the diplomacy side and the legal side should take them into account among the many other factors that inform decision-making.

Going beyond awareness, I also think practitioners should rely on insights developed from behavioral social science research in setting and responding to deadlines, at least to a modest extent. An easy case is where a practitioner is choosing between options which have different implications from a behavioral perspective but otherwise look equally good. Madeline Albright's testimony on the Chemical Weapons Convention is an example. She could have framed ratification by the entry-into-force date as a gain for the United States, or she could have framed nonratification by that date as a loss for the United States. If framing does not matter, than either approach should sound equally persuasive, but if framing can trigger loss aversion, then the latter approach would do more to accomplish her goal of US ratification. Therefore, she should have – and did – frame nonratification by the entry into force date as a loss for the United States.

Other situations will require more complicated calculations. Consider, for example, the issue of how to set optimal compliance deadlines. On the one hand, projections about when compliance can be achieved are likely to be overoptimistic. And if deadlines are too early, then they can no longer serve as a useful boundary for separating actors striving in good faith from actors who are willfully noncompliant. Moreover, once these deadlines are past, even good faith actors may be less motivated to achieve compliance, since their default has become noncompliance. On the other hand, deadlines help motivate action, especially since "work expands so as to fill the time available for its completion."[86] If deadlines are set to compensate for the planning fallacy and to accommodate the slowest actors, then actors who could comply more promptly may nonetheless wait until the deadlines and the least capable actors may wait too long to get started. These kinds of calculations will necessarily be heavily context-dependent, but there should be a thumb on the scale in favor of design choices that accord with behavioral insights.

2.3 CONCLUSION

Where the use of deadlines and other procedural design mechanisms are concerned, scholars of both diplomacy and international law should

---

[86] *Parkinson's Law*, ECONOMIST (Nov. 19, 1955), http://www.economist.com/node/14116121.

consider the relevance of existing empirical research in psychology and behavioral economics. The case study of the Chemical Weapons Convention offered in this chapter shows how this research might help explain features of international legal design and improve it going forward. The discussion here is only a tentative starting point. Much more work is needed to establish just how relevant the various strands of this research are and, more generally, how deadlines can best be used in international legal practice. In the meantime, practitioners would do well to consider the insights offered by behavioral research as they set deadlines – and as they engage in international decision-making more generally.

3

Cooperating without Sanctions

Epistemic Institutions versus Credible Commitments Regimes in International Law

Timothy Meyer

3.1 INTRODUCTION

Like domestic law, international law has experimented in recent decades with new approaches to changing legal subjects' behavior. Realist and institutionalist scholarship in international law and international relations generally assumes that states will cheat on their obligations if doing so is in their interest. On this view, the basic challenge for international institutions is to establish a set of "credible commitments" that states will abide by even in the face of incentives to cheat. To make a commitment credible, an international agreement must alter state incentives so that states will find it in their interest to comply with their commitments, a task usually accomplished through the imposition of some form of sanction for violation. To promote compliance, international lawyers became obsessed with mechanisms for detecting and sanctioning cheating, while international law scholars debated the level and significance of compliance with international law.[1]

Below the radar, however, a variety of international regimes began to emerge that seek to coordinate state behavior without resorting to, or at least without relying exclusively upon, credible commitments. Instead, these regimes produce information – scientific information, advice from experts, or information about practices and policies in other states – relevant to an underlying cooperative problem. They might, for instance, produce reports

---

[1] *See, e.g.*, George W. Downs, David M. Rocke & Peter N. Barsoom, *Is the Good News about Compliance Good News about Cooperation?*, 50 INT'L ORG. 379 (1996); Oona Hathaway, *Do Human Rights Treaties Make a Difference?*, 111 YALE L.J. 1935 (2002); JACK L. GOLDSMITH & ERIC A. POSNER, THE LIMITS OF INTERNATIONAL LAW (2005); ANDREW T. GUZMAN, HOW INTERNATIONAL LAW WORKS: A RATIONAL CHOICE THEORY (2008); BETH A. SIMMONS, MOBILIZING FOR HUMAN RIGHTS: INTERNATIONAL LAW IN DOMESTIC POLITICS (2009).

compiling scientific research on the health risks associated with nonionizing radiation,[2] or they might disseminate information about the relative cost-effectiveness of different forms of renewable energy technology.[3] In its purest form, this kind of cooperation uses informational strategies to push states to adopt policies domestically without actually requiring them to do so as a matter of international law. These regimes, in other words, seek to achieve coordinated policymaking across states without engaging the sanctions long thought critical to international law.

This chapter takes a first cut at describing this newer mode of international cooperation and contrasting it with the traditional conceptions of international cooperation. I refer to the way in which states organize the process of creating shared knowledge relevant to international cooperation as epistemic cooperation. Epistemic regimes are international regimes that coordinate behavior principally by changing states' perceptions of the desirability of adopting domestic measures through this process of creating shared knowledge.[4] The International Renewable Energy Agency is perhaps the purest form of an epistemic regime. Rather than requiring states to adopt policies regarding renewable energy, the institution provides states expert information and advice in a variety of forms to encourage them to do so. Other examples include the Rotterdam Convention on Prior Informed Consent,[5] the Basel Convention on Hazardous Waste,[6] the Cartagena Protocol on Biosafety,[7] and the Framework Convention on Tobacco Control.

I contrast epistemic regimes with *credible commitment regimes*, which define a legally required standard of conduct and aim to create sanctions for failing to meet that standard.[8] Examples of credible commitment regimes

---

[2] Oren Perez, *The Hybrid Legal-Scientific Dynamic of Transnational Scientific Institutions*, 25 Eur. J. Int'l L. (2014).

[3] Timothy Meyer, *Epistemic Institutions and Epistemic Cooperation in International Environmental Governance*, 2 Transnat'l Envtl. L. 15 (2013).

[4] *Id.* at 16–17. Epistemic regimes are similar to epistemic institutions, which I have described elsewhere. *See id. Epistemic institutions* refer to the discrete international institutions engaged in the production of shared knowledge among states. *Id. Epistemic regimes* refers to international regimes that rely principally on epistemic cooperation to change state behavior, rather than embedding an epistemic institution within a larger credible commitment regime.

[5] Rotterdam Convention on the Prior Informed Consent Procedure for Certain Hazardous Chemicals and Pesticides in International Trade, Sept. 10, 1998, 2244 U.N.T.S. 337 [hereinafter Rotterdam Convention].

[6] Basel Convention on the Control of Transboundary Movements of Hazardous Wastes and their Disposal, Mar. 22, 1989, 1673 U.N.T.S. 57 [hereinafter Basel Convention].

[7] Cartagena Protocol on Biosafety to the Convention on Biological Diversity, May 15, 2000, 39 I.L.M. 1027 (2000) [hereinafter Cartagena Protocol].

[8] Credible commitment regimes are somewhat analogous to command-and-control regulations domestically.

include elements of the climate change regime, such as the Kyoto Protocol, where review and monitoring mechanisms to ensure compliance with emissions reductions commitments has become a central component; the World Trade Organization with its highly effective dispute settlement system; and arms control agreements, which frequently contain verification procedures. Of course, epistemic regimes and credible commitment regimes represent ideal types only. In practice, states often blend the two approaches, using epistemic strategies within credible commitment regimes.[9] The distinction, however, highlights two different modes of attempting to influence states to coordinate their policy decisions.

I argue that in designing international institutions, states increasingly choose epistemic regimes over credible commitment regimes because the former can, in some instances, reduce the costs of coordinating regulatory standards across nations. Epistemic regimes make coordination easier by reducing the transaction costs of bargaining over and enforcing international legal rules. In Section 3.2, I describe how international scholarship has focused on credible commitment regimes. Credible commitment regimes create a range of transaction costs in the name of constraining states to comply with an internationally required legal standard. Like epistemic regimes, credible commitment regimes often produce information. They do so, however, primarily to support the enforcement of legal commands. In credible commitment regimes, information is chiefly about reducing the risk of cheating through monitoring.

In Section 3.3, I develop the notion of epistemic regimes, where information plays the central, and very different, role. Here, institutions encourage states to produce and share information about a cooperative problem, but (at least in its pure form) the institution does not mandate particular outcomes. Instead, the hope is that the production of information will cause states to

---

[9] In other words, states can make the design choice at the level of a particular obligation or policy issue, rather than at the regime level. The WTO's Agreement on Sanitary and Phytosanitary Measures (SPS Agreement) reflects just such a compromise. The SPS Agreement is itself a credible commitment regime, containing legally binding obligations backed by the threat of enforcement through the WTO's Dispute Settlement Body. However, the SPS Agreement contains harmonization provisions that provide a safe harbor for states that adopt the international standards established by international standard setting bodies such as the Codex Alimentarius Commission or the International Office of Epizootics. At the same time, states can select a level of protection higher than that embodied in international standards if they can demonstrate that their standards are based upon a risk assessment, which can include relying on data developed by other countries. In this way, the SPS Agreement links its binding rules to a process of information sharing and nonbinding standard setting that occurs outside the WTO.

adjust their view of what is in their own self-interest. Information can, at least in some circumstances, result in coordination through decentralized choices by states.

Section 3.4 provides an initial analysis of the conditions under which states will prefer epistemic regimes versus credible commitment regimes. Neither is better across the board. Rather, following transaction costs economics, I argue that which is better depends on which regime minimizes the transaction costs of coordinating state behavior. Epistemic regimes save the transaction costs of having to actually agree on a legal rule and also reduce the cost of contracting over and implementing costly enforcement mechanisms. On the other hand, epistemic agreements may be inferior at actually coordinating state behavior both because they do not pick a single standard for all states and because they are not backed by sanctions. Transaction cost economics predicts that states should select epistemic agreements when the costs of contracting over specific legal rules and enforcement procedures are larger than the costs of failing to coordinate on the basis of information alone. I identify three circumstances that are particularly relevant to this tradeoff: problem structure, the credibility of information, and value- or capacity-based limits on officials' openness to scientific or expert recommendations.

3.2 CREDIBLE COMMITMENT REGIMES

One of the central problems in international law and international relations scholarship has been identifying the conditions under which states will not cheat on their legal obligations. Scholars working in the realist and institutionalist traditions commonly assume that states act self-interestedly with respect to their legal obligations.[10] They will therefore violate their legal obligations when it is in their interest to do so, taking into account any incentives the international regime provides for compliance. This assumption accords with the empirical observation that states do indeed violate their obligations, often in high-stakes situations or when faced with political pressure from domestic constituencies.[11]

---

[10]   See, e.g., Andrew T. Guzman, *How International Law Works: Introduction*, 1 INT'L THEORY 285 (2009); ROBERT O. KEOHANE, AFTER HEGEMONY: COOPERATION AND DISCORD IN THE WORLD POLITICAL ECONOMY (1984).

[11]   Scholars have debated the extent to which international law actually causes compliance with its rules, or whether compliance, when observed, is merely epiphenomenal. *See, e.g.*, Downs, Rocke & Barsoom, *supra* note 1; GOLDSMITH & POSNER, *supra* note 1. Some commentators have gone so far as to argue that international law is not "law" because it lacks a centralized system of enforcement to compel compliance. *See* Anthony A. D'Amato, *Is International Law Really "Law"?*, 79 Nw. U. L. REV. 1293 (1985) (arguing against those who "react with a sort of

The credible commitment paradigm is the chief prism through which scholars and commentators have tackled this compliance problem. In its purest form, the credible commitment paradigm holds that international legal commitments must be self-enforcing.[12] To be self-enforcing, in turn, an international agreement must counter any incentives states have to cheat on their obligations by establishing incentives to comply. Scholars have emphasized that credible, self-enforcing commitments are important for multiple reasons. Without them, international agreements may be prone to opportunistic renegotiation.[13] States may also not trust their counterparties, leading to breakdowns in cooperation.[14] Perhaps most importantly, however, a number of commentators suspect that in the absence of credible commitments little meaningful cooperation will occur as states instead succumb to the temptation to cheat on their obligations.[15]

A traditional rational choice approach to analyzing credible commitment regimes divides cooperative problems into two broad categories: bargaining problems and enforcement problems.[16] Bargaining problems involve states selecting the substantive terms on which they will cooperate. For example, how much will states reduce their greenhouse gas emissions? What products will be subject to tariff bindings and at what rate will they be bound? Enforcement involves ensuring that states actually honor the substantive commitments they make during the bargaining stage. Enforcement can involve establishing monitoring mechanisms, such as inspection regimes in arms control agreements or the complicated negotiations over a verification regime during the 2015 Paris climate change negotiations; formal dispute resolution; or the unilateral or collective imposition of sanctions.

Both bargaining and enforcement can entail significant transaction costs. Of course, states bargain over enforcement issues when designing treaties. In this sense, a distinction between transaction costs from bargaining and transaction costs from enforcement may seem artificial. However, the distinction is

---

indulgence when they encounter the term 'international law,' as if to say, 'well, we know it isn't *really* law'.").

[12] *See, e.g.,* Robert E. Scott & Paul B. Stephan, *Self-Enforcing International Agreements and the Limits of Coercion,* 2004 Wis. L. Rev. 551 (2004).

[13] Anne van Aaken, *International Investment Law Between Commitment and Flexibility: A Contract Theory Analysis,* 12 J. Int'l Econ. L. 507 (2009).

[14] Andrew H. Kydd, Trust and Mistrust in International Relations (2005).

[15] *See, e.g.,* International Regimes (Stephen D. Krasner ed., 1983); Robert Axelrod & Robert O. Keohane, *Achieving Cooperation Under Anarchy: Strategies and Institutions, in* Cooperation Under Anarchy 226 (Kenneth A. Oye ed., 1986).

[16] *See* James Fearon, *Bargaining, Enforcement, and International Cooperation,* 52 Int'l Org. 269 (1998).

meant to highlight the source of the transaction costs: Are transaction costs the result of choosing a substantive standard with which states should comply (what I shall call "bargaining costs") or are they the result of measures taken to enforce cooperation (what I shall refer to as "enforcement costs")?

Bargaining costs are a function of a number of variables. First, scholars generally believe that the transaction costs of negotiations increase with the number of parties to the negotiation.[17] Second, bargaining costs increase with the degree of distributional tension between the parties. As parties stand to gain more from reaching an agreement that reflects their preferred cooperative terms, they will hold out longer. This can be costly in terms of time and may necessitate expanding the scope of negotiations in order to reach a compromise. For example, all states may prefer a legal regime under which Antarctica remains demilitarized, as the Antarctic Treaty requires.[18] In such a situation, bargaining over substantive rules will be relatively cheap, allowing states to select a legal rule with ease.[19] In other situations, the degree of distributional tension among states may be quite high. Treaties that award a legal right to some states but not others provide a clear illustration of this point. The Nuclear Nonproliferation Treaty lets five states possess nuclear weapons but bans all other states from doing so.[20] Somewhat less starkly, the choice in environmental negotiations between technical standards or emissions reductions often has significant distributional consequences. States that have put in place the best available technology prior to treaty negotiations prefer that the treaty require use of the best available technology for the simple reason that the treaty then requires nothing more of them. In negotiating the Convention on Long-Range Transboundary Air Pollution, for example, the United States favored a legal rule requiring the use of best available technology, so that it would not be penalized for having invested already in developing and deploying such technology.[21] For other countries, however, using the best available technology might be more expensive than merely reducing emissions through other means.

Like bargaining problems, enforcement problems can be easy or hard. In some cases, states have little reason to cheat once they agree on the legal rule.

---

[17] *See, e.g.*, Barbara Koremenos, *Contracting around International Uncertainty*, 99 AM. POL. SCI. REV. 549 (2005).

[18] Antarctic Treaty, Dec. 1, 1959, 12 U.S.T. 794.

[19] Indeed, explicit bargaining may not be necessary if states are able to coordinate their behavior without communication. As I explain in Section 3.4, though, the ability to forego cooperation is not simply a function of the distributional tension over the legal rule.

[20] Treaty on the Non-Proliferation of Nuclear Weapons, June 12, 1968, 21 U.S.T. 483.

[21] DAVID HUNTER, JAMES SALZMAN, & DURWOOD ZAELKE, INTERNATIONAL ENVIRONMENTAL LAW & POLICY 526 (4th ed. 2011).

Such situations are often referred to as coordination problems, because states merely need to coordinate on a particular behavior. After doing so, cooperation is self-enforcing. For example, once the International Civil Aviation Organization determines that air traffic controllers and pilots must all speak English, states have no reason to cheat on this standard. Cheating simply increases the odds of an accident.[22] In other situations, states do have an incentive to cheat. For example, parties to a climate change agreement may find that they have little incentive to honor their emissions reductions commitments. Honoring their commitments may be more individually costly than disregarding them. States therefore cheat on their commitments, getting the benefits of emissions reductions from those states that do comply with their commitments. Outside of the public goods context, arms control agreements present a similar problem. States have an incentive to arm themselves regardless of their legal commitments. If other states do not arm themselves, the cheating state gets a strategic advantage; if other states cheat too, the cheating state is at least not at a disadvantage.

Incentives to cheat create enforcement costs for states because states must then create incentives for states to comply. States might, for example, create a tribunal to which they would grant, ex ante, jurisdiction over disputes, as in the case of the World Trade Organization's Dispute Settlement Body. Alternatively, they might create a system in which a vote of the member states can deny noncompliant parties access to certain markets. Environmental regimes such as the Convention on the International Trade in Endangered Species and the Kyoto Protocol allow the Conference of the Parties to deny access to international markets for protected species or emissions trading markets.[23] These enforcement costs occur both during initial negotiations and afterwards. During the initial negotiations, states must bargain over the creation of enforcement procedures. After an agreement is in place, states must spend time and resources actually enforcing the agreement, such as by litigating disputes or imposing sanctions on violators.

Critically, in some circumstances transaction costs in credible commitment regimes can have a zero-sum character. James Fearon has shown that as states

[22] Critically, the fact that a focal point is self-enforcing once it has been identified does not mean that there is no distributional tension in selecting the focal point. States may care deeply which rule is selected, even though they will cooperate over whichever rule is chosen. The selection of English as a language for air traffic controllers again illustrates the point. Non-English speaking countries all bear some cost not born by English speaking countries in selecting English. There is thus some distributional tension at the bargaining stage, even if there is little tension in state interests' at the enforcement stage.

[23] Convention on International Trade in Endangered Species of Wild Fauna and Flora, July 1, 1975, 27 U.S.T. 1087; Kyoto Protocol, Dec. 11, 1997, 37 I.L.M. 22.

become more confident that an agreement will be successfully enforced, they will hold out longer for their preferred substantive terms.[24] In other words, bargaining costs rise as enforcement costs fall. This insight has a number of important implications.

First, it means that easy enforcement problems can still be difficult cooperative problems due to high bargaining costs. States may have difficulty reaching an agreement, even though an agreement would be relatively easy to enforce were they able to reach one. This situation is most likely to occur when states try to select precise cooperative terms in the presence of distributional tension. Fearon, for instance, argues that international cooperation on macroeconomic policy suffers from bargaining concerns over which states will bear the economic costs of adjusting to any new international norms, rather than concerns over cheating after an agreement has been reached.[25] Similarly, the managerial school of international relations pioneered by Abram and Antonia Chayes posits that concerns about deliberate cheating are overblown.[26]

Second, it means that improvements in the technology of enforcement – such as the proliferation of international tribunals in recent years – do not necessarily reduce the overall transaction costs associated with credible commitment regimes. Better enforcement, in other words, does not necessarily make cooperation easier. Unless states find some other way to reduce bargaining costs, lowering enforcement costs may simply shift transaction costs from enforcement to bargaining as states hold out for a deal with which they know they must live for a long time. Relatedly, improvements in enforcement technology may cause states to negotiate more intensely over the enforcement provisions of an agreement. The negotiations over the Trans-Pacific Partnership (renamed the Comprehensive and Progressive Trans-Pacific Partnership after the United States elected not to ratify the agreement) illustrate the point. Investor-state dispute settlement has become sufficiently effective at reaching the conduct of developed states that countries like Australia held out for specific limitations on the scope of investor-state dispute settlement under the agreement.[27] The result was a provision giving individual governments the right to prevent tobacco companies from bringing investor-state claims.[28]

---

[24] Fearon, *supra* note 16.
[25] *Id.* at 287.
[26] ABRAM CHAYES & ANTONIA CHAYES, THE NEW SOVEREIGNTY (1998).
[27] Jess Hill, *TPP's Clauses That Let Australia Be Sued Are Weapons of Legal Destruction, Says Lawyer*, GUARDIAN (Nov. 9, 2015, 9:58 PM), https://www.theguardian.com/business/2015/nov/10/tpps-clauses-that-let-australia-be-sued-are-weapons-of-legal-destruction-says-lawyer.
[28] Comprehensive and Progressive Trans-Pacific Partnership (CPTPP) art. 29.5, GOV'T OF CAN., https://www.international.gc.ca/trade-commerce/trade-agreements-accords-commer ciaux/agr-acc/tpp-ptp/text-texte/29.aspx?lang=eng.

The fact that enforcement provisions must themselves be bargained over results in front-loading the transaction costs associated with credible commitment regimes.[29] This front-loading, in turn, can make reaching agreement much more difficult. This effect may explain in part the slow pace of negotiations in major multilateral institutions such as the UNFCCC and the WTO. States know how to solve enforcement problems through dispute resolution provisions and trade sanctions. Where they have done so, as in the WTO, states are reluctant to agree to new trade terms unless the terms are significantly in their favor. Where they haven't, as in the UNFCCC, negotiations drag on as states hold out for the inclusion of more effective enforcement provisions.

Information plays a key role in credible commitment regimes, although one different from that which it plays in epistemic regimes. At the bargaining stage, states may have asymmetric knowledge about each other's capabilities or the state of the world. As James Morrow has shown, in the presence of distributional tension, informational asymmetry can be a significant drag on negotiations because states do not have an incentive to share information.[30] More generally, states may be faced with uncertainty about the world that is costly to resolve. Bargaining in the presence of uncertainty requires investments in either developing information necessary to determine what policies are in a state's interests or negotiating mechanisms within the regime to reduce uncertainty's costs.

Information about violations is also critical in credible commitment regimes. For this reason, monitoring and enforcement mechanisms are designed to elicit information about possible violations. Such information is a necessary condition for the reciprocal actions and reputational penalties that ultimately create an incentive for states to comply with credible commitment regimes. For example, bilateral arms control agreements between the United States and the Soviet Union often contained very detailed verification procedures.[31] These procedures were designed to produce information about the other side's activities. By placing observers in the other country or conducting site inspections, the legal regime facilitated monitoring. If one state spotted a violation, it could quickly take reciprocal action.

---

[29] This suggests an empirically testable hypothesis. If one believes that the technology of enforcement has improved, then we should see fewer multilateral agreements tackling public goods.

[30] James D. Morrow, *Modeling the Forms of International Cooperation*, 48 INT'L ORG. 387 (1994).

[31] *See, e.g.*, Eugene Rumer, *A Farewell to Arms . . . Control*, CARNEGIE ENDOWMENT FOR INT'L PEACE (Apr. 18, 2018), https://carnegieendowment.org/2018/04/17/farewell-to-arms-.-.-.-control -pub-76088.

States have tried a number of techniques to reduce the transaction costs associated with bargaining and enforcement in credible commitment regimes. Provisions that permit periodic renegotiation have the effect of spreading bargaining costs over time. Making an agreement soft law, for example, eases the way to agreement both by reducing the subsequent penalty for noncompliance and making exit, and therefore renegotiation, easier.[32] Exit provisions and explicit renegotiation provisions accomplish the same end.[33] They thus alleviate some of the bargaining costs by deferring them to the future.[34]

Where enforcement is concerned, international tribunals or monitoring bodies, such as human rights committees, may be a relatively efficient way to produce and publicize information about violations. These free-standing organizations bear the costs of producing information necessary for enforcement and can vouch for its credibility. The existence of these institutions, however, can shift transaction costs to bargaining over substantive terms. For example, in 2013 the United States declined to ratify the Convention on the Rights of Persons with Disabilities in part because members of the US Senate worried about the Disabilities Committee's role in implementing the Convention.[35] Specifically, they worried that the Committee's pronouncement about what counts as compliance with the Convention would change the United States' obligations without the United States' consent.

International legal rules are also often designed to make state-led monitoring more efficient. The International Convention for the Prevention of Pollution from Ships (MARPOL) illustrates this proposition. For many years, states attempted to control the emission of oil pollution from ships through rules (contained in a treaty known as the International Convention for the Prevention of Pollution of the Sea by Oil or OILPOL) stipulating when

---

[32] Timothy Meyer, *Shifting Sands*, 27 EUR. J. INT'L L. 161 (2016); Kal Raustiala, *Form and Substance in International Agreements*, 99 AM. J. INT'L L. 581 (2005).

[33] Timothy Meyer, *Power, Exit Costs, and Renegotiation in International Law*, 5 HARV. INT'L L.J. 379 (2010); Laurence R. Helfer, *Exiting Treaties*, 91 VA. L. REV. 1579 (2005); Barbara Koremonos, *Loosening the Ties that Bind*, 55 INT'L ORG. 289 (2001).

[34] Yet each of these mechanisms has drawbacks. Soft law agreements, because they are not legally binding, may be disfavored by domestic constituencies who see validation in the legal nature of an agreement. *See* Raustiala, *supra* note 32. Creating the possibility of renegotiation can also expose states to the possibility of opportunistic renegotiation that leaves them worse off, limiting the upside to exit or sunset clauses.

[35] *Hearing on the Convention on the Rights of Persons with Disabilities Before the S. Comm. on Foreign Relations*, 103d Cong. (2013) (statement of Timothy Meyer, Assistant Professor, University of Georgia School of Law) (responding to concerns about the Disability Committee).

and where ships could discharge oil.[36] The ocean is a vast place, however, and monitoring what ships did on the high seas proved to be impossible. In the 1970s, governments therefore negotiated a set of design standards for ships and bookkeeping requirements that, when complied with, would make unlawful discharges of oil more difficult.[37] Most prominently, states required ships to maintain segregated ballast tanks. These design standards greatly reduced monitoring costs. No longer did governments have to scour the seas hoping to catch ships in the act of discharging oil. Instead, governments merely needed to verify whether the ship complied with the design and bookkeeping standards, a task that can be performed in port.

As these examples make clear, information's role in credible commitment regimes is principally to expose violations – a necessary predicate to the enforcement of international rules. Credible commitment regimes aim to reduce the transaction cost of producing this information through the use of standing tribunals and monitoring bodies, as well as substantive rules that are relatively easy to monitor. Information also plays an important role in bargaining over the substantive rules to be enforced, although whether information reduces or increases the transaction costs of bargaining likely depends on the circumstances. Moreover, producing information more efficiently within a credible commitment regime does not necessarily reduce the transaction costs associated with the regime as a whole. If information makes bargaining over substantive rules easier, states may hold out over the enforcement terms. If the transaction costs associated with enforcement fall, states have an incentive to bargain harder over the substantive terms. The gains from efficiently producing information within credible commitment regimes are thus limited. The result is that some international regimes may be infeasible when designed as credible commitment regimes.

3.3 EPISTEMIC COOPERATION

Many modern international law agreements provide a different role for information. Instead of facilitating compliance with binding legal obligations, states produce information as part of a strategy to encourage states to change and coordinate their policies in a decentralized fashion. Oftentimes, however, the legal regimes that facilitate the production of information do not require

---

[36] For a fuller account of MARPOL's innovative enforcement scheme, see HUNTER, SALZMAN & ZAELKE, *supra* note 22.

[37] International Convention for the Prevention of Pollution from Ships, Feb. 17, 1973, 34 U.S.T. 3407, 12 I.L.M. 1319.

states to coordinate policies based on the information produced. Instead, the hope is that the provision of information by itself will change states' understanding of what policies are in their interest. States will then change their behavior – hopefully in a way that coordinates state policies to solve problems with international dimensions – without needing to select and enforce credible legal commitments. By reducing these transaction costs, states may be able to create international regimes to coordinate their behavior on issues where a credible commitment regime, with its bargaining and enforcement costs, would not succeed. Epistemic regimes, in other words, expand the set of issues over which states can cooperate.

Examples of epistemic institutions that work in this way abound. Examples include the International Renewable Energy Agency,[38] the Rotterdam Convention on Prior Informed Consent,[39] the Basel Convention on Hazardous Waste,[40] the Cartagena Protocol on Biosafety,[41] and the Framework Convention on Tobacco Control,[42] to name only a few. Each of these agreements is a legally binding treaty that requires states to produce information. States are not legally obligated to act upon that information. Rather, the information provides a basis for states to select the policy they desire within a legal framework that provides states with discretion. These institutions seek to guide state choices, rather than to mandate them.

Perhaps the clearest example of epistemic regimes are agreements requiring states to share information with each other about potentially hazardous materials. These regimes allow states to make unilateral decisions about how to regulate hazardous substances on the basis of shared pool of information. Consider the Cartagena Biosafety Protocol, which creates a legal framework governed the trade in living genetically modified organisms (LGMOs).[43] That treaty provides for a Biosafety Clearing-House. Member states are obligated to report to the Biosafety Clearing-House any legal measures or decisions they have made with respect to the release of LGMOs, as well as any related risk assessment data.[44] Then, countries to which LGMOs are exported (that is, importing countries) are able to make decisions about whether to permit the trade in LGMOs if they are intended

---

[38] *Treaties in Force*, 2019 U.S. Dep't St. 1, 511, https://www.state.gov/wp-content/uploads/2019/07/2019-TIF-Multilaterals-7-31-2019-1.pdf.

[39] Rotterdam Convention, *supra* note 5.

[40] Basel Convention, *supra* note 6.

[41] Cartagena Protocol, *supra* note 7.

[42] World Health Organization Framework Convention on Tobacco Control, Feb. 27, 2005, 2302 U.N.T.S. 166 [hereinafter Convention on Tobacco Control].

[43] Cartagena Protocol, *supra* note 7.

[44] *Id.* at art. 20.

for release into the environment.[45] Moreover, such decisions are supposed to be based on a risk assessment that takes into account relevant scientific information including, presumably, information produced through the Clearing-House.[46] Exporters may also request importing states to review their decisions limiting the import of living LGMOs if they believe circumstances have changed.[47] Ultimately, however, the decision remains with the importing state. While the international regime seeks to provide information to states for use in selecting their policies, and seeks to ensure that states use and rely upon the scientific information that exists, at the end of the day the treaty leaves the precise rules on importing living GMOs to the discretion of individual states.

This approach does not, therefore, direct coordination of countries' policy choices in the manner that credible commitment regimes do. The law does not require specific steps that each state must take to satisfy its legal obligations. At the same time, though, the agreement clearly aims to coordinate state policies at some level. Article 1 of the Protocol provides that "the objective of this Protocol is to contribute to ensuring an adequate level of protection in the field of the safe transfer, handling and use of" LGMOs. While the Protocol does not determine what policy constitutes "an adequate level of protection," it establishes a process of information sharing through which states can make that decision for themselves. That process need not lead to convergence over time, although it seems likely to promote coordination as compared to a world without information sharing.

The chief advantage of this approach for international law is that it reduces the transaction costs of creating and implementing legal regimes. States can avoid the bargaining and enforcement costs associated with credible commitment regimes by leaving the ultimate policy choice to individual states. Epistemic regimes reduce transaction costs at the bargaining stage because states do not need to agree on specific substantive behaviors on which they will converge. Instead, they rely on decentralized action by states to develop a focal point. International regimes merely coordinate the production of information, rather than enshrining and enforcing the chosen focal point. Creating epistemic regimes will, of course, still require bargaining over information-producing agreements, as well as a commitment of resources to support any treaty bodies. But relative to credible commitment regimes, epistemic institutions do not

---

[45] *Id.* at arts. 7–10.
[46] *Id.* at art. 15.
[47] *Id.* at art. 12.

require the same kind of bargaining and enforcement resources. They do not need, for example, the same kinds of procedural rules used in institutions such as the Conference of the Parties (COP) to the UNFCCC.[48] Moreover, because they are not engaging in substantive rulemaking, the risk that the institution will become paralyzed by holdout states – a form of "governance risk" – is greatly reduced.[49]

At the same time, states can coordinate their policy choices in pursuit of a shared aim by producing information that causes states to view unilaterally adopting particular policies as in their interest. While the ultimate level of coordination may often turn out to be less under an epistemic regime, the reduced costs associated with regime may deliver a coordination at a reduced cost.

A comparison between the International Renewable Energy Agency (IRENA) and the climate change regime illustrates how epistemic cooperation can reduce bargaining costs and therefore facilitate policy coordination. IRENA is a stand-alone international institution with no formal ability to set legal rules for its member states, nor does its founding treaty create substantive obligations for states to implement particular renewable energy policies. Instead, IRENA's mission is to assemble information about renewable energy technologies, opportunities for renewable energy in particular countries, as well as practices and policies states have implemented to support renewable energy.[50] It also facilitates cooperation among its member states, as it has done in promoting the introduction into Africa of biofuel technology developed in South America.[51] These activities facilitate the diffusion of renewable energy and renewable energy technology without binding international legal rules requiring renewable energy's adoption – an enterprise that would surely have been considerably more contentious.

By contrast, parties to the UNFCCC struggled for years to negotiate a legally binding successor agreement to the Kyoto Protocol. The difficulty in negotiations arose from the need to obtain the agreement of a wide set of states with greatly diverging interests. Oil-producing states, for example,

---

[48]   Diplomatic Conference on Certain Copyright and Neighboring Rights Questions, *Rules of Procedure*, WIPO CRNR/DC/9 (Dec. 5, 1996).

[49]   Timothy Meyer, *Global Public Goods, Governance Risk, and International Energy*, 22 DUKE J. COMP. & INT'L L. 319 (2012).

[50]   Conference on the Establishment of the International Renewable Energy Agency, *Statute of the International Renewable Energy Agency (IRENA)*, IRENA/FC/Statute (Jan. 26, 2009).

[51]   International Renewable Energy Agency (IRENA), Report of the Director-General, *Medium-Term Strategy 2018-2022*, A/8/11 (Jan. 13, 2018), https://www.irena.org/-/media/Files/IRENA/A gency/About-IRENA/Assembly/Eighth-Assembly/A_8_11_MTS-2018-2022.pdf? la=en&hash=07546C5D6CB968EEEDBEBE322136DEF2AB389AFB.

opposed immediate and robust measures to transition away from a carbon-intensive economy. Developing countries like China and India similarly argued for a longer time horizon for any obligations they might undertake, so as not to prejudice their economic development objectives. The United States, for its part, resisted binding commitments to emissions reductions unless developing countries such as China and India agree to the same. Coupled with the consensus rules that prevail in the UNFCCC, this confluence of interests caused bargaining costs within the UNFCCC to skyrocket.

As a consequence of these bargaining difficulties, when several governments (most notably the German government) began to push for the creation of IRENA, they argued that it should not be housed in either the UNFCCC or the International Energy Agency.[52] Their rationale rested in part on a concern that nesting IRENA within larger institutions would subject the new organization to the political constraints arising from the operation of those institutions.[53] By contrast, establishing IRENA as a stand-alone institution with no law-creating powers would greatly reduce the bargaining costs around IRENA's operation. This structure meant that IRENA member states did not have to spend time and resources negotiating specific renewable energy standards. Instead, IRENA was liberated to carry out its primary missions of assembling information about renewable energy technologies, opportunities, and best practices, and disseminating that information to member states.[54]

Epistemic institutions likewise reduce transaction costs at the enforcement stage. There are several reasons for this. Most obviously, epistemic regimes have little to enforce, given that states lack significant substantive obligations. Enforcement costs are not, of course, zero. States still have procedural obligations related to sharing information, funding any related international organization, and perhaps capacity building in developing country members.

Second, if information successfully shifts states' understanding of their payoffs, states may no longer perceive themselves as having an interest in cheating. States have, in effect, changed their behavior because their understanding of their interests has changed. Katerina Linos provides some of the most compelling work on this subject.[55] She shows that policies across a range of issue areas, including family, health, and employment law, diffuse due to nonbinding recommendations from international organizations. These

---

[52] Thijs van de Graaf, *How IRENA Is Reshaping the Global Energy Architecture*, Eur. Energy Rev. (2012), http://www.europeanenergyreview.eu/site/pagina.php?id53615.

[53] *The Case for an International Renewable Energy Agency*, Ger. Gov't White Paper, Apr. 10–11, 2008, http://www.wcre.de/en/images/stories/The_case_for_IRENA.pdf.

[54] *See* Meyer, *supra* note 3, at 38–42.

[55] *See* Katerina Linos, The Democratic Foundations of Policy Diffusion (2013).

recommendations influence how voters feel about policy proposals, driving governments – especially governments in countries with internationally oriented voters – to adopt policies encouraged but not necessarily required by international regimes. The work of the Intergovernmental Panel on Climate Change provides another example. The IPCC has shifted perceptions in many nations (although by no means all), causing domestic constituencies and therefore governments to understand climate change regulation as increasingly in their interest.[56]

Third, epistemic regimes may also reduce sovereignty costs. States no longer perceive themselves as required to take certain action. In some countries, this may actually encourage states to take action, removing as it does an antagonistic relationship with international institutions. Moreover, epistemic agreements typically give states greater discretion in selecting their policies. This flexibility also allows nations to tailor policies to their own political, social, and economic situations in a way that binding legal rules might not, especially if they are detailed.

***

Credible commitment regimes and epistemic institutions represent two different strategies for coordinating state behavior. Credible commitment regimes, the traditional focus of much of international scholarship, involve states collectively agreeing on a legal rule to govern their conduct and then providing sanctions to deter states from cheating. The goal is to move state behavior in the direction of compliance with the legal rule. Both of these stages – bargaining and enforcement – are costly. In some instances, states may therefore prefer to cooperate over the production of information through epistemic regimes. These institutions change how states perceive the payoffs from selecting different policies. In their pure form, epistemic regimes permit states to make unilateral choices over policies, but they seek to guide those decisions through information production and often by requiring states to justify their decisions on the basis of that information. Epistemic regimes thus reduce both sovereignty costs and the transaction costs associated with bargaining and

---

[56] Intergovernmental Panel on Climate Change, Special Report on the Ocean and Cryosphere in a Changing Climate (2019), https://report.ipcc.ch/srocc/pdf/SROCC_FinalDraft_FullReport.pdf; Matthew Taylor, Matthew Weaver & Helen Davidson, *IPCC Climate Change Report Calls for Urgent Action to Phase Out Fossil Fuels – As It Happened*, Guardian (Oct. 8, 2018), https://www.theguardian.com/environment/live/2018/oct/08/ipcc-climate-change-report-urgent-action-fossil-fuels-live?page=with:block-5bbabd21e4b0b8830be6b6ac.

enforcement. At the same time, they can move state behavior in the direction of common goal, sometimes more effectively than credible commitment regimes, in which the common goal can be watered down during bargaining over the content of legal obligations or in which states can still fail to achieve compliance. The next section turns to considering the trade-offs involved in choosing between credible commitment and epistemic regimes.

3.4 EPISTEMIC AGREEMENTS VERSUS CREDIBLE COMMITMENTS

The choice between an epistemic regime and a credible commitment regime thus implicates a trade-off between transaction costs. Using epistemic agreements saves states the transaction costs of having to actually agree on a legal rule and also saves them the cost of contracting over and implementing costly enforcement mechanisms. On the other hand, under some circumstances, epistemic agreements will be inferior at actually coordinating state behavior. States may not trust the information produced or may still lack the incentive to coordinate their behavior in the absence of the threat of sanctions. Transaction cost economics predicts that states should select an epistemic regime when the costs of contracting over specific legal rules and enforcement procedures are larger than the costs of failing to coordinate on the basis of information alone.[57] In other words, epistemic regimes save on bargaining and enforcement costs, but possibly do so at the expense of effectiveness. Under what conditions will states prefer epistemic regimes because of the saved transaction costs, and under what conditions will the transaction costs inherent in credible commitment regimes be worth it?

3.4.1 *Problem Structure*

The structure of a cooperative problem influences whether credible commitments or epistemic strategies are a better choice. In some situations, simply providing information is enough to encourage states to adopt different standards that are more in line with the international regime's purpose. Influencing the information states have at their disposal is therefore sufficient

---

[57] In practice, of course, states may choose to do both. For example, agreements like the Biosafety Protocol may provide legally binding rules with which states must comply, as well as information-producing mechanisms such as the Biosafety Clearing-House. But even in agreements in which states mix the two forms, they face this same tradeoff at the level of an individual obligation. States can always replace an information-production obligation coupled with discretion with a binding legal rule backed by the threat of sanction.

to drive coordination.[58] In other situations, however, changing the information available to states still leaves them with an incentive to leave in place the status quo. In these situations, credible commitment regimes will outperform epistemic regimes.

Efforts to coordinate state responses to the risks of tobacco use illustrate a problem structure ripe for epistemic cooperation. First, tobacco regulation is a global problem. Tobacco moves in international trade and tobacco companies such as Phillip Morris are huge multinational enterprises with presence in many different nations. These companies can use their power, resources, and influence to block the adoption of tobacco regulation and to spread misinformation. Through these tactics, powerful multinational companies like tobacco companies can effectively prevent regulation that is in the long-term health interests of nations and in the fiscal interests of governments that must cope with the resulting health care costs. Indeed, Phillip Morris has aggressively used international economic law agreements to challenge domestic regulations such as plain packaging rules.[59] The global nature of the tobacco trade and tobacco companies thus makes tobacco regulation very much an international problem.

Second, though, the health benefits of regulating tobacco are largely internalized by the regulating state. Respecting this "internalization principle" means that governments have the right incentives to regulate if they understand the costs and benefits of different domestic regulatory regimes.[60] They do not, in other words, have strong incentives to choose their domestic control regime based on what other states choose to do with respect to tobacco. While it has a significant international dimension, tobacco control is not a collective action problem.

Third, information can change how states – or voters and interest groups within those states – understand the costs and benefits of regulating, or failing to regulate, tobacco products. Developing countries may be unaware of the severe health consequences of tobacco regulation or of the financial costs of health care arising from tobacco-related disease. Providing information about

---

[58]   Of course, in some situations the objective of an international regime may purely be the provision of information, with no implicit or explicit goal of encouraging states to adopt new standards. In such situations, epistemic regimes will by definition be better, since the international regime's purpose is not to change state behavior.

[59]   Philip Morris Asia Ltd. v. Australia, Case No. 2012-12 (Perm. Ct. Arb. 2017), https://pcacases .com/web/sendAttach/2190.

[60]   *See* ROBERT D. COOTER, THE STRATEGIC CONSTITUTION 107 (2000).

these costs and the benefits of regulation can lead states to make different regulatory choices domestically.

The Framework Convention on Tobacco Control (FCTC), the first international treaty dealing with tobacco, is designed to take advantage of this problem structure.[61] While the FCTC contains binding obligations to adopt tobacco control measures, in a number of areas the treaty does not direct states to take specific measures – despite the fact that its aim is to "protect present and future generations from the devastating health, social, environmental and economic consequences of tobacco consumption."[62] Instead, it provides for an epistemic strategy for coordinating state behavior. Articles 9 and 10, dealing with the regulation of tobacco products and tobacco product disclosures, stipulate that the FCTC's COP should adopt specific measures in conjunction with "competent international bodies." In practice, this institutional arrangement has meant that the COP looks to the World Health Organization and its Tobacco Free Initiative (TFI) to provide scientifically informed recommendations, which then become the basis for guidelines on tobacco regulation and disclosure. The WHO's recommendations, however, have value beyond just the FCTC COP. Regardless of whether the COP decides to adopt the WHO recommendations, states faced with tobacco problems have an incentive to regulate on the basis of the scientifically informed recommendations. Once benefits from regulation are made clear through information sharing and international risk assessment processes, countries internalize the benefits from reducing their own exposure to tobacco, regardless of the stringency of regulation in other countries. And the evidence is that the FCTC's strategy has worked. While room for more effective implementation remains, reviews have found the FCTC to be effective in spreading tobacco control regulation globally, leading in turn to lives saved.[63]

Adopting this epistemic structure eased the negotiation and adoption of the FCTC. During negotiations some nations, led by the United States, pushed back against broader limitations on tobacco advertising, promotion, and sponsorship, as well as a legally binding ban on handing out free tobacco samples.[64] Insisting on writing legally binding standards into the treaty could

---

[61] Convention on Tobacco Control, *supra* note 42.

[62] *Id.* at art 2.

[63] Janet Chung-Hall, Lorraine Craig, Shannon Gravely, Natalie Sansone & Geoffrey T Fong, *Impact of the WHO FCTC Over the First Decade: A Global Evidence Review Prepared for the Impact Assessment Expert Group*, 28 TOBACCO CONTROL 119 (2019) (reviewing the literature on the FCTC's effectiveness and assessing implementation of the FCTC by member states).

[64] Sean D. Murphy, *Adoption of Framework Convention on Tobacco Control*, 97 AM. J. INT'L L. 689 (2003).

well have caused negotiations to founder. Instead, drafting broad standards giving states discretion to act in accordance with recommendations from the WHO allowed the agreement to go forward with the idea that states might unilaterally adopt controls in accordance with expert recommendations.

The structure of cooperating on sustainable fisheries presents a contrasting example in which information, although necessary to effective international cooperation, does not remove the collective action problem. Overfishing is a major problem, with global fish stocks depleted or depleting.[65] Overfishing threatens the livelihood of nations and people dependent on fishing for the livelihood, as well as the health of populations that depend on fish as a primary food source.[66]

To combat this threat, nations have agreed to international regimes that establish levels of fishing that are sustainable and allocate quotas among fishing nations.[67] But knowing what constitutes a sustainable catch of Southern Bluefin tuna, for example, does not necessarily change a state's incentives to regulate its catch of tuna. Overfishing is a classic tragedy of the commons.[68] While each fisherman (or nation) gets the entire benefit of each additional fish he catches, he receives only a portion of the future benefit from preserving fish stocks. Thus, restraining tuna fishing is costly to a state in economic terms. At the same time, such costly restraint may not preserve fish stock for future economic exploitation. Other states may simply step in and catch more fish today. Effective environmental coordination in fisheries thus requires not only providing scientific information about what constitutes a sustainable catch; it also requires legal rules and enforcement procedures that enhance the costs of defection.

Not surprisingly, regional fisheries conventions – such as the International Convention for the Conservation of Atlantic Tunas, the Convention for the Conservation of the Southern Bluefin Tuna, and even the International Convention on the Regulation of Whaling (ICRW) – impose legally binding quotas on the catch of regulated species. These legally binding rules are supported by a series of enforcement mechanisms, including jurisdiction

---

[65] Margaret A. Young, Trading Fish, Saving Fish: The Interaction between Regimes in International Law 6 (2011).

[66] David Farrier & Linda Tucker, *Access to Marine Bioresources: Hitching the Conservation Cart to the Bioprospecting Horse*, 32 Ocean Dev. & Int'l L. 213, 229 (2001).

[67] *See, e.g.*, Convention for the Conservation of Southern Blue-Fish Tuna, May 10, 1993, 1819 U.N.T.S. 360; International Convention for the Regulation of Whaling, Dec. 2, 1946, 161 U.N.T.S. 72.

[68] Garret Hardin, *The Tragedy of the Commons*, 162 Sci. 1243 (1968).

before the International Tribunal for the Law of the Sea and the International Court of Justice.[69]

3.4.2 *Information Credibility*

The role of information credibility is the second feature that affects the relative costs of epistemic regimes versus credible commitments. Epistemic regimes essentially ask states to trust that the information produced and shared within the regime is fair, accurate, and reliable, that is, credible. In some instances, however, states may have reason to doubt this. Information generating capacities vary across countries, as do information assessing capacities. Developed states such as members of the European Union or Japan have the ability to conduct complicated scientific research, as well as to replicate studies done elsewhere. Developing countries may lack these capacities. In some circumstances, they may also fear that information producing governments will slant the information to produce results in their own interest. If developing states so fear, they may be unwilling to regulate domestically based on information produced internationally. As a result, to be effective epistemic regimes must create confidence in the information they produce. Where an epistemic agreement is not able to produce such confidence, a credible commitment regime may be superior.

The regulation of trade in hazardous materials provides a case in point. The so-called Chemicals Conventions – the Rotterdam Convention on Prior Informed Consent, the Stockholm Convention on Persistent Organic Pollutants, and the Basel Convention on Hazardous Waste – each place global restrictions on trade in certain kinds of toxic materials. Each convention has the same basic architecture, with a few salient differences. The treaties provide a set of legally mandated controls that apply to covered materials. Toxic materials are, in turn, added to the list of covered materials by decision of the COPs following a risk assessment procedure. These risk assessment procedures are the epistemic piece of the chemicals regime, which blends epistemic and credible commitment strategies.

---

[69] Indeed, these tribunals have heard a number of disputes involving fishers. *See* Whaling in the Antarctic (Austl. v. Japan; N.Z. Intervening), Judgment, 2014 I.C.J. 226 (Mar. 31, 2014); Southern Bluefin Tuna Cases (N.Z. v. Japan, Austl. v. Japan), Case No. 2-3, Order of Aug. 27, 1999, 1999 ITLOS Rep. 280; Southern Bluefin Tuna Cases (N.Z v. Japan, Austl. v. Japan), Jurisdiction and Admissibility, 23 R.I.A.A. 1 (Int'l Trib. L. Sea 2000). These cases have had mixed results, however, in generating compliance. After losing the whaling case at the ICJ, Japan withdrew from the International Convention on the Regulation of Whaling and, in 2019, resumed commercial whaling. *Japan Resumes Commercial Whaling After 30 Years*, BBC (July 1, 2019).

The Chemicals Conventions raise difficult issues about scientific capacity and information credibility precisely because of the asymmetric information between developed and developing states, as well as differing economic incentives. Many toxic substances are produced and exported by developed countries. In some situations, countries will ban substances domestically while permitting their export. Developing countries, unaware of the risk, will continue to import the substance. Developing countries may thus distrust claims that potentially toxic substances are safe. On the opposite extreme, developed countries may wish to ban trade in toxic substances such as DDT because the so-called "circle of poison" means that DDT used in developing countries is reimported in developed countries on, for example, food products.[70] Developing countries, however, may distrust information about the extent of the harmful effects of DDT. These countries often use DDT to combat malaria. They therefore will want to be sure about the scale of the harmful effects so that they can weigh those effects carefully against the potentially significant health benefits of DDT.

Although they have similar architectures, the Rotterdam and Stockholm Conventions deal with these credibility issues differently. The Rotterdam Convention is more of an epistemic regime, while the Stockholm Convention involves more credible commitments. For its part, the Rotterdam Convention requires states to report their own "final domestic regulatory actions" controlling toxic substances.[71] Multiple reports from around the globe trigger a risk assessment, which can result in a listing decision.[72] The effect of a listing decision is that each state is then entitled to make a choice as to whether it consents to the import of the listed material.[73] Requiring that information reported internationally be based on domestic regulatory actions boosts the credibility of the information. Other states know that a final regulatory action means that a state is sufficiently confident that a substance is toxic that it wishes to ban the substance to protect its own population. Having created that confidence in the quality of information, Rotterdam leaves the ultimate decision on trade controls to individual states.[74]

---

[70] Evan Mascagni & Shannon Post, *The Circle of Poison*, AL JAZEERA (Nov. 15, 2016), https://www.aljazeera.com/programmes/specialseries/2016/11/circle-poison-pesticides-developing-world-161115084547144.html.

[71] Rotterdam Convention, *supra* note 5.

[72] *Id.*

[73] *Id.*

[74] The Rotterdam Convention does provide legal rules restricting trade with those countries that have chosen not to consent to the import of a listed substance. Rotterdam Convention, *supra* note 5. In this sense, the Rotterdam Convention is not purely an epistemic agreement.

The Stockholm Convention balances these pressures differently. Instead of requiring states to produce information about domestic regulatory decisions and using that information to initiate the listing process, any state can make a listing proposal.[75] The state must include with its proposal certain required information for the risk assessment. Like the Rotterdam Convention, the Stockholm Convention follows the proposal with a risk assessment designed to assess the credibility of the scientific information appended to the proposal.[76] But unlike Rotterdam, the information attached to the proposal is not necessarily accompanied by a signal, such as domestic regulation, that testifies to its credibility. This information producing requirement raises much more serious concerns about the credibility of information appended to a proposal. In particular, it makes more serious informational demands on states seeking international regulation. For developing states that lack scientific capacity, these risk assessments under the Stockholm Convention may require information processing capacity that they lack. Technical and financial assistance for developing states can help alleviate these considerations. Indeed, during initial efforts to regulate persistent organic pollutants under the Convention on Long-Range Transboundary Air Pollution, the United States and northern European countries stepped in and provided funding for newly independent Eastern European states to participate in the risk assessment process. They did so precisely to address this capacity problem, although reports indicate that the targeted states remained relatively inactive in the assessment process.[77]

But where technical and financial assistance are insufficient, credible commitment regimes may offer a better solution than epistemic regimes. Lacking the signals about credibility that come from the Rotterdam Convention's linking of information and domestic regulation, a choice architecture like that provided by Rotterdam is inappropriate for the Stockholm Convention. With less confidence in the reliability of the information, states may be unwilling to voluntarily regulate in situations in which regulation is optimal. Rather than imposing a prior informed consent regime, Stockholm therefore bans or restricts the trade in listed chemicals directly. The listing decision, in other words, directly engages legal commitments to offset the potentially less credible information produced at the front end of the process.

---

[75] Stockholm Convention on Persistent Organic Pollutants, May 22, 2001, 40 I.L.M. 532 (2001).
[76] *Id.*
[77] Henrik Selin & Noelle Eckley, *Science, Politics, and Persistent Organic Pollutants: The Role of Scientific Assessments in International Environmental Co-operation*, 3 INT'L ENVTL. AGREEMENTS: POL. L. & ECON. 17, 25 (2003).

3.4.3 *Limits to Officials' Engagement with Information*

Credible commitment regimes may also be preferable when states are unwilling or unable to regulate on the basis of information. Modern international governance increasingly tries to make scientific information the basis for regulation. This is evident in a wide range of regimes, from the SPS Agreement to the Chemicals Conventions discussed above. Basing regulation on scientific information, however, may not be effective or desirable in certain circumstances. It may not be effective because not all states or government officials view scientific information as a valid basis for decision-making. Alternatively, they may be unable under some circumstances to engage in the deliberations necessary for epistemic strategies to work. Finally, epistemic regimes may be inappropriate when policymakers (or the domestic constituencies that motivate them) question the value-neutrality of scientific or expert-produced information. It may be undesirable in some circumstances because scientific information is not value-neutral in the way that the move to science sometimes supposes it is. I unpack these three points below.

First, government officials may not necessarily view scientific information as a valid basis for policymaking in specific issue areas. This point is distinct from issues regarding the credibility of scientific information. Here, government officials may resist the notion of regulating based on science or expertise, rather than worrying about the content of the scientific or expert advice. For example, three Nigerian states boycotted efforts by the WHO to eradicate polio.[78] The boycotts were led by religious groups such as the Supreme Council for Sharia in Nigeria.[79] The underlying causes of the boycott were complex. In part, they had roots in issues about the credibility of Western-provided health services stemming from Pfizer Trovan drug trials in Nigeria, and in part they were tied to political themes of conflict between the Western world and Muslim communities.[80] They also, however, stemmed from a divide in how scientific information was understood by religious leaders who supported the boycott and the targeted community that had little experience with the delivery of health services.

In situations in which the validity of science- or information-based regulation is itself contested, credible commitments may be a sounder basis for international cooperation. Epistemic strategies do not engage government officials' decision-making processes in the way necessary to coordinate state

---

[78] A. S. Jegende, *What Led to the Nigerian Boycott of the Polio Vaccination Campaign?* 4 PLOS Med. 417 (2007).

[79] *Id.*

[80] *Id.*

behavior. Legal rules that provide a command backed by at least some sanction may engage a different kind of decision-making process by government actors. States may respond to a legal mandate even if they reject the scientific information or expert advice underlying it. The international moratorium on whaling, under the auspices of the International Convention on the Regulation of Whaling, offers a case in point.[81] Although they engage in whaling now, nations such as Iceland, Japan, and Norway respected the moratorium on whaling for a number of years despite disagreeing with the (weak) scientific basis for the moratorium.[82]

Second, capacity-constrained states might respond better to (clear) legal commands that tell them what behavior to expect. In the absence of the expertise or resources to evaluate different policies in light of the information produced by epistemic regimes, information may fail to provide incentives for capacity-constrained states to change their behavior. Although of course capacity constraints can limit states' information processing ability during ordinary times, the international law governing response to natural disasters provides a stark illustration of circumstances under which officials may be unable to regulate based on epistemic strategies. Following natural disasters, humanitarian relief from abroad can be critical to ensuring the survival and recovery of affected populations. National governments may, however, be slow to permit humanitarian relief into the country, in part out of fear of relaxing border controls, as was the case after Cyclone Nargis hit Myanmar in 2008, causing the worst natural disaster in the nation's history.[83] More frequently, during crises processing information about what should be allowed in to the country and what should not may be too taxing on government officials' limited resources. Decision-making capacity that relies on assessing information may thus be unreliable. Legal obligations that do not place the same kind of information assessment demands on decision-makers may be a superior form of regulation. Efforts to develop a disaster law framework thus might be improved through the drafting of conventions governing how affected states, as well as assisting states, must respond.[84]

[81]   Phillip Shabecoff, *Commission Votes to Ban Hunting of Whales*, N.Y. TIMES, Jul. 24, 1982.
[82]   Steinar Andresen, *The Whaling Regime, in* STEINAR ANDRESEN, TORA SKODVIN, ARILD UNDERDAL & JORGAN WETTESTAD, SCIENCE AND POLITICS IN INTERNATIONAL ENVIRONMENTAL REGIMES: BETWEEN INTEGRITY AND INVOLVEMENT 37, 45 (2000).
[83]   Pam Steele, *Disaster Preparedness: Lessons from Cyclone Nargis*, GUARDIAN, Jul. 16, 2013.
[84]   *See, e.g.,* Guidelines for the Domestic Facilitation and Regulation of International Disaster Relief and Initial Recovery Assistance, INT'L FED'N OF RED CROSS (IFRC), http://www.ifrc.org/en/what-we-do/idrl/idrl-guidelines/.

Finally, making international cooperation information-based is not value-neutral and can have significant distributional consequences.[85] The decision to base regulation on scientific information – as opposed to religious or social values, for example – is itself a value judgment that one need not necessarily accept. To return to the example of whaling, the International Whaling Commission (IWC) has maintained its moratorium on commercial whaling since the 1980s. The IWC's own scientific committee has stated that the moratorium is not justifiable on scientific grounds.[86] Whaling stocks could tolerate some level of whaling without endangering their existence. Nevertheless, countries like the United States have successfully opposed lifting the moratorium. They do so not because of any relevant scientific information, but because they (or the domestic interest groups that support their policies) believe that it is morally objectionable to kill whales. Interestingly, the United States has also supported an exception to the moratorium for indigenous populations.[87] Again, the justification for this exception flows from some other value, in this case a desire to preserve native cultures in which whaling plays an important role, rather than from scientific information.

Although often framed as a dispute about the application of the precautionary principle, the long-running fight within the World Trade Organization over trade in genetically modified organisms has elements of a dispute about values as well.[88] European consumers, in particular, object to genetically modified foods. Their objections appear in part to be based on a general objection to modifying the genes of living beings, rather than any scientific reason to think that GMOs are harmful as a general matter.[89]

Presenting information-based regimes as value-neutral can present two different kinds of challenges. First, it may lead states to question the legitimacy of the entire legal regime. If the values underlying the information produced

[85] *See* On Amir & Orly Lobel, *Stumble, Predict, Nudge: How Behavioral Economics Informs Law and Policy*, 108 COLUM. L. REV. 2098, 2118 (2008).
[86] Dennis Normile, *Scientists Renew Objections to Japan's Whaling Program*, SCI. MAG. (June 19, 2015, 12:15 PM), https://www.sciencemag.org/news/2015/06/scientists-renew-objections-japan-s-whaling-program.
[87] *Aboriginal Subsistence Whaling*, INT'L WHALING COMM'N, https://iwc.int/aboriginal.
[88] Panel Report, *European Communities – Measures Affecting the Approval and Marketing of Biotech Products*, WTO Doc. WT/DS291 (adopted Nov. 21, 2006).
[89] Particular genetically modified organisms can of course be harmful in particular circumstances. Genetically modified crops, for example, may threaten crop diversity, a long-term risk to the security of the food supply. Heather Landry, *Challenging Evolution: How GMOs Can Influence Genetic Diversity*, SCI. IN THE NEWS (Aug. 10, 2015), http://sitn.hms.harvard.edu/flash/2015/challenging-evolution-how-gmos-can-influence-genetic-diversity/.

by the regime are not widely shared, the entire cooperative endeavor may become suspect. The epistemic aspects of the trade regime have come under stress in part because it is not clear that a widespread consensus exists on whether the current state of scientific information is the appropriate basis on which to determine the permissibility of trade restrictions on genetically modified foods. Credible commitment regimes, on the other hand, tend to rely on the process through which legal rules are created, contested, and enforced to confer legitimacy on the outcomes.[90] Credible commitment regimes, by formulating legal rules in accordance with processes perceived to be fair, may thus outperform epistemic agreements in the presence of value-driven conflicts.

Second, as the whaling example shows, information-based regulation within credible commitment regimes can in some situations be vulnerable to exploitation by powerful states that are not committed to the underlying scientific premise. Powerful states may pressure other states to adopt non-science-based regulations, such as the blanket moratorium on commercial whaling. In such situations, a purely epistemic regime may be preferable as a way to limit the possibility of power politics influencing the choice of legal rule.

The blanket moratorium on commercial whaling again illustrates the point. The preamble to the ICRW provides that "that the whale stocks are susceptible of natural increases if whaling is properly regulated, and that increases in the size of whale stocks will permit increases in the numbers of whales which may be captured without endangering these natural resources." This language makes clear that at its founding member states viewed the ICRW as a sustainable management regime. The American-led efforts to keep the whaling moratorium in place have undermined this view of the ICRW. As its regulation of whaling has come to be value-driven, rather than science-driven as originally contemplated, the legitimacy of the ICRW itself has come under increasing pressure. Major whaling nations such as Japan, Iceland, and Norway have at various times defied the ban, left the ICRW, and founded the North Atlantic Marine Mammal Commission, an alternative regime to promote responsible whaling.[91] An epistemic regime could have avoided

---

[90] *See, e.g.,* Daniel Bodansky, *The Legitimacy of International Governance: A Coming Challenge for International Environmental Law*, 93 Am. J. Int'l L. 596 (1999).

[91] David D. Caron, *The International Whaling Commission and the North Atlantic Marine Mammal Commission: The Institutional Risks of Coercion for Consensual Structures*, 89 Am. J. Int'l L. 154 (1995).

the tensions that have arisen due to the nonscientific basis for the moratorium.[92]

Finally, just as capacity constraints can limit the effectiveness of epistemic regimes, they can also expose epistemic regimes to manipulation by powerful states. As discussed above, lack of capacity may lead states to make worse choices within epistemic regimes than they would in the presence of legal rules that embody a collective and bargained-for judgment as to how states should behave. Moreover, sophisticated states may exploit this lack of capacity for their own benefit. Developed states might, for example, push for a prior informed consent regime in hazardous waste, rather than a treaty that outright bans trade in a substance. Because of deficiencies in how states translate information into domestic regulation, prior informed consent regimes may allow sophisticated states to ban environmental practices they deem too risky but still profit from the fact that less scientifically sophisticated states still engage in the practice.

The Basel Convention on Hazardous Waste provides an illustrative example. The Basel Convention creates a prior informed consent regime for trade in hazardous waste as between parties.[93] Specifically, before a shipment of hazardous waste can proceed, the parties must exchange written notice of consent as well as confirmation that environmentally sound disposal plans are in place in the importing country. Developed countries favored this regime because it allowed them to continue to trade in hazardous waste. Developing countries, on the other hand, objected on the grounds that these rules were ripe for exploitation.[94] The parties engaged in the trade might forge necessary documents, and developing states might not be in a position to determine what constituted environmentally-sound disposal of particular hazardous wastes. As a consequence, thirty-nine African nations refused to sign the Basel Convention, and instead negotiated among themselves the Bamako Convention, a credible commitment regime that bans outright importing hazardous waste into Africa.

3.5 CONCLUSION

International cooperation is changing, although scholars have been slow to notice the change. Like domestic regulation, information-based regimes are increasingly complementing or supplanting credible commitment regimes.

---

[92] Of course, the legally binding rules may have been necessary to allow whaling stocks to recover earlier in the life of the ICRW. In this sense, multilateral regimes may have life cycles that make different strategies appropriate for different time periods. *See* Harlan Grant Cohen, *Multilateralism's Life Cycle*, 112 AM. J. INT'L L. 47 (2018).

[93] Basel Convention, *supra* note 6, at art. 6.

[94] HUNTER, SALZMAN & ZAELKE, *supra* note 22, at 965.

This shift is an opportunity to improve international cooperation in a variety of ways. It offers the possibility of reducing bargaining and enforcement costs and simultaneously moving away from tired conversations about whether the lack of centralized enforcement means that international law is not really "law." At the same time, however, treaty designers need to be sensitive to the fact that information-based regulation comes with significant drawbacks. It may fail to produce coordination when credible commitment regimes would. It also has the potential to create backlashes in situations in which the underlying value of scientifically driven governance is not widely shared.

4

Egocentric Bias in Perceptions of Customary International Law

Ryan M. Scoville[*]

Customary international law (CIL) is "general practice accepted as law."[1] Positivist in orientation, this formulation establishes that the task of ascertaining CIL is fundamentally empirical: a proper analysis will identify both the extent to which states around the world engage in a practice and their reasons for doing so. Only those practices that garner sufficient global adherence will qualify.

It is increasingly clear, however, that government officials, academic commentators, and private lawyers often fail to adhere to this understanding. In a citation analysis covering decades of published opinions, Stephen Choi and Mitu Gulati recently found that international courts "do not come anywhere close to engaging in the type of analysis" that the traditional doctrine requires.[2] Stefan Talmon reached a similar conclusion in reviewing decisions from the International Court of Justice.[3] Others, meanwhile, have observed deficiencies in CIL assessments in legal scholarship and opinions from municipal courts.[4] Perhaps the most significant problem is underinclusivity. Far from collecting and evaluating evidence of practice from around the globe, analysts often engage in inductive reasoning on the basis of small and convenient

---

[*] For comments on earlier drafts, I thank Milan Markovic and Tim Meyer.

[1] Statute of the International Court of Justice art. 38(1)(b).

[2] Stephen J. Choi & Mitu Gulati, *Customary International Law: How Do Courts Do It?*, in CUSTOM'S FUTURE: INTERNATIONAL LAW IN A CHANGING WORLD 117 (Curtis A. Bradley ed., 2016).

[3] Stefan Talmon, *Determining Customary International Law: The ICJ's Methodology Between Induction, Deduction and Assertion*, 26 EUR. J. INT'L L. 417, 441 (2015).

[4] *See generally* Nikki C. Gutierrez & Mitu Gulati, *Custom in Our Courts: Reconciling Theory with Reality in the Debate About* Erie Railroad *and Customary International Law*, 27 DUKE J. COMP. & INT'L L. 243 (2017) (conducting a citation analysis of decisions by US federal courts); Ryan M. Scoville, *Finding Customary International Law*, 101 IOWA L. REV. 1893 (2016) (conducting a citation analysis of decisions by US federal courts and the academic publications cited therein).

samples.[5] In such cases, the pronouncements that result are little more than the declarant's crude estimates of international norms.

This methodology renders the identification of CIL vulnerable to certain types of judgment error that are well known to social psychologists but unfamiliar to many legal scholars and law practitioners. Specifically, a long line of empirical research has established that, due to egocentric biases, individuals often fare poorly at discerning norms. This chapter identifies and explains two of those biases, and then explores their relevance and implications for efforts to identify customary international law. In doing so, the chapter seeks to offer a fresh form of interdisciplinary analysis on a topic that lawyers often approach as a pure matter of legal doctrine.[6]

4.1 TWO BIASES IN THE PERCEPTION OF NORMS

Several decades of experiments in social psychology have shown that egocentric biases can distort norm perception. For present purposes, the most significant biases are the False Consensus Effect and the False Uniqueness Effect. This part explains each phenomenon.

4.1.1 *The False Consensus Effect (FCE)*

The FCE holds that individuals tend to perceive their own behaviors and judgments as exhibiting greater normativity than do dissimilar others.[7] A subject will tend to view his own position as "relatively common and appropriate to existing circumstances while viewing alternative responses as uncommon, deviant, or inappropriate."[8] He will also tend to perceive those who share his position as relatively diverse in their attitudes, values, and interests, and those who do not as relatively homogeneous.[9] To be

---

[5] *See, e.g., id.* at 1909–1916 (reporting this tendency in U.S. federal courts).

[6] For exceptions to this tendency, see, for example, JACK L. GOLDSMITH & ERIC A. POSNER, THE LIMITS OF INTERNATIONAL LAW (2006) (offering a game-theoretic account of CIL); ANDREW T. GUZMAN, HOW INTERNATIONAL LAW WORKS: A RATIONAL CHOICE THEORY (2008) (same).

[7] Glenn S. Sanders & Brian Mullen, *Accuracy in Perceptions of Consensus: Differential Tendencies of People with Majority and Minority Positions*, 13 EUR. J. SOC. PSYCHOL. 57, 68 (1983).

[8] Lee Ross, David Greene & Pamela House, *The "False Consensus Effect": An Egocentric Bias in Social Perception and Attribution Processes*, 13 J. EXPERIMENTAL SOC. PSYCHOL. 279, 280 (1977).

[9] George R. Goethals, Shelley Jean Allison & Marnie Frost, *Perceptions of the Magnitude and Diversity of Social Support*, 15 J. EXPERIMENTAL SOC. PSYCHOL. 570, 578–580 (1979).

clear, the FCE "has no direct bearing on whether subjects will overestimate, underestimate, or accurately estimate the actual consensus for
their own behavior."[10] At its core, the theory is strictly about the relativity
of norm appearances among individuals comprising a heterogeneous
population.

Consider two brief illustrations: (1) X enjoys *Lost in Translation* but his
colleague does not. The FCE holds that they will likely arrive at different
estimates of both the size and nature of the film's fan base, with X's
estimate being materially higher and envisioning fans with a relatively
variegated set of aesthetic preferences. Moreover, this will probably occur
regardless of whether a majority of moviegoers share his opinion. (2)
Y protests a government policy but her colleague supports it. The FCE
posits that they will likely make different projections about the number
and diversity of those who protest. Where Y might perceive large demon-
strations representing a substantial cross section of the public, her colleague will be more inclined to see limited opposition from an ideologically
narrow group of malcontents. And again, all of this will likely happen
regardless of whether most citizens actually protest. Experiments suggest
that the FCE is typically moderate but nevertheless variable in
magnitude,[11] persists even after substantial exposure to a reference
population,[12] survives de-biasing measures such as education,[13] and manifests in a wide variety of contexts, including election predictions,[14] con-
troversies over public policy,[15] and legal disputes.[16]

Why does the FCE occur? Many researchers propose unintentional, cognitive influences. Some suggest that individuals perceive norms in self-
referential ways due to homophily, or the common tendency to socialize
primarily with similar others, the effect of which is a propensity to extrapolate
normativity from interpersonal experiences that are not necessarily

---

[10]   Brian Mullen, Jennifer L. Atkins, Debbie S. Champion, Cecilia Edwards, Dana Hardy, John
       E. Story & Mary Vanderklok, *The False Consensus Effect: A Meta-analysis of 115 Hypothesis
       Tests*, 21 J. EXPERIMENTAL SOC. PSYCHOL. 262, 263 (1985).
[11]   Mullen et al., *supra* note 10, at 267.
[12]   Sanders & Mullen, *supra* note 7, at 66.
[13]   Joachim Krueger & Russell W. Clement, *The Truly False Consensus Effect: An Ineradicable
       and Egocentric Bias in Social Perception*, 67 J. PERSONALITY & SOC. PSYCHOL. 596, 601
       (1994).
[14]   Adeline Delavande & Charles F. Manski, *Candidate Preferences and Expectations of Election
       Outcomes*, 109 PROC. NAT'L ACAD. SCI. 3711, 3715 (2012).
[15]   Terri Mannarini, Michele Roccato & Silvia Russo, *The False Consensus Effect: A Trigger of
       Radicalization in Locally Unwanted Land Use Conflicts?*, 42 J. ENVTL. PSYCHOL. 76 (2015).
[16]   Lawrence Solan, Terri Rosenblatt & Daniel Osherson, *False Consensus Bias in Contract
       Interpretation*, 108 COLUM. L. REV. 1268 (2008).

representative within a broader population.[17] Others point to the availability heuristic.[18] On this account, a comparative ease of cognitive access to one's own position yields relatively high estimates of its commonality.[19]

A separate line of research proffers a motivational explanation, suggesting that individuals perceive their own attitudes and behaviors as relatively common and appropriate because they derive value from doing so. Perceived agreement with peers might subjectively validate personal behaviors and beliefs that would otherwise fuel uncertainty or discomfort.[20] The perception of agreement might also facilitate harmonious social interactions,[21] satisfy personal dispositional needs,[22] and honor vested interests.[23] Although there is uncertainty about their relative importance,[24] these explanations are not necessarily antagonistic to one another.

One of the most important findings about the FCE is that it is a bit of a misnomer as applied to majority positions. Even while making relatively high projections regarding the commonality of their own attitude or behavior, members of the majority tend to *underestimate* the objective extent of that commonality.[25] Members of the minority, in contrast, will not only make relatively high estimates of the commonality of their own position, but also

---

[17] *See* Willem Bosveld, Willem Koomen, Joop van der Plight & Janine W. Plaisier, *Differential Construal as an Explanation for False Consensus and False Uniqueness Effects*, 31 J. EXPERIMENTAL SOC. PSYCHOL. 518, 519 (1995) (discussing this research).

[18] *Cf.* Amos Tversky & Daniel Kahneman, *Availability: A Heuristic for Judging Frequency and Probability*, 5 COGNITIVE PSYCHOL. 207 (1973) (explaining the availability heuristic).

[19] Bosveld et al., *supra* note 17 at 519 (discussing this research).

[20] James A. Kitts, *Egocentric Bias or Information Management? Selective Disclosure and the Social Roots of Norm Misperception*, 66 SOC. SCI. Q. 222, 224 (2003); *see also* Steven J. Sherman, Clark C. Presson & Laurie Chassin, *Mechanisms Underlying the False Consensus Effect: The Special Role of Threats to the Self*, 10 PERSONALITY & SOC. PSCYHOL. BULL. 127, 135–136 (1984) (suggesting that this is a particularly powerful determinant of the FCE).

[21] Norman Miller & Gary Marks, *Assumed Similarity Between Self and Other: Effect of Expectation of Future Interaction With That Other*, 45 SOC. PSYCHOL. Q. 100 (1982).

[22] Michael H. Kernis, *Need for Uniqueness, Self-Schemas, and Thought as Moderators of the False-Consensus Effect*, 20 J. EXPERIMENTAL SOC. PSCYHOL. 350 (1984).

[23] William D. Crano, *Assumed Consensus of Attitudes: The Effect of Vested Interest*, 9 PERSONALITY & SOC. PSYCHOL. BULL. 597 (1983). *But see* Leandre R. Fabrigar & Jon A. Krosnick, *Attitude Importance and the False Consensus Effect*, 21 PERSONALITY & SOC. PSYCHOL. BULL. 468 (1995) (finding that the subjective importance of the perceiver's attitude does not affect the size of the FCE).

[24] *Cf.* Mullen et al., *supra* note 10, at 263 ("[T]he mechanisms underlying the false consensus effect have not been clearly delineated.").

[25] Joachim Krueger & Russell W. Clement, *Estimates of Social Consensus by Majorities and Minorities: The Case for Social Projection*, 1 PERSONALITY & SOC. PSYCHOL. REV. 299, 312 (1997); Sanders & Mullen, *supra* note 7, at 65.

overestimate in doing so.[26] Moreover, the minority's overestimation will normally diverge from actuality to a greater extent than the majority's underestimation.[27] In short, majorities and minorities both experience perceptual distortion, but minorities are uniquely prone to perceive a consensus that does not exist.

The explanations for this dynamic vary. Some are motivational: if unconfident about their respective estimates, members of a population might hedge by selecting a conservative figure somewhere near 50 percent, resulting in a negative error of underestimation on the part of the majority and a positive error of overestimation by the minority.[28] Or, if it is uncomfortable to be in the minority, individuals who hold that status may experience a uniquely strong motivation to overestimate the pervasiveness of what distinguishes them.[29] An explanation of the cognitive variety is that the majority overestimates the prevalence of the minority position because encounters with the minority are atypical, vivid, and thus easy to recall in memory.[30]

4.1.2 *The False Uniqueness Effect (FUE)*

The FUE is simply the opposite of the FCE: a tendency to perceive one's own behaviors and attitudes as *less* normative than do dissimilar others. If, for instance, one person can run a seven-minute mile and another cannot, the former might perceive her feat as less common than the other. The FUE can also manifest as a form of stereotyping, where subjects underestimate the commonality of their own behaviors and judgments within a group to which they do not belong.[31] For example, in American politics, a Republican might perceive that her position on an issue is less popular among Democrats than it is in fact. Research on this phenomenon is comparatively limited but suggests that the FUE can serve a motivational purpose – a subject might derive satisfaction from perceiving that her behavior is extraordinary, even when it is not.[32] In certain circumstances, the FUE also occurs due to the difficulty

---

[26]   Sanders & Mullen, *supra* note 7, at 65

[27]   *Id.*

[28]   *Id.* at 67–68.

[29]   *Id.* at 59.

[30]   *Id.* at 67.

[31]   Brian Mullen, John F. Dovidio, Craig Johnson & Carlyn Copper, *In-group – Out-group Difference in Social Projection*, 28 J. EXPERIMENTAL SOC. PSYCHOL. 422 (1992).

[32]   Jerry Suls, C.K. Wan, David H. Barlow & Richard G. Heimberg, *The Fallacy of Uniqueness: Social Consensus Perceptions of Anxiety Disorder Patients and Community Residents*, 24 J. RES. PERSONALITY 415, 429 (1990); *see also* Bosveld et al., *supra* note 17, at 519 (discussing the motivational logic of the FUE).

of detecting an opinion or behavior that is privately held among members of a population.[33]

In the sense that both entail a low estimate of the normativity of personal behaviors and perspectives, the FUE and the majority's encounter with the FCE appear similar. There is, however, a critical difference, as the estimates in each case will tend to be low in relation to different things. A person in the majority who experiences the FCE will likely underestimate only in relation to the *actual* normativity of her position; that estimate will still be high in comparison to the estimates of dissimilar others. The estimate of a person who experiences the FUE, in contrast, will be low relative to the estimates of dissimilar others. For example, imagine that 70 percent of moviegoers hold a favorable view of *Lost in Translation*, that X is part of the majority who liked the film, and that Y is part of the minority who disliked it. If X and Y experience the FCE, X might estimate that 60 percent of viewers enjoyed the film while Y might estimate 40 percent. But if X and Y experience the FUE, it is more likely that X will estimate that 40 percent enjoyed the film while Y estimates 60 percent.

4.2 RELEVANCE TO ESTIMATES OF CIL

Having outlined the basic nature of the FCE and FUE, the question now is whether these phenomena have any relevance to estimates of customary international law. Strictly speaking, the answer is uncertain. No one has tested for, much less confirmed, the operation of egocentric bias in this context. Nevertheless, by comparing the circumstances that give rise to the FCE and FUE on one hand and pronouncements about CIL on the other, it is possible to develop a reasonable hypothesis. The argument here is that the FCE and FUE are plausibly relevant, such that underinclusive research on state practice and *opinio juris* could very well intensify an omnipresent risk of egocentric perception even when judges, lawyers, and legal scholars attempt to estimate CIL in good faith.

4.2.1 *Self-Projection in Inductive Reasoning*

The most salient feature of the FCE and FUE is that they manifest as flaws of inductive reasoning – a subject knows something about themselves and perhaps a group of similar others, and overuses that information to draw

---

[33] Deborah E. S. Frable, *Being and Feeling Unique: Statistical Deviance and Psychological Marginality*, 61 J. PERSONALITY 85 (1993).

conclusions about a larger population, while a dissimilar other also knows
something about *themselves* and associated others, and in like fashion overuses
that different information to draw conclusions about the same population.[34]
That is, variable perceptions of normativity arise because the diversity of
human experience supplies different data points from which to make inferences about society at large, and subjects give more or less weight to self-
associated data than is statistically appropriate. Unable to step entirely beyond
one's own reality, each subject projects it onto or deems it inapplicable to
others without fully comprehending their differences and similarities. The
FCE and FUE are unlikely to be relevant unless efforts to identify CIL involve
a similar process.

Whether they do is complicated by the absence of a single methodology for
determining CIL. A common view holds that there are two. On one hand,
a "traditional" approach is said to prioritize evidence of state practice over
opinio juris and identify custom through an inductive process, whereby the
interpreter collects evidence of specific instances of official practice and then
uses that evidence to make inferences about the norm.[35] On the other hand,
a "modern" approach is said to privilege *opinio juris* and identify CIL deduc-
tively from accepted rules or principles of international law.[36]

The traditional approach appears vulnerable to egocentric bias if one
accepts that estimates of international normativity often proceed from
a particular type of data sample. This is a sample comprising an assemblage
of conveniently accessible legal authority and – whether consciously or not –
personal perspective. In such estimates, the premise for the conclusion about
CIL is neither a syllogism nor a comprehensive survey of state practice and
opinio juris, but rather a modest collection of evidence from a subset of states,
the singular datum of the analyst's preexisting attitude regarding the conduct
or putative norm in question, and an embedded sensibility that these trans-
parent parts are sufficiently indicative of an otherwise opaque whole. This is
an implicitly probabilistic logic that is structurally similar to the reasoning that
has opened the door to the FCE and FUE in laboratory testing.

The modern approach, in contrast, might appear to evade the problem of
egocentric perception. Once appropriate rule-premises are identified, the
deduction of norms does not require any probabilistic reasoning; the central
task is simply to identify the legal conclusions that *must* follow as a matter of

---

[34]   Krueger & Clement, *supra* note 13, at 596.
[35]   Anthea Elizabeth Roberts, *Traditional and Modern Approaches to Customary International
       Law*, 95 AM. J. INT'L L. 757, 758 (2001).
[36]   *Id. But see* Talmon, *supra* note 3, at 429–434 (critiquing this taxonomy).

abstract logic. If there is no estimate of normativity from specific cases, including that of personal perspective, there is in theory no opportunity for the FCE and FUE to influence the analysis.

Yet this understanding reflects a rather superficial view of the modern approach. For an interpreter, it may be quite easy to imagine any number of seemingly uncontroversial premises from which specific rules necessarily follow. But the idea that the international community accepts those premises as such is not self-evident; it is instead an extrapolation from the interpreter's own training, ideology, and experience, which subjectively and perhaps idiosyncratically construct the given premises as appropriate starting points for syllogistic reasoning.[37] Put differently, deduction becomes possible *following* the identification of rule-postulates, but is likely based on one or more implicit acts of inductive reasoning by which the interpreter surmises the dominant international position on the legitimacy, meaning, and relevance of those postulates for the case at hand. Indeed, the modern approach itself appears normative not because of deduction, but rather in light of an interpreter's estimate of the degree of global consensus on the normativity of deduction.

To take the argument a small step further, the possibility of egocentric tint seems unlikely to disappear even when deduction proceeds from an easily identifiable and widely accepted treaty-based rule. Consider the *Arrest Warrant* case as an example. There, the International Court of Justice deduced primarily from the Vienna Convention on Diplomatic Relations that the Minister of Foreign Affairs for the Democratic Republic of the Congo was entitled as a matter of CIL to full immunity from Belgian criminal jurisdiction.[38] Given its subject matter and nearly universal adherence,[39] the treaty would seem to provide an uncontroversial basis for deduction. Yet the Court's reasoning still provoked four separate dissents, three of which disagreed that immunity for a foreign minister logically followed from the treaty. Judges al-Khasawneh, Oda, and van den Wyngaert each distinguished the Vienna Convention as pertaining to diplomatic agents who reside abroad, rather than foreign ministers, and implicitly privileged the inductive logic of the traditional approach by emphasizing the absence of state practice in favor

---

[37] *See id.* at 420 ("The syllogism assumes an audience that accepts its premises.").

[38] Arrest Warrant of 11 April 2000 (Dem. Rep. Congo v. Belg.), Judgment, 2002 I.C.J. Rep. 3 (Feb. 14).

[39] *See generally* Vienna Convention on Diplomatic Relations, Apr. 18, 1961, 500 U.N.T.S. 95; *see also Vienna Convention on Diplomatic Relations*, U.N. TREATY COLLECTION, https://treaties.un.org/pages/ViewDetails.aspx?src=TREATY&mtdsg_no=III-3&chapter=3&lang=en (reporting 191 parties to the treaty as of May 19, 2017).

of immunity.[40] In effect, the judges adopted different estimates of the leading international perspective on the relevance and meaning of the postulates from which deduction proceeded, and different estimates of the normativity of the deductive method itself.

The present suggestion is that while those estimates may have partially reflected certain objective rule-evidence, it is plausible that they also channeled personal perspectives to a degree that is statistically inappropriate. More concretely, it is plausible that the dissenting judges perceived the Court's use of the Vienna Convention as relatively nonnormative in material part because that usage appeared atypical in the context of each dissenter's own experience. Likewise, it is plausible that the dissenters perceived the Court's use of the deductive method as relatively nonnormative in material part because they personally employ that method less frequently in their own estimates of CIL. In short, while the internal logic of the modern approach evades the FCE and FUE, its embrace and application appear vulnerable to the precise mode of reasoning that risks perceptual distortion. The task now is to evaluate whether any other variables might negate that risk.

4.2.2 *Object of Estimation*

Most studies have tested for the FCE and FUE in estimates regarding the commonality of a subject's *personal* attitude or behavior within a reference population.[41] Individuals who purport to identify CIL, in contrast, will typically estimate the commonality of a *state* action, and the difference could be consequential. For example, estimates of CIL might evade the motivational forces that have otherwise contributed to bias if analysts do not gain or lose anything from over- or underestimating the commonality of positions or actions that are not their own.[42] Similarly, the availability heuristic might operate only weakly, if at all, when analysts' own behaviors and perspectives are not directly in question.[43]

Nevertheless, there is reason to suppose that a material risk of bias will persist. Consider a scenario in which lawyers must determine whether CIL

---

[40] Arrest Warrant of 11 April 2000, *supra* note 38, at 137, 143–151 (dissenting opinion of Judge van den Wyngaert); *id.* at 95, 95–97 (dissenting opinion of Judge al-Khasawneh); *id.* at 46, 52 (dissenting opinion of Judge Oda).

[41] *See, e.g.,* Mannarini et al., *supra* note 15, at 78–79 (testing for the FCE by asking a sample of residents of Turin, Italy to estimate the total number of residents who share their personal opinion on the merits of a new infrastructure project).

[42] *Cf. supra* section 4.1.1 (discussing the motivational forces that underlie the FCE and FUE).

[43] *Cf.* Bosveld et al., *supra* note 17, at 519 (discussing the availability heuristic's contribution to misperception).

embraces the "unwilling or unable" test under the jus ad bellum.[44] Many are likely to approach the task not as a tabula rasa, but instead with preexisting instincts or even fully formed perspectives on the existence and contours of the norm, regardless of whether they have carefully studied the matter in advance. To that extent, they *will* hold personal positions that are available for over-utilization in estimates of global normativity and thus resemble the subjects who have experienced the FCE and FUE in empirical testing.[45]

It is plausible, moreover, that these positions reflect the documented contributors to egocentric estimation. The sense of validation that flows from the perception that one is correct could supply a motive to perceive a concurring global settlement on the test's legitimacy.[46] Professional socialization within a distinctive national or subnational legal culture might amount to a form of selective exposure that spurs lawyers to impute universality to ideas about the test that are parochial in fact.[47] And as personal perspectives that are more accessible in cognition than competing viewpoints, the lawyers' attitudes about the unwilling-or-unable test might subjectively appear common and appropriate.[48]

In other cases, a state action or position might be attributable to the individual analyst. This will not hold true with legal scholars and private practitioners, who lack direct influence over government policy, but it is plausible with high-ranking officials, who might at one point or another address the international normativity of policies that they personally

---

[44] *See generally* Ashley S. Deeks, *"Unwilling or Unable": Toward a Normative Framework for Extraterritorial Self-Defense*, 52 VA. J. INT'L L. 483 (2012) (describing the test and its status under CIL).

[45] Views about CIL, as opposed to views about the commonality of conduct that may or may not be lawful as a matter of CIL, are unique in the sense that they bear a circular relationship to the task of estimating international legal normativity: to have a belief about CIL is, by definition, to suppose precisely that an act or position has acquired general support in state practice and *opinio juris*. Insofar as that supposition rests on rigorous research, either by the subject or others with whom she has socialized, the follow-on belief about normativity is unlikely to be erroneous even if egocentric, and even if acquired with little or no effort. In such circumstances, egocentric perception is unproblematic. But the inverse is also likely to be true: under-substantiated conclusions might generate pervasive misperceptions within a social network by shaping the beliefs of a professional audience that lacks the time, interest, expertise, or resources to scrutinize the merits. In short, it is certainly possible that any given belief about CIL will be correct, but it is hardly guaranteed. Indeed, given the evidence that conclusions about CIL often rest on underinclusive examinations of state practice, it is plausible that even common beliefs about CIL within a national or subnational legal community lack global resonance. *See supra* notes 2–4. In this sense perceptions of CIL are no different than perceptions of other types of norms.

[46] *Cf.* Kitts, *supra* note 20, at 224 (discussing this type of motivation for misperception).

[47] *Cf.* Bosveld et al., *supra* note 17, at 519 (discussing the role of selective exposure).

[48] *Cf.* Tversky & Kahneman, *supra* note 18, at 207 (explaining the availability heuristic).

helped to develop and implement. Thus, President Putin and his advisors might reasonably view a Russian position on international humanitarian law as their own, given the locus of power within the Russian government, and President Xi and his advisors might do likewise with respect to a Chinese position on the law of the sea. If that is correct, then the motivational and cognitive forces that interfere with the capacity to draw appropriate inferences about the commonality of personal positions might also apply to certain official efforts to identify customary international law, even assuming those efforts are undertaken in good faith.[49]

Consider also the nature of a typical question about CIL. A number of experiments have found that the FCE tends to be larger when a question primes a subject to causally attribute their position on an issue to the nature of the issue itself, rather than to personal characteristics or experiences.[50] In one representative study, the test procedure required each subject to answer two questions, one about whether the subject prefers city or country life and the other about the basis for their preference.[51] Where the latter question called upon subjects to explain themselves by reference to the characteristics of the option they selected (e.g., "what is it about cities that is attractive?"), the subjects exhibited the FCE in subsequent estimates of the commonality of their answer.[52] But when researchers changed the question and called upon subjects to offer personalized explanations (e.g., "what is it about cities that *you* find attractive?"), the FCE disappeared in follow-on estimates of commonality.[53] Underlying this difference, it appears, is the supposition that attitudes are more likely to be widely held when they are derived

---

[49] Compared to scholars and judges, foreign policy officials are probably more inclined to ascertain CIL strategically to promote national interests, rather than dispassionately for the sake of neutral exposition. To that extent, accuracy of estimate may be less of a concern in foreign policymaking. But that is not to say that accuracy is irrelevant in such a context. It could be useful for officials to know the true condition of state practice with respect to an issue, and perceptual distortion could prove problematic even when accuracy is not the principal goal. The FCE, for example, could exacerbate cross-national differences of understanding and thereby undermine the efficacy of CIL. It could also inspire undue confidence that a national position is normative, and thus intensify disagreements with foreign counterparts.

[50] *See, e.g.,* Thomas Gilovich, Dennis L. Jennings & Susan Jennings, *Causal Focus and Estimates of Consensus: An Examination of the False-Consensus Effect,* 45 J. Personality & Soc. Psychol. 550, 558 (1983); Miron Zuckerman, Robert W. Mann & Frank J. Bernieri, *Determinants of Consensus Estimates: Attribution, Salience, and Representativeness,* 42 J. Personality & Soc. Psychol. 839, 840–844 (1982).

[51] Gilovich et al., *supra* note 50, at 552–554.

[52] *Id.*

[53] *Id.*

from external circumstances that others also encounter, rather than personal dispositions or histories that are unique to each individual.[54]

It is plausible that this dynamic contributes to perceptual distortion in estimates of CIL by cloaking the self-projection of otherwise conscientious analysts. The rule of law calls upon interpreters to justify their conclusions not by reference to personal preferences, but rather common rules and standards. Indeed, legal doctrine is in numerous ways overtly hostile to the idea that outcomes should depend on the proclivities of the expositor.[55] In this sense, the law is similar to the depersonalizing primes that have spurred subjects to attribute their positions to circumstance rather than themselves. As applied here, the implication is that an analyst who in good faith reaches a particular conclusion about CIL is less likely to suspect that the conclusion is attributable to personal inclinations, and thus more likely to estimate that others acting in good faith will concur. Those others, after all, will presumably apply the same doctrine and operate within an international context that contains the same objective evidence of state practice and *opinio juris*.

4.2.3 *Effort Involved in the Estimate*

Studies documenting the FCE and FUE usually involve subjects who estimate normativity in a casual fashion, with minimal effort and without the benefit of representative sampling or formal research about the reference population. One typical experiment entailed a simple telephone survey in which undergraduate students were informed of a potential tuition surcharge, asked their opinion about a proposal for collecting that surcharge, and then called upon to estimate the percentage of their peers who share their opinion.[56] In this and other similar cases, self-projection was unsurprising because there was no real alternative; without public information of a particular social preference, and without an opportunity to study the population's positions in advance, the primary and even exclusive basis for estimation was the subject's own attitude.[57]

An interpreter of CIL, in contrast, might arrive at a conclusion only after months or more of research and deliberation, whether for academic inquiry,

---

[54] *Id.* at 558.

[55] *See, e.g.*, U.N. Secretary-General, *The Rule of Law and Transitional Justice in Conflict and Post-Conflict Societies*, ¶ 6, U.N. Doc. S/2004/616 (Aug. 23, 2004) (defining the rule of law as requiring "independent[] adjudicate[ion]" and measures to ensure "fairness in the application of the law" and "avoidance of arbitrariness").

[56] Crano, *supra* note 23, at 599–600.

[57] *See* Delavande & Manski, *supra* note 14, at 3715 (making this observation).

the presentation or resolution of a claim in litigation, or the formulation of government policy.[58] There is room for skepticism that the FCE and FUE will similarly manifest in these circumstances. Thorough examination of a representative collection of original sources might help to offset the availability heuristic and the influence of homophily by injecting new evidence of state practice and *opinio juris* into the analyst's epistemic bubble.[59] Indeed, at least one study has found that case sampling can shape consensus estimates even when the subject possesses relevant knowledge of their own perspective on an issue, such that congruent sample-based information reinforces the effects of egocentrism while incongruent sample-based information attenuates those effects.[60] Moreover, with a relatively small reference population of approximately 190 states, it may be possible to undertake a comprehensive survey that produces a definitive pronouncement of CIL, rather than a bias-prone estimate.

Yet the use of information about foreign state practice and *opinio juris* is often quite limited. Courts, law practitioners, and legal scholars do not consistently or even typically pursue thorough and inclusive research before estimating CIL.[61] This is understandable insofar as strict application of the traditional doctrine presents a number of daunting challenges, including identifying relevant evidence despite language barriers, collecting that evidence from disparate sources, and correctly interpreting the evidence in light of the rules and cultures of the various legal systems from which it originates.[62]

---

[58] As examples of particularly inclusive surveys of state practice, see Expert Declaration of Professor Philip Alston, United Nations Special Rapporteur on Extrajudicial, Summary or Arbitrary Executions at 44, Wiwa v. Royal Dutch Petroleum Co., 626 F. Supp. 2d 377 (S.D.N. Y. 2009) (Nos. 96 Civ. 8386 (KMW) (HBP), 01 Civ. 1909 (KMW) (HBP)) (surveying state practice with respect to the question of whether CIL prohibits summary execution); Declaration of Stefan Talmon at 6, Almog v. Arab Bank, PLC, 471 F. Supp. 2d 257 (E.D.N. Y. 2007) (Nos. 04–CV–5564(NG) (VVP) & 05–CV–0388(NG) (VVP)) (collecting evidence of state practice and *opinio juris* on the meaning of "terrorism" under CIL).

[59] *See* Mullen et al., *supra* note 10, at 280 (raising this possibility).

[60] James A. Kulik & Shelley E. Taylor, *Premature Consensus on Consensus? Effects of Sample-Based Versus Self-Based Consensus Information*, 38 J. Personal. & Soc. Psychol. 871, 876 (1980).

[61] *See, e.g.*, Choi & Gulati, *supra* note 2, at 117 (reporting that international tribunals typically do not undertake extensive surveys of state practice and *opinio juris*); Gutierrez & Gulati, *supra* note 4, at 271–84 (same for federal judicial opinions in the United States); Scoville, *supra* note 4, at 1908–1934 (same for federal judicial opinions in the United States and many of the academic works cited therein); Talmon, *supra* note 3, at 441 (same for the International Court of Justice).

[62] *See, e.g.*, Anthea Roberts, *Comparative International Law? The Role of National Courts in Creating and Enforcing International Law*, 60 Int'l & Comp. L.Q. 57, 88–89 (2011) (discussing research limitations encountered by those who might seek to conduct research on foreign law).

The probable effect, however, is that CIL in practice encounters a material risk of perceptual distortion, even if CIL in theory does not. Without rigorous surveys, there is ample room for an analyst's personal views to fill the empirical void and, in turn, drive estimates of international norms.

There is evidence, moreover, that egocentric bias can persist even in the event of substantial research. Social psychologists have found that the FCE can influence judgment even when a subject is exposed to information about a reference population prior to the estimation of normativity,[63] and even after extended exposure to the population itself.[64] One study, for example, found that US citizens tend to hold substantially different expectations about election outcomes, that these expectations bear a strong, positive association with voters' candidate preferences, and that the differences manifest notwithstanding the widespread availability and salience of information about popular opinion in the form of polling data.[65] Another found that overgeneralization in the presence of sampling data is particularly likely when the data sources share the interpreter's own preferences and values.[66] Thus, for Western lawyers and legal scholars, a survey of state practice that is heavily Eurocentric or otherwise occidental may be far less effective at negating egocentric bias.[67] If anything, such a survey might amplify bias by contributing to selective exposure.[68]

4.2.4 *Nature of the Reference Population*

The most typical experiment on the FCE is one that calls upon small groups of undergraduate students to estimate the commonality of a personal behavior or perspective among their peers.[69] Such testing consistently reveals that bias can manifest in estimates of norms pertaining to relatively small and homogeneous social environments.[70] On some accounts, this is unsurprising because the perceived nature of the reference population rationalizes the act of self-projection – if a subject believes that a group is fairly small and monolithic,

---

[63] Sherman, Presson & Chassin, *supra* note 20, at 136.

[64] Sanders & Mullen, *supra* note 7, at 66.

[65] Delavande & Manski, *supra* note 14, at 3715.

[66] Mark D. Alicke & Edward Largo, *The Role of the Self in the False Consensus Effect*, 31 J. EXPERIMENTAL SOC. PSYCHOL. 28, 45 (1995).

[67] *Cf.* Scoville, *supra* note 4, at 1909–1914 (documenting an American and occidental focus in U.S. judicial opinions on customary international law).

[68] *Cf.* Bosveld et al., *supra* note 17, at 519 (discussing the effect of selective exposure).

[69] For example, Andrew D. Gershoff, Ashesh Mukherjee & Anirban Mukhopadhyay, *What's Not to Like? Preference Asymmetry in the False Consensus Effect*, 35 J. CONSUMER RES. 119, 120–122 (2008).

[70] *See id.*

believes that she has a lot in common with its members, and holds a particular preference, it is reasonable to assume that the preference is normative within the group.[71]

The reference population involved in an estimate of CIL, however, is quite different. While there are fewer than 200 states, the judges, academics, lawyers, and others who opine on and contribute to the development of CIL are numerous. Moreover, these professionals are geographically dispersed, culturally diverse, and frequently limited in their contact with one another. In the United States, for example, significant foreign legal experience is often lacking even among professors of international law,[72] and the same appears to be true of countries such as France and Russia.[73] Insofar as the assumption of similarity is harder to justify in these circumstances, self-projection may be less likely.[74]

That said, such an assumption appears to be quite common. It would seem to be implicit in any analysis that draws conclusions about international norms from a small handful of cases, and it is not difficult to rationalize. Ideas about globalization might contribute by highlighting the interconnectedness of states. The terminology of CIL might itself contribute by positing the existence of a broad category of shared norms. And the size of the reference population might play a role.

To elaborate on this last point, one study found that while "[l]ittle false consensus appears in . . . groups of limited size," the FCE tends to be "much stronger" within large populations.[75] The proffered explanation is selective exposure – in a large and diverse population, it is easier for members to sort themselves, socialize primarily with similar others, and misperceive the broader commonality of norms that pertain in homophilic relationships.[76] This suggests that egocentric bias could be even more robust in estimates of CIL than it has been in many of the experiments to date,[77] given that the international community is both large and infused with a diverse collection of cultural, political, legal, epistemic, and other communities that create

---

[71] *Cf.* Jacob Shamir & Khalil Shikaki, *Self-Serving Perceptions of Terrorism Among Israelis and Palestinians*, 23 Pol. Psychol. 537, 540 (2002) (suggesting that perceptions of dissimilarity within an international population might discourage self-projection).

[72] Ryan Scoville & Milan Markovic, *How Cosmopolitan Are International Law Professors?*, 38 Mich. J. Int'l L. 119, 126–129 (2016).

[73] Anthea Roberts, Is International Law International? (2017).

[74] *See* Shamir & Shikaki, *supra* note 71, at 540 (making this argument with respect to the international community).

[75] Kitts, *supra* note 20, at 234.

[76] *Id.*

[77] *Cf.* Scoville, *supra* note 4, at 1916 (discussing selective exposure as a potential contributor to parochialism in municipal estimates of CIL).

plentiful opportunities for selective exposure. To return to the example of the unwilling-or-unable test, on what literature have proponents and critics of the test versed themselves in the relevant arguments and data points? What are the dominant nationalities of the authors of that literature? And with whom do the proponents and critics socialize in professional settings? Unless the answers to these questions exhibit a diversity of nationalities and perspectives, it is a significant leap to assume that any given position reflects a global understanding. And yet, that appears to be precisely the assumption that is made.

4.3 AN ILLUSTRATION FROM US LITIGATION

As an illustration of the argument so far, consider *Sarei v. Rio Tinto PLC*, a 2009 decision from a federal district court in the United States.[78] There, residents of Papua New Guinea sued Rio Tinto for conducting mining operations in a manner that violated an alleged rule of CIL against environmental degradation.[79] The court rejected this claim, concluding that it was "based on international law norms that have not, as yet, achieved the status of matters of 'universal concern.'"[80] The principal basis for this conclusion, however, was not an exhaustive investigation of state practice and *opinio juris*, but rather a collection of nonbinding precedents from other American courts.[81] In citing to those precedents, the court treated them as sufficient evidence of the dominant international position. Assuming a dispassionate judge, on what logic is it possible that the FCE nevertheless influenced this analysis?

First, the judge must have approached the task already in possession of relevant views. One possibility is that she held a preexisting view about the defendant's alleged conduct: she supposed that environmental degradation is common and in turn doubted the normativity of a rule against it. Other possibilities involve views about the law itself: the judge believed, even if only vaguely, that CIL fails to prohibit environmental degradation. Or, the judge held no belief regarding the normativity of the alleged prohibition but nevertheless felt that US pronouncements on international law, including those from other federal judges, tend to be globally normative and legitimate.

These positions would inevitably derive from personal experience. Perhaps the judge observed or read about so much pollution in her lifetime that she simply could not make sense of the idea that environmental degradation is

---

[78] Sarei v. Rio Tinto PLC, 650 F. Supp. 2d 1004 (C.D. Cal. 2009).
[79] *Id.*
[80] *Id.* at 1025.
[81] *Id.* at 1024–1026.

unlawful on the basis of customary practice. Perhaps years of professional socialization from legal training, conferences, conversations with colleagues, and exposure to news media and legal scholarship led her to believe that CIL fails to prohibit the defendant's conduct, or that the analysis of other federal judges is worthy of credence even where nonbinding.

Second, the operation of the FCE would require that the judge's relevant views are less than universally held. Perhaps other analysts live and work in settings where environmental degradation is sufficiently uncommon to render sensible a belief that it is unlawful on the basis of customary practice. Perhaps others have acquired views about CIL from socialization in legal communities that are more critical of environmental harm, or that look upon the pronouncements of US federal courts with greater skepticism.

The third requirement is that the judge's estimate of CIL advanced at least in part from the nonuniversal premises that are her personal beliefs. The FCE could have manifested, in other words, only if the judge subconsciously ascribed outsized representativeness to her own views. But this is hardly implausible. It is what subjects have repeatedly done in empirical testing. It is encouraged by common narratives about globalization and American hegemony, which suggest that normative positions in domestic legal culture are also normative abroad.[82] It was likely the judge's only real option, given the apparent dearth of accessible evidence of foreign and international perspectives.[83] And even if the parties had supplied such evidence, research on the FCE indicates that the judge's belief could have remained overly influential.[84]

At this point in the process, the literature suggests that the FCE will have occurred, as the judge's act of projecting personal belief onto the international community will have generated a relatively high estimate of the percentage of foreign actors who concur. In turn, given the traditional test for CIL under the doctrine of sources,[85] the judge's estimate will have encouraged the conclusion that CIL fails to prohibit environmental degradation. What is intriguing is that such a process reverses the commonly presumed sequence of analysis; the judge's personal beliefs about what is normative will have materially influenced the assessment of state practice and *opinio juris*, rather than the other way around.

---

[82]   *Cf.* Harold Hongju Koh, *Is International Law Really State Law?*, 111 HARV. L. REV. 1824, 1853–1854 (1998) ("[I]nsofar as customary international law rules arise from traditional State practice, the United States has been, for most of this century, the world's primary maker of and participant in this practice.").

[83]   *See Sarei*, 650 F. Supp. 2d, at 1024–26.

[84]   Sherman, Presson & Chassin, *supra* note 20, at 136; Sanders & Mullen, *supra* note 7, at 66.

[85]   Statute of the International Court of Justice art. 38(1)(b).

This is not necessarily to say that *Sarei* was wrongly decided. Given US influence, any judge would do well to consider the US position in estimating the existence and contours of a global norm.[86] The FCE does, however, raise the possibility that the judge's limited consideration of foreign and international practice created additional space for her personal views about the normativity of either the underlying conduct or the purported rule to quietly influence the estimate of CIL to a greater degree than is statistically appropriate. It also raises the possibility that judges from other countries reach materially different estimates on the basis of personal beliefs about the norm or associated conduct.

4.4 IMPLICATIONS

Assume now for the sake of argument that the FCE and FUE *are* relevant, and that egocentric bias frequently manifests at least in those estimates of CIL that are based on under-inclusive analyses of state practice and *opinio juris*. What follows?

4.4.1 *Differences Over CIL*

First, the research offers a new way to understand disagreements over the contours of CIL. If the FCE and FUE manifest in this context, then perceptions can vary even when all parties undertake good faith efforts to estimate the normativity of a practice, hold equally high regard for international law, apply the same doctrine of sources, and share common interests. Government officials, private lawyers, and legal scholars may disagree with one another simply because their preexisting experiences and perspectives lead them subconsciously to perceive the commonality and diversity of support for alleged norms in different ways. This might occur in the context of debates about humanitarian intervention, mass surveillance, or the law of the sea, among many other topics. The challenge from this perspective is one of either similarly socializing legal analysts or somehow limiting self-projection so that the inductive reasoning of diverse actors yields common conclusions.

In this regard, a social psychological lens compliments existing research in the field of comparative international law, which seeks to identify and explain cross-national differences in how states understand and value international norms.[87] Some in this field suggest that differences arise as states rationally

---

[86] See Koh, *supra* note 82, at 1853–1854 (discussing US influence over contemporary CIL).

[87] *See generally* Anthea Roberts, Paul B. Stephan, Pierre-Hugues Verdier & Mila Versteeg, *Comparative International Law: Framing the Field*, 109 AM. J. INT'L L. 467 (2015) (discussing the purposes and challenges of comparative international law).

pursue divergent national interests,[88] while others highlight the significance of municipal legal cultures.[89] The FCE, in contrast, would posit that differences arise because legal analysts from around the world approach the task of estimating CIL with different epistemic priors. These actors acquire unique experiences and ideas and then subconsciously project them onto the international community to a degree that is unwarranted.[90] To be sure, interests and culture might operate as some of the underlying sources of the experiences and ideas that are projected, but even where that is true, research on the FCE helps to explain how those variables matter. They matter, that is, not necessarily because actors consciously and strategically interpret CIL in light of them, but rather as subconscious determinants of social perception.

In suggesting a cause of normative discord, the FCE in turn hints at measures for improving the efficacy of CIL. If selective exposure contributes to the excessive self-projection that in turn fosters disagreement and cross-national variation, then lawyers and academics might profitably work to mitigate selective exposure. They might seek out opportunities to study international law from foreign perspectives, including by reading foreign journals on international law, attending conferences abroad, and working in foreign legal settings. Even if these experiences fail to produce acceptance of foreign perspectives, they may very well engender an appreciation for the diversity of opinion that can exist and in doing so encourage analysts to estimate CIL with greater caution.

4.4.2 Majority Positions, Persistent Objectors

The FCE and FUE also offer what seems like a new way to think about majority and minority perspectives on any given dimension of CIL. The tendency for members of a majority to underestimate the normativity of their position raises the possibility that some norms exist without recognition as such, and that some recognized norms garner even broader support than one might suspect.[91] As an example of the latter, acts of torture in Syria might by their salience create the

---

[88] For example, Anu Bradford & Eric A. Posner, *Universal Exceptionalism in International Law*, 52 Harv. Int'l L.J. 1, 23 (2011).

[89] For example, Jed Rubenfeld, *Unilateralism and Constitutionalism*, 79 N.Y.U. L. Rev. 1791, 1974–1975 (2004); *see also* William E. Butler, *International Law and the Comparative Method*, *in* International Law in Comparative Perspective 25, 36 (William E. Butler ed., 1980) (summarizing potential influences).

[90] *Cf.* Roberts, *supra* note 73, at 72–89 (comparing the professional backgrounds of international law professors at elite schools in Australia, China, France, Russia, the United Kingdom, and the United States); Scoville & Markovic, *supra* note 72, at 126–129 (discussing the professional backgrounds of US professors of international law).

[91] Krueger & Clement, *supra* note 25, at 312; Sanders & Mullen, *supra* note 7, at 65.

false impression that anti-torture norms enjoy weaker global adherence than they do in fact.[92] Likewise, extensive media coverage of China's claim to "historic rights" over the resources in the South China Sea might give rise to a mistaken perception that such claims are relatively common.[93] Awareness of this tendency might contribute to the stability of current norms.[94]

In similar fashion, the FUE suggests a risk of underestimating the generality of personally familiar practices and perspectives. To name just one example, it has become clear that a majority of states obligate their law students to complete a course on public international law en route to a law degree,[95] but commentators virtually never identify this practice as potential evidence of CIL. Few have suggested, in other words, that CIL requires states to oblige their law students to study international law. One possible explanation is that it has been difficult, at least historically, to survey comprehensively the curricula of foreign law schools, the effect of which has been to render invisible much of the evidence of relevant practice.[96] Another possibility is that analysts instinctively stereotype differences between the domestic systems of higher education with which they are familiar and the systems that operate in foreign states, and thus presume uniqueness. To identify this and other domains in which the FUE might operate is to draw attention to previously unacknowledged regularities of state practice that could warrant treatment as emerging custom.

On the flip side, the tendency for members of a minority to overestimate the normativity of their perspectives – and to overestimate to a greater degree than the majority underestimates – suggests a problem with the persistent objector rule. In its classic formulation, this rule holds that a state can exempt itself

[92] *Id.* at 67.
[93] *See* South China Sea Arbitration (Phil. v. China), PCA Case Repository Case No. 2013–19, Judgment, ¶ 180–187 (2016) (discussing China's claim).
[94] There is moderate tension between the FCE and the apparent frequency of positive identifications of CIL, in the sense that the FCE tends to associate with objectively low majority estimates of the normativity of majority positions. How could positive identifications be common if the majority exhibits a tendency for objective underestimation? There are a few possible answers. One is that these analysts underestimate, but not by so much that they perceive a norm as lacking general and consistent support. Another is that some of the analysts in fact hold minority views and are thus inclined to overestimate. Still another possibility is that the analysts often materially underestimate, such that positive identifications of CIL would be even more common if the FCE did not occur.
[95] *See generally* Ryan M. Scoville, *Who Studies International Law? A Global Survey*, PIL MAP, http://PILMap.org (2015) (reporting national percentages of law schools in which public international law is a compulsory topic of study).
[96] *Cf.* Frable, *supra* note 33, at 85 (identifying difficulties in detecting the private behavior of others as a contributor to the FUE).

from nascent CIL by making clear its opposition in a timely fashion.[97] China or Russia, for example, might avoid a budding norm on the law of the sea or human rights by persistently expressing disapproval. But if officials in minority states experience the FCE, then they may not perceive a disfavored normative shift at all, in which case they will not feel the need to object. Indeed, where the magnitude of the FCE is substantial, minority states might mistakenly perceive an emerging majority as the minority and thus insist upon persistent objection as the prerequisite for any exemption from what is in fact a minority position. At some point this actual minority might realize its true status, but by then the position of the majority may have already crystalized into a norm, rendering any objection untimely.[98] This would further complicate the task of reconciling CIL with the principle of state consent.[99]

Such a dynamic would also help to explain a longstanding puzzle: persistent objection seems like it should be an attractive option for sovereign states confronted with legal positions they oppose, but states almost never invoke the doctrine. Writing in 1985, Ted Stein predicted that states would do so with greater frequency in an age of multilateral lawmaking, which he viewed as presenting "more salient targets [for objection], more obvious occasions, and more visible means of objecting to rules that they find uncongenial."[100] Yet recent commentary suggests ongoing desuetude.[101] How could this be? Some have conjectured that states do not persistently object because doing so risks disapproval from much of the international community.[102] While this may often be true, the evidence on the FCE suggests that perceptual distortion might also play a role. That is, sometimes government officials might decline to persistently object simply because they have mistakenly perceived their position as one that enjoys majority status.

---

[97] Jonathan I. Charney, *The Persistent Objector Rule and the Development of Customary International Law*, 56 Brit. Y.B. Int'l L. 1 (1986).

[98] *See id.* at 3 (discussing formulations of the rule that require any objection to occur early on in the life of the norm).

[99] *See* Andrew T. Guzman, *Saving Customary International Law*, 27 Mich. J. Int'l L. 115, 141–145 (2005) (identifying tensions between traditional understandings of CIL and international law's formal embrace of the consent principle).

[100] Ted L. Stein, *The Approach of the Different Drummer: The Principle of the Persistent Objector in International Law*, 26 Harv. Int'l L.J. 457, 472 (1985).

[101] *See, e.g.*, Curtis A. Bradley & Mitu Gulati, *Withdrawing from International Custom*, 120 Yale L.J. 202, 239, 245 (2010) (suggesting that states rarely invoke the right); Patrick Dumberry, *Incoherent and Ineffective: The Concept of Persistent Objector Revisited*, 59 Int'l & Comp. L.Q. 779, 791–794 (2010) (same).

[102] *See, e.g.*, Dumberry, *supra* note 101, at 791 (suggesting that states rarely use the concept of persistent objector because invoking it "would show a State's isolation from the rest of the international community").

4.4.3 *Emergence and Change*

Given the traditional requirement of *opinio juris*, commentators have long recognized that the emergence and evolution of CIL present a conundrum – namely, it is unclear how innovator states could perceive as legally obligatory a new practice that existing CIL either prohibits or does not address. One possibility is that they do not: these states are knowing scofflaws, or at least opportunists, whose conduct fails to qualify as evidence of CIL but nevertheless normalizes a previously aberrant practice over time, such that other states, through a sort of social alchemy, gradually come to perceive the practice as obligatory. Curtis Bradley and Mitu Gulati have identified such a process as one of the only ways to change inefficient or outdated CIL, given the traditional understanding that states cannot withdraw from custom.[103] Another possibility is that innovator states *do* perceive their conduct as legally obligatory and are simply mistaken. François Gény suggested such a scenario as early as 1899, writing that "an error seems at least at the beginning of a usage a *sine qua* condition for the conviction that such a usage is binding."[104] Notably, both possibilities rely on the occurrence of error and differ only on who commits it, with the subject being either the states that come to perceive the innovator's conduct as normative or the innovator itself.

Yet the precise causes of error have been underspecified,[105] and this has fueled skepticism that it plays a role. According to Michael Byers, for example, the error thesis "is unsatisfactory because it is inconceivable that an entire legal process – and, since the customary process provides the basis for the law of treaties, an entire legal system – could be based on a persistent misconception."[106] Perhaps sharing this view, a number of commentators have proffered alternative explanations.[107]

---

[103] Bradley & Gulati, *supra* note 101, at 212, 260. In their view, the only other option is for states to adopt a new norm by consensus. *Id.* at 260.

[104] François Gény, Méthode d'Interpretation et Sources en Droit Privé Positif 251–252 (Jaro Mayda transl. 1963).

[105] *See, e.g.*, Peter E. Benson, *François Gény's Doctrine of Customary Law*, 20 Can. Y.B. Int'l L. 267, 277 (1982) (arguing that Gény "has not properly established the objective basis of the supposed error" that leads to new CIL).

[106] Michael Byers, Custom, Power and the Law of Rules: International Relations and Customary International Law 131 (1999).

[107] *See, e.g.*, John Finnis, Natural Law & Natural Rights 238–245 (2d ed. 2011) (reframing *opinio juris* as a belief that "it is desirable that in [a certain] domain there be some determinate, common, and stable pattern of conduct and corresponding authoritative rule," and that a "particular pattern of conduct, Ø, is (or would be if generally adopted and acquiesced in) an appropriate pattern for adoption as an authoritative common rule.").

The evidence on the FCE, however, suggests that misperception is entirely plausible as an explanation for the origin and evolution of CIL. If the FCE manifests in this context, international contacts and other harmonizing influences will simply be insufficient to offset the instinctive overuse of self-associated data on the part of those who estimate CIL. On this view, norms can emerge and change not simply because of misperception, but more specifically because of shifts in the predominance of competing forms of egocentrically biased estimates among coalitions of actors in different states.

4.4.4 *Parochialism*

CIL analyses often seem to exhibit a parochial bias. To name just one example, there is considerable evidence that American courts and scholars frequently identify norms primarily by reference to the practices and views of the United States and Western Europe.[108] The most cynical interpretation of this tendency is that American legal analysts cherry-pick evidence of CIL in order to promote American empire, sustain the marginalization of peripheral states, and mold the law to reflect US interests. Social psychology, in contrast, suggests a far more innocent explanation – namely, that analysts cite primarily to Western sources because they genuinely perceive that American and Western norms reflect global consensus. This perception might arise from the selective exposure that comes from professional socialization within a particular domestic legal context that takes some norms for granted and discounts others.[109] It might also arise for reasons that are motivational but subconscious. The projection of Western views onto a diverse collection of states fosters an appearance of consensus, which could be comforting, especially on matters such as human rights.[110]

4.4.5 *A Supplement to Rational Choice*

Finally, the FCE and FUE suggest that social psychology could be a fruitful supplement to rational-choice accounts of CIL, which have garnered considerable attention in recent years.[111] The principal expositors of such accounts posit that CIL amounts to a collection of behavioral patterns that arise as states rationally pursue national self-interests.[112] The small point of intersection with

---

[108]   See Scoville, *supra* note 4, at 1909–1912, 1924–1934.
[109]   *Id.* at 1916 (making this argument).
[110]   *Id.*
[111]   See, e.g., GOLDSMITH & POSNER, *supra* note 6; GUZMAN, *supra* note 6.
[112]   See, e.g., Eric A. Posner & Jack L. Goldsmith, *A Theory of Customary International Law*, 66 U. CHI. L. REV. 1113, 1120–1139 (1999).

social psychology is that both rational choice theory and motivational explanations for egocentric bias propound the relevance of interests. But the commonality ends there. Rational choice theory takes the state as the primary unit of analysis, while the present approach focuses on the myriad individuals who attempt to identify CIL. Rational choice assumes strategic action, while the FCE and FUE highlight the role of instincts, beliefs, and nonrational processes. And in seeking to explain how CIL arises and whether it is effective, rational choice presents itself as an ontology of custom. In contrast, the theory of egocentric bias is essentially epistemological in its focus on the processes by which actors identify CIL. In a sense, these are complimentary projects, for it is hard to theorize on the nature of CIL without first understanding the social and cognitive variables involved in its identification.

At the same time, the FCE and FUE also suggest a weakness in rational choice theory. Simply put, the relativity of norm perceptions could interfere with states' ability to rationally pursue national self-interests on matters of CIL. Even if all states hold a reputational interest in compliance,[113] for example, some of them might adopt or persist in minority positions on the mistaken view that those positions are normative. Similarly, some states might hesitate to embrace or promote a majority position on the mistaken perception that it enjoys only limited international support. In both of these scenarios, states will fail to optimize their reputations for compliance, and variations in state practice will persist.

4.5 CONCLUSION

Experiments on the False Consensus Effect and False Uniqueness Effect suggest intriguing ways to think about the epistemology of customary international law. For those who seek to promote the efficacy of international norms, the implications range from promising in the case of the FUE to potentially disquieting in the case of the FCE. Further work is in order to ascertain the prevalence and intensity of egocentric bias in this domain.

---

[113]   *See* GUZMAN, *supra* note 6, at 73 (positing the importance of states' reputational interests in explaining compliance with CIL).

5

Explaining the Practical Purchase of Soft Law

Competing and Complementary Behavior Hypotheses[*]

Tomer Broude and Yahli Shereshevsky

Why do international and domestic legal actors *employ* and even *apply* international soft law sources, that by any definition, are not formally binding and are technically unenforceable? Definitions of soft law abound.[1] Broadly construed, soft law includes binding international commitments that are in substance vague and imprecise, therefore reducing the costs of compliance.[2] A more commonly accepted definition focuses on the lack of formal binding effect of a norm.[3] In this chapter we pursue the latter approach, focusing on the nonbinding nature of soft law, with a rather inclusive position as to the outputs that are treated as soft law in the literature, that is, not only sources that have been made directly by states or intergovernmental institutions (such as United Nations (UN) General Assembly (GA) Resolutions), but also soft law created by a wide range of actors, ranging from the secretariats of international organizations, expert committees established under treaties, decisions of international tribunals, to civil society organizations and industry groups.

While our chapter focuses on the use of soft law, the more commonly asked query is why do international legal actors – primarily states and international intergovernmental organizations and their agents, but also nongovernmental organizations – bother to *create* and even "adopt" copious texts that have no formally binding legal effect. In other words, what explains the existence of

[*] The authors wish to thank Anne van Aaken, Harlan Cohen, Tim Meyer and Eyal Zamir for extremely helpful comments, and Rebecca Baskin-Zafrir, Shahar Bruckner, Noa Hirsh and Tomer Treger, for diligent research assistance.

[1] *See* Gregory C. Shaffer & Mark A. Pollack, *Hard vs. Soft Law: Alternatives, Complements and Antagonists in International Governance*, 94 MINN. L. REV. 706, 712 (2009).

[2] Kenneth W. Abbott & Duncan Snidal, *Hard and Soft Law in International Governance*, 54 INT'L ORG. 421 (2000).

[3] *See, e.g.*, Andrew T. Guzman & Timothy L. Meyer, *International Soft Law*, 2 J. LEGAL ANALYSIS 171, 174 (2010).

international "soft law"? This is indeed a longstanding puzzle in the study of modern international law. Some classical international lawyers simply dismiss the significance of soft law, deeming it "non-law,"[4] "redundant,"[5] and even "undesirable,"[6] to some extent obviating the question. Others, in contrast, consider soft law, or its more recent terminological counterpart, "informal law"[7] to be a central feature of contemporary international regulation and global governance,[8] though not necessarily quite the future of international law.[9] To them, it is just a different kind of law, created for the same reasons that "hard" law is made. In between, sophisticated explanations have been suggested by rational choice scholars for the emergence of soft law.[10]

In this chapter, we shift the focus from the *creation* of soft law to an understudied yet closely related question that we find no less important, particularly in the context of *International Law As Behavior*, the topic of this volume. Given the actual and indeed ubiquitous existence of international soft law (as "nonlaw on-the-books," so to speak), why do legal actors (including state and nonstate parties to disputes and negotiations, legal counsel, domestic and international courts and tribunals, etc.) apply and employ it in their conduct and justifications thereof, despite the explicit lack of legal obligation – and indeed authority – to do so? With few exceptions,[11] discussions of soft law appear to assume that soft law does (or alternatively, does not)[12] influence behavior once it is made, albeit to varying degrees, often taking hard (binding) law as a comparative benchmark, without explanatory analysis.[13] Thus, for example, Guzman and Meyer assume that soft law is considered by states as normative guidance for conduct and focus on the lower costs for non"compliance" with it.[14] Shaffer and Pollack, while providing empirical examples of the use of soft law in relation to hard law,

---

[4]   Prosper Weil, *Towards Relative Normativity in International Law*, 77 AM. J. INT'L L. 413 (1983).

[5]   Jan Klabbers, *The Redundancy of Soft Law*, 65 NORDIC J. INT'L L. 167 (1996).

[6]   Jan Klabbers, *The Undesirability of Soft Law*, 67 NORDIC J. INT'L L. 381 (1998).

[7]   Joost Pauwelyn, Ramses A. Wessel & Jan Wouters, *Informal International Law Making: An Assessment and Template to Keep It Both Effective and Accountable*, in INFORMAL INTERNATIONAL LAWMAKING 500 (Joost Pauwelyn et al. eds., 2012).

[8]   Jean Galbraith & David T. Zaring, *Soft Law as Foreign Relations Law*, 99 CORNELL L. REV. 735 (2014).

[9]   JOEL P. TRACHTMAN, THE FUTURE OF INTERNATIONAL LAW: GLOBAL GOVERNMENT (2013).

[10] Guzman & Meyer, *supra* note 3.

[11] *See* DINAH L. SHELTON, COMMITMENT AND COMPLIANCE: THE ROLE OF NON-BINDING NORMS IN THE INTERNATIONAL LEGAL SYSTEM (2003).

[12] JOHN J. KIRTON & MICHAEL J. TREBILCOCK, HARD CHOICES, SOFT LAW: VOLUNTARY STANDARDS IN GLOBAL TRADE, ENVIRONMENT, AND SOCIAL GOVERNANCE (2004).

[13] Bryan H. Druzin, *Why Does Soft Law Have Any Power Anyway?*, 7 ASIAN J. INT'L L. 361 (2016) (providing an exception, discussed further *infra* notes 75, 82).

[14] Guzman & Meyer, *supra* note 3, at 177.

assume that soft law has real normative purchase, but do not explain, directly or indirectly, how this power comes to be.[15] Trachtman even views the expectation that soft law will affect state behavior as one of its defining elements.[16]

We contend that these two key functional questions relating to soft law – why is it *made*? and why is it *used*? – are strongly and analytically interrelated.[17] International legal actors will invest time, effort, and attention to the creation of soft law, insofar as its existence influences future conduct – their own behavior and that of other agents and actors. The key – or at least one key – to explaining the proliferation of international soft law lies, therefore, in an understanding of why soft law, once created, holds practical purchase over behavior, decision-making, justification, and argumentation. To be sure, because by definition soft law is not formally binding, one cannot speak of "compliance" in a strict legal-positivist sense. Nevertheless, as far as "a state of conformity or identity between an actor's behavior and a specified rule" is concerned,[18] compliance with soft law surely exists, and when compliance is viewed as a choice,[19] adherence to soft law lends itself to a replication, *mutatis mutandis*, of rational and behavioral analyses of compliance with formally binding rules. The purchase of international soft law is not, however, limited to compliance as such; it can be addressed, used, and employed influentially even in the absence of compliance.[20] Moreover, we identify a dialectic relationship between these key questions, not only because the expectation of

---

[15] Shaffer & Pollack, *supra* note 1.

[16] TRACHTMAN, *supra* note 9, at 32. Trachtman defines soft law as "rules ... that ... are: (i) non-binding under formal international law ...; (ii) prepared in contexts similar to those in which binding international law is prepared; (iii) prepared in a form similar to that in which binding international law is prepared; and (iv) expected to affect state behavior." In this article, our primary interest is in unpacking the fourth component of this definition: Why is soft law expected to affect state behavior?

[17] *See, e.g.*, SHELTON, *supra* note 11, at 11 ("[C]ompliance with soft law cannot be separated from the issue of why states have recourse to soft law forms for their international commitments.").

[18] Kal Raustiala & Anne-Marie Slaughter, *International Law, International Relations and Compliance, in* THE HANDBOOK OF INTERNATIONAL RELATIONS 538, 539 (Walter Carlnaes, Thomas Risse & Beth Simmons eds., 2002).

[19] Peter Haas, *Choosing to Comply Theorizing from International Relations and Comparative Politics, Commitment and Compliance, in* COMMITMENT AND COMPLIANCE: THE ROLE OF NON-BINDING NORMS IN THE INTERNATIONAL LEGAL SYSTEM 43 (Dinah L. Shelton ed., 2003) [hereinafter COMMITMENT AND COMPLIANCE].

[20] For example, in the 2005 *Mara'abe* case regarding the separation barrier between Israel and Palestinian occupied territories, the Israeli Supreme Court chose not to simply dismiss as irrelevant the International Court of Justice (ICJ) Advisory Opinion on the same issue because the latter was non-binding. HCJ 7957/04 Mara'abe v. Prime Minister of Israel 60(2) PD 477 (2005) (Isr.); Legal Consequences of the Construction of a Wall in the Occupied Palestinian Territory, Advisory Opinion, 2004 I.C.J. Rep. 136 (July 9). Rather, in what can certainly be understood as a case of non"compliance" or at least lack of conformity with international soft

future influence feeds into the adoption of soft law, but because the costs of its creation may become a factor in its subsequent effective normative influence.

Within the limited scope of this chapter, our ambition is not to present, let alone to prove, a unified explanation for the power and practical purchase of soft law. Rather, we aim to review a broad range of competing yet complementary falsifiable hypotheses regarding the reasons for the use of soft law and its effects on behavior. After a stylized discussion of the diverse range of ways in which soft law is indeed applied and employed despite its lack of formal status as a source of international law, with a focus on international and domestic courts (Section 5.1), we describe and explicate in context a series of "standard" rational choice conjectures for soft law's influence, mainly derived from existing literature (Section 5.2), ranging from simple signaling and coordination points to network effects. We then move on to propose alternative explanations derived from psychology and behavioral economics that can provide additional – though not necessarily better, across the board – explanations for the effective use and influence of soft law (Section 5.3). In our concluding comments (Section 5.4), we focus on the dynamic, dialectic relationship between soft lawmaking and soft law adherence and influence, suggesting that makers of soft law understand, ex ante, the influence of soft law, ex post – the expectation that it will ultimately possess practical purchase.

5.1 THE NORMATIVE PURCHASE OF SOFT LAW IN INTERNATIONAL AND DOMESTIC COURTS AND TRIBUNALS

Working within the rather broad inclusive definition of soft law that we have espoused for present purposes – although limited to the notion of unbindingness – in this section, we wish to establish the prevalence of referential use of international soft law, in its "infinite variety of forms,"[21] by legal actors, after its creation. By referential use we mean the citation of soft law sources, without a deeper exploration of either context or weight. A comprehensive empirical survey of the use of soft law in this sense would be a truly daunting task, and we therefore restrict ourselves to broadly representative examples of such use of soft law, use that is surprisingly common when one recalls that soft law lacks formal binding power. This is a gap that demands explanation.

---

law – setting aside the underlying questions of international "hard" law – the Israeli Court chose to devote considerable attention to addressing the Advisory Opinion and to explaining why there are justified substantive and procedural differences between its ruling and that of the ICJ.

[21] Christine Chinkin, *Normative Development in the International Legal System, in* COMMITMENT AND COMPLIANCE, *supra* note 19, at 21, 25.

Moreover, within the limited scope of this chapter, we will concentrate on a discussion of the referential use of international soft law by one set of actors: international and domestic courts and tribunals (with an emphasis on their *use* of soft law, not on their contribution to its creation). While acknowledging that this focused approach risks losing much of the scope and texture of the use of international soft law, especially with respect to more recent or peripheral soft law sources (e.g., the Code of Conduct for Health Systems,²² which may have significant administrative impact, but – at least so far – not in courts), we find this focus to be useful for gauging the use and purchase of soft law for several reasons. First, as opposed to inner bureaucratic reasoning, conducted non-transparently within governmental and nongovernmental organizations, court decisions are relatively accessible to public scrutiny, and can provide us with a visible indication of the use of soft law. Second, the use of international soft law within international intergovernmental organizations, which could also be accessed, is often *self*-referential (e.g., nonbinding UN Human Rights Council (HRCon) Resolutions that refer to previous nonbinding HRCon Resolutions or to the nonbinding work of subsidiary organs and special procedures), whereas references made by independent entities such as courts are more indicative of practical purchase. Third, on the input side, the use of international soft law by courts is often in reaction and response to argumentation by state parties or nongovernmental actors based on soft law, making such argumentation more observable.²³ And fourth, perhaps most importantly on the output side, the referential employment of international soft law by courts indicates that the judicial decision-makers believe that such reference has legitimate purchase with their "mandate-providers"²⁴ and the addressees of the jurisprudence.

To emphasize a point already made above, we are not interested here in "compliance" or conformity with soft law sources, but rather with the explicit,

---

²² WORLD HEALTH ORGANIZATION, NGO CODE OF CONDUCT FOR HEALTH SYSTEMS STRENGTHENING (2008), http://www.who.int/workforcealliance/news/Code%20booklet%20 lowres.pdf?ua=1.

²³ In fact, parties to disputes often make arguments more far-reaching in their use of soft law than courts are willing to endorse. For example, in Construction of a Road in Costa Rica along the San Juan River (Nicar. v. Costa Rica), Judgment, 2015 I.C.J. Rep. 665, 99–100, Nicaragua argued before the International Court of Justice (ICJ) on the basis of the International Law Commission (ILC)'s *Draft Articles on Prevention of Transboundary Harm from Hazardous Activities*. In its judgment (¶ 190), the ICJ described the argument but did not address it; in their Separate Opinions, Judge Bhandari (¶ 21) and especially Judge *ad hoc* Dugard (¶¶ 7, 9, 17–18) made positive reference to these Draft Articles, whereas Judge Donoghue (¶ 19) cautioned against overstating their role "in the assessment of state practice and *opinio juris*."

²⁴ YUVAL SHANY, ASSESSING THE EFFECTIVENESS OF INTERNATIONAL COURTS 6–7 (2014).

expressive referential use made of soft law. This ultimately means a primary focus on the employment of soft law in legal argumentation and justification of action or inaction. In so doing, we thus exclude conduct and decisions that are substantively in conformity with soft law solely for parallel, doctrinal "hard law" reasons,[25] due to so-called spontaneous cooperation,[26] or arise out of other "realist" self-interested reasons, and where such justification is sufficient, and are therefore not of concern here. We also generally exclude a second zone of conduct and decision-making that overtly turns a blind eye to soft law, whether out of doctrinal purism, simple ignorance, or expedient disregard. We are, rather, interested in the (wide) middle ground, in which legal actors find it necessary and pertinent to *refer* to soft law in the construction of their arguments and justifications regarding behavior under international law. This approach corresponds generally with the literature on the use of citations as a tool to measure influence[27] – the reference to soft law as an indication of its effect.

Put differently, because soft law is nonbinding, there is absolutely no formal a priori reason to make express reference to it in argumentation for conduct or justification of decisions. Thus, when legal actors do refer to soft law, they have chosen to do so, presumably because they consider it helpful to their goals, either in justifying their actions and decisions, or in influencing the actions and decisions of interlocutors; or because they genuinely consider it as normatively relevant. International and domestic courts are no exception in this respect. Here, however, we must carefully distinguish between the motivation for the use by courts of existing soft law, on the one hand (which can be viewed as simply instrumental or, quite differently, normatively sincere), and its behavioral sources, on the other hand – that is, *why* is soft law considered instrumental or normatively relevant, despite an absence of legal effect?

Several caveats and precisions are in order here. Note that much the same could be said about the use of foreign and comparative law in domestic contexts, or taken *ad absurdum*, as far as motivation for the use of soft law is concerned, about references to poetry in legal contexts, such as the

---

[25] For example, reference to soft law may become superfluous, when the source has 'hardened' through a treaty or domestic law. *See, e.g.*, Kenneth W. Abbott & Duncan Snidal, *Pathways to International Cooperation, in* THE IMPACT OF INTERNATIONAL LAW ON INTERNATIONAL COOPERATION: THEORETICAL PERSPECTIVES 50 (Eyal Benvenisti & Moshe Hirsch eds., 2004).

[26] BENJAMIN MILLER, WHEN OPPONENTS COOPERATE: GREAT POWER CONFLICT AND COLLABORATION IN WORLD POLITICS 9 (1995).

[27] Richard A. Posner, *An Economic Analysis of the Use of Citations in the Law*, 2 AM. L. ECON. REV. 381 (2000).

courtroom;[28] but however liberal our understanding of soft law may be, it is nonetheless limited to references made to nonbinding rules,[29] that are similar to references made to legally binding rules.[30] Thus, we are primarily interested in those cases in which legal actors assimilate soft law to hard law and use it in fashions that are comparable to the use of binding, hard, sources of international law, mainly treaty and custom. This can be done in several ways, ranging from "raw" application that ignores the deficient formal status of a soft law source, through introduction of the soft law source as an interpretative device, to persuasive reference that is supplementary to (but distinct from) arguments made on the basis of hard law. Moreover, reference to soft law can also be made in a negative, distinguishing sense, in order to explain why it is not dispositive, so to speak, to a course of action, beyond its lack of formal bindingness.

Turning first to the use of soft law in *international* courts, it is evident that referential recourse to soft law is quite widely practiced, even if one excludes references made for merely descriptive and factual purposes,[31] or where otherwise nonbinding decisions have been granted special status, such as UNGA Resolutions on UN membership.[32] However, care is usually exercised to ensure that the reference is made within a semblance of acceptable international legal doctrinal framework of application or interpretation, though not always with optimal clarity. For example, the ICJ has over the last decades struggled with the legal status of generally nonbinding UNGA Resolutions and, in particular, their relationship with customary international law. In *Nicaragua*,[33] the ICJ developed the use of soft law (*in casu*, UNGA Resolution 2625)[34] as evidence of *opinio juris* for the legal purpose of

---

[28] David Cole, *Poetry in the Courtroom*, N.Y. REV. BOOKS (Aug. 11, 2017), www.nybooks.com /daily/2017/04/11/poetry-in-the-courtroom-gavin-grimm/.

[29] *Cf.* TRACHTMAN, *supra* note 9.

[30] While outside the scope of the chapter, our behavioral analysis might be relevant to the influence of comparative law on judicial decision making, as we briefly discuss in Section 5.3.3.

[31] For example, INT'L CT. JUST., Memorial of Timor-Leste, Questions Relating to the Seizure and Detention of Certain Documents and Data (Timor-Leste v. Australia), ¶¶ 2.8, 2.12 (Apr. 28, 2014), https://www.icj-cij.org/files/case-related/156/18698.pdf (referencing UNGA Resolutions as part of the history of Timor-Leste).

[32] Competence of the General Assembly for the Admission of a State to the United Nations, Advisory Opinion, 1950 I.C.J. Rep. 4 (Mar. 3).

[33] Construction of a Road in Costa Rica along the San Juan River (Nicar. v. Costa Rica), Judgment, 2015 I.C.J. Rep. 665, ¶¶ 99–100 (Dec. 15).

[34] G.A. Res. 2625 (XXV), Declaration on Principles of International Law Concerning Friendly Relations and Cooperation Among States in Accordance with the Charter of the United Nations (Oct. 24, 1970).

determining the formation of custom, a concept subsequently developed in *Nuclear Weapons*[35] and relied upon in other cases. To be sure, this doctrinal use is not free from analytical doubts,[36] but we need not, for present purposes, enter this doctrinal debate; and we have already clarified that our interest is not in "compliance," but in the prevalence of referential use. What is important, then, is that in combination with hard law sources, the ICJ makes referential use to soft law, where expedient or substantively relevant for legal construction.

The use of nonbinding sources by the ICJ in similar fashion is not limited to UNGA Resolutions and transcends the interaction with custom. With respect to Human Rights Committee (UNHRC) "case-law," the ICJ in *Diallo*[37] stated specifically that although it "is in no way obliged to adopt UNHRC interpretations," it "should ascribe great weight" to them (opening the door for comparative-interpretative use of this type of soft law). The ICJ has also referred to the 1992 Rio Declaration for support,[38] without establishing its customary status. Most recently, and perhaps most dramatically, the ICJ in the *Whaling* case,[39] made extensive and creative use of the formally nonbinding, technical output of institutions established under the International Convention for the Regulation of Whaling, not as "subsequent practice" for the purpose of interpretation,[40] but rather as necessitating due regard in light of the duty to cooperate.[41]

Other international courts and tribunals use international soft law in similar ways – and again we need not engage in a thorough doctrinal discussion of this use; what is pertinent here is that soft law is referred to as law, despite its nonbinding status. The European Court of Human Rights has referred comparatively to UNHRC Individual Communications;[42] the WTO Appellate

---

[35] Legality of the Threat or Use of Nuclear Weapons, Advisory Opinion, 1996 I.C.J. Rep. 226 (July 8) [hereinafter Nuclear Weapons].

[36] M. D. Öberg, *The Legal Effects of Resolutions of the UN Security Council and General Assembly in the Jurisprudence of the ICJ*, 16 Eur. J. Int'l L. 879 (2005).

[37] Ahmadou Sadio Diallo (Guinea v. Dem. Rep. Congo), Judgment, 2010 I.C.J. Rep. 639, ¶ 66 (Nov. 30).

[38] U.N. Conference on Environment and Development, *Rio Declaration on Environment and Development*, U.N. Doc. A/CONF.151/26 (Vol. I) (Aug. 12, 1992); *see* Nuclear Weapons, *supra* note 35, ¶ 30.

[39] Whaling in the Antarctic (Austl. v. Japan), Judgment, 2014 I.C.J. Rep. 226 (Mar. 31).

[40] International Convention for the Regulation of Whaling, with Schedule for Whaling Regulations, Dec. 2, 1946, 62 Stat. 1716, 161 U.N.T.S. 72.

[41] Margaret A. Young & Sebastían R. Sullivan, *Evolution Through the Duty to Cooperate: Implications of the* Whaling Case *at the International Court of Justice*, 16 Melb. J. Int'l L. 311 (2015).

[42] For example, Mouvement Raelien Suisse v. Switzerland, 2012-IV Eur. Ct. H.R. 373, 444 (referring to Coleman v. Australia, U.N. Hum. Rts. Comm., No. 1157/2003, U.N. Doc. CCPR/C/87/D/1157/2003 (2006)).

Body has turned, for interpretative and other operative purposes, to soft law
sources as diverse as "Agenda 21"[43] (a UN document produced by subsidiary
organs)[44] and the OECD Arrangement on Officially Supported Export
Credits,[45] which played a key role in the analysis in the Brazil-US cotton subsidy
dispute.[46] Reference by international tribunals to the ILC Articles on State
Responsibility (ARSIWA)[47] is understandably relatively common, given the
customary international law status of many of its provisions and the blurry line
between those provisions and others of a more "controversial" nature. Among
the latter referred to by international tribunals,[48] are Article 40, cited by the
Inter-American Court of Human Rights,[49] and Article 51, which has found its
place in WTO jurisprudence.[50] Similarly, the ARSIWA commentaries have
been referred to by the International Tribunal for the Law of the Sea (ITLOS).[51]

Moving on to *domestic* courts, here we find a surprisingly high degree of
judicial willingness to refer to international soft law. In the United Kingdom,
courts have made positive references to General Comments of the UNHRC
and the UN Committee on the Rights of the Child.[52] South Africa's highest
courts have made significant referential use of General Comments of the UN
Committee on Economic, Social and Cultural Rights (CESCR) in the

[43] *See* U.N. Conference on Environment & Development, *Conference Agenda* (Jun. 3, 1992),
      https://sustainabledevelopment.un.org/content/documents/Agenda21.pdf.
[44] Appellate Body Report, *United States – Import Prohibition of Certain Shrimp and Shrimp
      Products*, WTO Doc. WT/DS58/AB/R (adopted Oct. 12, 1998).
[45] Org. for Econ. Co-op. & Dev. [OECD], *Arrangement on Officially Supported Export Credits*,
      OECD Doc. TAD/PG(2019)1 (Jan. 2, 2019).
[46] Panel Report, *United States – Subsidies on Upland Cotton*, WTO Doc. WT/DS267/R
      (adopted Sept. 8, 2004). *See also* Shaffer & Pollack, *supra* note 1 (analyzing the interaction
      between hard and soft law in the WTO).
[47] Int'l Law Comm'n, Rep. on the Work of Its Fifty-Third Session, U.N. Doc. A/56/10 (2001).
[48] JAMES CRAWFORD, THE CREATION OF STATES IN INTERNATIONAL LAW (2d ed. 2006).
[49] Juridical Condition and Rights of Undocumented Migrants, Advisory Opinion OC-18/03,
      Inter-Am. Ct. H.R. (ser. A) No. 18 (Sept. 17, 2003) (separate opinion of Cançado Trindade, J., ¶
      70); Myrna Mack Chang v. Guatemala, Judgment, Inter-Am. Ct. H.R. (ser. C) No. 101 (Nov.
      25, 2003) (separate opinion of Cançado Trindade, J.).
[50] For example, Arbitration Report, *United States – Tax Treatment for Foreign Sales Corporations –
      Recourse to Article 22.6*, ¶ V.58 n.52, WTO Doc. WT/DS108/ARB (Aug. 30, 2002).
[51] Arctic Sunrise (Neth. v. Russ.), Case No. 22, Order of Nov. 22, 2013, ITLOS Rep. 230, ¶ 337.
[52] *See* Kasey McCall-Smith, *Interpreting International Human Rights Standards: Treaty Body
      General Comments as a Chisel or Hammer?*, *in* TRACING THE ROLE OF SOFT LAW IN
      HUMAN RIGHTS 27 (Stephanie Lagoutte, Thomas Gammeltoft-Hansen & John Cerone
      eds., 2016) (referring, among others, to Derrick Agyeman v. Sec. of State for Foreign and
      Commonwealth Affairs, Sec. of State for the Home Dep't, Admin CO/8185/2006, 2010 EWHC
      2180, ¶ 12–13 (Aug. 11, 2010); RT & KM (among others) v. Secretary of State UKSC 38 ¶ 33
      (2012); and DS (Afghanistan) v. Secretary of State for the Home Department EWCA Civ. 305,
      ¶ 65 (2011).

interpretation of constitutional rights to housing, education, and water.[53] In Israel, we have found examples of what may be called "distinguishing" referential use. Thus, in the *Dirani* case,[54] an Israeli District Court referred to UNHRC General Comment 31, in order to demonstrate that international law did *not* require the State of Israel to respect and ensure ICCPR rights to the plaintiff, as at the time he was outside of Israel's jurisdiction and effective control (nevertheless the Court allowed the tort case to proceed).[55] Otherwise, Israeli Courts at all levels (including the Supreme Court), have made referential use of international soft law, mainly treaty monitoring body General Comments[56] (instrumental in developing economic and social rights in Israel)[57] and UN High Commissioner for Refugees (UNHCR) Guidelines[58] and Working Group conclusions,[59] but also UNGA Resolutions such as the Rio Declaration[60] and the Declaration on the Rights of Disabled Persons.[61]

Similar referential use to international soft law can be found in the courts of India,[62] Pakistan,[63] Bangladesh,[64] Uganda,[65] Kenya,[66] and Italy.[67] Even

[53] *See* Mpange v. Sithole 2007 (6) SA 578 (W) at paras. 51–52 (S. Afr.); S v. Mazibuko 2008 (4) All SA 471 (ZAGPHC) (A1246/2006) 106 at paras. 36, 124, 128 (S. Afr.); Residents of Joe Slovo Community, Western Cape v. Thubelisha Homes (CCT 22/08) (2009) at para. 232; Juma Musjid Primary School & Others v. Essay N.O. (CCT 29/10) [2011] ZACC 13 (11 Apr. 2011) at para. 40.

[54] Int'l Comm. of the Red Cross, State of Israel v. Dirani, Civil Appeal 1461/00, ¶ 43 (Dec. 19, 2005).

[55] *See also* Iris Canor, Tamar Gidron & Haya Zandberg, *Litigating Human Rights Violations Through Tort Law: Israeli Law Perspective*, *in* DAMAGES FOR VIOLATIONS OF HUMAN RIGHTS: A COMPARATIVE STUDY OF DOMESTIC LEGAL SYSTEM 193 (Ewa Bagińska ed., 2016).

[56] *See, e.g.*, HCJ 2245/06 Dobrin v. Israel Prison Service, IsrLR 2006(2) 1, 28 (2006) (Isr.).

[57] HCJ 11437/05 Kav LaOved v. Ministry of Interior 64(3) PD 122 ¶ 48 (2011) (Isr.); HCJ 3071/05 Luzon v. Gov't of Israel 63(1) PD ¶ 9, 17 (2008) (Isr.); HCJ 10662/04 Hassan v. Nat'l Ins. Inst. 65(1) PD ¶ 51 (2012) (Isr.).

[58] *See, e.g.*, HCJ 7146/12 Adam v. The Knesset IsrSC ¶ 92 (2013) (Isr.) (unpublished), http://versa.cardozo.yu.edu/sites/default/files/upload/opinions/Adam%20v.%20Knesset.pdf.

[59] *Id.* at ¶ 91.

[60] CC (Jer) 9582/99 Livni v. Shabo, Tak-Magistrate 2005(2) 6844, 6863–6864 (2005) (Isr.).

[61] CC (Jer) 1136/10 Cnafo v. EASYGO, ¶¶ 7–10 (2010) (Isr.).

[62] Essar Oil Ltd. v. Halar Utkarsh Samiti (2004) 2 SCC 392 ¶ 8 (India); Karnataka Indus. Areas Dev. Bd. v. Kenchappa, AIR 2006 SC 2546 (India); Research Found. for Sci. Tech. & Nat. Res. Policy v. Union of India (2005) WP 657/1995 (India).

[63] Zia v. WAPDA (1994) PLD (SC) 693, ¶ 9 (Pak.).

[64] Farooque v. Gov't of Bangladesh (2001) 17 BLD (AD) 1 (App. Div. 1996).

[65] Supreme Court Feb. 11, 2004, Onyango-Obbo & Mwenda v. Attorney General of Uganda, Constitutional Appeal No. 2/2002, ILDC 166, *in* ANDRE NOLLKAEMPER, NATIONAL COURTS AND THE INTERNATIONAL RULE OF LAW 156 (2011).

[66] Waweru v. Republic of Kenya (2004) 2006 eKLR Case No. 118, ILDC 880 (H.C.K.) (Kenya).

[67] Cass., sez. un., 16 ottobre 2007, n. 21748, ILDC 1431 (It.), *in* NOLLKAEMPER, *supra* note 65, at 146.

United States jurisprudence, with its uneasy relationship with foreign and international law,[68] is not shy of making referential use of international soft law, in a variety of settings.[69] What is striking in all these cases of referential use of international soft law in domestic courts, is that in contrast to the similar use by international tribunals, there is little to no attempt to justify this use through doctrinal means, despite the absence of binding effect – not only because of the softness of the sources in question, but because of their lack of incorporation into domestic law.

Overall, taking international and domestic courts as an indicator, there is little doubt that referential use is made of international soft law in a broad range of scenarios, for argumentation and justification, despite the lack of "hard" binding effect. We turn now to a series of rational choice hypotheses as to why this might be so.

5.2 RATIONAL CHOICE AND THE USE OF SOFT LAW

5.2.1 *From Rational Design to Rational Use and Back Again*

In standard rational choice theory, human decision-makers are assumed, under prevailing conditions of resource scarcity, to act as utility-maximizing and self-interested beings that respond to incentives (positive and negative) in accordance with stable preference priorities. In international law and economics, these assumptions are often applied to states as rational actors.[70] As noted already, this framework has been theoretically applied to the question of why states and other international actors bother to create international soft law – the "rational design"[71] of soft law – with an assumption, explicit or implicit, that such soft law is followed or otherwise influences behavior, argumentation, and justification. In the previous section, we demonstrated that international

---

[68] *See, e.g.*, Robert J. Delahunty & John C. Yoo, *Against Foreign Law*, 29 HARV. J.L. & PUB. POL'Y 291–330 (2005), http://scholarship.law.berkeley.edu/cgi/viewcontent.cgi?article=1670& context=facpubs). This is worthy of further exploration; we do not make any claims regarding the context or tone of such reference here.

[69] *See, e.g.*, Int'l Ass'n of Machinists v. Org. of Petroleum, 477 F. Supp. 553 (C.D. Cal. 1979) at 567 (referring to UNGA Resolutions); Flores v. S. Peru Copper Corp., 253 F. Supp. 2d 510 (S.D.N.Y. 2002) at 521 (referring to the Rio Declaration); Abay v. Ashcroft, 368 F.3d 634 (6th Cir. 2004), and 400 F.3d 785 (9th Cir. 2005) (referring to UNGA Resolutions and to treaty monitoring body General Comments).

[70] *See, e.g.*, Andrew T. Guzman, *The Design of International Agreements*, 16 EUR J. INT'L L. 579, 586 (2005).

[71] Barbara Koremenos, Charles Lipson & Duncan Snidal, *The Rational Design of International Institutions*, 55 INT'L ORG. 761 (2001).

soft law does indeed carry such practical purchase, at least in the jurisprudence of international and domestic courts and tribunals, but likely well
beyond. In this section, we will endeavor to unpack the leading rational choice
explanations for the creation of international soft law,[72] to "reverse engineer"
rational choice explanations – as hypotheses, no more – for this evident
referential *use* of soft law, subsequent to its creation.

Guzman and Meyer essentially suggest four rational choice-inspired explanations for the creation of international soft law. As noted above, we identify
close linkages between soft-law creation and its subsequent use, and so we will
pursue these lines of thinking, adapting them to the judicial context; this
should not detract as such from application to the nonadjudicative situations
in which soft law may matter.

The first explanation posited relates to "simple" and "straightforward"
coordination problems,[73] in which soft law can ostensibly provide a focal
point for cooperation, where states have a "high degree of certainty" that the
rules will remain "self-enforcing in the future," and the costs of creating soft
law are low. Although not explicitly defined as such, it appears that the
reference here is to situations in which the actors are not so much concerned
with the content of the rule arrived at as with the existence of a rule.
The second explanation is termed "loss avoidance theory," whereby states
create soft law as part of a trade-off, recognizing that while soft law (compared
to hard law) will diminish *chances* of "compliance," it will also reduce the
costs of noncompliance. Here too, a degree of adherence to soft law – albeit
reduced – is assumed, not explained. The third explanatory theory is labeled
(somewhat confusingly) "delegation theory"; the gist of it is that soft law is
actually adopted where (some) states intend to violate it in order to "unilaterally amend suboptimal legal rules"[74] without incurring significant costs
from violation. In this regard, it is a theory that explains nonconformity with
soft law rather than conformity, but it can be useful in explaining various
referential uses of soft law, especially with respect to the potential use of soft
law in the progressive creation of hard law. The fourth explanation, referred to
by Guzman and Meyer as "international common law"[75] focuses on the
international soft law produced by international courts and tribunals, arguing
in essence that (some) such institutions are used by states to constrain other
states' behavior. Let us now see how these explanations translate into

---

[72] *See* Guzman & Meyer, *supra* note 3.
[73] *Id.* at 176.
[74] *Id.* at 178.
[75] *Id.*

rationales for the use of international soft law; we will also briefly address the distinct network effects explanation put forward by Druzin.[76]

5.2.2 *Simple or Rather, Noncontroversial Coordination Problems*

The simplest (though not the most illuminating) explanation for referential use to international soft law sources arises when these sources are considered to be noncontroversial or otherwise noncontested in ways that exact costs. This would appear to be the main situation that Guzman and Meyer have in mind in their discussion of soft law sources as focal points for cooperation. In these scenarios, the creation of soft law is relatively uncostly because actors prefer the existence of a rule over the absence of one and do not have significant substantive preferences regarding the content of the rule. Once the rule exists, parties will adhere to it, and by extension, courts will cite it. Guzman and Meyer give as an example the choice of Olympic Games' venues by the International Olympic Committee (IOC).[77] Although the choice of Olympic venue is certainly controversial ex ante, it is not easily defectable ex post. Moreover, this example is not an ideal-type for a discussion of international soft law in any case; a determination by the IOC is formally binding upon IOC members, and the IOC is an organization incorporated under Swiss law, and in that respect, its determinations are hard law, if not under public international law. It is indeed somewhat difficult to think of noncontroversial rules that could serve the purpose of soft law in this way. Voluntary international standards, such as those of the Codex Alimentarius Commission for example, are a source that has been discussed intensively as soft law, but cannot be said to be noncontroversial across the board.[78] The International Maritime Organization's International Code of Signals[79] may be noncontroversial – which color and shape of flag spells which letter of the alphabet should not be a significant issue – and some internet standards might also fit the bill.

The idea is nevertheless compelling: once a standard exists, however uncontroversial, however nonbinding, it can be assumed that all prior bargaining and coordination costs have been absorbed – whether the negotiation was costly or not is seemingly of no importance to the subsequent user of the norm. The rule may be used and referred to, at least for argumentation and justification purposes. In these cases, the transaction costs of somehow altering

---

[76]   Druzin, *supra* note 13.
[77]   Guzman & Meyer, *supra* note 3, at 189.
[78]   JOINT FAO/WHO FOOD STANDARDS PROGRAMME, CODEX ALIMENTARIUS COMMISSION: PROCEDURAL MANUAL (23d ed. 2013).
[79]   INT'L MAR. ORG. [IMO], INTERNATIONAL CODE OF SIGNALS (4th ed. 2005).

the soft rule will rightly be considered to be greater than the advantages of referring to it – especially if there are no significant preferences regarding the content of the rule – and for all relevant actors, the soft rule may be deemed optimal. The use of soft law as a focal point might serve in some cases to solve coordination problems even if the relevant actors have conflicting interests.[80] Moreover, from the perspective of international and domestic courts and tribunals, and of other actors, referential use of soft law in these circumstances bears little or no cost, whereas the benefits of using it in persuasive support of arguments and determinations is clear. Under these circumstances, recourse to existing soft law is quite understandable from a rational choice perspective.

5.2.3 *Loss Avoidance Theory and Its Obstruction*

Setting aside assumptions regarding the noncontroversial nature of a given soft law norm, the central observations of Guzman and Meyer in their "loss avoidance" theory boil down to this: soft law, in contrast to hard law, will (unsurprisingly) be less influential and formative toward the behavior of states and other international actors. This is mainly because soft law generates lower costs to non"compliance" both for the "violating" party and for the compliant parties that wishes to retaliate. At the same time, soft law may create less value for actors because it generates less cooperation. Moreover, creating soft law may be a relatively low cost stepping-stone toward the establishment of binding hard law at a later stage. Hence, states (and to belabor the point – other actors) may opt for the low cost and lesser (immediate) value of soft law – basically a "little ventured, little gained" strategy.

While this theory can explain the creation of soft law in many instances, how does it inform the high referential use of existing soft law? Once a soft law rule is created, it is not clear that the low cost (or "loss avoidance") strategy applies. Courts and tribunals, both domestic and international, and actors arguing before them, appear to take soft law seriously, as we have demonstrated. This suggests that states and other actors consider soft law sources as meaningful, and are intent on maximizing adherence to norms even if they are nonbinding. Reputational costs of noncompliance with soft norms can be significant, at least to the extent that such costs are significant at all, even with respect to hard norms.[81] The creation of soft law may be driven by loss

---

[80]   Tom Ginsburg & Richard H. McAdams, *Adjudicating in Anarchy: An Expressive Theory of International Dispute Resolution*, 45 Wm. & Mary L. Rev. 1229 (2004).

[81]   *See, e.g.*, Chris Brummer, Soft Law and the Global Financial System: Rule Making in the 21st Century 174 (2012) (regarding nonconformity with informal international financial regulatory standards).

avoidance theory, but its use – once a soft law norm is created – is not necessarily impacted by the idea of loss avoidance – quite the contrary. Actors may adopt soft law instead of hard law in order to reduce future losses, but it is not entirely clear that they will be successful in this respect. Indeed, the use of soft law by international actors might be less common than the use of hard law, but given its use and potential influence, it is hard to predict the costs of noncompliance with soft law. Non"compliance" with soft law bears its costs, and this can even induce "compliance" or at least normative relevance, for example, through the referential use made by tribunals and other actors. In short, soft law is used once it is there, because it is there, because actors have made it – and their efforts to make it less costly in terms of compliance have not been factored in successfully.

5.2.4 *"Delegation" Theory – the Weakness of Strategic Noncompliance*

Under this theory,[82] international soft law is sometimes adopted as a provisional compromise of sorts, a benchmark from which some actors – particularly powerful states – actually intend to diverge, or are at least prepared to do so, in order to influence the conduct of other actors after the soft benchmark has been arrived at, and to bring it closer to its preferences. Soft law presumably incurs lower non"compliance" costs than hard law, while divergence from it – again, presumably – somehow exerts strategic pressure on other actors to change their conduct in similar ways.

Moving from the creation of soft law to its deployment, it is not quite clear how this theory would work beyond realist or institutional power politics, and why a soft law instrument would actually be necessary or influential in this regard. From a standard rational choice perspective, there is no reason to think that weaker states would be more amenable to accepting the stronger states' preferences on either the applicable international rule or standard of conduct, merely because there has been a soft law understanding on a rule or standard that is apparently closer to their own preferences, let alone because this rule or standard is being violated by the stronger state. All this is said in comparison to a situation where there is no soft law rule to begin with.

We are, however, at present interested in explanations for the subsequent use of soft law, and if we adopt this theory's premises, it is not inconceivable that a party to an understanding, a party to a dispute, or a third-party decision-maker, would make referential use of international soft law as a benchmark, even if to

---

[82] Guzman & Meyer, *supra* note 3.

undermine its normative content – a negative use of international soft law that can bolster argumentation and justification, without reliance on soft law as true source of law. Indeed, we have seen several examples of such use in Section 5.1, that we referred to as "distinguishing" referential use. More obviously, weaker (or stronger) parties in this equation will continue to refer to the soft law benchmark against those wishing to diverge from it. Nevertheless, we consider this a less persuasive explanation, both for soft law creation and its utilization.

5.2.5 *International Common Law*

To complete the picture, Guzman and Meyer use the term – international common law – primarily to characterize the creation of international soft law *by* international courts and tribunals. This is indeed an important issue. However, in this current chapter we are mostly interested in the ways in which soft law, already in existence, is *used* in practice, even when formally disallowed, by international courts and tribunals (as a proxy for its wider use). The use of soft law by courts and tribunals, in order to establish soft law, risks being circular and self-referential (otherwise known as "tenterhooking"), although it may also be viewed as an element in the creation of network effects, which we discuss briefly immediately below. It is, however, conceivable that a court or tribunal would refer to soft law in order to enhance its own influence, by increasing the legitimacy of the decision – as we have seen in several of the examples in Section 5.1.

5.2.6 *Another Explanation? Network Effects or Ineffects*

In a recent article, Druzin suggests that soft law norms gain their power through network effects, when the value of the norm to its users grows over time, due to the number of users – a variable that in itself is clearly significant (also in the legal sense of *opinio juris*, toward the creation of customary international law).[83]

Network effects can provide, in our view, a plausible explanation for some referential use of soft law, but not a significant one. International and domestic tribunals may indeed be swayed to use international soft law for these (ultimately reputational, in a positive sense) causes, in particular when the soft law source in question has already been referred to by other courts (e.g., the extensive use of UNHCR guidelines in refugee status cases). Thus, somewhat circularly, if a soft law norm is used, it is used; it is less clear how network effects would explain the referential use of soft law sources to begin with.

---

[83] Druzin, *supra* note 13.

5.3 BEHAVIORAL ECONOMICS AND THE USE OF SOFT LAW

5.3.1 *The Shift to Behavioral Economics*

The rational choice hypotheses described above regarding the widespread referential use of international soft law are appealing, at least in their relative parsimony. In this section, we propose a number of alternative hypotheses, shifting our focus to the fields of psychology (both social and cognitive). While we do not, in this article, submit experimental and/or empirical evidence that supports these hypotheses, we do propose that they are no less plausible than the standard rational choice explanations, and thus are well worthy of consideration and future empirical investigation.

In principle, we suggest that at least part of the reason that soft law instruments are influential in the ways described above is the mere fact that they actually exist. This explanation builds on two behavior-related observations. First, evidently, numerous actors in the international law universe accord value to a genuine application of relevant legal norms to a particular situation. Second, in many cases the self-same actors do not hold a strong preference as to the substantive determination of the legal question at hand. Imagine a situation in which an international actor is facing a legal question where soft law is the most accessible, convenient, and detailed source of (normative) information, or as in some cases the only available legal source – and in some cases, the "first available information." Will it affect the decision or justification offered by this international actor? It seems probable that such material, though "soft" sources, will feed into the decision. The following section suggests behavioral explanations for this likelihood.

Notably, the behavioral mechanisms that we will refer to work best – though hardly exclusively – when the relevant actors are imperfectly knowledgeable with regard to the specific legal question, especially when they are expected to provide legal reasoning for the position they maintain. The literature provides anecdotal support for this pattern. For example, the lack of international humanitarian law expertise in US courts has been found to have opened the possibility of greater influence of experts in the field through the filing of amici briefs,[84] making decisions more susceptible to the influence of soft law. Another study has found that soft norms had a strong influence as an argumentative tool when used by the High Commissioner on National Minorities

---

[84]   Naz K. Modirzadeh, *Folk International Law: 9/11 Lawyering and the Transformation of the Law of Armed Conflict to Human Rights Policy and Human Rights Law to War Governance*, 5 HARV. NAT'L SEC. J. 225 (2014).

of the Organization for Security and Cooperation in Europe (OSCE), especially when the actors to whom the communications were directed had little knowledge of the relevant binding international law norms.[85] Nonetheless, as explained below, these behavioral mechanisms can be relevant even when highly knowledgeable international legal experts, such as international judges (and their clerks, and counsel arguing before them), are involved.

The following section does not provide an in-depth discussion of the relevant psychological mechanisms nor does it address all of the potential mechanisms that are relevant to the power of soft law. Rather, we briefly describe the literature, mostly the law and behavior literature, and its potential relevance to the power of soft law, in the mode of "theoretical application" for the sake of raising hypotheses.[86] In doing so we follow the path of several authors who have discussed the relevance of such behavioral insights in other legal contexts, most notably as possible explanations for path dependence in corporate contracting,[87] the adherence to the doctrine of stare decisis,[88] and the phenomenon of constitutional stickiness.[89]

Our aim is not to suggest that such mechanisms are necessarily the main explanation for the practical purchase of international soft law, or to suggest that they have an effect in all circumstances. Rather, we try to bring into the international soft law literature a body of research that has not received enough attention in this context and might have important implications to the study of soft law. In the following section, we offer several such psychological mechanisms that might have an effect on the power of soft law. Then we will briefly discuss these mechanisms in the context of different types of soft law and international legal actors.

5.3.2 *Status Quo Bias*

The status quo bias is the tendency of individuals to prefer the perceived current state of affairs over alternatives, even if the latter may be objectively more desirable. The status quo bias has been widely demonstrated in numerous studies.[90] In the legal context, the status quo bias has been used to explain

---

[85] *Id.*

[86] Tomer Broude, *Behavioral International Law*, 163 U. PA. L. REV. 1099, 1132 (2013).

[87] Marcel Kahan & Michael Klausner, *Path Dependence in Corporate Contracting: Increasing, Returns, Herd Behavior and Cognitive Biases*, 74 WASH. U. L.Q. 347 (1996).

[88] Goutam U. Jois, *Stare Decisis in Cognitive Error*, 75 BROOK. L. REV. 63 (2009).

[89] Ozan Varol, *Constitutional Stickiness*, 49 U.C. DAVIS L. REV. 899 (2016).

[90] For example, William Samuelson & Richard J. Zeckhauser, *Status Quo Bias in Decision Making*, 1 J. RISK & UNCERTAINTY 7 (1988); Ilana Ritov & Jonathan Baron, *Status-Quo and Omission Bias*, 5 J. RISK & UNCERTAINTY 49 (1992); M. Schweitzer, *Disentangling Status*

different decision-making tendencies. For example, it has been suggested as a possible explanation for the tendency of courts to follow the practice of stare decisis,[91] and the reluctance of (domestic, non-apex) appellate court judges to overturn lower courts decisions.[92] Another study has demonstrated that contract default rules – rules that in themselves have no binding effect – create status quo bias that makes it harder to contract around it.[93] While the status quo bias is closely related to the omission bias, which is the tendency of individuals to prefer inaction over action, it is also explained independently by a reluctance to change the perceived current state of affairs regardless of the requirement for an action or inaction.[94]

We hypothesize that courts refer to soft law in those situations in which they perceive that it reflects the status quo. We contend that courts tend to rely more on soft law in those situations in which they perceive that it reflects the normative status quo (despite its nonbinding effect), reflecting a type of status quo bias. An empirical challenge to this proposition is whether soft law instruments are indeed perceived as the status quo by the relevant actors. Alternatively, these actors might be merely making argumentative instrumental use of these instruments *qua* status quo, or for other ends, such as pushing hard law (such as custom) in a particular direction. Ostensibly, unlike the constitutional norms or common-law jurisprudential precedents, nonbinding soft law might be perceived as a *change* to the formal status quo rather than the prevailing legal state of affairs. Nonetheless, as already mentioned, in many cases, soft law instruments are the main legal material pertaining to a legal issue when no alternative but the silence (or dearth, or vagueness) of formal international law on the issue is available. Indeed, in such cases, it is reasonable to assume that soft law will be perceived – or presented – as the current status quo. Cases in point are the ILC's Draft Articles on the Responsibility of International Organizations (DARIO)[95] or the so-called

Quo and Omission Effects: An Experimental Analysis, 58 ORG. BEHAV. & HUM. DECISION PROCESSES 457 (1994).

[91] Jois, *supra* note 88.
[92] Chris Guthrie & Tracey E. George, *The Futility of Appeal: Disciplinary Insights into the 'Affirmance Effect' on the United States Court of Appeals*, 32 FLA. ST. U. L. REV. 185 (2005).
[93] Russell B. Korobkin, *Inertia and Preference in Contract Negotiation: The Psychological Power of Default Rules and Form Terms*, 51 VAND. L. REV. 1583 (1998).
[94] Schweitzer, *supra* note 90.
[95] Int'l Law Comm'n [ILC], *Draft Articles on Responsibility of States for Internationally Wrongful Acts*, U.N. Doc. A/56/10 Supp. No. 10, IV.E.1 (Nov. 2001). *See also* HR 6 September 2013, ILM 2014, 53(3) m.nt. Amir Čengić (Nederland/Nuhanović) (Neth.) (discussion by the Supreme Court of the Netherlands).

"Ruggie Principles" in Business and Human Rights.[96] Both of these lack formal binding effect, but have rapidly become normative benchmarks, referentially, as if they reflected a legal status quo.

Perhaps the clearest example of such a perception are decisions of international courts. Specifically, relying on our broad definition of soft law and the literature discussion of the role of the status quo bias in adherence to the doctrine of stare decisis in domestic courts, the tendency in international law to rely on precedent even though there is no formal obligation to do so can be explained by the status quo bias.[97] In any case, future research on the actual perceptions of the status of soft law is desirable to promote our understanding as to the role of the status quo bias in this regard.

5.3.3 *Social Influences: the Reputational and the Informational*

As discussed, international soft law is created by states as well as by nonstate actors. Behind those state and nonstate actors are individuals, often renowned international law experts, either practitioners or academics. In addition, in many cases, soft law is the product of cooperation between many different actors.[98] Thus, when examining the practical purchase of soft law, the influence of social positions, including those of authority, on the decisions made by individuals should be explored. Our proposition here is that legal actors may increase references to international soft law in order to better conform – at least in perception – with the international epistemic community; this could be explained in either of the tracks we discuss below – meeting others' expectations, and reducing informational uncertainty.

In his seminal study on conformity, Solomon Asch divided participants into groups and asked them to decide which of three comparison lines match a standard line that was presented to them.[99] In each group one participant was an uninformed "naïve" participant while the other participants were "confederates," who were aware of the experimental goals and dynamics. Asch found that the naïve participants tended to yield to the other participants' positions even when their responses were quite obviously wrong. The

---

96 Hum. Rts. Council, *Guiding Principles on Business and Human Rights: Implementing the United Nations' "'Protect, Respect and Remedy' Framework"*, A/HRC/17/31 (Mar. 21, 2011).

97 Harlan Grant Cohen, *Theorizing Precedent in International Law, in* INTERPRETATION IN INTERNATIONAL LAW 268 (Andrea Bianchi, Daniel Peat & Matthew Windsor eds., 2014).

98 Kenneth W. Abbott, Philipp Genschel, Duncan Snidal & Bernhard Zangl, *Two Logics of Indirect Governance: Delegation and Orchestration*, 46 BRIT. J. POL. SCI. 719 (2016).

99 Solomon E. Asch, *Studies of Independence and Conformity: I. A Minority of One Against a Unanimous Majority*, 70 PSYCHOL. MONOGRAPHS 1 (1956).

tendency to conform to the majority was further established in numerous subsequent experiments.[100] Conformity to such group positions is explained in two main ways. The first is social normative influence, which is the proclivity of individuals to meet the expectations of others. The second is informational influence, which is the tendency of individuals to reduce uncertainty in situations that involve ambiguity as to the correct answer.[101]

In contrast to the potential influence of soft law, much of the research on such decisional conformity in social psychology has been conducted on relatively small groups that were physically present in relation to determinations of facts or opinions. However, another set of studies on what is usually referred to as cascades, has been conducted on much more broadly defined groups. The literature on *informational* cascades assumes that people tend to rely on their own private information as well as on signals conveyed by others. For example, some people tend to rely on the New York Times bestseller list when deciding to buy a book.[102] Informational cascades might lead to overreliance on others' positions even if all individuals act rationally. Consider a case in which people are asked to determine the composition of an urn that is full of red and white balls.[103] Each participant draws one ball out of the urn and needs to determine whether it has more red or white balls. The other participants are not informed of the color of the ball that each participant draws but are informed of their determinations regarding the composition of the urn. Assume that the first two participants draw white balls. It is rational for them to determine that there are more white than red balls in the urn – the first one has only her white ball to rely on, and the second one has his white ball and the determination of the first participant that there are more white balls. Now assume that the third participant draws a red ball, it is still rational for her to determine that there are more white balls in the urn, since against her red ball she knows that the first two participants determined that there are more white balls. The same is true to the next participant that also draws a red ball and relies on the three previous

[100] Rod Bond & Peter B. Smith, *Culture and Conformity: A Meta-Analysis of Studies Using Asch's (1952b, 1956) Line Judgment Task*, 119 PSYCHOL. BULL. 111 (1996); Robert B. Cialdini & Noah J. Goldstein, *Social Influence: Compliance and Conformity*, 55 ANN. REV. PSYCHOL. 591 (2004).

[101] Robert B. Cialdini & Melanie R. Trost, *Social Influence: Social Norms, Conformity, and Compliance*, in THE HANDBOOK OF SOCIAL PSYCHOLOGY 151 (Daniel T. Gilbert, Susan T. Fiske & Gardner Lindzey eds., 1998).

[102] Sushil Bikhchandani, David Hirshleifer & Ivo Welch, *Learning from the Behavior of Others: Conformity, Fads, and Informational Cascades*, 12 J. ECON. PERSP. 151 (1998).

[103] This example is based on the study of Lisa R. Anderson & Charles Holt, *Information Cascades in the Laboratory*, 87 AM. ECON. REV. 847 (1997).

participants who determined that there are more white balls in the urn. It is easy to see how even in cases in which there are in fact more red balls in the urn, rational people will make the wrong decision based on signals from other people. This example demonstrates that informational cascades can occur among rational actors with the same status as those who convey the information. When those who provide the information are somehow highly regarded – in terms of reputation, expertise, and the like – the significance that will be attributed to the information they provide can be expected to increase. Academic citations of other academic sources could serve as another relevant example of an informational cascade, where it is not always clear whether the number of sources who support a particular position reflects an accumulation of independent individual private information or rather a repeated reliance on and echoing of other academic sources, that might also primarily rely on other sources, etc.

A similar and related phenomenon could be attributed to *reputational* cascades. It can be assumed that normative conformity is often socially beneficial. Thus, individuals might agree to the positions of others due to the benefit of conformity and the negative costs of dissent. Since the costs and benefit of conformity increase the more actors are involved, it is reasonable to assume that when a given number of people hold a specific position – such as referential use to an otherwise nonbinding "soft law" norm – it becomes highly costly to hold to a different position.[104]

In the legal context, social influences in this vein have been discussed primarily in the context of following the precedents of peer courts.[105] It has been suggested that when deciding a case, courts of appeal take into account the informational signaling of other courts' decisions, and that this might lead to informational cascades.[106] It has also been suggested that the use of comparative law – like international soft law, not formally binding – is prone to such informational and reputational cascades.[107]

Different factors affect the tendency of individuals to conform to group positions. On one hand, the tendency to yield to others is reduced when the individual has eminent social status, has greater confidence in this position, or

---

[104] Timur Kuran & Cass R. Sunstein, *Availability Cascades and Risk Regulation*, 51 STAN. L. REV. 683 (1999).

[105] Andrew F. Daughety & Jennifer F. Reinganum, *Hush Money*, 30 RAND J. ECON. 661 (1999); Adrian Vermeule, *Many Minds Arguments in Legal Theory*, 1 J. LEGAL ANALYSIS 1 (2009).

[106] Eric Talley, *Precedential Cascades: An Appraisal*, 73 S. CAL. L. REV. 87 (1999).

[107] Eric A. Posner & Cass R. Sunstein, *The Law of Other States*, 59 STAN. L. REV. 131 (2006).

when there are dissenting voices among the group. On the other hand, the tendency to conform increases in complicated or ambiguous cases, when a position is pronounced in public, the majority of those who hold the position is increased, and when people perceive themselves as part of the social group of those who provide the information.[108]

Turning more concretely to international soft law – again, as a theoretical application that may produce useful hypotheses, not as a positive claim – consider the question of whether a particular provision in a particular constitutive international treaty has gained the status of customary international law. When an international actor – *in casu*, an international or domestic tribunal – is faced with such a question, it is faced with both its own "private" information regarding the existing evidence of state practice and *opinio juris* in this case, as well as information on other international legal actors' positions that is often revealed through soft law instruments. It might be rational for this expert actor to follow the position of other experts as relevant information. For example, using our broad definition of soft law, this could be an ICJ judgment, an ILC output, or UNHRC statement, assuming that these statements were based on their private information. At a certain point, it might be reasonable for the actor to give more weight to other experts' opinions than its own position. It can also decide to follow their positions due to their high reputation and a reluctance to be perceived as an outlier in the international law experts' community.

5.3.4 *The Difficulty to Discount Information*

Another contention, closely connected to some of the previous, is that the influence of soft law might be related to the effect of exposure to information, especially when the information seems relevant. Different behavioral phenomena address the effects of such exposure to relevant and irrelevant materials. These include, inter alia, anchoring, priming, order effects, and more generally, reference points and reference dependence, that are tightly associated with the status quo bias previously discussed.[109] Studies have also focused on the (in)ability to ignore information in legal and juridical contexts, setting aside the exact psychological mechanisms.

---

[108] John D. DeLamater, Daniel J. Myers & Jessica L. Collett, Social Psychology (8th ed. 2015).

[109] Eyal Zamir, Law, Psychology, and Morality: The Role of Loss Aversion (2015).

Many studies have demonstrated that it is difficult to ignore inadmissible evidence even under instructions to ignore such information.[110] Such difficulty to ignore information has been found among both juries and judges.[111] Different explanations have been offered for this difficulty including motivational explanations that focus on the desire of juries and judges to reach a result that they perceived as just and mental contamination explanations that relate to cognitive phenomena in which initial information affects the processing and interpretation of new information.[112] We posit here that similar effects may apply to nonbinding rules, their application and interpretation.

There are some notable exceptions to the findings related to the inability to ignore or discount information. First, studies have found that in probable cause cases, judges were able to ignore the hindsight effect of inadmissible evidence on the result of the search.[113] It has been suggested that the ability to ignore the information in these cases was based on the amount of case law on probable cause that enabled the informed judges to rely on their legal knowledge to overcome their intuition. Second, a notable example that is closer to the use of soft law is a recent study that demonstrated the ability of international law experts (in contrast to international law students) to ignore the influence of preparatory work under the rules of treaty interpretation.[114] The authors suggested that the unique expertise in interpreting legal text (in contrast to evaluating evidence) might enable the international law experts to ignore the preparatory work text. It was also suggested that the long-standing criticism of international law as not being "real law" might have driven international law experts to be more formal in their application of legal rules. It is important to note that in both cases (inadmissible evidence and the use of preparatory work) the use of the material was expressly prohibited,[115] while the use of soft law is not forbidden but at best formally inapplicable to the legal question. Experts who determined that the use of preparatory work was allowed were influenced by its

---

[110] Nancy K. Steblay, Harmon M. Hosch, Scott E. Culhane & Adam McWethy, *The Impact on Juror Verdicts of Judicial Instruction to Disregard Inadmissible Evidence: A Meta-Analysis*, 30 LAW & HUM. BEHAV. 469 (2006).

[111] Andrew J. Wistrich, Chris Guthrie & Jeffrey J. Rachlinski, *Can Judges Ignore Inadmissible Information? The Difficulty of Deliberately Disregarding*, 153 U. PA. L. REV. 1251 (2005).

[112] *Id.*

[113] J. J. Rachlinski, Chris Guthrie & Andrew J. Wistrich, *Probable Cause, Probability, and Hindsight*, 8 J. EMPIR. LEGAL STUD. 72 (2011); Wistrich et al., *supra* note 111.

[114] Yahli Shereshevsky & Tom Noah, *Does Exposure to Preparatory Work Affect Treaty Interpretation? An Experimental Study on International Law Students and Experts*, 28 EUR. J. INT'L L. (2017).

[115] The findings on the use of preparatory work involved cases in which the participants held a strict reading of the hierarchy between articles 31–32 to the VCLT and determined that the text is clear and reasonable.

substance. A third study that might be relevant to our discussion is a recent study on US federal judges that did not find the exposure to a weak international criminal law precedent affected the decisions of the judges.[116]

Based on these studies, it is unclear whether the mere exposure to soft law will affect the decision-making process of relevant international law experts. We should acknowledge that there are differences between exposure to factual evidence, on the one hand, and exposure to norms, on the other hand. Moreover, difficulties can apply. While there is no international legal rule that prohibits reference to international soft law, such norms are not considered formal sources of international law; nevertheless, it appears that they may not be ignored by judicial decision-makers. Taking into account the motivational and cognitive explanations, it seems that much of the potential influence of the text depends on the perception of soft law as relevant/irrelevant to the case and on the ability of international law experts to use their knowledge of the subject matter to mitigate the influence of the soft law. These conditions might yield different results for different types of soft law instruments and for different type of international law actors, as we discuss in section 5.3.5 below.

A specific type of cognitive bias that has been used to explain similar influences of nonbinding legal materials is anchoring. Such use of anchoring is rather far from the way in which it is treated in the psychological literature and the following paragraphs address both. Under this line of explanations, soft law might serve as a meaningful *anchor*, namely an initial reference point or benchmark that affects the position of the relevant actors (decision-makers). In the psychological and behavioral economic legal literature, "anchoring" primarily refers to the effect of cognitive exposure to a number before making a numerical judgment. Research has shown that when exposed to such numbers the numerical judgment that follows is adjusted from the initial (substantively irrelevant) number.[117] In the paradigmatic example of the study of anchoring, the participants were asked to make a comparative assessment with regard to a specific question (e.g., is the number of elephants in the Serengeti National Park more or less than 1000?), and then to estimate the exact number. For example, in a study in which the participants were asked (among other questions) to estimate the length of the Mississippi River, the median result from those who were questioned about whether the length is longer or shorter than 2,000 miles was 1,500, while the median of those who

[116] Holger Spamann & Lars Klöhn, *Justice Is Less Blind, and Less Legalistic, than We Thought: Evidence from an Experiment with Real Judges*, 45 J. LEGAL STUD. 255 (2016).
[117] Amos Tversky & Daniel Kahneman, *Judgment Under Uncertainty: Heuristics and Biases*, 185 SCI. 1124 (1974).

were presented with the number of 70 miles was 300.[118] These results have been replicated in numerous studies. Many studies have specifically examined the effect of anchoring on legal (numerical) judgments and have demonstrated that such anchors can affect legal decisions. For example, a recent study on active trial judges from Canada and the US, demonstrated that when exposed to a compensation "cap," judges tended to award larger compensation than judges who were not exposed to such anchors.[119]

The study of anchoring often involves random numbers. Nonetheless, it has been suggested that anchoring can involve meaningful numbers – that is, relevant information[120] and even nonnumerical anchors.[121] The notion of anchoring as including nonnumerical anchors has been addressed in the legal literature in two contexts: first, that standard contractual terms might have an anchoring effect that affects contractual design;[122] and second, that existing constitutional norms might have an anchoring effect that contributes to the stickiness of constitutional norms.[123]

Taking the notion of nonnumerical anchors to the realm of international soft law might shed a little light on its practical purchase. In many situations, soft law instruments will be the first piece of "legal information" encountered by actors facing decisions regarding future and past behavior. The proviso that the instrument in question is not binding (and hence, irrelevant from a purely legal perspective) may be insufficient to overcome the adoption of the expression of soft law as an anchor (or other form of reference point) that is likely to affect their position on the subject matter.

To be sure, some cautionary notes are required. First, while the notion of nonnumerical relevant anchors has been discussed in the legal literature, and in other contexts such as business management,[124] it is quite distant from its ordinary use in the psychological literature and no empirical studies have explored this notion yet, suggesting new research horizons.[125] Second,

---

[118]   Karen E. Jacowitz & Daniel Kahneman, *Measures of Anchoring in Estimation Tasks*, 21 PERSON. & SOC. PSYCHOL. BULL. 1161 (1995).

[119]   Jeffrey J. Rachlinski, Andrew J. Wistrich & Chris Guthrie, *Can Judges Make Reliable Numeric Judgments? Distorted Damages and Skewed Sentences*, 90 IND. L.J. 695 (2015).

[120]   Hans Van Der Heijden, *Evaluating Dual Performance Measures on Information Dashboards: Effects of Anchoring and Presentation Format*, 27(2) J. INFO. SYS. 21 (2013).

[121]   Yuval Feldman, Amos Schurr & Doron Teichman, *Anchoring Legal Standards*, 13 J. EMPIR. LEGAL STUD. 298 (2016).

[122]   Kahan & Klausner, *supra* note 87.

[123]   Varol, *supra* note 89.

[124]   John S. Hammond, Ralph L. Keensey & Howard Raiffa, *The Hidden Traps in Decision Making*, 84 HARV. BUS. REV. 118 (2006).

[125]   *But see* Feldman et al., *supra* note 121 (suggesting such studies should be made in the context of contractual design).

anchoring is most relevant in cases where the anchor is the first available information. Soft law is not always the first available information, and in such cases anchoring cannot explain the use of soft law. Third, research has demonstrated that knowledge might reduce the effect of anchoring.[126] This further strengthens our suggestion that the behavioral force of soft law works best in cases of less knowledgeable international legal actors.[127] It is important to note though that even domestic judicial decision-makers and international legal experts are not always knowledgeable in all circumstances, and may be swayed by anchoring. Indeed, as mentioned, studies have demonstrated that anchoring can affect acting trial judges when they make decisions involving much discretion and vagueness. Specifically, in the context of soft law, the vagueness and indeterminacy of the legal question in many cases seems to reduce the significance of expertise.[128] In any case, we should stress that the idea of soft law as a cognitive anchor is very different from the rational choice notion of soft law as a focal point for coordination. While the discussion of focal points for coordination accepts the possibility of the use of third parties' materials (such as ICJ judgments),[129] it focuses on the rational use of these materials to solve coordination problems. The notion of broadly understood cognitive anchors or reference points that we offer here stresses the involuntary reactions to previously created materials. In practice, there may be overlaps between the two, but they are conceptually different.

5.3.5 *Behavioral Insights and Questions: Varying International Actors and Varying Types of Soft Law*

We believe that the behavioral insights discussed in this chapter have the potential to explain at least part of international soft law's significant influence, or more accurately, to provide general hypotheses in this respect. Regardless of the actual rational and psychological processes that lead to this impact, the common feature of these explanations is the visibility and centrality of the soft norm that transcend its formal status. The mere availability of the norm might best explain the practical power of soft law. However, the potential effect of soft law norms might vary depending on (1) their nature, that is, the subset of soft law involved; and (2) the actors engaged in soft law creation and

---

[126]   Andrew R. Smith, Paul D. Windschitl & Kathryn Bruchmann, *Knowledge Matters: Anchoring Effects Are Moderated by Knowledge*, 43 Eur. J. Soc. Psychol. 97 (2013).

[127]   *See also* Shereshevsky & Noah, *supra* note 114.

[128]   *See* Feldman et al., *supra* note 121 (demonstrating that anchoring affected participants in the context of vague legal standards).

[129]   Ginsburg & McAdams, *supra* note 80.

application. In this section we briefly discuss the potential implications of such differences.

First, regarding the type of soft law – as noted, soft law is ultimately a vague concept that includes very different type of outputs. The broad definition of soft law we have embraced, for example, includes, inter alia, divergent sources and reference points such as treaties not in effect, guiding principles adopted by intergovernmental organizations, and international tribunals' case law. It is not clear that the influence of these different outputs on the conduct, argumentation, and justification of international actors will be homogenous. More specifically, it appears that there might be a significant difference between two types of soft law. One type is an output of an international actor that is not formally binding, but either claims to represent existing law (making it a claimant to hard law status) or leaves the normative status vague. For example, while international case law is not binding, its substance often claims to represent the lex lata on the subject matter, though often not proclaimedly so. Another example is ILC or UNHRC outputs that often – perhaps deliberately – leave vague whether they perceive the output to represent customary law.[130] The second type encompasses soft law that does not claim to represent the lex lata, and even excludes this from the outset. The strongest examples of this type of soft law are a variety of guiding principles that explicitly include a statement regarding the nonbinding nature. It seems reasonable that the influence of the first type of outputs, which resembles in many ways the discussion of nonbinding precedents, will be greater than the second type of soft law, but this is of course a question best put to more empirical testing.

Second, the identity of the actors who create and apply soft law are also significant factors to be further researched. While all soft law is by definition nonbinding, it should be quite straightforward and clear that not all actors are expected to create equally influential soft law. The more authoritative and respected the actor, the more influential it is expected to be. In addition, the more actors are involved, the tendency to yield to the group judgment discussed above increases and so does the perception of the output as a kind of status quo.

The identity of the actor who uses soft law can also be of import in this respect. As we mentioned previously, behavioral insights may be expected to be more salient – as a descriptive matter – when the actors that use soft law are

[130] Laurence R. Helfer & Timothy Meyer, *The Evolution of Codification: A Principal-Agent Theory of the International Law Commission's Influence, in* CUSTOM'S FUTURE: INTERNATIONAL LAW IN A CHANGING WORLD 305 (Curtis A. Bradley ed., 2016).

less informed of the hard law context or do not perceive themselves as highly regarded experts on the specific subject. Based on these insights, it is possible to hypothesize that domestic courts or generalist international tribunals might rely on soft law more than specialized tribunals. Similarly, it might be expected that weaker actors – for example, particular tribunals or states – will be more influenced by soft law, taking into account the insights on social influence. There is some evidence that the effect of soft law on international law experts might be less strong than other relevant actors. Following his discussion of the influence of soft law on government officials, Steven Ratner stated that one exception to the tendency to rely on soft norms was a small group of foreign ministry specialists who insisted on the relevance of the hard/soft law distinction.[131] In addition, one of the authors has demonstrated in another context the ability of international law experts to ignore irrelevant information in the process of treaty interpretation.[132] It must be noted, though, that this study examined the ability to ignore information when it is explicitly prohibited to use such information, while the use of soft law in many cases in the decision-making process is permissible or undefined. Moreover, as the more general literature on legal precedents and academic fashions suggest,[133] experts can be influenced from the positions of others as well, especially when the legal questions at hand are ambiguous and complicated.

5.4 CONCLUSIONS: THE "EVEREST EFFECT"?

In this chapter, our modest goal has been to set out a series of plausible and potentially falsifiable (to the extent that appropriate research plans may be developed and pursued) hypotheses regarding a significant research puzzle in public international law: Why do international and domestic legal actors employ and even apply international soft law sources, that by definition, are not formally binding and are technically unenforceable? We have done this by recourse to two main theoretical strands: standard rational choice theory, and behavioral economics based on insights from cognitive psychology. We do not claim that any of these hypotheses can explain all types of uses of all types of soft law. In fact, we have circumscribed our discussion to the use of soft law by domestic and international courts and tribunals, although our discussion can

---

[131]   Steven R. Ratner, *Does International Law Matter in Preventing Ethnic Conflict?*, 32 N.Y.U. J. Int'l L. & Pol. 591 (1999–2000).

[132]   Shereshevsky & Noah, *supra* note 114.

[133]   Daughety & Reinganum, *supra* note 105; Cass R. Sunstein, *On Academic Fads and Fashions*, 99 Mich. L. Rev. 1251 (2001).

be relevant to the use of soft law by a wider set of actors. As explained in Section 5.1, we consider this to be broadly representative of the use of international soft law, for a variety of reasons, but there is no question that the referential use of legal sources by courts and tribunals is a special case. We also do not claim that either of the strands – rational choice and behavioral economics – provides a better or more persuasive set of explanations. This is ultimately an empirical question whose answers on future research.

In these brief concluding comments, we will focus on what we identify as a central common thread to both strands. In all forms of analysis, international soft law is employed and applied by courts and tribunals (and actors arguing before them), because it is there – what we might call the "Everest effect," in reference to George Mallory's alleged quip when asked why he wanted to climb Mt. Everest. In our own exploration of various – and hardly exclusive – explanations for the use of soft law, the fact that a soft law source exists is accorded weight that greatly transcends its formal effect, its non"bindingness." The existence of a soft law source can be viewed as reducing transaction costs in decision-making; and can impact the cognition of decision-makers faced with choices in complex and uncertainty-ridden settings.

As we suggested in the introduction, we identify a dialectic relationship between the causes for the creation of soft law, on one hand, and its subsequent use, on the other. The latter essentially explains the former. International soft law is created because of an expectation that it will be used influentially in the future. This expectation is well-founded, as we have seen on a legal-empirical basis in Section 5.1, and for the theoretical reasons discussed in Sections 5.2 and 5.3. Moreover, the not inconsequential costs of international soft law's creation often become a factor in its subsequent effective normative influence. It signals to decision-makers that a meaningful compromise has been reached, even if nonbinding, which has implications in both research strands. This creates a dynamic, dialectic relationship between soft lawmaking and soft law adherence and influence. At the meta-level, it appears that the makers of international soft law – governmental and nongovernmental negotiators, lobbyists, and advocates – understand or at least perceive, ex ante, the influence of soft law, ex post – the expectation that it will have practical purchase. Hence, international soft law is produced and used, as an important element of "international law as behavior," that continues to defy legal doctrinal logic.

6

Toward an Anthropology of International Law

Galit A. Sarfaty

With the growing importance of global legal institutions, new forms of global law, and transnational social movements around legal issues, anthropologists are studying the multiplicity of sites where international law operates. Scholars have examined the practices of international courts and tribunals and their conceptions of justice in relation to those of local communities.[1] They have studied the global impact of law-oriented nongovernmental organizations on postcolonial consciousness.[2] They have also analyzed the production of international treaties by transnational elites and their localization and translation on the ground.[3] By drawing on anthropological literature and applying ethnographic tools in their own analysis, legal scholars can gain insights into how international law is produced and operates in practice.

Ethnographic methods constitute an underutilized but rich tool for international law scholars. An anthropological approach can be applied to study a range of legal phenomena, including the organizational behavior of international institutions; the internalization of international legal norms in local communities; and regulatory tools of global governance. It can uncover the reasons why certain laws are adopted and internalized, the process by which

---

[1] See, e.g., KAMARI CLARKE, FICTIONS OF JUSTICE: THE INTERNATIONAL CRIMINAL COURT AND THE CHALLENGE OF LEGAL PLURALISM IN SUB-SAHARAN AFRICA (2009); RICHARD A. WILSON, THE POLITICS OF TRUTH AND RECONCILIATION IN SOUTH AFRICA: LEGITIMIZING THE POST-APARTHEID STATE (2001).

[2] See, e.g., John L. Comaroff & Jean Comaroff, Law and Disorder in the Postcolony: An Introduction, in LAW AND DISORDER IN THE POSTCOLONY 1 (Jean Comaroff & John L. Comaroff eds., 2006).

[3] See, e.g., SALLY ENGLE MERRY, HUMAN RIGHTS AND GENDER VIOLENCE: TRANSLATING INTERNATIONAL LAW INTO LOCAL JUSTICE (2006); Kay Warren, The 2000 UN Human Trafficking Protocol: Rights, Enforcement, Vulnerabilities, in THE PRACTICE OF HUMAN RIGHTS: TRACKING LAW BETWEEN THE GLOBAL AND THE LOCAL 242 (Mark Goodale & Sally Engle Merry eds., 2007) [hereinafter THE PRACTICE OF HUMAN RIGHTS].

laws are enforced, the interaction between legal and nonlegal norms, and the internal decision-making of legal institutions. This chapter analyses the unique insights that anthropology contributes to our understanding of international law behavior. After describing what an anthropological approach to international law entails, I review key contributions that scholars have made in three areas: (1) the cultures of international organizations and international tribunals; (2) the transnational circulation and localization of international legal norms; and (3) the knowledge practices and technologies of governance in international law. Finally, I illustrate the value of an anthropological approach by providing a case study of the culture of the World Bank, based on extensive ethnographic research.

6.1 WHAT IS AN ANTHROPOLOGICAL APPROACH TO INTERNATIONAL LAW

Anthropological theory and methods enable the study of how international law operates in practice, from how it is produced on a global scale to its localization on the micro-level. As Sally Engle Merry observes, the discipline's "focus on the meanings and practices of small social spaces, whether in villages or the corridors of international tribunals, enables a far deeper understanding of how the various facets of international law actually work."[4] Through ethnographic research, anthropologists analyze individual actions, systems of meaning, power dynamics, and the political and economic contexts that shape the operation of international law. They recognize disjunctures between how laws are written and how they are implemented on the ground, as well as further variations in how they affect different communities. In the context of Harold Koh's transnational legal process theory of norm compliance, an anthropological approach sheds light on the norm emergence and internalization phases by which international norms penetrate domestic legal systems on the local level.[5]

Ethnographic research involves in-depth, case-oriented study, including long-term fieldwork and in-depth interviews. Conducting fieldwork, or what

---

[4] Sally Engle Merry, *Anthropology and International Law*, 35 ANN. REV. ANTHRO. 99, 106 (2006).

[5] Transnational legal process is "the theory and practice of how public and private actors – nation-states, international organizations, multinational enterprises, non-governmental organizations, and private individuals – interact in a variety of public and private, domestic and international fora to make, interpret, enforce, and ultimately, internalize rules of transnational law." Harold Hongju Koh, *Transnational Legal Process*, 75 NEB. L. REV. 181, 183–184 (1996); *see also* Harold Hongju Koh, *The 1998 Frankel Lecture: Bringing International Law Home*, 35 HOUS. L. REV. 623 (1998) [hereinafter Koh, *1998 Frankel Lecture*].

anthropologists call "participant observation," means that one is usually "living with and living like those who are studied. In its broadest, most conventional sense, fieldwork demands the full-time involvement of a researcher over a lengthy period of time ... and consists mostly of ongoing interaction with the human targets of study on their home ground."[6] For instance, an ethnographer studying the everyday workings of an international institution would engage in direct, firsthand observation of employees' daily behavior and participate in their activities, such as training workshops, seminars, and project meetings. In addition, he or she would often carry out archival work and interpretive analysis of documents. In the context of studying international law, fieldwork is frequently multisited to allow researchers to analyze such phenomena as the transnational circulation of global norms and local settings where multiple legal orders intersect – or what scholars call "global legal pluralism."[7] By tracking the flow of laws, institutions, people, and ideas across locales and jurisdictions, multisited "deterritorialized" ethnography is a useful tool in the study of international law.[8]

Unlike other disciplinary scholars, anthropologists offer a more interpretive understanding of culture as a political process of constructing and negotiating meanings, which are continuously contested. According to Jean and John Comaroff, culture is "the historically situated field of signifiers, at once material and symbolic, in which occur the dialectics of domination and resistance, the making and breaking of consensus."[9] Therefore, an anthropological perspective on culture analyzes contestation over cultural meanings and practices, shifting relations of power, and historical change. In contrast, scholars in management and psychology frequently treat "culture" as an object that is static, uniform, and can be

---

[6] JOHN VAN MAANEN, TALES OF THE FIELD: ON WRITING ETHNOGRAPHY 2 (1988).

[7] *See, e.g.,* PAUL SCHIFF BERMAN, GLOBAL LEGAL PLURALISM: A JURISPRUDENCE OF LAW WITHOUT BORDERS (2012); Sally Engle Merry, *International Law and Sociolegal Scholarship: Towards a Spatial Global Legal Pluralism,* 41 STUD. L. POL. & SOC'Y 149 (2008); Ralf Michaels, *Global Legal Pluralism,* 5 ANN. REV. L. & SOC. SCI. 243 (2009); Francis Snyder, *Governing Economic Globalisation: Global Legal Pluralism and European Law,* 5 EUR. L.J. 334 (1999); Gunther Teubner, *"Global Bukowina": Legal Pluralism in the World Society, in* GLOBAL LAW WITHOUT A STATE 3 (Gunther Teubner ed., 1997); Richard A. Wilson, *Reconciliation and Revenge in Post-Apartheid South Africa: Rethinking Legal Pluralism and Human Rights,* 41 CURRENT ANTHRO. 75 (2000).

[8] For a discussion of multisited ethnography, see ARJUN APPADURAI, MODERNITY AT LARGE: CULTURAL DIMENSIONS OF GLOBALIZATION (1996); GEORGE MARCUS, ETHNOGRAPHY THROUGH THICK AND THIN (1998).

[9] JEAN COMAROFF & JOHN COMAROFF, OF REVELATION AND REVOLUTION: CHRISTIANITY, COLONIALISM, AND CONSCIOUSNESS IN SOUTH AFRICA 21 (1991).

defined and measured.[10] For instance, organizational culture is presented as "an objectified tool of management control,"[11] such that companies can invest in corporate culture as a way of instilling unifying values and practices among employees.[12] Anthropological research aims at answering a question rather than testing a hypothesis. Unlike other methods, it is not based on prior assumptions or models. Rather, hypotheses and theories emerge from the data, and are constantly evaluated and adjusted as the research progresses.[13] The following concisely summarizes the cycle of ethnographic research: "In ethnography ... you learn something ('collect some data'), then you try to make sense out of it ('analysis'), then you go back to see if the interpretation makes sense in light of new experience ('collect more data'), then you refine your interpretation ('more analysis'), and so on. The process is dialectic, not linear."[14] Therefore, when ethnographers interview subjects, they "do not automatically assume that they know the right questions to ask in a setting."[15] Interviews are usually unstructured or semi-structured with open-ended questions developed in response to observations and ongoing analysis. The questions are designed to seek respondents' interpretations of what is happening and allow them to describe problems, policy solutions, and their rationales in their own words.

While it provides unique insights into international law behavior, participant observation also brings distinct challenges as a methodology. In addition to the time and resources required to conduct long-term fieldwork and the access that must be attained to relevant institutions/communities, researchers must juggle multiple positionalities.[16] For instance, in the context of my ethnography of the World Bank and its approach to human rights, being a participant observer

[10] Edgar H. Schein, *What is Culture, in* REFRAMING ORGANIZATIONAL CULTURE 243–253 (Peter J. Frost et al. eds., 1991).

[11] Susan Wright, *"Culture" in Anthropology and Organizational Studies, in* ANTHROPOLOGY OF ORGANIZATIONS 1, 4 (Susan Wright ed., 1994).

[12] *See* TERRENCE E. DEAL & ALLAN A. KENNEDY, CORPORATE CULTURES: THE RITES AND RITUALS OF CORPORATE LIFE (1982).

[13] John Comaroff argues that "anthropology always rests on a dialectic between the deductive and the inductive, between the concept and the concrete, between its objectives and its subjects, whose intentions and inventions frequently set its agendas." MICHELE LAMONT & PATRICIA WHITE, WORKSHOP ON INTERDISCIPLINARY STANDARDS FOR SYSTEMATIC QUALITATIVE RESEARCH 37 (2005), http://www.nsf.gov/sbe/ses/soc/ISSQR_workshop_rpt.pdf.

[14] MICHAEL H. AGAR, THE PROFESSIONAL STRANGER: AN INFORMAL INTRODUCTION TO ETHNOGRAPHY 62 (1996).

[15] HELEN B. SCHWARTZMAN, ETHNOGRAPHY IN ORGANIZATIONS 54 (1992).

[16] *See* Iris Jean-Klein & Annelise Riles, *Introducing Discipline: Anthropology and Human Rights Administrations,* 28 POL. & LEGAL ANTHRO. REV. 173 (2005).

meant taking on at least three roles and concurrently serving as both an insider and an outsider.[17] One role was that of an external researcher, analyzing the institution from an outsider's point of view. The second role was as intern and consultant, participating firsthand in the work of the institution and interacting with other employees in the context of their day-to-day work. Finally, I briefly took on the role of an advocate, while serving as a human rights focal point for the World Bank's Europe and Central Asia region. My background in human rights legal advocacy and my previous work on indigenous rights gave me a preconceived assumption that the Bank should become more involved in promoting and protecting human rights. This attitude colored my framing of questions to interviewees and the analysis of my data, thus confirming that there is a "slippage between the role of activist and scholar and [an] impossibility of separating them."[18] After all, "[a]cademic and activist endeavors are never autonomous, despite our analytical assumptions of separateness."[19] My personal engagement with the subject of my research clearly shaped my study in various ways, but it also gave me access I might not have had otherwise. Ethnographers commonly face similar challenges as they strive to engage with their object of study while maintaining a scholarly objectivity.

6.2 WHAT ANTHROPOLOGISTS OF INTERNATIONAL LAW STUDY

The best way to understand how anthropologists study international law is to review some of their major contributions. While there are numerous areas of focus for anthropologists, I will highlight a few important ones here: (1) the cultures of international organizations and international tribunals; (2) the transnational circulation and localization of international legal norms; and (3) the knowledge practices and technologies of governance in international law. Please note that this is not a comprehensive literature review of the field, but rather a sampling of a few key contributions.

6.2.1 *The Cultures of International Organizations and International Tribunals*

Ethnographic research of international organizations (IOs) uncovers the formal and informal norms and the decision-making processes within the

---

[17]   See GALIT A. SARFATY, VALUES IN TRANSLATION: HUMAN RIGHTS & THE CULTURE OF THE WORLD BANK (2012).

[18]   Sally Engle Merry, *Anthropology and Activism: Researching Human Rights Across Porous Boundaries*, 28 POL. & LEGAL ANTHRO. REV. 243 (2005).

[19]   *Id.*

institutions that shape state behavior. Ethnographers examine organizations from the top-down as well as the bottom-up, focusing not only on their leadership and administrative structure, but also on the tasks and incentives of staff. Treating organizational culture as "continually emergent, continually negotiated, and continually in play,"[20] anthropologists study what is considered "normal" and what is not,[21] and how and why certain meanings and discursive forms become authoritative in particular settings and circumstances.[22]

Previous scholarship in international relations (IR) and international law has devoted little attention to the norm dynamics that operate within IOs, and has emphasized the role of states in shaping IO behavior. The rational actor theories that have historically dominated international relations – realism and functionalism – are largely state-centric in their analyses of how IOs behave.[23] IOs play a larger role in the models developed by neoliberals and institutionalists, who disaggregate the state and focus on the actions and interests of individuals, interest groups, and political institutions that shape state preferences. Constructivist accounts have further departed from traditional IR theory by ascribing more autonomy to IOs, which serve as vehicles for socializing states into complying with norms.[24] Yet while constructivists have moved international relations away from state-centric theories, they are only beginning to offer empirical accounts of IO behavior.[25]

Even though legal scholars have increasingly treated IOs as an object of study, they have concentrated on factors other than the institutions' organizational cultures and internal politics. Interest-based models are rooted in a rationalist account of state interests and behavior.[26] Norm-based models, including managerial theory and the transnational legal process school, have focused on why states

---

[20]   Allen Batteau, *Negations and Ambiguities in the Cultures of Organization*, 102 AM. ANTHRO. 726 (2001).

[21]   *See* MARY DOUGLAS, PURITY AND DANGER: AN ANALYSIS OF CONCEPTS OF POLLUTION AND TABOO (1966).

[22]   Wright, *supra* note 11, at 22.

[23]   *See, e.g.*, ROBERT O. KEOHANE, AFTER HEGEMONY: COOPERATION AND DISCORD IN THE WORLD POLITICAL ECONOMY (1984); NEOLIBERALISM AND ITS CRITICS (Robert O. Keohane ed., 1986); KENNETH N. WALTZ, THEORY OF INTERNATIONAL POLITICS (1979).

[24]   *See, e.g.*, John Gerard Ruggie, *What Makes the World Hang Together: Neo-Utilitarianism and the Social Constructivist Challenge*, 52 INT'L ORG. 855 (1998); Alexander Wendt, *Anarchy is What States Make of It: The Social Construction of Power Politics*, 46 INT'L ORG. 391 (1992).

[25]   MICHAEL BARNETT & MARTHA FINNEMORE, RULES FOR THE WORLD: INTERNATIONAL ORGANIZATIONS IN GLOBAL POLITICS 6 (2004); Michael Barnett & Martha Finnemore, *The Politics, Power, and Pathologies of International Organizations*, 53 INT'L ORG. 699 (1999).

[26]   *See, e.g.*, JACK L. GOLDSMITH & ERIC A. POSNER, THE LIMITS OF INTERNATIONAL LAW (2005).

comply with international norms.[27] Scholars have also measured the extent of countries' implementation of and compliance with treaties over time.[28] In addition, a growing literature on mechanisms of norm socialization seeks to explain how law influences state behavior.[29] None of this scholarship, however, has investigated the process of norm development within IOs. What ethnographic research offers is an account of what David Kennedy calls "the vocabularies, expertise, and sensibility of the professionals who manage . . . background norms and institutions [that] are central elements in global governance."[30]

Through its unique methodology of long-term fieldwork, ethnographic research can provide a comprehensive analysis of the organizational cultures of IOs and how they change. Anthropological analysis entails an investigation of ambiguities, among them slippages between formal institutional representations and actual practice, internal tensions experienced by employees over the values that guide their behavior, and clashes between domains of expertise. Researchers examine these ambiguities in a variety of areas of organizational life: the institutional mission, operational policies, management structure, and the production and circulation of knowledge. For example, in my study of the culture of the World Bank, I revealed the competing subcultures and other internal contestations that have impeded human rights norm internalization.[31] This analysis focused on bureaucratic obstacles including the internal incentive system and power dynamics between staff economists and lawyers. A recent initiative to push human rights forward at the Bank demonstrates that norms have to be adapted to the structural, functional, and cultural distinctiveness of an institution. For instance, in order to appeal to the dominant subculture of economists, internal advocates had to frame human rights as quantifiable and instrumentally valuable to achieving the Bank's economic development goals. Through ethnographically studying the World Bank, I was able to explain the conditions under which certain legal norms are adopted and internalized on the micro-level, as well as how those norms are diffused worldwide.

Anthropologists have recently contributed important insights into the study of international institutions, including not only their organizational cultures

[27] *See* Abram Chayes & Antonia Handler Chayes, The New Sovereignty: Compliance with International Regulatory Agreements (1995); Harold Hongju Koh, *Why Do Nations Obey International Law?*, 106 Yale L.J. 2599 (1997).

[28] *See* Engaging Countries: Strengthening Compliance with International Environmental Accords (Edith Brown Weiss & Harold K. Jacobson eds., 1998).

[29] *See, e.g.*, Ryan Goodman & Derek Jinks, *How to Influence States: Socialization and International Human Rights Law*, 54 Duke L.J. 621 (2004).

[30] David Kennedy, *Challenging Expert Rule: The Politics of Global Governance*, 27 Sydney L. Rev. 1, 7 (2005).

[31] *See* Sarfaty, *supra* note 17.

but also their interactions with civil society, states, transnational corporations, and local communities. A recently published volume of essays, entitled *Palaces of Hope: The Anthropology of Global Organizations*, brings together the growing body of work by anthropologists of global institutions, from the World Trade Organization to the United Nations (UN) Human Rights Council.[32] In the words of editors Ronald Niezen and Maria Sapignoli:

> The research in this field gives a human face to these world-reforming institutions. *Palaces of Hope* demonstrates that these institutions are not monolithic or uniform, even though loosely connected by a common organizational network. They vary above all in their powers and forms of public engagement. Yet there are common threads that run through the studies included here: the actions of global institutions in practice, everyday forms of hope and their frustration, and the will to improve confronted with the realities of nationalism, neoliberalism, and the structures of international power.[33]

Anthropologists have devoted particular attention to the practices of international courts and tribunals as they explore contestations over justice. Richard Wilson's work on the South African Truth and Reconciliation Commission illustrates its impact in urban African communities in Johannesburg and its effect (or lack thereof) on popular ideas of justice such as retribution.[34] Kamari Clarke's study of the International Criminal Court (ICC) and the international rule of law movement documents the making of the Rome Statute and the implications of ICC activity in Africa.[35] Her work demonstrates how international institutions and transnational networks are transforming sovereignty in postcolonial Africa and legitimating new relations of global inequality. Anthropological studies such as Clarke's contribute to our understanding of the workings of international tribunals and suggest that conceptions of justice are highly contextualized and pluralistic.

6.2.2 *The Transnational Circulation and Localization of International Norms*

Ethnographic studies of local lawmaking within communities and the transnational circulation of international norms can provide insights into the

---

[32] *See* PALACES OF HOPE: THE ANTHROPOLOGY OF GLOBAL ORGANIZATIONS (Ronald Niezen & Maria Sapignoli eds., 2017).

[33] *Id.* at 1.

[34] *See* Wilson, *supra* note 1.

[35] *See* Clarke, *supra* note 1; *see also* KAMARI CLARKE, AFFECTIVE JUSTICE: THE INTERNATIONAL CRIMINAL COURT AND THE PAN-AFRICANIST PUSHBACK (2019).

micro-level mediation process among local, state, and international law. Scholars from a variety of disciplines have analyzed the diffusion of international norms across borders, but their focus on states has neglected the ways in which norms are translated on the local level. International legal scholars have described the transnational legal process whereby transnational actors interact and cause international norms to become internalized into domestic structures.[36] They have also analyzed how international law changes state behavior, through legal means such as treaty ratification or social forces such as acculturation.[37] Political scientists have explained how transnational advocacy networks use international law to pressure states, and thus create a boomerang effect toward domestic policy change.[38] In addition, they have described how state governments become socialized to conform to international human rights norms.[39] Yet as one scholar noted, "more is needed to fully flesh out the idea of transnational legal process in order to see how norm internalization actually takes place outside of the official organs of government."[40] What is missing is an analysis of the local – that is, how local communities internalize international norms, and in particular, how these norms interact with local and state norms and shape local institutions.

Ethnographic studies can illuminate local processes and fill the gaps that exist in legal scholarship. Anthropologists examine the process of international norm diffusion on the ground – where international law is shaping the ways in which local actors construct their laws and legal institutions. Based on participant observation and fieldwork, they analyze how international norms become embedded in local communities and circulate transnationally. Scholars have demonstrated that local groups do not just absorb international norms or redeploy them against states; they are also transformed by these norms in a variety of ways, particularly in their laws and governing institutions. For example, when indigenous communities are exposed to international human rights law (e.g., through interaction with an NGO or their own participation in an international campaign), they may adapt local laws in relation to the international

---

[36]   *See, e.g.*, Koh, *Transnational Legal Process, supra* note 5; Koh, *1998 Frankel Lecture, supra* note 5.

[37]   *See* Goodman & Jinks, *supra* note 29.

[38]   *See* Margaret Keck & Kathryn Sikkink, Activists Beyond Borders: Advocacy Networks in International Politics (1998).

[39]   *See* The Power of Human Rights: International Norms and Domestic Change (Thomas Risse-Kappen, Stephen C. Ropp & Kathryn Sikkink eds., 1999).

[40]   Paul Schiff Berman, *From International Law to Law and Globalization*, 43 Colum. J. Transnat'l L. 485, 545 (2005).

norms that they have internalized.[41] Local actors may design innovative governing structures that borrow from state and international law while also adapting cultural norms.[42] Ethnographic research such as this case study can thus contribute to our understanding of how international norms affect local lawmaking and how local actors negotiate between conflicting normative commitments (including local, state, and international norms).

Anthropological studies have offered insights into the translation process by which legal norms become meaningful on the ground.[43] As an observer of diplomatic negotiations at the UN as well as the workings of grassroots feminist organizations in several countries, Sally Engle Merry examines how human rights become "vernacularized" in local settings as they are appropriated and then translated into local terms.[44] When legal norms are localized, they are not just transplanted but are adapted in a variety of ways. Merry's work also raises a paradox in the vernacularization process for international legal norms. Norms such as human rights frequently need to resonate with local cultural understandings (including institutional and national cultures) if they are to be accepted by community members. At the same time, they must often reflect universal principles if they are to establish their legitimacy and maintain their transformative character.[45] As Richard Wilson confirms, there are limits to vernacularization, for instance when human rights contradict local conceptions of justice and security.[46]

My own work on the World Bank extends Merry's insights by revealing another limit of vernacularization: the critical costs that ensue when translation goes too far.[47] I describe how Bank lawyers have recently translated human rights into an economic framework to resonate with the disciplinary group that is dominant within the institution. They have thus attempted to depoliticize rights by vacating their emancipatory dimension, including their normative valence and legal framework. The strategy of

---

[41] See Galit A. Sarfaty, *International Norm Diffusion in the Pimicikamak Cree Nation: A Model of Legal Mediation*, 48 HARV. INT'L L.J. 441 (2007).

[42] *Id.*

[43] There is a rich literature on the translation of human rights norms at the local level. *See, e.g.*, THE PRACTICE OF HUMAN RIGHTS, *supra* note 3; MARK GOODALE, SURRENDERING TO UTOPIA: AN ANTHROPOLOGY OF HUMAN RIGHTS (2009); CULTURE AND RIGHTS: ANTHROPOLOGICAL PERSPECTIVES (Jane K. Cowan et al. eds., 2001).

[44] MERRY, *supra* note 3.

[45] *Id.*

[46] See Richard A. Wilson, *Tyrannosaurus Lex: The Anthropology of Human Rights and Transnational Law*, in THE PRACTICE OF HUMAN RIGHTS, *supra* note 3, at 342.

[47] See Sarfaty, *supra* note 41.

"economizing" human rights has internally divided Bank lawyers, some of whom fear that it impoverishes the rights discourse and undermines its core values. Employees have also struggled with how to reconcile Bank norms (as defined by the institution's operational policies), international human rights norms on women and health (as defined by the UN), and cultural and domestic legal norms in the states where they operate. The internal dynamics within the Bank over the entrance of human rights norms reveals how international institutions can become sites of legal pluralism, where bureaucratic norms, international legal norms, and domestic norms overlap and possibly conflict.

Anthropologists have contributed to the growing literature in international law on legal pluralism, which describes the process by which multiple legal orders interact.[48] A leading theorist is legal scholar and anthropologist Sally Falk Moore, who rejects classic notions of legal pluralism that refer to a state-centered hierarchy of legal systems that are static and noninteracting.[49] She instead describes concurrent legal orders as a network of "semi-autonomous social fields," defined by their rulemaking capacity and their vulnerability to outside forces.[50] Building on Moore's work, anthropologists have recognized "the dialectic, mutually constitutive relation between state law and other normative orders," the dynamics of power between them, and the fluid nature of legal identities.[51] For instance, Sally Engle Merry's framework of spatial global legal pluralism "incorporates dimensions of power, meaning, and social relationships into a legal pluralist framework along with an analysis of spatial relationships."[52] This version of legal pluralism conceptualizes the spatial dimensions of laws in order to analyze their transnational movement and the places where they intersect, overlap, and conflict. It is a theoretically rich framework for understanding "the way pockets of legal regimes jump to new regions through transplants, global legal institutions, ratification of human rights treaties, the creation of special tribunals, and myriad other processes."[53] Building on rich ethnographies, theories of legal pluralism attempt to understand local settings where multiple legal orders interact.

---

[48] *See, e.g.*, sources cited *supra* note 7.
[49] *See, e.g.*, LEOPOLD POSPISIL, ANTHROPOLOGY OF LAW: A COMPARATIVE THEORY (1971).
[50] *See* SALLY FALK MOORE, LAW AS PROCESS: AN ANTHROPOLOGICAL APPROACH 24, 57 (1978).
[51] Sally Engle Merry, *Legal Pluralism*, 22 L. & SOC'Y REV. 869, 880 (1988).
[52] Merry, *supra* note 7, at 151.
[53] *Id.* at 24.

6.2.3 *Knowledge Practices and Technologies of Governance in International Law*

Anthropologists are uniquely suited to studying the knowledge practices and technologies of governance that are implicated in international law.[54] These legal forms (such as audits, surveys, and data tools) comprise techniques for producing truth and representing knowledge, which are embedded in the ways in which identities are constituted and power is exercised. Scholars have uncovered the distinct forms of technical knowledge that inform lawmaking. By identifying knowledge practices and analyzing documents as cultural texts, they reveal the impact of these technologies on global governance.

For an excellent example of this area of study, one can look at an anthropologically informed project based out of New York University School of Law on the use of indicators in global governance.[55] As a second-order abstraction of statistical information, indicators rely on numbers to represent social phenomena and evaluate performance. Backed by technical expertise and designed to produce comparability, these tools are shaping decision-making by global regulatory bodies. Given their propensity to simplify complex concepts and translate them into quantifiable measures, indicators are often used to regulate more intangible, value-laden issues such as the rule of law (as in the Freedom House indicators), corruption (as in Transparency International's Corruption Perceptions Index), and human rights (as in the indicators developed by the Office of the UN High Commissioner for Human Rights to monitor treaty compliance).[56] They attempt to imbue a technocratic rationality into decision-making and, by doing so, render domains (however complex, such as health or criminality) calculable and susceptible to evaluation and intervention.

---

[54] For anthropological studies on technologies of governance, see AUDIT CULTURES: ANTHROPOLOGICAL STUDIES IN ACCOUNTABILITY, ETHICS, AND THE ACADEMY (Marilyn Strathern ed., 2000) [hereinafter AUDIT CULTURES].

[55] *See* Kevin E. Davis et al., *Indicators as a Technology of Global Governance*, 46 LAW & SOC'Y REV. 71 (2012). This article was published as part of a larger research project on indicators and global governance, based at New York University School of Law and sponsored by the National Science Foundation and the Carnegie Corporation of New York. The project featured a network of scholars from several countries and organized a series of conferences to develop an empirically driven research agenda on this topic. *See Indicators*, INST. INT'L L. & JUST., http://www.iilj.org/research/IndicatorsProject.asp (last visited Jan. 24, 2017).

[56] *See Freedom in the World 2010*, FREEDOM HOUSE, https://freedomhouse.org/report/freedom-world/freedom-world-2010 (last visited Jan. 24, 2017); *Global Corruption Barometer 2009*, TRANSPARENCY INT'L, http://www.transparency.org/whatwedo/publication/global_corruption_barometer_20091 (last visited Jan. 24, 2017); Office of the U.N. High Commissioner for Human Rights (OHCHR), *Report on Indicators for Promoting and Monitoring the Implementation of Human Rights*, U.N. Doc. HRI/MC/2008/3 (June 6, 2008).

Ethnographic work has revealed that a guise of neutrality and objectivity exists behind indicators and other quantitative tools of governance that masks underlying power relations.[57] The effectiveness of these tools depends on experts with specialized skills and esoteric knowledge – "[e]xperts hold out the hope that problems of regulation can remove themselves from the disputed terrain of politics and relocate onto the tranquil yet seductive territory of truth."[58] In order to command scientific authority, indicators rely on numbers as they serve as second-order abstractions of complex phenomena. In her study of human rights indicators, Sally Engle Merry contends that "numbers convey an aura of objective truth and facilitate comparisons. [They] conceal their political and theoretical origins and underlying theories of social change and activism."[59] Merry further notes that "[a] key dimension of the power of indicators [and other technologies of audit] is their capacity to convert complicated, contextually variable phenomena into unambiguous, clear, and impersonal measures."[60] Numbers display governmentality because they serve as a technology of power that constitutes populations and makes individuals calculable and therefore governable – both by others and themselves. They create "a promise of control" through the administration of everyday life – for instance, they reassure citizens "against the uncertainties of poverty, crime, unemployment, and more recently environmental and technological risk."[61]

Other anthropological work has provided important insights into the technocratic rationalities of international law and their political effects. In her book *The Network Inside Out*, Annelise Riles provides an ethnographic account of the knowledge practices of UN bureaucrats and Fijian activists preparing for and participating in the UN Fourth World Conference on Women.[62] Through her analysis of artefacts of institutional life (such as

---

[57]   *See, e.g.*, THE QUIET POWER OF INDICATORS: MEASURING GOVERNANCE, CORRUPTION, AND RULE OF LAW (Sally Engle Merry et al. eds., 2015); SALLY ENGLE MERRY, THE SEDUCTIONS OF QUANTIFICATION: MEASURING HUMAN RIGHTS, VIOLENCE AGAINST WOMEN, AND HUMAN TRAFFICKING (2016); Galit A. Sarfaty, *Regulating Through Numbers: A Case Study of Corporate Sustainability Reporting*, 53 VA. J. INT'L L. 575 (2013); AnnJanette Rosga & Margaret Satterthwaite, *The Trust in Indicators: Measuring Human Rights*, 27 BERKELEY J. INT'L L. (2009).

[58]   PETER MILLER & NIKOLAS ROSE, GOVERNING THE PRESENT: ADMINISTERING ECONOMIC, SOCIAL AND POLITICAL LIFE 69 (2008).

[59]   Sally Engle Merry, *Measuring the World: Indicators, Human Rights, and Global Governance*, 52 CURRENT ANTHRO. S83 (2011).

[60]   *Id.*

[61]   SHEILA JASANOFF, STATES OF KNOWLEDGE: THE CO-PRODUCTION OF SCIENCE AND THE SOCIAL ORDER 33 (2004).

[62]   *See* ANNELISE RILES, THE NETWORK INSIDE OUT (2000).

documents, funding proposals, newsletters, and organizational charts), Riles demonstrates the political-aesthetic dimensions of the knowledge produced through the UN document-drafting process. Her research has also analyzed legal reasoning in global financial markets based on fieldwork among financial regulators and lawyers in Japan.[63] Riles's study sheds light on the practices of global finance, including the set of legal knowledges that form the technique of collateral. This ethnographic work serves as a useful model for the use of anthropological tools to study bureaucratic practices and techniques that constitute international law.

6.3 CASE STUDY: THE CULTURE OF THE WORLD BANK

The dilemma of human rights at the World Bank is a microcosm through which to study the negotiation of competing values within a global governance institution. Scholars and policymakers have debated the question of why the Bank has not adopted a human rights policy or agenda despite a number of factors that would suggest otherwise, including internal and external pressure over the past two decades as well as the agency's own pro-human rights rhetoric. The answer to this puzzle lies in the Bank's organizational culture, which is ideologically and discursively framed in such a way that its employees have resisted engaging with human rights in their work. Existing theories behind the marginality of human rights at the institution exclusively focus on the legal restrictions in its Articles of Agreement and the politics among member countries on its Board of Executive Directors. I argue that this approach has underemphasized the internal dynamics within the bureaucracy, including the production and circulation of knowledge and the interaction among professional groups whose actions may depart from the interests of member states. My study of the Bank's organizational culture uncovers the power dynamics and contestation within the institution, particularly with respect to human rights.[64]

6.3.1 *The Ambiguities of Organizational Life*

Studying the organizational culture of a bureaucracy entails an investigation into its ambiguities, including slippages between formal institutional representations

---

[63] *See* ANNELISE RILES, COLLATERAL KNOWLEDGE: LEGAL REASONING IN THE GLOBAL FINANCIAL MARKETS (2011).

[64] The following section draws from my earlier research that was published in *Values in Translation: Human Rights and the Culture of the World Bank* (Stanford University Press, 2012). The data is thus current as of 2012.

and actual practice, internal tensions within employees over the values that guide their behavior, and clashes between domains of expertise. I examine such ambiguities in a variety of areas of organizational life: the institutional mission, incentives, operational policies, construction of knowledge, management structure, and expert communities.

An organization has a "mission" when a clearly defined direction and principal goals lie behind its operations. While the Bank's explicit mission is poverty alleviation, the Bank has multiple implicit mandates, which have developed over time in response to internal and external pressure. In the 1960s, the Bank broadened its scope of activities to include health, education, agriculture, and housing, and later introduced policy-based lending, the environment, and gender, followed by such issues as indigenous peoples and legal and judicial reform.[65] This expansion of the Bank's activities has led critics (both internal and external) to accuse the institution of "mission creep," or the shifting of activities away from an organization's original mandate.[66]

Within the institution and in the minds of employees themselves, the core mission of the Bank and the activities that can be considered consistent with it have continually been debated. Employees often hold perspectives based on their disciplinary backgrounds, although there are exceptions. For example, many of the personnel in the Social Development Department, who are often sociologists and anthropologists, not only view human rights as part of the Bank's mandate, but advocate for a rights-based approach to development.[67] Within the Legal Department, some lawyers share this view, while others acknowledge that they are internally divided over the issue.

One lawyer to whom I spoke described a dilemma he faced in Swaziland, which has one of the largest AIDS problems in the world but also one of the most repressive regimes. Should the Bank stop lending to the country because it unfairly locked up 500 dissidents, even if it meant closing down its AIDS project, which was significantly helping its poor population? He noted that another problematic issue is whether bringing in human rights would create a double standard – punishing borrower countries for human rights violations while not doing so for donor countries. According to the lawyer: "Those are really difficult questions. I mean, it is easier when you are an academic sitting in a university, ... and it's another thing where you are sitting on a chair and making decisions and facing the reality every day. So how do you deal with the

---

[65] Daniel D. Bradlow, *The World Bank, the IMF, and Human Rights*, 6 TRANSNAT'L L. & CONTEMP. PROBS. 47, 56 (1996).

[66] Jessica Einhorn, *The World Bank's Mission Creep*, 80 FOREIGN AFF. 22, 22 (2001).

[67] Interview with official, Legal Department, World Bank, in Washington, DC (Jan. 4, 2006).

situations?"[68] Another employee expressed similar frustration at the clash between her moral beliefs and the pragmatic reality of carrying out projects:

> I find it sometimes easier to take the moral high ground and say that this is good because it's good, and we need to respect people, and I'm all for that. But then you're in Ethiopia, and ... you face this issue of a pro-poor government that has been doing real things to relieve poverty but apparently they can't handle the political space of the opposition. So what do you do? How do you have a dialogue? What arguments can you put on the table? It was not so easy.[69]

In an organization like the Bank where "the objectives of the institution are a little unclear, the norms are a little unclear, the roles are a little unclear, [and where] there are so many nationalities [and] so many disciplines," there is uncertainty among employees as to what their priorities should be at work.[70]

Since employees are not trained as to how to balance competing priorities, they end up "shoving [them] back somewhere" even though they never disappear.[71] Without guidance from the Bank on how to resolve these dilemmas, some employees have organized their own support groups, such as the Friday Morning Group, to openly discuss difficult issues that implicate ethics and values.[72] Others, perhaps frustrated with the uncertainty of what to do in these instances, try to abandon responsibility for the moral implications of their actions by hiding behind the political prohibition in the Bank's Articles of Agreement and claiming that ethical issues don't appear in Bank policies. Finally, there is a subset of staff members who explicitly embrace social justice as their end goal, beyond any Bank protocol. As one employee put it: "So if I'm going get fired because I'm trying to do something right, then fine, I don't belong here. That's my attitude."[73] Thus, there is a range of attitudes among employees who are largely left alone to determine how they will personally manage ethical dilemmas.

---

[68] Interview with official, Legal Department, World Bank, in Washington, DC (Mar. 9, 2006).
[69] Interview with official, Poverty Reduction and Economic Management Network, World Bank, in Washington, DC (May 4, 2006).
[70] Interview with official, Development Research Group, World Bank, in Washington, DC (Mar. 14, 2006).
[71] Interview with official, Independent Evaluation Group, World Bank, in Washington, DC (Nov. 16, 2005).
[72] The Friday Morning Group (also known as the Values in Development group), which had its last meeting in 2009, began in 1981 to discuss how employees' differing religious traditions help them resolve daily ethical dilemmas at work.
[73] Interview with official, Social Development Department, Latin America and the Caribbean Region, World Bank, in Washington, DC (Nov. 15, 2005).

Socialization conditions employees as to the unstated assumptions behind their work and the issues that are taboo, to be neither discussed nor worked on. Socialization refers to "a systematic means by which [organizations] bring new members into their culture."[74] It can occur through recruitment procedures, training, informal conversations with peers, and rituals that validate the organizational culture. Norm socialization processes inculcate employees with the generally accepted values and expected behavior in the organization. Managers can also send signals as to what is valued by spending time on and asking questions about particular issues, but not others.[75] Through such mechanisms of organizational control, the power distribution becomes a social fact and is thus institutionalized and perpetuated.[76]

One mechanism by which socialization occurs is through incentives (both pecuniary and nonpecuniary), which "tell people specifically what is valued and comparatively more important in the particular setting and how, therefore, to allocate attention and effort among competing objectives."[77] The Bank's incentive system could be summed up in this statement: "The culture of the Bank is getting a project to the Board .... You get your intellectual brownie points from your peers in the Bank by saying that I have taken a 200 million dollar project to the Board in so many months, and so many years. That's what gives you standing."[78] While this incentive is not explicitly stated in staff manuals, it becomes part of the common knowledge of employees soon after they join the Bank. The emphasis on lending targets originates in former President Robert McNamara's tenure in the 1970s, and reflects the Bank's need to justify its legitimacy and relevance by rapidly disbursing funds to borrower countries.

Several problems with this incentive system were articulated by an employee:

> It's very easy to measure money out the door but hard to assess your contribution to results. How do you know that it was your project that achieved [a particular result]? Also, managers move [to different departments] and there are big lags in things – people think you can change a country in two years, but you can't. You need to have a very sophisticated system for assessing your contribution to development in your specific area. And that's hard to do, and it's hard to do it in the time period where they can hold you accountable for that.[79]

---

[74] Richard Pascale, *The Paradox of "Corporate Culture": Reconciling Ourselves to Socialization*, 27 Cal. Mgmt. Rev. 26, 27 (1985).

[75] *Id.*

[76] Jeffrey Pfeffer, Power in Organizations 299 (1981).

[77] *Id.* at 111.

[78] Interview with official, World Bank Institute, World Bank, in Washington, DC (Nov. 10, 2005).

[79] Interview with official, East Asia and Pacific Region, World Bank, in Washington, DC (Nov. 9, 2005).

As this statement emphasizes, there is a lot of movement among staff, with most people from the operational units moving every three to seven years.[80] Since projects often take many years to yield results, promotion is not tied to favorable long-term outcomes. Rather, it is based on the number of projects approved and the size of those projects in terms of money lent – outputs that could be quantitatively measured. Moreover, staff movement makes it difficult to hold managers responsible for detrimental effects resulting from their projects. One frequently can't find a causal relationship between a manager's actions and a project's long-term effects, since many external factors (e.g., the political conditions on the ground) come into play. Once long-term deleterious effects have been realized, managers have long since left their department and are rarely reprimanded in their current positions. There are also tacit forms of promotion that employees discover through their conversations with colleagues and their personal observations of their peers' career trajectories. One employee had been told by one of her higher-ranked colleagues that in order to be promoted, "the relationship to the client doesn't matter at all. Or the impact of your projects. What matters is the perception of senior management about your skills and your ability to convey, particularly to the Board and to senior management, a good image of yourself. That's what matters at the Bank."[81]

The short-termism in the Bank's incentive system has been further exacerbated in the age of neoliberalism, which celebrates ephemerality and the short-term contract.[82] The market has become an ethical code, and the pursuit of self-interest has become a moral value. In the words of a Bank employee working on budget reform:

> There's an expectation expressed explicitly that says [that] your target is to deliver $22 billion worth of loans, for example. And then a lot of the behavior you drive is the result of putting in place that very precise target. Because you drive behavior that encourages the institution to do whatever it takes to hit the target. The goal is [to] hit the target. It's not [to] do the right thing.[83]

The pressure to extract as many material results as possible within a short time frame has resulted in unintended consequences like environmental degradations, as confirmed by a Bank manager:

---

[80] *Id.*
[81] Interview with official, East Asia and Pacific Region, World Bank, in Washington, DC (Nov. 9, 2005).
[82] David Harvey, The Condition of Post-Modernity: An Enquiry into the Origins of Social Change 166 (2005).
[83] Interview with official, Human Resources, World Bank, in Washington, DC (May 5, 2006).

[W]ithin the bank, [we] tend to be much more focused on a short run, even when there are not crises. If there are microeconomic crises and so on, I mean, obviously we're trying to focus on that. But even when things are going relatively well, and you're trying to promote growth and so on, you may be thinking only in terms of five years, and not really thinking still enough about the environmental implications as [you are] some of the actions that you may be supporting in order to promote growth, which is important for poverty reduction. But over the long run, you could actually be undermining things. For example . . . [t]he nonrenewable resources eventually are going to run out.[84]

Rather than being concerned with the long-term environmental and social consequences of their activities, workers are guided by and rewarded for immediate material gains.

There is thus a focus on outcomes, rather than outputs, in "procedural organizations" like the Bank, where the ways in which staff members "go about their job is more important than whether doing those jobs produces the desired outcomes."[85] As a result, there is a disincentive for ensuring the performance of projects once money has been disbursed. According to some accounts, employees are promoted if they are "following what the big donors in that region want[] . . . [r]egardless of whether there were bad impacts on the ground."[86] A strong emphasis is placed on how well people write and present in public, and less on what they achieve on the ground. Many employees have observed that promotion "doesn't have any kind of relationship with performance, in [one's] operations or with the clients."[87] Employees are not held accountable for the implementation of their projects or their negative evaluation by the Bank's Inspection Panel or Independent Evaluation Group.[88] One person even observed a negative correlation between quality of projects and

[84] Interview with former official, Social Development Department, Latin America and the Caribbean Region, World Bank, in Washington, DC (Apr. 5, 2006).
[85] JAMES WILSON, BUREAUCRACY: WHAT GOVERNMENT AGENCIES DO AND WHY THEY DO IT 164 (1989).
[86] Interview with official, East Asia and Pacific Region, World Bank, in Washington, DC (Nov. 9, 2005).
[87] Interview with official, Environment Department, Latin America and the Caribbean Region, World Bank, in Washington, DC (Nov. 15, 2005).
[88] *Id.* The World Bank Inspection Panel is a quasi-independent forum created in 1993 for local citizens to file complaints against the Bank for failure to follow its own policies. The Independent Evaluation Group, previously known as the Operations Evaluation Department, evaluates the Bank's activities to identify lessons learned and improve accountability.

promotion. In regard to two projects that received negative Inspection Panel evaluations, their managers were nevertheless promoted to be sector leaders (the heads of thematic departments).

Hence we see how Bank operations reflect an audit culture, "leading to a system of project evaluation in which what is really being evaluated is the procedural efficiency of action in terms of the agency's mission rather than its substantive impact on the lives of human beings."[89] This form of governmentality has disciplinary effects on its subjects – "[a]udit thus becomes a political technology of the self: a means through which individuals actively and freely regulate their own conduct."[90] In other words, "[e]xperts and bureaucrats are subjectified in two ways: as objects of calculations and as relays for calculations."[91] Thus the logic of auditability can penetrate not just management practice but also the individuals themselves, including how they conceptualize themselves as professionals and make sense of situations. Do they set targets for themselves and cast themselves as depersonalized units, thus adopting the norms of conduct that the organization is governed by?

In my experience at the Bank, I saw this phenomenon most starkly among social scientists working on social development, who struggled against their own professional norms in order to adapt to the procedural rationality of the Bank. According to one anthropologist,

> [I]t's very hard to be a task manager, and social scientists have not really been trained in terms of doing things in a structured, systematic, and timely manner, and com[ing] up with practical solutions that could then be integrated into the project cycle. We're trained to be critics – social critique, right? – and to identify problems and issues and challenges and complexity on the ground. That's our advantage. And that doesn't get you very far in a project cycle within an organization like the Bank. So we've had to change our way of working ... [W]hat we learned, I think, through working with the Bank is that the traditional anthropologist's or social scientist's approach to things in terms of going out there and experiencing the world and coming out with an ethnography or something similar, it doesn't work. It doesn't work time-wise, and it doesn't work because there's no consistency in the way different people work.[92]

89 John Gledhill, *Neoliberalism, in* A COMPANION TO THE ANTHROPOLOGY OF POLITICS 341 (David Nugent & Joan Vincent eds., 2004).

90 Cris Shore & Susan Wright, *Coercive Accountability: The Rise of Audit Culture in Higher Education, in* AUDIT CULTURES, *supra* note 56, at 57, 62.

91 NIKOLAS ROSE, POWERS OF FREEDOM: REFRAMING POLITICAL THOUGHT 152 (1999).

92 Interview with official, Social Development Department, Latin America and the Caribbean Region, World Bank, in Washington, DC (Mar. 15, 2006).

Some employees recognize the penetration of the logic of auditability within fellow staff members and criticize their focus on lending targets rather than project impact: "I remember this guy telling me so proudly that my loan is the biggest loan ever done for education in Africa. I thought, 'Why is this so important?'"[93] Others consciously commoditize themselves as a form of self-regulation, in order to improve their fit and therefore their career prospects within the organization. For instance, in an orientation workshop for new employees working on social development, one of the speakers announced: "We have to be very concrete, implementable, able to come up with clean policy recommendations."[94] The speaker suggested that staff in social development have to sell themselves to the powerful country directors and increase demand for their services.

One final characteristic of the Bank's audit culture is the Independent Evaluation Group (previously known as the Operations Evaluation Department), which reports directly to the Board. The IEG staff audit the auditors, so to speak, by evaluating Bank projects, programs, and strategies and recommending ways to improve performance. In the words of Michael Power, they function as "a second order control of the first order control system, [or a] control of control."[95] A member of the IEG stated that the department may be only "criticizing for the sake of criticizing," and is thus more concerned with the system in place to govern quality than improving the quality of performance.[96] The department's independence is also questionable – a number of employees described to me how particular IEG reports had been watered down as a result of management pressure before being publicly disseminated. Despite the lofty mission of the IEG and its supposed image as the conscience of the institution, its reports are frequently not followed up on and its recommendations have not significantly changed staff behavior or the overall incentive system.

6.3.2 *A Clash of Expertise*

There are over 10,000 Bank employees, including about 7,000 based in the Washington, DC headquarters and 3,000 in the field offices. This ratio is the

---

[93] Interview with official, East Asia and Pacific Region, World Bank, in Washington, DC (Nov. 9, 2005).
[94] Interview with official, Social Development Orientation, World Bank, in Washington, DC (Jan. 10, 2006).
[95] Michael Power, The Audit Society: Rituals of Verification 82 (1997).
[96] Interview with official, Independent Evaluations Group, World Bank, in Washington, DC (Apr. 5, 2006).

result of decentralization efforts during the administration of former President James Wolfensohn (1994–2005), when many headquarters employees were moved to the more than 100 country field offices. Today, employees come from about 160 different countries and include economists, political scientists, lawyers, sociologists, anthropologists, environmentalists, financial analysts, and engineers, among others. There are about 3,000 economists, while the number of noneconomist social scientists grew steadily from about a dozen in the 1970s and early 1980s to over 200 in 1998 to as many as 446 in 2002.[97] At the same time, the number of engineers, once an influential expert group at the Bank, has decreased. Thus, the dominance of staff members with particular expertise has shifted over time.

Staff behavior is shaped by various factors, including employees' prior experience, political ideology, personality characteristics, and professional or disciplinary background.[98] I focus on this last factor because my interviews and observations point to it as one of the strongest sources of identification among the staff, as well as a basis for sharp internal division. Having undergone specialized formal education, employees derive much of their working knowledge and skills from their professional background and are strongly influenced by professional norms. They perceive their disciplinary background as a key factor in determining their status and opportunities for career advancement within the organization. Many employees that I spoke to noted the dominant status of economists as compared to other professionals – "They're sort of the first class citizens, and everybody else is a second class citizen."[99] According to a staff lawyer, "[t]he mainstream way of convincing and persuading people is an economistic way of seeing things. Unfortunately, all the other disciplines, like social development for example, are forced to use that language to make their case."[100] Those employees who are most successful at doing so will have more opportunities to rise within the organization. One employee noted that "there are even people who are labeled as economists who may not have been trained as economists, just because that's the most legitimate discipline."[101] For instance, a staff member with a political science background told me that she calls herself a political economist in order to gain credibility within the institution.

---

[97]   Gloria Davis, World Bank, A History of the Social Development Network in the World Bank, 1973–2002 18 (2004); World Bank, An OED Review of Social Development in Bank Activities 8 (2004).

[98]   Wilson, *supra* note 86, at 55.

[99]   Interview with former official, Social Development Department, Latin America and the Caribbean Region, World Bank, Washington, DC (Apr. 5, 2006).

[100]   Interview with official, Legal Department, World Bank, Washington, DC (May 1, 2006).

[101]   Interview with former official, World Bank, Washington, DC (May 15, 2006).

Professional groups may exhibit competing preferences over goals for the organization, including visions for what development means and how it can be achieved. Composed of multiple, often competing, groups of professionals, the Bank's organizational culture is an "epistemic community," a "network of professionals with recognized expertise and competence in a particular domain and an authoritative claim to policy-relevant knowledge within that domain or issue-area."[102] It is useful to study the role and status of professional groups by analyzing them as part of an interdependent system, where jurisdictional boundaries are in dispute.[103] They speak distinct languages arising from their disciplinary training, which may impede understanding and collaboration. In an analysis of policy debates over the topic of social capital, a few employees observed: "In DEC [the Development Economics research unit], and among country economists and country managers, talk revolves around quantification, statistical significance, and formal models. Among operational staff, the grammar is different – it revolves around usability and, among many of the social scientists, around social and political change."[104] The expert communities exhibit multiple, often competing versions of rationality or so-called "value-spheres," deriving from their varying technical knowledge and administrative expertise.[105] Power relations between professional communities are apparent in turf wars, where departments try to assert their authority and influence within the larger organization. As Wendy Espeland argues, "authority is relational [in that] the authority of one field can be appreciated only in the context of its relations to other fields, other experts, and other forms of authority."[106]

6.3.3 *The Prestige of Economists and the Dominance of Economic Knowledge*

The dominant subculture within the organization is that of economists, whose expertise ranks as the most valuable in this evidence-based institution and whose language is the dominant mode of communication and

[102] Peter Haas, *Introduction: Epistemic Communities and International Policy Coordination*, 46 INT'L ORG. 1, 3 (1992); *see also* KARIN KNORR-CETINA, EPISTEMIC CULTURES: HOW THE SCIENCES MAKE KNOWLEDGE (1999).
[103] ANDREW ABBOTT, THE SYSTEM OF PROFESSIONS: AN ESSAY ON THE DIVISION OF EXPERT LABOR (1988).
[104] Anthony Bebbington et al., *Exploring Social Capital Debates at the World Bank*, 40 J. DEV. STUD. 33, 44 (2004).
[105] MAX WEBER, ECONOMY AND SOCIETY: AN OUTLINE OF INTERPRETIVE SOCIOLOGY (1978).
[106] Wendy Espeland, *Authority by the Numbers: Porter on Quantification, Discretion, and the Legitimation of Expertise*, 22 LAW & SOC. INQUIRY 1107, 1125 (1997).

rationality. Based on rigorous models and quantitative analysis, the discipline of economics makes claims to objectivity and universalism. These characteristics are particularly desirable in fostering efficient operations at the Bank, which entail the application of universal models to address development problems in any country, regardless of geography, history, or culture. Moreover, economic rationality reinforces the Bank's apolitical image and neoliberal ideology. Before further explaining why economics has become so dominant, I will describe the influential position that economists hold within the institution.

Economists have influence way beyond their numbers. They fill the majority of senior management positions (although they do not make up the majority of the staff), and their way of thinking prevails within the institution, including how they define development success. Moreover, they generally hold the prestigious country director positions, which bear responsibility for dialogue with country ministers and budget allocation to the sectoral units at the headquarters. Importantly, however, the Bank employs economists of different persuasions, including neoclassical and institutionalist, who are also placed in contention for authority.

Economists have their own prestigious research group, the development economics research unit (or DEC), which hires top economists and recent doctorate holders, mostly from US and UK universities. No comparable effort is made to recruit top members of other professions as to recruit economists into DEC, and no serious career-track exists for noneconomists as there does for economists. DEC economists produce high-quality academic papers that influence the Bank's staff, public policymakers in member countries, and the academic community. Since employees in operations rarely have enough time to write academic papers, and those in the network are often not afforded an opportunity to research topics of their own choosing, DEC serves as an important platform for transmitting new ideas across the institution.

The dominance of a single profession may be harmful for the Bank, as one senior economist acknowledged:

> In my view, the limitation of the Bank up to this point is that we've been wedded to one discipline: economics. So fashions and trends and fads in that discipline have affected the fashions and trends and fads of economic development at the Bank. So why shouldn't the fads and fashions of anthropology or political science affect it? Why shouldn't those fads and fashions be debated?[107]

---

[107] Interview with official, Development Research Group, World Bank, Washington, DC (Feb. 14, 2006).

Noneconomists often feel obliged to translate their writing and speech into economists' language and to quantify their observations to gain legitimacy for their ideas. Although noneconomists lack the theoretical training, many strive to learn "a craft version" of the economics knowledge system.[108] What distinguishes the economics professional from the legal one, for example, is that one can claim to be an economist without advanced training or licensing, while one cannot claim to be a lawyer without passing the bar exam.[109] Staff members with other backgrounds may even call themselves economists to gain status: I met a public sector specialist with a public policy background who chose the title of political economist for this reason. This form of "workplace assimilation" has discouraged informed debate between different disciplinary perspectives and has created a sense of inferiority among some who are not economists.[110]

6.3.4 The Status of Lawyers and the Culture of the Legal Department

Lawyers have not typically served as the intellectual leaders among the staff or key players in policymaking and agenda setting, with the occasional exception of general counsels. The great majority of lawyers at the Bank serve in the Legal Department, which is dominated by transactional specialists who work on loan agreements and advise the staff on operational policies and law-related issues.[111] Aside from a small number in operations who work on legal and judicial reform and other public sector projects, lawyers typically do not serve as project team leaders and their participation in projects is usually limited to technical legal tasks. Unlike economists, lawyers are not encouraged to spend their time writing academic papers. Although the Legal Department has organized seminars in order to foster intellectual dialogue on legal topics (e.g., a two-day Legal Forum in December 2005 and a seminar series with external academics), lawyers are mainly expected to be skilled in a practitioner-based knowledge.

A senior lawyer, who had recently been hired as a consultant in the Legal Department, was struck by lawyers' lack of prestige in the Bank and the absence of academically minded legal thinkers. He remarked:

---

[108]   ABBOTT, supra note 103, at 65.
[109]   Marion Furcate, The Construction of a Global Profession: The Transnationalization of Economics, 112 AM. J. SOC. 145, 151 (2006).
[110]   Id.
[111]   See Joseph J. Norton, International Financial Institutions and the Movement Toward Greater Accountability and Transparency: The Case of Legal Reform Programmes and the Problem of Evaluation, 35 INT'L LAW. 1443, 1457 (2001).

This place does not necessarily attract the most creative, energetic lawyers. There are many good lawyers here, but many of the people driving legal development are not here. And I don't think this place has the same attraction for lawyers as it does for economists ... One could also think about how one could strengthen the legal environment here. One way is to give it a more prominent place in the thinking of the institution. It's very often seen as a support service. But for human rights law and other issues, it would be worth bringing lawyers more to the core ... You should also have more lawyers in the operations.[112]

Another staff lawyer affirmed this view:

It's almost that the lawyers we get in the Legal Department are accidentally good when they're good. We're not getting the top [in the field] and there are no intellectuals ... [Y]ou're not really attracting the best minds because if you come here for a few years, it would be very hard to publish at the level so that you can get back into a university. So I think what that means is that there is not an intellectual leadership in those areas. It's not that these people are not excellent practitioners. There's just not that intellectual backing [as there is for economists, who have DEC, the Development Economics research unit].[113]

The lawyer who made the above statement further noted that, given the dominance of economists, he felt a need to constantly justify the importance of law and its institutions. In order to gain recognition from social scientists, he had to appeal to hard data that would measure the law's impact. A senior economist agreed, stating that most lawyers in the Bank are bureaucratic lawyers who shouldn't be telling the world how to change their legal systems. Based on his experience, "lawyers are usually not social scientists, [so] more lawyers ought to be trained in social science or need to be collaborating with social scientists."[114]

The reputation of the Bank's Legal Department has historically stood at a higher level and has shifted over time, often in line with the strength of leadership by the general counsel. The appointment and dismissal of the general counsel is the responsibility of the Bank's President. The role of the general counsel "may vary according to the organization, the time period, and even the personalities involved."[115] When the Bank's general counsel has

---

[112] Interview with official, Legal Department, World Bank, Washington, DC (Dec. 8, 2005).

[113] Interview with official, Legal Department, World Bank, Washington, DC (Jan. 4, 2006).

[114] Interview with official, Development Research Group, World Bank, Washington, DC (Feb. 14, 2006).

[115] William E. Holder, *The International Monetary Fund: A Legal Perspective*, 91 AM. SOC'Y INT'L L. 201, 207 (1997).

played an influential role in the institution, lawyers in the Legal Department
have been given an opportunity to go beyond the traditional duties listed above
and at times have served as policymakers, innovators, and institution
builders.[116] For example, during Shihata's tenure the Legal Department
played a key role in designing the Inspection Panel[117] and launching both
the Multilateral Investment Guarantee Agency and the Global Environment
Facility.[118] In addition, Shihata's legal opinions on governance and the rule of
law paved the way for the introduction of legal and judicial reform projects
onto the Bank's agenda.[119] Yet the general counsels after Shihata, as well as the
Legal Departments that they supervised, have been relegated to a weaker
position in Bank policymaking and institution building. Moreover, since
Shihata's departure, there has been a high turnover of general counsels, all
of whom have served less than five years as compared with Shihata's fifteen.
The Legal Department's increasingly weak leadership in Bank decision-
making following the Shihata period has made it difficult for lawyers to assert
substantial influence on the issue of human rights.

Perhaps because of their lower status and their desire to preserve jurisdictional control over legal issues, lawyers – and those in the Legal Department in
particular – exhibit a culture of secrecy. This feature is evident in their
response to the 2006 Legal Opinion on Human Rights, including its limited
distribution and their reluctance to talk about it openly, as well as in their
everyday practices. The legal opinion represented a significant departure from
the previous interpretation of the role of human rights in Bank operations.

The act of managing the circulation of information and controlling what
lies in the public domain endows members of the Legal Department with
a social power within the economist-dominated institution. They have exclusive control over the interpretation of opinions and internal legal notes, which
is expected given that they hold specialized expertise in this area. Yet what may
seem surprising is that they also have exclusive *access* to the opinions and legal
notes, even when they directly relate to an employee's work. If a Bank
employee who is not in the department entered the department's intranet
site, she would have access to all documents except the section on legal
opinions. She would be immediately prompted to provide a password,

---

[116] Richard W. Edwards Jr., *The Role of the General Counsel of an International Financial Institution*, 17 KAN. J.L. & PUB. POL'Y 254, 257 (2008).
[117] *Id.* at 261.
[118] Ibrahim Shihata, *Role of the World Bank's General Counsel*, 91 AM. SOC'Y INT'L L. 214, 221 (1997).
[119] Andres Riga, *Roundtable of International Financial Institutions General Counsels*, 91 AM. SOC'Y INT'L L. 199, 200 (1997).

which is only given to members of the department. This has not always been the case. Legal opinions used to be accessible to all Bank staff, but the practice ended when lawyers were feeling challenged by nonlawyers in operations, who had criticized some of their legal interpretations.[120] Moreover, there is a special law library of the Bank that provides only limited access to Bank employees who are not in the Legal Department.

Access to opinions and the law library is even restricted to the small number of lawyers who work in units outside of the Legal Department. I spoke to a lawyer in operations who had been writing a working paper on a human rights-related topic that required citation to former general counsel Shihata's legal opinions. When he attempted to gain access to the opinions in the law library, the librarian refused to show him the opinions because he was not a member of the Legal Department (even though he was a lawyer). After becoming suspicious of why someone outside the Legal Department would request access to the opinions, the librarian called a senior counsel in the Legal Department to follow up on the employee. The senior counsel informed the lawyer's boss in operations that the lawyer should not be writing on this topic, since interpretation of the legal opinions is the exclusive work of the Legal Department. The senior counsel did not want anyone outside of the department – even a lawyer – to challenge the department's interpretive authority.

As is the case for any department or organization, there is internal conflict within the Legal Department. There are those lawyers who favor a conservative, formalistic interpretation of legal issues, while others adhere to a progressive one. For example, the 2006 Legal Opinion on Human Rights did not represent a unity of views within the department over the Bank's Articles of Agreement. It was drafted by a group of five lawyers led by then-General Counsel Roberto Dañino and was circulated within the department for comment. While there was a general convergence of views and no strong opposition, some lawyers preferred a more cautious approach and later questioned its status as an official legal opinion.

Even after the opinion was released, resistance surfaced from within the department to openly discussing and publicizing it. An informal group of lawyers approached one of their superiors about ways to foster open dialogue inside the department on the opinion's practical implications. The lawyers considered this an opportune time to spark an internal conversation about the role of human rights, which they considered long overdue. Yet they knew that proposing a Bank-wide discussion would have been too radical at that

[120] Informal interview with officials, World Bank, Washington, DC (July 26, 2006).

moment, since it might have appeared to challenge the authority of the Legal Department. Instead, they suggested a safer alternative: a brown-bag lunch that would be restricted to members of the department. (Brown-bag lunches are low-key events, as opposed to day-long seminars or conferences.) Nonetheless, the senior official in question rejected such an event because he viewed the subject as "too controversial."[121] This resistance demonstrates a cautious attitude among members of the department and an unwillingness by some lawyers to promote discussion of new ideas. Thus, internal conflict inhibited the Legal Department from presenting a united position on human rights and from leading staff in an open discussion in light of the 2006 legal opinion.

6.3.5 *Concluding Thoughts on the Bank's Culture*

One cannot analyze the diffusion of norms within an institution without understanding its organizational culture, including norm socialization processes, the incentive system, power dynamics among professional groups, and internal contestations within departments. The World Bank's organizational life exhibits a variety of ambiguities – for example, slippages between the institution's official mission and multiple implicit mandates, clashes between domains of expertise, and ethical dilemmas among employees as they balance competing values and priorities. Its incentive system, which is largely based on lending targets and favors short-term results rather than long-term impacts, has resulted in the under-implementation of the Bank's social and environmental policies. The logic of auditability penetrates not only the system of project evaluation but also the staff members themselves, who struggle to adapt to the procedural rationality of the Bank.

The culture of the Bank is perhaps most apparent in how it values different forms of knowledge and thus how it effects power. Economic knowledge is the most privileged form as reflected in the institution's definition of development success as well as the status given to different expert communities and their respective value-spheres. The dominance of economists and the lower status of lawyers have shaped how human rights have entered the institution. While the 2006 legal opinion had the potential to usher in a new approach to human rights, internal conflict and a culture of secrecy within the Legal Department contributed to the opinion's limited impact. Although the opinion remained in legal limbo with no champion to promote it, a small group of lawyers

<hr/>

[121] Personal communication with official, Legal Department, World Bank, Washington, DC (Feb. 2, 2006).

persevered in their quest to push the human rights agenda forward through other means. Internal advocates attempted to appeal to the dominant sub-culture of economists by framing human rights as quantifiable and instrumen-tally valuable to achieving the economic development goals of the Bank. They pursued an incremental strategy from the bottom-up through country-level pilot projects, rather than a top-down operational policy that would require Board approval. My research demonstrates that this strategy met with early success because its leaders learned from the failures of prior attempts as they adapted their approach to the Bank's organizational culture.

7

Transnational Collaborations in Transitional Justice

Elena Baylis[*]

Hybrid tribunals are the international legal community's response to the perceived weakness of fully international criminal tribunals in engaging national audiences and promoting reform of national legal systems in post-conflict states.[1] But despite locating themselves in the concerned post-conflict states or employing national attorneys, judges, and staff to serve alongside their international counterparts, hybrid criminal tribunals have not found these structural changes to be a quick fix. Instead, like international tribunals, they have also struggled to achieve their desired national legacy.[2]

There are of course many dynamics affecting hybrid tribunals' performance in general and national impact in particular. In this chapter, I focus on just one of these elements: the transnational collaboration between "internationals" and "nationals" that is one of the core features of hybrid tribunals. (In the hybrid courts and in other international interventions in domestic systems, the individuals who are citizens of the concerned country are referred to as "nationals," and those who are from other countries are considered "internationals."[3])

In so doing, I aspire to address a gap in the literature on hybrid courts which, while it has addressed many aspects of these tribunals, has not yet closely examined the inner workings of the collaborative structures on which these

[*] Thanks to the editors, Harlan Cohen and Tim Meyer, for inviting me to contribute to this volume, and to the United States Institute of Peace, the University of Pittsburgh Global Studies Center, and the University of Pittsburgh School of Law for grants supporting a research study on which this chapter draws, as well as to all those who participated in and assisted with that study.
[1] Laura Dickinson, *The Promise of Hybrid Tribunals*, 97 AM. J. INT'L L. 295 (2003).
[2] Padraig McAuliffe, *Hybrid Tribunals at Ten: How International Criminal Justice's Golden Child Became an Orphan*, 7 J. INT'L L. & INT'L REL. 1, 6–7 (2011).
[3] Elena Baylis, *Function and Dysfunction in Post-Conflict Justice Networks and Communities*, 47 VAND. J. TRANSNAT'L L. 625 (2014).

tribunals rely. In this sense, this chapter is part of the second generation of legal scholarship on post-conflict justice. The first generation of legal scholarship was focused on establishing the primary norms, processes, and institutions of the field and defending their legitimacy. Now attention is, appropriately, shifting to questions of implementation and effectiveness: how those norms, processes, and institutions are being shaped in practice and what their impact has been thus far and could be.

In addition to its relevance to the post-conflict justice literature, this also represents a case study of the broader phenomenon of international-national collaborations, which occur in a variety of transnational legal contexts.[4] With this chapter, I explore the interpersonal and communal aspects of these transnational collaborations between nationals and internationals, building on my work theorizing those aspects of collaborations among internationals in international criminal law and rule of law initiatives.[5]

In undertaking this analysis, I rely on the theoretical framework that I have developed in several earlier articles, which emphasizes the part played by individual actors in developing international law in practice, through their roles as members of communities of practice and transnational legal networks, and as representatives of organizations. Specifically, I rely here on the premise that not only are individual actors and their actions relevant to an under-standing of international law, but that international law and its institutions and processes are shaped and enacted through the actions of individuals, both singly and in their network, communal, and organizational affiliations.[6] In this context, the communities and networks formed by individuals facilitate the development and transfer of norms and skills that are core purposes of hybrid courts' collaborative aspects.[7]

I begin by examining the primary types of national-international interaction that take place in hybrid courts so as to identify key characteristics of those

---

[4] Elena Baylis, *Transitional Justice and Development Aid to Fragile and Conflict-Affected States*, in Justice Mosaics: How Context Shapes Transitional Justice in Fractured Societies 370 (Roger Duthie & Paul Seils eds., 2017) (development context).

[5] Elena Baylis, *Reassessing the Role of International Criminal Law: Rebuilding National Courts Through Transnational Networks*, 50 B.C. L. Rev. 1 (2009) [hereinafter Baylis, *International Criminal Law*]; Elena Baylis, *Tribunal-Hopping with the Post-Conflict Justice Junkies*, 10 Or. Rev. Int'l L. 361 (2008) [hereinafter Baylis, *Tribunal-Hopping*] (invited symposium article); Baylis, *supra* note 3; Elena Baylis, *What Internationals Know: Improving the Effectiveness of Post-Conflict Justice Initiatives*, 14 Wash. U. Global Stud. L. Rev. 243 (2015) [hereinafter Baylis, *What Internationals Know*].

[6] Baylis, *International Criminal Law*, *supra* note 5; Baylis, *Tribunal-Hopping*, *supra* note 5; Baylis, *supra* note 3; Baylis, *What Internationals Know*, *supra* note 5.

[7] Baylis, *supra* note 3.

interactions. In keeping with my treatment of this subject as an example of the broader phenomenon of transnational collaborations, I draw from a set of interviews with internationals who have worked in several transnational settings, including hybrid courts, other international criminal tribunals, and rule of law initiatives. From this broad dataset, I identify common threads in the experiences of transnational collaboration in these settings, as well as useful lessons for hybrid courts from other contexts. In addition to my interviews with hybrid court internationals, I also focus particularly on my interviews with rule of law internationals; because transnational collaborations are central to the work of this field, rule of law internationals tend to be conscious of and attentive to the characteristics of their relationships with national actors.[8]

In addition to characteristics relating to particular types of interactions, transnational collaborations are complicated in hybrid tribunals by two overarching factors. The first is the inherent conflicts between the day to day activities required to carry out the tribunals' substantive and collaborative aims, which internationals resolve in part by drawing on their conceptualizations of their aims and their perceptions of their roles and capabilities. The second is nationals' dual position of being both actors for the tribunal and a primary audience for the tribunals' actions. These and other distinctions between nationals and internationals make it difficult to develop viable transnational communities within tribunals that would promote effective collaboration.

There is a common theme connecting the identified qualities and factors: the collaboration between nationals and internationals in hybrid courts is governed by the dynamics of their personal interactions and of the other communities in which the collaborators are immersed, such as the relevant national political community, rather than by principles of law. Accordingly, I conclude that, in attempting to structure transnational collaborations for success, we should neither look only to legal theories nor abandon all effort at theorization and dismiss these dynamics as mere practicalities of implementation. Instead we should look for insights to theories that address these kinds of personal and community dynamics, such as organizational theory, systems theory, and theories of communities of practice.

In addition, hybrid courts are just one example of transnational collaboration; these questions and issues arise in other contexts as well. Accordingly, this chapter explicitly draws lessons from other contexts, especially rule of law initiatives, and its analysis is also applicable to other contexts beyond hybrid courts. As such, the best practices and other tools and technologies developed

---

[8] *See infra* Appendices A and B.

by fields that focus predominantly on transnational collaboration are also a fruitful source for strategies for hybrid courts.

7.1 BACKGROUND AND SCOPE

The history of the modern development of transitional justice and international criminal law and the place of hybrid courts in that narrative are well known. In brief, the field of international criminal law centers on trials for atrocities such as genocide, war crimes, and crimes against humanity. Domestic courts in post-conflict countries may not be well-positioned to hear such cases, whether due to lack of jurisdiction over these crimes, limited capacity after a conflict or authoritarian government, insufficient political consensus, or other reasons. The first internationalized criminal courts were fully international. The International Criminal Tribunals for the former Yugoslavia and for Rwanda were staffed by international judges, attorneys, and administrators; they were located outside the concerned countries; and they applied solely international law. The next set of internationalized courts was composed predominantly of hybrid tribunals. These hybrid courts and chambers combined international and national components: all were primarily located in the concerned countries, all had both national and international staff, and all were authorized to apply both national and international law. The International Criminal Court is the notable exception to this hybrid trend, and as it became active, the interest in developing hybrid courts temporarily waned. Many expected the ICC to eliminate the need for further ad hoc courts, whether international or hybrid.

However, as it became evident that the International Criminal Court could not address all situations, and as regional dissatisfaction with the court has grown in Africa, an interest in establishing new hybrid courts has resurged.[9] The Extraordinary African Chambers in Senegal were established to try Hissène Habré for atrocities committed in Chad, and the Kosovo Specialist Chambers and the Special Criminal Court in the Central African Republic were founded to investigate and prosecute crimes committed in those countries. Hybrid courts have also been proposed but not yet established for Syria, South Sudan, Sri Lanka, and the Democratic Republic of Congo, among others.[10]

---

[9] Beth Van Schaack, *The Building Blocks of Hybrid Justice*, 44 DENVER J. INT'L L. & POL'Y 100 (2015).

[10] *Id.* at 102. In addition, the Special Tribunal for Lebanon was established in 2009 and the Kosovo Regulation 64 Panels evolved into the EULEX program in Kosovo.

My focus in this chapter is on the relationships between internationals and nationals, rather than on the many other features of hybrid tribunals and their work that can affect their performance, such as their structures, funding, political settings, and so on, which many others have ably analyzed.[11] I also will not address personnel issues that are common to many kinds of organizations, such as hiring and employment policies, corruption, and similar concerns.[12] While I will not review the literature on hybrid courts or post-conflict justice in detail here, I will highlight one characteristic of the field that is important to the analysis that follows: several aspects of the work done by hybrid courts are inherently difficult. In particular, relationships between internationals and nationals are inherently complex, as described in Section 7.2; post-conflict justice can only ever partially redress the atrocities committed during a conflict; and reforming national legal systems is a multifaceted, long-term task on which hybrid courts can expect to have only an indirect impact. So the fact that there is complexity, conflict, and difficulty in the work of hybrid courts and other post-conflict justice initiatives is not in itself a critique; we should expect this and should expect also that it will not be entirely mitigated no matter what structures or processes are established. The purpose of this chapter is not to critique the existence of conflict and difficulty but to better understand its nature and to propose mitigating strategies where possible.

Finally, a preliminary note on the scope of the interview data used here. At the end of this chapter, Appendix A provides information about the study methodology, and Appendix B sets forth aggregate information about the interviewees. While the appendices describe the study and its methods in some detail, for purposes of engaging with the issues discussed in this chapter, the reader should have in mind the following fundamental aspects of the nature, scope, and limits of the study and of the information gathered in the interviews.

Most importantly for purposes of this chapter, these interviews were all with internationals and include conversations with nationals only if they had taken on an international role by working on international initiatives outside their home country. This is because the interviews that comprise my dataset are taken from a study that had a different purpose and that deliberately focused on internationals. A study focused on the perceptions of nationals would be a valuable further contribution and would undoubtedly yield additional factors affecting international-national relations from

---

[11] *Id.* at 101; Dickinson, *supra* note 1, at 295, 297; McAuliffe, *supra* note 2, at 1.
[12] *See* Baylis, *What Internationals Know, supra* note 5.

the perspective of nationals.[13] For example, nationals would be able to describe the extent to which they find their hybrid court experiences to be transferable to the national justice system. They could assess whether they had found the existing teamwork and mentoring structures to be useful in conveying legal skills and expertise. Nationals could also provide insight on the effectiveness of external collaborations and outreach from the perspective of those targeted by the outreach as well as the perspective of those carrying it out.

In addition, this was a qualitative study based on thoughtful analysis of interviewees' perceptions of their work experiences. Most interviews were recorded and transcribed with the permission of the interviewees; I coded the transcripts for relevant concepts and experiences, and analyzed the coded materials. Furthermore, the study was designed to identify themes that arose across a variety of institutional and national contexts and to look for convergences and divergences in how those themes emerged in different settings. Accordingly, the study includes participants from many different institutions and settings, but frequently there are only a few participants from any particular institution or setting.[14] Finally, while the participants have worked in a wide variety of institutional contexts and post-conflict settings, the vast majority of interviewees are, by nationality, from the United States, the United Kingdom, and other European and Commonwealth countries, despite outreach to internationals from all regions.[15] As such, my analysis focuses on the experiences and perspectives of people from those regions and, when relevant, the practices and policies of the governments and other institutions with which they have interacted. The information provided by

[13] See the Appendices for further details about the study and its methodology.
[14] As detailed in Appendix B, my interviewees include people working for or with all of the international and hybrid criminal tribunals (ICC, ICTY, ICTR, ECCC, SCSL, STL, Timor-Leste Special Panels, Bosnia Special War Crimes Chamber), as well as the United Nations, Organization for Security and Co-operation in Europe, European Union, agencies of the U.S. government, agencies of several other governments, the U.S. and British armed forces, ABA-CEELI/ABA-ROLI, and numerous other institutions, nongovernmental organizations, and private contracting companies. My interviewees have worked in or on a wide range of post-conflict countries, including but not limited to Iraq, Afghanistan, Lebanon, Timor-Leste, Cambodia, Nepal, Liberia, Sierra Leone, Rwanda, Congo, Uganda, Sudan, South Sudan, Somalia, Kenya, Peru, Colombia, Guatemala, Haiti, Cyprus, Georgia, and all the countries of the former Yugoslavia. Because most of the interviewees requested anonymity, their names and institutional affiliations are not divulged, but aggregate information about the interviewees and their professional experiences is provided in Appendix B.
[15] This was not an aspect of the study design; rather, it is a description of the study results. Internationals from all regions were invited to participate in the study, but those who responded came disproportionately from the listed regions.

my interviewees suggests that the experiences of internationals from other regions may differ from those examined here.

7.2 TRANSNATIONAL COLLABORATION

Transnational collaboration is a core component of hybrid tribunals' mandates. One aspect of this transnational collaboration is internal to the tribunals: a distinguishing characteristic of virtually all hybrid courts as compared to national or international courts is that they employ both national and international actors in key positions.[16] In Bosnia and Herzegovina, for example, international and national judges served together in the War Crimes Chamber, and both international and national prosecutors worked in the Special Department for War Crimes; one sees similar arrangements in the hybrid tribunals in Sierra Leone and Cambodia.[17] One exception is the new Kosovo Specialist Chambers, which employ only international staff; however, other hybrid entities in Kosovo have utilized both international and national staff.[18]

A key purpose of building transnational collaboration into the structure of hybrid tribunals in this way is facilitating capacity-building among the national staff of the tribunals.[19] In this context, capacity-building includes both the technical legal skills necessary to conduct international criminal law trials, as well as the broader rule of law norms of due process and the role of the legal system.[20] On the technical side, practice in the legal analysis, writing, and argumentation required to conduct hybrid court trials according to international standards is expected to hone national practitioners' skills, which can then be utilized in national courts. In addition, national attorneys attain knowledge of international criminal law and procedure, which may be

---

[16]   Dickinson, *supra* note 1, at 295; Sarah Nouwen, *'Hybrid Courts': The Hybrid Category of a New Type of International Crimes Court*, 2 UTRECHT L. REV. 190, 204–206 (2006).

[17]   Nouwen, *supra* note 16; Bogdan Ivanišević, Int'l Ctr. Transitional Just., *The War Crimes Chamber in Bosnia and Herzegovina: From Hybrid to Domestic Court* 6–7 (Jan. 1, 2008).

[18]   *Frequently Asked Questions*, KOSOVO SPECIALIST CHAMBERS & SPECIALIST PROSECUTOR'S OFFICE, https://www.scp-ks.org/en/newsmedia/frequently-asked-questions (last visited Aug. 16, 2019). The Extraordinary African Chambers in the Senegalese courts is also unusual in that the national staff are not from the state where the crimes occurred or of which the defendant is a national, but rather are from the Senegalese justice system.

[19]   JANE STROMSETH, DAVID WIPPMAN & ROSA BROOKS, CAN MIGHT MAKE RIGHTS? BUILDING THE RULE OF LAW AFTER MILITARY INTERVENTIONS 274 (2006). Other stated aims of international involvement include enhancing the perception of the court as legitimate and unbiased and improving the quality of the trials. *See* Dickinson, *supra* note 1, at 298, 302–305.

[20]   STROMSETH ET AL., *supra* note 19, at 275; McAuliffe, *supra* note 2, at 14–15.

relevant in trying similar cases in national courts. Also, national practitioners gain experience with court systems like case management and the workings of the registry.[21] Since hybrid courts can typically only hear a few cases, leaving the vast majority of atrocity crimes to the national courts, this skill and knowledge transfer is particularly important to hybrid courts' national legacy.

On the "norm diffusion" or "norm cascade" side,[22] the experience of working in an institution with a commitment to due process for defendants, justice for victims, and unbiased proceedings that are not subject to political influence or bribery is meant to inculcate a sense of respect for rule of law that will then carry over into domestic legal communities.[23] More broadly, hybrid courts' proceedings are also meant to demonstrate that courts can address atrocities and can try politically powerful actors. The engagement of national staff in prosecuting such cases is a more directed version of the "demonstration effect" that hybrid courts are intended to produce in the population at large.[24]

While capacity-building has thus far primarily focused on national staff, there are some instances in which national actors have been tasked with mentoring international actors.[25] There would be significant value in more reciprocal collaborative arrangements in future hybrid courts, as proposed by the Office of the High Commissioner for Human Rights (OHCHR) in its 2008 report on hybrid courts. For example, international staff would benefit from training on domestic legal institutions, laws, and trial practices, as well as the national legal culture, history, and political and professional setting.[26] Internationals should already have a robust understanding of and experience with international criminal law and complex trials, as this expertise is expected to be a core component of the value they add to a hybrid tribunal; however, if not, training and mentoring in these areas would also be critically important.

In addition, hybrid tribunals also engage in external transnational collaborations when pursuing outreach and when engaging directly with victims and witnesses. These activities are not exclusive to hybrid courts, but hybrid

---

[21] McAuliffe, *supra* note 2, at 15.

[22] Martha Finnemore & Kathryn Sikkink, *International Norm Dynamics and Political Change*, 52 INT'L ORG. 887 (1998).

[23] STROMSETH ET AL., *supra* note 19, at 275. Of course, this is an idealized understanding of how hybrid courts operate. *See also* McAuliffe, *supra* note 2, at 35–36.

[24] OFF. OF THE U.N. HIGH COMMISSIONER FOR HUM. RTS. (OHCHR), RULE-OF-LAW TOOLS FOR POST-CONFLICT STATES: MAXIMIZING THE LEGACY OF HYBRID COURTS 17–18, U.N. Sales No. 15.XIV.1 (2008); Van Schaack, *supra* note 9, at 104; STROMSETH ET AL., *supra* note 19, at 258–261.

[25] McAuliffe, *supra* note 2, at 38 (citing the example of Bosnian judges mentoring international judges).

[26] OHCHR, *supra* note 24, at 29–32.

tribunals are placed within the concerned country in order to facilitate this engagement with the national community, and hybrid tribunals have placed a particular emphasis on local outreach and engagement as compared to the international criminal tribunals.[27] The outreach role is commonly understood in a fairly narrow way, as being aimed primarily at marketing or information dissemination, and so this chapter will focus on collaborations between hybrid courts and national non-governmental organizations ("NGOs") and other national entities in pursuit of that aim. However, it is worth noting that some organizations have advocated practicing outreach in a more robust way to deliberately develop the courts' relationships with and impact on key national communities, national and local courts, and civil society.[28]

Practically speaking, transnational collaboration is carried out in several forms, which I will discuss in turn: teamwork, mentoring, encouraging national ownership, and external partnerships. Although I am dividing collaboration into these categories for the purpose of drawing out particular qualities of transnational engagement, these are not discrete activities, but rather, overlap in practice.

7.2.1 *Teamwork with National Staff*

One aspect of transnational collaboration in hybrid courts is teamwork between national and international colleagues. In some instances, tribunal employees are formally paired in international-national teams. International and national judges serve together on the same panels in most of the hybrid tribunals.[29] Some tribunals also pair international and national employees to work jointly in the prosecutor's office and other offices, as in the Extraordinary Chambers in the Courts of Cambodia, which has Co-Investigating Judges and Co-Prosecutors who share authority.[30] In other instances, internationals and nationals work side by side but not necessarily hand in hand, as occurred in the Special Department for War Crimes in Bosnia and Herzegovina, where individual prosecutors typically managed their own cases.[31]

---

[27] Nouwen, *supra* note 16, at 209; Clara Ramirez-Barat & Maya Karwande, Int'l Ctr. Transitional Just., *Outreach Strategies in International and Hybrid Courts: Report of the ICTJ-ECCC Workshop* 18 (Apr. 1, 2010); OHCHR, *supra* note 24, at 18–20.

[28] Ramirez-Barat & Karwande, *supra* note 27, at 7; OHCHR, *supra* note 24, at 18–20.

[29] Dickinson, *supra* note 1, at 295; Nouwen, *supra* note 16, at 204–06; Ivanišević, *supra* note 17, at 11.

[30] Agreement Between the United Nations and the Royal Government of Cambodia Concerning the Prosecution Under Cambodian Law of Crimes Committed During the Period of Democratic Kampuchea arts. 3–4, Cambodia-U.N., Jun. 6, 2003, 2329 U.N.T.S. 117.

[31] As of 2008, only three cases had been tried jointly by teams of national and international prosecutors, out of 48 trials altogether. *See* Ivanišević, *supra* note 17, at 11–12.

Teamwork is intended to serve the purposes of capacity-building and norm transfer by serving as a mode of "on-the-job training" and "cross-fertilization of international and domestic norms."[32] Norm communication and skill development are expected to occur organically in the context of shared work activities. Nationals are then meant to convey those skills and norms into the national setting in the course of their concurrent or subsequent work in the national judicial system.

These processes are treated as natural in theory, and they can occur organically in practice in some contexts.[33] As one international who had worked in a hybrid court explained: "I think that [mentoring and capacity-building] is an aspiration. I don't think it's necessarily one of the core mandates. But I think it will end up being that way to some extent. . . . And there's certainly lots of . . . nationals that will have a greatly increased skill set as the tribunal works toward the end of its mandate."[34] So in the teamwork model, capacity-building and norm transfer are viewed as positive secondary effects that are expected to follow from the collaborative structure alone, without deploying additional resources or directly tasking internationals with engaging in supportive work. But in practice in hybrid courts, the OHCHR observes that: "while interactions with counterparts (both local and international) may provide a valuable opportunity for professional development, experience shows that such interactions have been, at best, ad hoc and need to be carefully managed to be beneficial."[35] In particular, internationals often problematize their working relationships with nationals. One international described his/her hybrid court experience working with nationals as complex:

> [W]ith my national colleagues, it was hard to build trust basically and to not alienate them and to get to know them at first. . . . [T]here's a tenderness about the process when you're a highly-leveraged well-resourced person coming into a traumatized country, and the people with whom you've

[32] Dickinson, *supra* note 1, at 307.

[33] Theories of communities of practice suggest that people working together with a shared purpose tend to learn from each other and develop shared concepts and practices. *See generally* ETIENNE WENGER, COMMUNITIES OF PRACTICE: LEARNING, MEANING, AND IDENTITY (1998); EMANUEL ADLER, COMMUNITARIAN INTERNATIONAL RELATIONS: THE EPISTEMIC FOUNDATIONS OF INTERNATIONAL RELATIONS 13–26 (2005). In practice, experiences differ. For example, internationals working in international criminal law reported that they felt they were able to readily engage with other internationals on the job to learn and collaborate. *See* Baylis, *supra* note 3, at 656–659. However, internationals working in rule of law initiatives reported that while they did learn on the job, they found it difficult to collaborate effectively with other internationals. *Id.* at 659–660.

[34] Interview with I (May 12, 2011) (hybrid court context).

[35] OHCHR, *supra* note 24, at 28.

worked have seen many people like you come in. It's hard to build that
trust.[36]

Factors such as power dynamics, different employment structures and compensation for nationals and internationals, and resource, cultural, and language differences can all create barriers between internationals and nationals
that can interfere with their joint work.[37]

As such, transnational teamwork requires deliberate attention, cultural
sensitivity, and what is colloquially termed "people skills." Internationals
emphasized the importance of developing genuine, multifaceted, reciprocal
relationships with their national coworkers that are more deeply rooted than
the façade of workplace politeness that might suffice for other kinds of working
relationships. A rule of law international offered this description, which was
echoed by internationals working in hybrid courts:

> I had a very positive relationship with [my national coworkers], but I think
> that's also because I was very, very interested in the place and in the
> culture. ... And it wasn't easy at the beginning, because by the time
> I came, there was already a certain wariness with regard to the international
> community. There was this feeling of "they don't take us that seriously
> because we're just the locals." But in our institution ... they would seek out
> our advice and listen to what we had to say. But the reason why they did that
> was because we had a very, very strong personal relationship. With all of the
> lawyers that I worked with, I had a very strong personal relationship of trust
> and liking.[38]

Over and over, the concept that was emphasized by international interviewees
was trust, and the message they conveyed was that in transnational collaborations between internationals and nationals, trust would not emerge naturally
but must be deliberately cultivated.

Another factor contributing to the complexity of international-national
relationships is that internationals typically come from a wide variety of
countries, professional backgrounds, training, and cultures themselves.
While international criminal law may be gradually developing a cohesive
professional culture, its members still express a mélange of attitudes and
approaches to their work, even before the international-national divide is

---

[36] Interview with D (May 31, 2011) (hybrid court context).
[37] Suzannah Linton, *Cambodia, East Timor and Sierra Leone: Experiments in International Justice*, 12 Crim. L.F. 214 (2001); *see also* Interview with N (Apr. 14, 2011) (hybrid court context).
[38] Interview with R (Mar. 20, 2011) (ROL context). *See also* interview with P (Apr. 5, 2011) (hybrid court context).

added to the mix.[39] This raises a key question: Is there something about transnational collaboration between internationals and nationals that is different and perhaps more difficult than such collaborations between internationals from different states, or is this simply an example of the difficulties of transnational work more generally?

One vitally important difference relates to hybrid tribunals' aim of producing national impact. International employees' role is to contribute to that impact; national employees are there to contribute to it as well, to be sure, but they are also part of the national community to be influenced. This is true in two senses. First, national employees are key participants in advancing the capacity-building and norm transfer goals discussed in this section and the next. Also, national employees are part of the broader national political, legal, and social communities that hybrid courts ultimately seek to influence. This complicates national employees' relationships to the work of the court and to the transnational collaborations in which they are engaged. An international at a hybrid court explained:

> [I]nternationalized tribunals ... are inevitably enmeshed in very complex political environments and have many, many politicized aspects. ... And this creates lots of complexities in the relationships between the national and the international staff ... [W]hen they don't want our assistance any more, then we have to leave, and that's it. But our national colleagues don't get to leave. They still have to live here, in the same system, most likely with the same leaders. So they have to think about their future as well.[40]

Thus, nationals are both actors and the intended recipients of the action, who are constantly impacted by national perceptions and receptions of the tribunals, while internationals are relatively isolated from those influences. Because these dynamics are important to all forms of transnational interaction, they are discussed further in the section on overarching factors.

Finally, another type of barrier to effective international-national interaction is organizational in nature. While some internationals at hybrid courts reported working daily in close one-on-one engagement with their national counterparts, others described more attenuated arrangements:

> [Y]ou have your own cases. And so ... you wouldn't normally interact, there wouldn't be a team of prosecutors on one case. There'd be one prosecutor on one case. And so, you didn't really have that sort of same connection. Yes,

---

[39] Baylis, *supra* note 3, at 665–672; Maria Derks & Megan Price, *The EU and Rule of Law Reform in Kosovo*, CLINGENDAEL INST. 1, 30–31 (Nov. 1, 2010), http://www.clingendael.nl/sites/defa ult/files/20110106_CRU_publication_mderks.pdf.

[40] Interview with J (Apr. 29, 2011) (hybrid court context). *See also* interview with P, *supra* note 38.

we'd work together; yes, we'd speak to each other; and of course, we'd communicate with each other. ... In a sense it was those [national and international] prosecutors and judges, and [international] legal officers and [national] legal officers, [international] interns and [national] interns, all a mixture. ... But in terms of day-to-day prosecution work, no, because you'd have your own case.[41]

Padraig McAuliffe identifies separate national and international work silos as a fundamental obstacle to capacity-building in the early hybrid courts. According to his analysis, not only do such arrangements create separation rather than collaborative working relationships, in addition, internationals tend to coopt key cases and control of institutional processes, isolating nationals within the institutions.[42] The OHCHR concurs that some hybrid courts have organizational divisions that hinder capacity-building; it also identifies defense offices in Sierra Leone and Bosnia as offering particular strong counterexamples of close collaborative working relationships between internationals and nationals.[43] Since hybrid courts are intended to facilitate active transnational collaboration, this should be prioritized in the structure of work teams and office geography; when this does not occur, it is even more difficult for internationals and nationals to engage in everyday interactions, much less to invest in the level of engagement required for trust-building and effective collaboration.

7.2.2 *Mentoring and Capacity-Building*

Another aspect of international-national collaboration in hybrid tribunals is mentoring or capacity-building. The teamwork approach to collaboration described above takes as its premise that skills and norms will be transferred to or developed by nationals organically while engaging in joint tasks with internationals. In contrast, mentoring and capacity-building initiatives presume that guidance will be required in this process and that providing a formal structure or specifically tasking internationals with providing that guidance will facilitate successful norm transfer and skill development.

As such, mentoring structures can be understood as responding to the perceived limitations of the teamwork approach. Optimally, mentoring would be complementary to and synergistic with team structures, so that nationals got the benefit both of working together with internationals and

---

[41] Interview with Xi (Nov. 20, 2010) (hybrid court context).
[42] McAuliffe, *supra* note 2, at 37.
[43] OHCHR, *supra* note 24, at 28, 32.

also of some structured guidance or of a deliberate progression in their work tasks. However, mentoring is also in some tension with the teamwork function described above. Mentoring relationships tend to highlight the perceived differences in power, authority, and capabilities that internationals identified above as complicating their relationships with nationals, especially when those differences exist between people who are ostensibly working together as equals.

One approach to addressing this tension is to designate internationals primarily as mentors or advisors, rather than primarily as coworkers with substantive responsibilities, who also do some mentoring and advising. This establishes the legitimacy of the mentoring role and enables internationals to focus on this aspect of the work.[44] In the Bosnian War Crimes Chamber's Criminal Defense Office, for example, the lawyers and administrative staff were all Bosnians; internationals participated in an oversight role as director and deputy of the office, and as temporary advisers, fellows, and interns, rather than as full-fledged coworkers.[45] In the Kosovo Special Prosecutor's office under EULEX, internationals were also tasked primarily with what is called "MMA" or "monitoring, mentoring and advising," although they did some substantive work as well.[46]

Another factor that relates to the substance of the mentoring relationship rather than the perception of it is internationals' capabilities to undertake such roles. Internationals typically have experience as attorneys, judges, or in other law-related functions, rather than as mentors or advisers. As a consequence, playing a mentoring role, as opposed to working side by side with national colleagues, does not tend to happen naturally of its own accord, as indicated in this report:

> Despite it being the primary function of EULEX, implementation of the EULEX MMA mandate turns out to be challenging in practice. The most common obstacle is that secondees tend to be accustomed to taking action. Shifting this mentality to a more passive MMA role requires a great deal of learned restraint and adapting to this role can reasonably take a couple of months to get accustomed to.[47]

In addition, internationals are often untrained in mentoring skills and so are learning how to mentor on the job, with predictable consequences for the consistency of mentoring practices.[48]

---

[44] Interview with Xi, *supra* note 41.
[45] Ivanišević, *supra* note 17, at 16–17.
[46] Derks & Price, *supra* note 39, at 31–32.
[47] *Id.* at 31.
[48] *Id.* at 32.

Another approach to this tension is for internationals to deliberately defer to nationals in spheres of national expertise or in matters of public prestige. The international judges in the Bosnian War Crimes Chamber publicly deferred to their national colleagues by having them serve as the presiding judges on each panel and minimizing their own participation in the questioning in public hearings, for example.[49]

A final concern about capacity-building and mentoring processes focuses on nationals and their role in transitioning learned skills or practices from the hybrid or internationalized work environment into the national setting. Because the transition of skills and norms to the national setting is a factor that relates to several types of transnational collaboration, it will be discussed further in the section on overarching factors.

7.2.3 *Facilitating National Buy-In and Ownership*

The concerns about sustainability and transition to national settings that internationals raised in the context of mentoring and capacity-building also relate to another aspect of transnational collaboration: encouraging (minimally) national buy-in for or (ideally) a sense of national ownership of the immediate work of the hybrid tribunal, as well as the legal skills, practices, and aims it is attempting to convey to nationals for the long-term. This buy-in or ownership can be pursued vis-à-vis tribunal employees, external partners, or broader communities.

Fostering a sense of national ownership of the work of the tribunal has been cited as one of the reasons for establishing hybrid tribunals that are located in the concerned post-conflict country and staffed in part with national employees rather than purely international tribunals.[50] But hybrid tribunals, like international tribunals, have found that the value of their work is not necessarily obvious to national constituencies simply by virtue of their closer national affiliation. Vis-à-vis the Extraordinary Chambers in the Courts of Cambodia, for example, many Cambodians have reportedly questioned the need to hold trials or hear a defense when the responsibility of those on trial is so well-known publicly.[51] Similarly, many Sierra Leoneans reportedly found the Special Court for Sierra Leone irrelevant in light of the small number of defendants it tried

[49] Ivanišević, *supra* note 17, at 11.
[50] Nouwen, *supra* note 16, at 198.
[51] Ramirez-Barat & Karwande, *supra* note 26, at 6.

while the vast majority of those known to have committed atrocities lived unhindered in their communities.[52]

Processes of consultation with national constituencies in the court development process are fundamental to fostering buy-in and ownership. Vis-à-vis national communities generally, internationals working in the rule of law sector repeatedly emphasized the importance of buy-in from the political community to enable the immediate success of their projects as well as their long-term transition goals.[53] In the hybrid court context, the judiciary is an important national constituency. For example, the Serious Crimes Unit in East Timor reportedly found itself facing fierce resistance from the Timorese judiciary who felt they had not been adequately consulted in its establishment.[54] Also critical is undertaking these processes with the understanding that the concerned national communities are multiple rather than singular, with different and often conflicting views. These distinctions can be particularly acute in post-conflict societies whose divisions are often the lines of delineation for the atrocities that are the very subject of the cases being heard before the tribunal.

Vis-à-vis tribunal employees and particular external partners, another approach is for internationals to take a secondary role and cede control to their national counterparts in the course of their collaborative activities, so that those individuals take ownership of the work. This is a strategy endorsed by some rule of law internationals:

> It's local empowerment. In a sense, being on the wall, being an advisor, being there when a balloon goes up. And trying to steer the ship or tack sails or trim the sails in terms of where you think you [can] provide critical redactive suggestions, which ideally have been based on practical experience. And for the most part to work subject to local nuance, to the local mores, to the ethics and the ethos that was on the ground.[55]

Some courts have pursued local ownership by gradually transitioning from international control to national control. In the Bosnian context, the strategy from the beginning was to gradually nationalize the hybrid tribunal as its reputation for legitimacy and fairness was established and as the capacity of the

[52] Rachel Kerr & Jessica Lincoln, *The Special Court for Sierra Leone: Outreach, Legacy and Impact, Final Report*, KING'S C. LONDON 1, 20 (2008), kcl.ac.uk/sspp/departments/warstudies/research/groups/wc/slfinalreport.pdf.

[53] Interview with Gamma (Aug. 23, 2011) (ROL context); interview with T (Feb. 7, 2011) (same).

[54] Linton, *supra* note 37, at 214.

[55] Interview with Chi (June 14, 2011) (ROL context). *See also* interview with Kappa (Dec. 2, 2010); interview with C (June 19, 2011); interview with D, *supra* note 36; interview with Mu (Dec. 6, 2010); interview with W (Dec. 8, 2010).

national staff increased. In the War Crimes Chamber, for example, the initial balance of authority on judicial panels was two international judges and one national judge; this was later reversed so that the national judges predominated, and eventually the court was entirely nationalized.[56]

Finally, achieving national ownership of the norms that are meant to be embodied in hybrid tribunals to the extent of reforming the national legal system requires more than can be accomplished within the context of a hybrid tribunal or panel. This is particularly relevant when the national judicial system suffers from political interference, corruption, or technical gaps which cannot be addressed by individual national actors returning to their national systems from hybrid settings.[57] Instead, structural mechanisms within the domestic judicial system, such as independent procedures for assigning cases, would be required, as well as the political will to make such procedures effective in fact rather than mere formalities. While hybrid courts may aspire to national impact, this sort of reform is the purview of rule of law initiatives.

7.2.4 *External Partnerships*

Some internationals in hybrid tribunals and other internationalized settings engage with nationals who are not coworkers. Investigators and prosecutors interview national witnesses and collaborate with nationals in gathering evidence. Outreach personnel partner with NGOs, government actors, and other entities and individuals to organize events and circulate information via media. In some hybrid tribunals, victims have the right to participate or seek reparations from the tribunal.[58]

For transnational collaborations within the hybrid tribunal workplace, there is no need to decide with whom to collaborate; unless one is in

---

[56]   Ivanišević, *supra* note 17, at 6–7.

[57]   Eur. Ct. of Auditors, Special Report No. 18: European Union Assistance to Kosovo Related to the Rule of Law (2012), http://www.eca.europa.eu/Lists/ECADoc uments/SR12_18/SR12_18_EN.PDF.

[58]   Ramirez-Barat & Karwande, *supra* note 16, at 7–14. Of course, one sweeping area of outreach work is mass communication strategies that are aimed at the national population as a whole, or at broad swaths of it. The Special Court for Sierra Leone, for example, focused its outreach efforts primarily on this kind of outward communication, including video screenings, radio programs, and in person lectures, town hall meetings, and school visits. *See* Stuart Ford, *How Special Is the Special Court's Outreach Section?*, *in* The Sierra Leone Special Court and Its Legacy: The Impact for Africa and International Criminal Law 4 (Charles Chernor Jalloh ed., 2014). While these efforts are of course important to the national impact of hybrid courts, I do not discuss them in detail here because they are based on one-way messaging rather than mutual, reciprocal collaboration.

a hiring position, that decision has already been made, and one works with one's coworkers, whoever they may be. But for those collaborating with other nationals, the first question is with whom they should engage. When addressing widespread atrocities like those that are commonly the subject of hybrid tribunals, investigators and prosecutors have to make many decisions about where to focus their investigations, with whom to affiliate in local government or militias, with which NGOs to partner, and so on. Likewise, those engaged in outreach must select associates from media, government, and NGOs, among others, for their work. The Extraordinary Chambers in the Courts of Cambodia, for example, has reportedly relied almost entirely on NGOs for its outreach work, while the Special Court for Sierra Leone connected with civil society primarily by liaising with a set of NGOs who had organized themselves into a court-related working group.[59]

The experience of rule of law internationals suggests that hybrid tribunals need more information than is superficially available in order to cooperate successfully with NGOs, civil society, and other external national parties. When internationals enter a post-conflict country, they are inserting themselves into local relational networks with ongoing flows of power, action, and information, and no small part of effective collaboration is developing an understanding of that network.[60] In part, this means identifying the relevant political and social interests that support tribunal-friendly aims, rather than relying on a national's mere status as a member of the government, the judicial system, an NGO, or another organization. But this is also a difficult and time-consuming process, as the rule of law internationals I interviewed often attested, for example:

> So when you get into the country, it's very important for you to be sure to whom you are talking. You have to know that those NGOs' support is more with the government, those NGOs they are from the opposition, and there are some NGOs who are not politically involved. ... After months and months, you have to have your own contacts and connections, and you can figure out which NGO is more political, or this one is not too much political. And this is

---

[59]   Ramirez-Barat & Karwande, *supra* note 16, at 5, 10.

[60]   Krackhardt identifies network members' conceptions of the network as an important subject of analysis in social networks, because those who have a better understanding of how the network works are able to exercise power beyond what one would expect based on their position in the network, their number of connections, and other measures of how important someone is in the network. *See* David Krackhardt, *Social Networks, in* Encyclopedia of Group Processes and Intergroup Relations 817, 817–818 (John M. Levine & Michael A. Hogg eds., 2010).

work that has to be done. But it's not easy. . . . [I]t's a lot of time because you have to know the people, you have to have good contacts.[61]

In addition to choosing partners carefully, establishing some mode of coordination can be critical. The Sierra Leonean court had the advantage of engaging with a self-organized group of NGOs, which streamlined coordination. Similarly, the Bosnian War Crimes Chamber created a network of NGOs in which particular NGOs were designated contact points for distributing information to others, offering it some degree of coordination and a close relationship with selected NGOs, although it necessitated an attenuated, secondhand relationship with most.[62]

Apart from shared interests and sympathetic politics, another important question is who is most influential and in what contexts. Several rule of law interviewees noted that internationals tend to focus on some part of the elite cadre in the post-conflict country, because they are the most accessible, as well as the most likely to speak internationals' languages. However, those are not necessarily the most locally influential people. Also, there may be a divide between the elite and the rest of the population, so that those most influential in the capital are not necessarily those most influential in the rest of the country. So while ease of accessibility and expressed interest play a role in determining who internationals tend to connect with, relying on these features can in some instances actually form a barrier to connecting with others who are more embedded in and powerful in local networks.[63] Along these lines, the Sierra Leone Special Court's Outreach section was criticized within Sierra Leone for focusing too much on elites, those who were literate, and those located in Freetown, rather than putting resources into reaching those in distant locales; of course those groups would naturally be easiest to contact from the Court's location in Freetown, and given the available modes of communication and the Court's resource constraints.[64]

In addition, as with national colleagues within the workplace, collaborating with nationals once again requires building mutual trust. This can mean making an effort to signal one's respect with one's behavior both within and without the collaboration itself. An international working at a hybrid court endorsed this view:

---

[61]   Interview with Upsilon (Mar. 29, 2011) (ROL context).
[62]   Ramirez-Barat & Karwande, *supra* note 16, at 10, 11.
[63]   Interview with Epsilon (Aug. 23, 2011) (ROL context); Interview with Gamma, *supra* note 53; Interview with T, *supra* note 53.
[64]   Kerr & Lincoln, *supra* note 52.

I think that the ability to get well outside the bubble obviously helps. These are not new ideas. You don't really want to be hanging with the ex-pat crowd, related to that. If you can pick up some language skills, that's great. People just see it. Even if you can't converse in the language, it's a sign of some respect to have some basics on that. Getting out and about, whether that's trying to locally travel in puta-putas instead of having a driver, etc. All those things help. And being able to deliver results helps as well.[65]

This was also a common perspective among rule of law internationals, for example:

So it was a normal sort of process of having to build up trust. The fact that I was a lawyer meant that there was sort of a reason for them to have some degree of mutual respect there. . . . I was treating them with respect. We had quite friendly meetings. We had to meet in a series of dilapidated bombed out buildings at times. And so we would bring tea and cakes to the meetings, and they would be serious meetings in which we're talking about the details of the law, but they were – especially as time went on – good-natured meetings in which we were occasionally having a laugh . . . By the end of the process, it was all hugging and presents and that sort of thing.[66]

7.3 INTERPERSONAL AND COMMUNAL DYNAMICS

7.3.1 *Internationals' Concepts and Conflicts*

In the day to day work of a tribunal, internationals can either focus on producing the products of litigation – investigations, briefs, arguments, out-reach-focused informational materials – as efficiently as possible, or they can put time and energy into working collaboratively with all team members or mentees. Collaborative structures like international-national teams and formal mentoring relationships are meant to enable synergies between collaboration practices and substantive work tasks. But there is an inherent conflict between engaging in the everyday activities that promote the substantive goal of litigation with its focus on immediate, measurable, concrete outputs, and engaging in the relationship-building and guidance that promote the long-term, far more intangible goals of building nationals' capacity to do the work or having national impact. [67]

---

[65]   Interview with Delta (Aug. 22, 2011) (hybrid courts context).
[66]   Interview with Kappa, *supra* note 55 (ROL context).
[67]   Interview with D, *supra* note 36 (hybrid courts context); Interview with P, *supra* note 38 (hybrid courts context); Interview with X (Nov. 29, 2010) (ROL context).

In determining what approach an international will take to her everyday activities, one important factor is how she conceives of her own individual purpose and role. In my discussions with internationals working in international criminal law, I found that litigators tended to be focused on the immediate, tangible goal of winning their individual cases as their primary aim.[68] Some looked beyond that immediate goal to the overarching purpose of building the field of international law.[69] With some exceptions, most internationals did not concern themselves with broad questions of national legacy, seeing those as questions solely for the outreach section of their tribunal, rather than as an issue for the tribunal as a whole. The issues of the reception of the tribunal's decisions in the national legal system and in the national public were typically deflected as being outside the purview of the tribunals altogether.[70] Interviewees who worked in hybrid or national settings tended to evince a greater awareness of the complexities of the national implications of their work, attributing that to their contact with nationals and immersion in the national setting, but they did not express a sense that the way they conducted their daily work activities would contribute positively to the tribunal's national impact.[71]

Thus, this narrow focus on the results of litigation as the predominant aim of the tribunal has important practical ramifications. It both reflects and reinforces internationals' tendency to focus on efficiently producing litigation materials as their predominant daily activity, to the detriment of a more collaborative approach. For naturally, if one measures one's success by the

[68] Baylis, *What Internationals Know, supra* note 5, at III(B)(2); interview with Beta (July 12, 2011) (international courts context).

[69] Baylis, *supra* note 3, at 662; interview with Eta (Sep. 6, 2011) (international courts context); interview with Psi (Apr. 16, 2011) (hybrid courts context).

[70] It is important to understand that this is not always the case in other settings of transnational collaboration. In rule of law programs, national impact is understood to be the primary purpose of the intervention, and rule of law internationals tend to focus on indicators of national impact as the measure of their success and on collaboration with nationals as a key component of their work, notwithstanding the difficulty of identifying and measuring tangible results. Rule of law interviewees also tended to express less satisfaction with the results of their work than did international criminal law interviewees; one reason for this may be the difficulty of identifying achievable tangible outcomes for their work, particularly short-term ones. *See* Baylis, *What Internationals Know, supra* note 5, at III(C)(1)–(2). Thus, one reason that internationals tend to favor focusing on immediate goals like the results of litigation may be that the results are far more tangible, measurable, and objective than the results of teamwork, capacity-building or outreach work. Another may be that this is the standard by which litigators are used to being judged in domestic settings, where courts also are not typically assessed according to their impact on the local political or social environment.

[71] Baylis, *supra* note 3, at 654; Baylis, *What Internationals Know, supra* note 5, at III(B)(1)(c), III(B)(2).

outcomes of one's cases, that is a compelling reason to favor focusing on producing substantive work product in one's everyday activities. Without the impetus of long-term national impact or even short-term capacity-building with one's national colleagues as a goal, taking time for collaborative activities will always get short shrift.[72]

This conception of aims also legitimizes and operates in a self-reinforcing dynamic with internationals' interrelated sense of themselves and their roles. Interviewees tended to conceive of themselves and their roles vis-à-vis the defined tangible goal of their jobs – as litigators, or as court administrators, or investigators – not as mentors, relationship-builders, or collaborators. They are not typically trained in strategies for collaborating and mentoring; it is not an activity that they have devoted time to and, as discussed above, they don't conceive it as being part of their core goals. As such, the extent to which these relationships do not function automatically but require active attention tends to come as a surprise to internationals. Rule of law interviewees, who tended to focus more on the relational aspects of their work, commented on this frequently: "What I learned that I didn't expect was how you really need to navigate the inter-personal more than I anticipated."[73] "It's very hard to step out of that [active] mode and be a mentor, trainer, advisor."[74] This comports with the dynamics that were mentioned in the previous section; that internationals are typically trained and experienced in their substantive subject area and find difficult and unfamiliar both the mentoring strategy of allowing others to do the work and the mentoring tasks of guiding others in that work.[75]

7.3.2 Nationals' Communities

In another paper, I have written at length about communities of practice. In the simplest sense, these are the informal groups through which people develop common practices and shared understandings of their work and what it means. In brief, communities of practice enable effective collaboration.[76]

Thus, a key question for hybrid tribunals is whether they are developing communities of practice that include both international and national

---

[72] Padraig McAuliffe observes a similar phenomenon on the organizational level, noting that hybrid institutions in Kosovo, Timor and Sierra Leone tended to prioritize the accountability purpose of these tribunals over their capacity-building functions. As a consequence, in his estimation, these entities consistently failed to achieve their capacity-building goals. McAuliffe, *supra* note 2, at 36; OHCHR, *supra* note 24, at 7.

[73] Interview with K (Apr. 20, 2011) (ROL context).

[74] Interview with Omega (Dec. 15, 2010) (ROL context).

[75] *Id. See also* interview with T, *supra* note 53 (ROL context).

[76] Baylis, *What Internationals Know, supra* note 5.

coworkers. In my previous work, I found that in order to successfully collaborate in communities of practice, community members should share common aims, identity, and professional culture.[77] While such communities may develop organically in settings where coworkers share common backgrounds or cultural understandings of their work, the differences among national and international colleagues may inhibit this development.

Here, one key difference identified above is that national tribunal employees are constantly operating on, experiencing, and processing the meaning of the tribunal in two contexts: within the tribunal as a workplace and within the national communities in which they live. In contrast, internationals are typically engaged with the work of the tribunal solely within the tribunal, and are not directly impacted by or sometimes even particularly conscious of the meaning of the tribunal's actions in the concerned post-conflict state.

This inevitably creates different attitudes toward the tribunals' actions and different understandings of the meanings of the work that complicate communication and joint action between internationals and nationals. Internationals can exempt themselves from worrying about national impact, focus solely on the immediate results of the litigation, and pin their success or failure on that, as discussed in the previous section. In contrast, nationals are constantly affected by national perceptions of and reception of the tribunals. Nationals are also implicitly tasked with the difficult process of transferring skills, practices, and norms into the domestic system when they return to it. So the domestic impact of the tribunal to some degree rests on their shoulders, but not in the sense that they are specifically tasked with it. Rather, what they intend to do with what they learn, and whether they are successful with it, eventually becomes part of the evaluation of and judgment of the tribunal and its success. Internationals, in contrast, leave the tribunal to go on to their next job somewhere else, and the national impact of the tribunal is not a measure of their success.

In addition to the difficulty of fostering a shared community of practice to develop internal understandings within hybrid courts, the transfer of practices, skills, and values into national settings is complicated by the participation of national colleagues in their own national communities of practice. That is, even if national colleagues participate in communities within hybrid tribunals and adopt the tribunals' norms within that context, those norms will have different meanings in the national contexts, as defined by the national communities of practice.

---

[77]   *Id.* at 678–679.

7.4 CONCLUSION

Hybrid courts rely on collaborative working relationships between internationals and nationals as a key mechanism for achieving their national legacy goals within the concerned post-conflict countries. In many hybrid tribunals, some of those collaborative relationships take place internally, as international and national judges, prosecutors, registry staff, and/or defense attorneys work side by side. At a minimum, hybrid tribunals must engage in external partnerships with national organizations for the purpose of outreach. These relationships between international and national actors are complicated by several factors, such as organizational divisions, cultural and linguistic barriers, the limits of teamwork and mentoring strategies, and the need to gradually develop trust within transnational collaborations.

Throughout internationals' discussions of their collaborative work with nationals, and throughout reports on the work of hybrid tribunals, the importance of the interpersonal qualities of these transnational relationships is emphasized again and again. But for internationals, the effort required to develop those relationships stands in tension with the tasks by which they judge the success and failure of their work in the tribunal. In contrast, the immediate and long-term national impact of the tribunal affects nationals directly through their immersion in multiple communities.

The analysis in this paper is meant to lay a foundation for further work by establishing several preliminary propositions. First, the interpersonal and communal aspects of transnational collaboration are vitally important to the success of hybrid courts and other international initiatives that rely on such collaborations. Also, by closely examining the qualities of these relationships through interviews and observation, we can identify characteristics and factors that will help us understand how they function; that is, these relationships can be analyzed and theorized. Finally, while these interactions can be theorized, they are not subject to legal theories. Instead, it is from organizational theory and international relations theory that we can draw applicable concepts such as communities of practice. In order to better understand and leverage these vital interpersonal and intercommunal dynamics, we should explore other ways of understanding them, drawn from organizational theory, network theory, leadership theory, and similar modes of analysis.

In particular, a systematic study of national perspectives on these questions could provide insight into several key questions raised in this chapter. For example, do national staff at hybrid courts feel that they are part of shared communities of practice with international employees? Are the skills and norms that they are exposed to in hybrid tribunals relevant to their national judicial institutions and national communities of practice? Internationals have identified developing trust as a key prerequisite to successful collaboration. It would be useful to know whether nationals also feel that trust is hard won and whether they agree with internationals' assessments of the strategies that are most effective in developing that trust.

Enabling effective transnational collaboration is central to the international community's aspirations for hybrid courts' potential domestic impact. The national staff of those tribunals represent an important constituency for the rule of law and accountability norms that hybrid courts represent, as well as a potential conduit for those norms into the concerned national legal and political communities. Similarly, effective partnerships with national constituencies are necessary if hybrid courts' outreach efforts are to be effective. Accordingly, the collaborative relationships between internationals and nationals must be carefully designed at the outset, along with the other core components of new hybrid tribunals.

APPENDIX A

Methodology

This chapter draws from a study I conducted on the movement and networking patterns of internationals working in post-conflict justice. It also explored how knowledge, skills, and legal norms were developed and transferred in the post-conflict justice context. The primary results of that study are reported in a pair of articles, "Function and Dysfunction in Post-Conflict Justice Networks and Communities" and "What Internationals Know: Improving the Effectiveness of Post-Conflict Justice Initiatives."[78] The study and those articles drew from the ideas introduced in an earlier essay, "Tribunal-Hopping with the Post-Conflict Justice Junkies."[79] This chapter addresses an issue that was raised but not fully explored in those earlier articles.

In the study, I chose to compare multiple post-conflict justice contexts for several reasons: to identify systemic patterns that are common across post-conflict justice settings; to explore changes in those patterns across different contexts and thereby to identify relevant factors that may be affecting those patterns; and in particular, to compare how those patterns emerge in the international criminal law and rule of law contexts. A holistic approach also

---

[78] Baylis, *supra* note 3; Baylis, *What Internationals Know, supra* note 5.
[79] Baylis, *Tribunal-Hopping, supra* note 5.

fit the nature of the subject. The studied behavior takes place across the entire field: individuals move from one organization and post-conflict setting to another over the course of their careers. Part of what I examined was the direction and nature of that movement and whether and how it connects disparate post-conflict settings and initiatives. Finally, while there have been numerous case studies and analyses of work in particular post-conflict contexts, like those cited in the introduction, these topics had not previously been explored across post-conflict contexts.

The study consisted of 50 interviews and an online questionnaire, which received 181 validated responses. The interviews and questionnaire were open to internationals who had worked in post-conflict justice. The purpose of conducting interviews was to investigate several complex and subjective questions: interviewees' experiences of network and community, their sense of their skills and knowledge and how those changed over time, the reasons for their job movements, and the relationship of all these factors to the effectiveness of post-conflict justice work, as they conceived of it. Interviews provided the opportunity to explore these issues with people who had a variety of experiences in post-conflict justice work and thus to gain different perspectives on the same issues. The interview format also enabled me to discuss these issues with interviewees in some detail, and thereby to attain a nuanced understanding of each interviewee's views.

The interviews were conducted via phone, Skype, and in person. All were conducted in English. Interviews lasted between thirty minutes and three hours. Most interviewees requested anonymity, and so I identify interviewees here only by an anonymous code and have redacted identifying details. I also requested permission from interviewees to publish the information provided in their interviews and to quote them in any publications. Most interviewees gave these permissions; those who did not are treated as background, or cited but not quoted, according to their preferences. More information about the interviewees is provided in Appendix B.

The opportunity to participate in an interview was publicized in several ways. Respondents to the online questionnaire were given the opportunity to volunteer for an interview after completing the questionnaire. The study was publicized through blogs and message boards concerning international law and post-conflict justice. I also requested names of possible interviewees from contacts who had worked for a variety of institutions, including international and hybrid criminal tribunals, the United Nations and other international organizations, the US government, and NGOs. I then used the snowball technique to identify further interviewees. Eventually, most of the information I gathered in each interview on the main questions of the study served primarily to corroborate or elaborate upon the information given by others, rather than generating new themes. At this point, I identified several trends in the data on which I wished to follow up and conducted a handful of interviews aimed at gaining information on those particular issues. These interviewees were identified by requesting suggestions from contacts and from prior interviewees who worked in the relevant areas.

I used a list of standard topics for the interviews, which were intended to get at the major questions of the study. However, while interested in testing my theories, I also wished to garner interviewees' own concepts of their experiences, and therefore, I endeavored to keep my questions open-ended and to follow up on themes introduced by interviewees, both within the interview and in interviews with others. When given permission by the interviewee, I recorded the interviews and had them transcribed; most interviews gave permission for recording. When interviewees did not give permission for recording, I took notes. I then coded and analyzed the transcripts and notes for relevant themes using NVivo research software. In analyzing the interviews, I focused on identifying those themes that arose repeatedly across a range of different institutions and countries and examining how they emerged in those different contexts. I also noted themes that appeared to be limited to particular institutions or settings. I have the transcripts and interview notes on file.

I attempted to counter the risks of self-selection and bias amongst the interviewees in several ways at different stages of the process. First, interviewees were identified through several different means of publicity and through people who had worked in a range of institutions in a variety of countries over different periods of time. The interviewees themselves worked in a wide variety of institutions and post-conflict settings, as set forth in the indexes in Appendix B. During the interviews, interviewees were also asked about their prior work experience, education, and reasons for getting involved in post-conflict justice work, so as to ensure that I had interviewees from a diversity of backgrounds and to provide insight into the starting point for their post-conflict justice experiences. I also invited interviewees to speak at length in response to my questions and to raise their own observations and concerns; this allowed for a more complete understanding of the interviewees' views and thus for a better assessment of the factors influencing their perspectives. Finally, in analyzing the interviews, I first coded the interviews for the topics under discussion and then reviewed the comments of different interviewees on each of those topics directly against each other, allowing for immediate comparison of the views of people from different contexts and for exploration and testing of the patterns that seemed to emerge. In developing my ideas, I focused on those themes that emerged repeatedly across different settings from people with varying perspectives.

Finally, as mentioned at the outset of the chapter, this is a qualitative study, based on analysis of the interview transcripts. Also, it has a limited set of participants. Appendix B provides additional detail about the interviewees and their relevant post-conflict justice experience. As for the interviewees' demographics, I spoke with thirty-one men and nineteen women. Of the fifty interviewees, twenty-six were US citizens, twenty-one came from European or Commonwealth countries, two from South America, and one from the Middle East. This was not an aspect of the study design; rather, it is a description of the study results. Internationals from all regions were invited to participate in the study, but those who responded came disproportionately from the listed regions. Accordingly, as noted at the outset of this chapter, the study's results and my analysis represent the perspectives and experiences of people from those regions.

APPENDIX B

Interview Indexes

TABLE 7.1 *Interviewees*

Interviewee	Interview Date	Field
A	7/16/11	ROL
Alpha	5/12/11	Both
B	6/22/11	ROL
Beta	7/12/11	ICL
C	6/19/11	ROL
Chi	6/14/11	ROL
D	5/31/11	Both
Delta	8/22/11	Both
E	6/2/11	Both
Epsilon	8/23/11	Both
Eta	9/6/11	ICL
F	4/14/11	Both
G	4/15/11	Both
Gamma	8/23/11	ROL
H	5/15/11	ICL
I	5/12/11	Both
Iota	9/12/11	ICL

TABLE 7.1 *(continued)*

Interviewee	Interview Date	Field
J	4/29/11	ICL
K	4/20/11	ICL
Kappa	12/2/10	ROL
L	4/15/11	ICL
Lambda	2/10/11	ROL
M	6/29/11	ROL
Mu	12/6/10	ROL
N	4/14/11	ICL
Nu	6/22/11	ROL
O	9/19/11	ICL
Omega	12/15/10	ROL
Omicron	11/30/10	ROL
P	4/5/11	ICL
Phi	2/9/11	ROL
Pi	12/7/10	ICL
Psi	4/16/11	ICL
Q	3/24/11	Other
R	3/20/11	ROL
Rho	3/29/11	ICL
S	3/9/11	ICL
Sigma	4/6/11	ICL
T	2/7/11	ROL
Tau	6/15/11	ICL
Theta	9/8/11	ICL
U	1/5/11	ROL
Upsilon	3/29/11	Both
V	12/14/10	ROL
W	12/8/10	ROL
X	11/29/10	Both
Xi	11/30/10	Both
Y	11/6/10	ROL
Z	11/29/10	ICL
Zeta	8/25/11	ROL

Table 7.1 notes
(1) Dates are in Month/Day/Year format.
(2) ROL = Rule of Law
ICL = International Criminal Law (includes domestic
accountability mechanisms)
Both = ROL and ICL
Other = Non-ICL accountability mechanism

TABLE 7.2 *Aggregate numbers of interviewees by institutional categories*

Institutional Category	Interviewees
ICL tribunals	27
International organizations	21
Foreign governments	14
NGOs	11
Private contracting companies	6
National post-conflict governments	4
Academic institutions	4
Independent consultants	4

Table 7.2 notes

"ICL Tribunals" includes international and hybrid tribunals as well as hybrid panels in national courts. This category includes defense attorneys.

"NGOs" includes both international and national post-conflict state NGOs.

Because I included hybrid panels in national courts in the "ICL tribunals" category, I did not include such panels in the "National post-conflict governments" category.

"Academic institutions" includes only people working in nonresearch, nonpublication capacities, for example, for academic institutions as contractors for other entities. People who were solely teaching, researching, or publishing about post-conflict justice were not included.

"Independent consultants" have their own consulting companies. They may contract directly with funders, private contracting companies, or both.

Interviewees may be included in multiple institutional categories.

These categories includes people working directly for these institutions and indirectly through contractors.

The number of contractors ("Private contracting companies" and "NGOs") is undercounted because people sometimes listed on their CVs or mentioned in their interviews only their funding organization. In addition, some ROL contractors with long careers did not list many of their projects, producing an undercount of both funders and contractors.

TABLE 7.3 *Aggregate numbers of interviewees by institutions*

Institution	Interviewees
UN	14
ICTY	11
US government	10
ICTR	9
SCSL	7 (+2 off-site)
ECCC	6 (+2 off-site)
ICC	6 (+1 off-site)
OSCE	6
EU	5
STL	4

TABLE 7.3 (*continued*)

Institution	Interviewees
UK government	4
Bosnia State Court	3
PAE/PAE-HSC	3
ABA-CEELI/ABA-ROLI	2
COE	2
ICTJ	2
A national NGO	2
A national post-conflict government	2
Italian government	2
RAMSI	1
Special Panel for Serious Crimes, Timor-Leste	1
World Bank	1
16 private contracting companies	1 person each
15 international NGOs	1 person each
4 academic institutions (in nonresearch capacities)	1 person each
4 independent consultants	1 person each
3 foreign (non-post-conflict) governments	1 person each
3 national NGOs	1 person each
3 national post-conflict governments	1 person each

Table 7.3 notes
This table follows the same guidelines as Table 7.2, as applied to institutions rather than institutional categories.
For tribunals, this table designates separately people who worked solely off-site.
Not all institutions are listed by name. I did not list the institution by name when I felt withholding the name was necessary to protect the identity of interviewees. Also, if there was only one person working for an institution, I consolidated institutions of the same type into a single category for the sake of space, on the understanding that it would be more useful to the reader to get a sense of the number of institutions in each category that were represented, rather than the name of each individual institution.

TABLE 7.4 *Aggregate Numbers of Interviewees by region*

Region	Total	In-country	Out-of-country
Balkans	28	17	11
Africa	25	13	12
Middle East	17	12	5
Asia	15	13	2
Non-Balkans Europe	4	4	0
Americas	3	3	0

TABLE 7.4 (*continued*)

Region	Total	In-country	Out-of-country
Oceania	1	1	0
Unknown	6	NA	NA

Table 7.4 notes

The "Unknown" category represents interviewees who did not list all the countries in which they had worked.

Even if a person worked in multiple countries in a region, I only counted them once for that region. Similarly, if a person worked in a region more than once, I only counted them once.

If someone worked both in-country and out-of-country on the same region, I only counted them in the in-country category for that state.

Individual interviewees may have worked in more than one region.

TABLE 7.5 *Aggregate numbers of interviewees by country*

Country/region	Total	In-country	Out-of-country
Former Yugoslavia	13	0	13
Kosovo	13	13	0
Sierra Leone	10	6	4
Bosnia-Herzegovina	9	9	0
Cambodia	9	6	3
Afghanistan	8	8	0
Rwanda	8	0	8
Other Africa	7	0	7
Iraq	6	5	1
Liberia	5	4	1
Lebanon	4	0	4
Timor-Leste	4	4	0
Georgia	2	2	0
The Philippines	2	2	0
Serbia	2	2	0
Somalia	2	1	1
Sudan	2	2	0
South Sudan	2	2	0
Uganda	2	1	1
Ukraine	2	2	0
Bolivia	1	1	0
Chile	1	1	0
Colombia	1	1	0
Congo	1	1	0
Costa Rica	1	1	0

TABLE 7.5 *(continued)*

Country/region	Total	In-country	Out-of-country
Croatia	1	1	0
Cyprus	1	1	0
Dominican Republic	1	1	0
Ecuador	1	1	0
Guatemala	1	1	0
Haiti	1	1	0
Honduras	1	1	0
Indonesia	1	1	0
Ivory Coast	1	1	0
Kenya	1	1	0
Malawi	1	1	0
Mozambique	1	1	0
Namibia	1	1	0
Nepal	1	1	0
Pakistan	1	1	0
Panama	1	1	0
Paraguay	1	1	0
Peru	1	1	0
Solomon Islands	1	1	0
Turkey	1	1	0
Venezuela	1	1	0
Zimbabwe	1	1	0
Unknown	6	NA	NA

Table 7.5 Notes

This Table follows the same guidelines as Table 7.4, as applied to states rather than regions. The "Former Yugoslavia" category primarily represents people who have worked at the ICTY. People who also worked specifically on a particular Balkan country were not included in the general "Former Yugoslavia" category; only those who had only worked generally on the region without working in a particular country were included.

The "Other Africa" category represents people who have worked at the ICC. As with the "Former Yugoslavia" category, people who had also identified a particular country in which they had worked were not included in the general "Africa" category.

8

Advancing Neuroscience in International Law

Anna Spain Bradley[*]

A fundamental purpose of international law is to shape the behavior of nations in ways that promote international peace and security.[1] International legal rules that prohibit the use of force, regulate states' conduct during war, and promote increased cooperation through trade all serve this aim. Historically, the central actor in this story has been the nation-state, leading to a rich array of theories about state behavior, such as realism, liberalism, and constructivism that continue to dominate the study of international law and international relations.[2] In the twenty-first century, international law is increasingly called upon to shape the behaviors of individuals, too. The challenges facing our world now and in the future – such as terrorism, climate change, noninternational armed conflict, cyberespionage – require international law to motivate and constrain the behavior of individuals in addition to nation-states.[3]

To do so, international legal scholars have sought new ways by which to understand and analyze human behavior. This had led to rich interdisciplinary engagement between international legal scholarship and the behavioral

---

[*] The author is grateful to Tomer Broude, R. McKell Carter, Harlan Cohen, Susan D. Franck, Jean Galbraith, Peter Huang, Tim Meyer, Michael S. Pardo, Marissa Kardon Weber, and Sukumar Vijayaraghavan for their helpful comments and editorial suggestions. Furthermore, the author notes that research for this chapter concluded in 2018 and does not account for updates since that time prior to publication.

[1] U.N. Charter art. 1.

[2] *See, e.g.*, Louis Henkin, How Nations Behave: Law and Foreign Policy (2d ed. 1979). For a helpful overview of theories of international law, see The Oxford Handbook of the Theory of International Law (Anne Orford & Florian Hoffman eds., 2016), as well as Foundations of International Law and Politics (Oona Hathaway & Harold Koh eds., 2005) [hereinafter Foundations].

[3] *See, e.g.*, Yuval Feldman, The Law of Good People: Challenging States' Ability to Regulate Human Behavior (2018); Anthea Roberts, Is International Law International? (2017); Karen J. Alter, The New Terrain of International Law (2014); Joel P. Trachtman, The Future of International Law (2013).

sciences and social sciences. One of the central objectives within this emergent scholarship is to establish that human behavior deviates from traditional assumptions of rationality in predictable ways.[4] As a result, the behavioral trend in international legal scholarship is upon us.[5]

Neuroscience, however, is critically missing from this interdisciplinary discourse in international law even as it is leading the way in providing novel, evidence-based understandings about connections between the brain and human behavior.[6] In simple terms, neuroscience investigates brain activity and cann address "how" and "why" questions by showing correlations between neural mechanisms associated with certain types of cognitive activity. For example, we have observed that some people who suffer from brain injuries have trouble making decisions. Behavioral studies contribute to this understanding by observing that people with certain brain injuries tend to fail to learn from previous mistakes and continue to make bad choices when playing a card game. Neuroscientific functional Magnetic Resonance Imaging (fMRI)-based research can deepen such understandings about how and why this happens by revealing, for example, that damage to a person's frontal lobe disrupts neural pathways associated with decision-making.[7] Future research in this area may advance or refine initial studies but, collectively, such findings help deepen our appreciation for the complexity of brain-behavior connections.

This chapter introduces neuroscience to the study of international law. The chapter begins by providing readers with a basic foundation for understanding

[4] *See, e.g.*, DAN ARIELY, PREDICTABLY IRRATIONAL, THE HIDDEN FORCES THAT SHAPE OUR DECISIONS (2010). For an overview of rational choice theory in international law, see Alan O. Sykes, *International Law, in* 1 HANDBOOK OF LAW & ECONOMICS 757 (A. Mitchell Polinsky & Steven Shavell eds., 2007).

[5] Emilie Hafner-Burton et al., *The Behavioral Revolution and International Relations*, 71 INT'L ORG. S1–S31 (2017). For additional works, see *infra* note 63.

[6] Public interest and professional engagement in neuroscience is growing. *See generally* EBEN ALEXANDER, PROOF OF HEAVEN: A NEUROSURGEON'S JOURNEY INTO THE AFTERLIFE (2012) (exploring how neuroscience helps us to learn more about the modern brain and how it heals); NORMAN DOIDGE, THE BRAIN THAT CHANGES ITSELF (2007) (discussing how the neuroplastic revolution has implications on different aspects of human life); MICHIO KAKU, THE FUTURE OF THE MIND 4 (2014) (describing the movement to understand how the human brain functions); SRINIVASAN PILLAY, YOUR BRAIN AND BUSINESS: THE NEUROSCIENCE OF GREAT LEADERS (2011) (describing how neuroscience is improving performance in the business environment); TARA SWART, KITTY CHISHOLM & PAUL BROWN, NEUROSCIENCE FOR LEADERSHIP: HARNESSING THE BRAIN GAIN ADVANTAGE 2 (2015) (describing the intersection between the brain and decision making).

[7] Nathalie Camille, Ami Tsuchida & Lesley K. Fellows, *Double Dissociation of Stimulus-Value and Action-Value Learning in Humans with Orbitofrontal or Anterior Cingulate Cortex Damage*, 31 J. NEUROSCI. 42 (2011). *See also* McGill University, *Decision-Making: What You Want vs. How You Get It*, SCIENCEDAILY (Oct. 23, 2011), https://www.sciencedaily.com /releases/2011/10/111021125707.htm.

the field of neuroscience. The second section describes the existing literature at the intersection of law and neuroscience, which forms the basis of interdisciplinary work known as neurolaw that emerged about a decade ago. The third section considers how to begin constructing the foundations, frameworks, and central agenda for interdisciplinary connections between neuroscience and international law. The fourth section maps out potential areas of study in international law that may benefit from neuroscientific insights. For example, neuroscientific studies about the biological basis for drug addiction may have implications for understanding mental states and intention in international criminal law. Advances in knowledge about brain activity associated with memory, fear, and decision-making offer important implications for the decision making practices of international judges and arbitrators as well as political appointees at international organizations. Having a neuroscientifically informed understanding of human cognition provides a foundation for understanding how international law should regulate artificial intelligence and other new technology that seek to emulate or deviate from how humans make choices. The chapter concludes by considering how neuroscience might inform, challenge, and advance existing theoretical and normative discourses in international law.

This chapter provides one of the first, if not the first, attempts to comprehensively analyze how neuroscience might inform international legal scholarship and what the appropriate frameworks and limitations for doing so are. The chapter describes what neuroscience is and the contributions it has made to understanding brains, behavior, and the connections between the two. It creatively engages how such findings might inform matters international law cares about, posing more questions than answers. The central assumption presented here is that research from neuroscience is relevant to the study of human behavior and, therefore, is relevant to the study of how international law can shape human behavior. The chapter does not make claims about the comparative value of neuroscience in comparison to other fields, such as psychology or behavioral economics, as such inquiries are best framed and answered by and between those in each respective discipline. Research in neuroscience is emergent and developing, challenging old notions and advancing new ones. Accordingly, the concepts and research presented here will, necessarily, evolve in relation to future research and scholarly engagement.

8.1 ON NEUROSCIENCE AND HOW TO USE IT

Many areas of international law concern human behavior. Law's inextricable connection to human behavior means that the study of how our brains shape

our actions and choices is paramount. We might wonder, for example, whether
or not international judges are affected by their emotion when they issue
judicial opinions that become subsidiary sources of law pursuant to Article
38.1d of the International Court of Justice's Statute.[8] Should the International
Law Commission take into account a perpetrator's age when defining crimes
against humanity? How does presenting photographs instead of a written report
change the UN Security Council's determination of whether or not a situation
poses a threat to international peace and security pursuant to Article 39 of the
UN Charter?[9] Before we can determine if and how neuroscience informs the
answers to such questions, we must first understand neuroscience's foundations,
methodologies, and limitations as a scientific discipline.

Neuroscience is the study of the brain, its organization, and its functions.[10]
The prevailing assumption is that thinking, feeling, and other mental activity
is linked to brain activity .[11] Our brains are composed of the following units:
We have neurons, the nerve cells that form the basic unit of the brain, which
promote or inhibit activity in our nervous system.[12] Glial cells, or glia, support
neurons structurally and assist in forming the fatty myelin that insulate
neurons improving electrical conduction.[13] The basic function of neurons is
to transform information in the brain, allowing for a wide-array of cognitive
functions that underlie behavior. They do so through molecules called neurotransmitters, which are diverse and varied in form and function. The major
neurotransmitters in the brain are glutamate and gamma amino butyric acid

[8]   I.C.J. Statute art. 38, ¶ 1 (describing the four sources of international law including, "subject to
      the provisions of Article 59, judicial decisions and the teachings of the most highly qualified
      publicists of the various nations, as subsidiary means for the determination of rules of law.").
[9]   U.N. Charter art. 39 ("The Security Council shall determine the existence of any threat to the
      peace, breach of the peace, or act of aggression and shall make recommendations, or decide
      what measures shall be taken in accordance with Articles 41 and 42, to maintain or restore
      international peace and security.").
[10] *See generally* MICHAEL S. GAZZANIGA, RICHARD IVRY & GEORGE MANGUN, COGNITIVE
      NEUROSCIENCE: THE BIOLOGY OF THE MIND (3d ed. 2008) (providing a general overview
      of the field); OWEN JONES, JEFFREY SCHALL & FRANCIS SHEN, LAW AND NEUROSCIENCE
      195–220 (2014).
[11] JONES ET AL., *supra* note 10. *But see* MICHAEL PARDO & DENNIS PATTERSON, MINDS,
      BRAINS, AND LAW: THE CONCEPTUAL FOUNDATIONS OF LAW AND NEUROSCIENCE 20
      (2013) (arguing that, within legal scholarship, one should make a conceptual distinction
      between the mind and the brain and not conflate empirical evidence about the brain with
      conceptual questions about other things such as knowledge).
[12] For an overview of the fundamentals of neurons, see Annabelle M. Belcher & Adina Roskies,
      Neuroscience Basics, in A PRIMER ON CRIMINAL LAW AND NEUROSCIENCE 4 (Stephen
      Morse & Adina Roskies eds., 2013); JAMES SCHWARTZ ET AL., PRINCIPLES OF NEURAL
      SCIENCE (5th ed. 2013); GAZZANIGA ET AL., *supra* note 10; LARRY SQUIRE ET AL.,
      FUNDAMENTAL NEUROSCIENCE (3d ed. 2013).
[13] Belcher & Roskies, *supra* note 12, at 4.

(GABA) that perform the basic excitatory and inhibitory functions, respectively. These systems are modulated by other neurotransmitters like acetylcholine, serotonin, and norepinephrine.[14]

Within the general field of neuroscience, there are subspecialties.[15] Neurophysiology studies function of neurons and circuits in the brain and the peripheral nervous system to address both the normal functioning of the nervous system and changes that occur in abnormalities and disease. Affective neuroscience is the study of emotion in the brain.[16] Neuroethics considers the implications of neuroscience and law on human ethics covering topics such as free will or cognitive enhancement.[17] Neuroanatomy is the study of the organization and connectivity of the brain, which allows us to map the regions of the brain.[18] This work helps explain how information flows through the brain, though much remains undiscovered.[19]

The macroscopic structures of the brain include the cerebrum, divided into right and left hemispheres, the cerebellum, and the brain stem. The brain is made up of gray matter where the neuronal cell bodies reside and white matter that consists of their processes (axons), the ensheathing myelin, and associated glial cells.[20] Direction in the brain is organized into the rostral/anterior (front), caudal/posterior (back), dorsal/superior (top), ventral/inferior (bottom); parts of the brain are often described using the direction you would go from the middle

---

[14] *Id.* at 10 (serotonin, the neurotransmitter known for aiding in sleep and histamines, the neurotransmitter known for its role in producing seasonal allergies, are two common examples).

[15] *See, e.g.*, NYU NEUROLOGY DEP'T, https://med.nyu.edu/neurology/training-education/neurology-residency/neurology-subspecialties.

[16] Antoine Bechara, *Human Emotions in Decision Making: Are They Useful or Disruptive?*, in NEUROSCIENCE OF DECISION MAKING 73, 76 (Oshin Vartanian & David R. Mandel eds., 2011) ("This mechanism for selecting good from bad options is referred to as decision making, and the physiological changes occurring in association with the behavior selection constitute part of *somatic states* (or somatic signals)."); S. M. McClure et al., *Conflict Monitoring Cognition-Emotion Competition*, in HANDBOOK OF EMOTION REGULATION 204, 222 (James J. Gross ed., 2007) (concluding that there are at least three types of decision making where emotions discernibly influence behavior).

[17] NEUROETHICS: DEFINING THE ISSUES IN THEORY, PRACTICE, AND POLICY 4–5 (Judy Illes ed., 2006); S. W. Anderson et al., *Impairment of Social and Moral Behavior Related to Early Damage in Human Prefrontal Cortex*, 2 NATURE NEUROSCI. 1032–1037 (1999); INT'L NEUROETHICS SOC'Y, http://www.neuroethicssociety.org/about.

[18] GAZZANIGA ET AL., *supra* note 10.

[19] *The Brain and Its Functions*, NEUROLOGYCHANNEL, http://thebrainlabs.com/brain.shtml; Interview with R. McKell Carter, Assistant Professor, University of Colorado, in Boulder, Colo. (Jan. 21, 2016) ("Because of neuroanatomists, we know things like the fact that there are likely spiraling information flows that compare predictions and outcome at a more and more abstract level through cycles between the stratum and cortex.").

[20] Belcher & Roskies, *supra* note 12, at 13.

to find that part. The cortex of the brain is broadly divided into lobes: frontal, parietal, temporal, and occipital lobes.[21] Underneath our cerebral cortex, there are further subcortical structures that include the amygdala, hippocampus, and cingulate cortex; the basal ganglia; the thalamus; the hypothalamus and pituitary gland; the brain stem; and the spinal cord. Neurons in these and other areas carry out neural processing, resulting in various cognitive functions.

Studies of this functional neuroanatomy have led to discoveries about where particular functions occur. For example, it is believed that the hippocampus processes new memories.[22] The amygdala is associated with a variety of neural functions associated with emotion. The temporal lobe processes auditory information, speech, and memory.[23] The parietal lobe processes somatosensory functions such as temperature, touch, and pain.[24] Executive functions involving planning and doing seem to take place in the frontal cortex.[25]

Despite this rich knowledge of brain regions and associated cognitive activity, newer studies and brain imaging technology reveal even further complexity. Research in neuroscience has advanced in recent years due to technological developments in noninvasive ways to study our brains. Referred to generally as neuroimaging, these technologies allow researchers to observe the brain in order to study brain structures, anatomical connectivity (e.g., how different regions of the brain connect), and functional connectivity (e.g., how different areas of the brain affect each other).[26] Neuroimaging methods include positron emission tomography (PET), measuring brain activated through radioisotopes; electroencephalography (EEG), measuring large-scale electrical activity; magnetoencephalography (MEG), measuring magnetic field activity; and Diffusion Tensor Imaging (DTI), used to study axon pathways throughout white matter in the brain.[27]

Today, many researchers rely on fMRI brain scans to test and to study cognitive processes and behavior, such as how moving your finger to scroll

---

[21]   *Id.* at 16.
[22]   Jones et al., *supra* note 10, at 213–214.
[23]   Belcher & Roskies, *supra* note 12, at 20.
[24]   *Id.*
[25]   *Id.*
[26]   Maria de la Iglesia-Vaya et al., *Brain Connections – Resting State fMRI Functional Connectivity*, in Novel Frontiers of Advanced Neuroimaging 51, 51–54 (Kostas Fountas ed., 2013) (describing the ways in which "exploring the neuroanatomy of the brain and the underlying connectivity of different functional areas [allow us to attain] new insights on the organization of the human brain.").
[27]   Jones et al., *supra* note 10, at 222–233; *see also* Jorge Armony & Patrik Vuilleumier, *Introduction* to The Cambridge Handbook of Human Affective Neuroscience 1 (Jorge Armony & Patrik Vuilleumier eds., 2013) [hereinafter Cambridge Handbook].

through an app on your iPhone activates certain parts of your brain.[28] Studies utilizing fMRI provide evidence showing that anatomically distinct regions of the brain need more blood during different types of reasoning.[29] For example, a particular set of brain areas do more work when using common decision-making biases such as framing effects.[30] The field of such research highlights the complexity of our brains while also discrediting commonly held but erroneous ideas, such as the "left brain" or "right brain" idea.[31] Much remains unknown as studies in the field continue to uncover how brains work. With these evolved neuroimaging techniques, studies can illustrate relationships between a behavior and associated areas of the brain that activate, finding, for example, that "increased amygdala reactivity predicts trait anxiety."[32] Neuroscience is beginning to account for the neurobiological basis that may explain certain neurogenetic mechanisms.[33] An emerging area is epigenetics, which is based on data that show that environmental factors early on in life can alter gene expression. These alterations can result in lifelong changes in behavior, such as underlying susceptibility to drug addiction, depression, and other behavioral and psychiatric disorders.[34]

For all of its promise, there are important limitations in applying findings from neuroimaging studies to international legal scholarship. First, new advancements and findings are occurring each year, suggesting that some earlier findings may be inaccurate or incorrect. Second, the results derived from neuroimaging-based studies are not entirely objective. The choices a researcher makes in designing and applying the test are subject to her

---

[28] GAZZANIGA ET AL., *supra* note 10, at 110, 152–158 (discussing how fMRI works, comparing it to PET scans, and discussing the reasons behind its popularity as a mechanism for scientists).

[29] Vinod Goel et al., *Dissociation of Mechanisms Underlying Syllogistic Reasoning*, 12 NEUROIMAGE 504, 512–513 (2000) (using an event-related fMRI study of syllogistic reasoning using sentences with and without semantic content and finding that the left-temporal system was recruited during content-based reasoning, but when performing the same reasoning task without semantic content, the parietal system was recruited).

[30] Joshua A. Weller et al., *Neural Correlates of Adaptive Decision Making for Risky Gains and Losses*, 18 PSYCHOL. SCI. 958 (2007).

[31] Interview with R. McKell Carter, *supra* note 19 ("There is no evidence of strong lateral bias in brain functioning. Language is an exception as it is left lateralized with subtle bias effects. Social processing occurs more frequently on the right side of the brain but the left side is still engaged.").

[32] A. R. Hariri, *Mapping Neurogenetic Mechanisms of Individual Differences in Affect*, in CAMBRIDGE HANDBOOK, *supra* note 27, at 575 (discussing how to "identify the underlying mechanisms driving variability in brain circuit function").

[33] *Id.* at 584.

[34] Eric J. Nestler, *Epigentic Mechanisms of Drug Addiction*, 76 NEUROPHARMACOLOGY 259–268 (2014); Eric J. Nestler, *Epigentic Mechanisms of Depression*, 71 JAMA PSYCHIATRY 454–456 (2014).

views and assumptions.[35] Third, many neuroimaging studies investigate a research question that has previously been studied in behavioral psychology, as it is the older and more established field. However, neuroscience has its own methodologies and assumptions. Accordingly, it is necessary for legal scholars not to conflate findings or limitations from one field to the other. Fourth, though neuroscience has advanced what we know about human behavior in new and exciting ways, its findings do not occur in isolation from other fields. Advancements in evolutionary biology and genetics, for example, are becoming particularly salient.[36] Neuroscience provides an important lens, but one that is best employed in conjunction with perspectives from other fields.

8.2 NEUROLAW

Neurolaw describes the emergent field of legal scholarship that aims to apply neuroscientific insights to questions of legal importance. This field of study arose in the first decade of the twenty-first century as legal scholars began to hold conferences and publish edited volumes in pursuit of applying neuroscientific insights to legal topics.[37] Around the same time, the US Supreme Court considered neuroscience-based evidence and theories in *Roper v. Simmons*, where the Court's prohibition on applying the death penalty to older minors was based, in part, on neuroscience-based theories about child development.[38] In 2010, in *Graham v. Florida*, the Court took account of neuroscientific data about the structural and functional differences between adolescent and adult brains for evidentiary purposes in a case about whether

---

[35] JONES ET AL., *supra* note 10, at 245 ("[N]euroimages are the product of a multiple step process involving many statistical and graphical choices.").

[36] *See, e.g.*, E. H. Shen, C. C. Overly & A. R. Jones, *The Allen Human Brain Atlas: Comprehensive Gene Expression Mapping of the Human Brain*, 35 TRENDS NEUROSCI. 711 (2012).

[37] *See, e.g.*, O. R. Goodenough, *Mapping Cortical Areas Associated with Legal Reasoning and Moral Intuition*, 41 JURIMETRICS 429, 431 (2001) (arguing for reconceptualizing law in response to neuroscience and awarded the Jurimetrics Research Award); LAW AND THE BRAIN (S. Zeki & O. R. Goodenough eds., 2006); GAZZANIGA ET AL., *supra* note 10; LAW, MIND, AND BRAIN (M. Freeman & O. R. Goodenough eds., 2009); Joshua I. Davis et al., *Four Applications of Embodied Cognition*, 4 TOPICS COGNITIVE SCI. 786 (2012) (considering legal consequences of embodied cognition); PARDO & PATTERSON, *supra* note 11 (describing the use of neuroscience in legal theory, criminal law, criminal procedure and theories of criminal punishment); Owen D. Jones et al., *Law and Neuroscience*, 33 J. NEUROSCI. 17624, 17624–17630 (2013) ("[A] distinct field of Law & Neuroscience (sometimes called 'neurolaw') has emerged in barely a decade.").

[38] Roper v. Simmons, 543 U.S. 551 (2005).

sentencing without parole for a juvenile was unconstitutional.[39] Due to increased interest among courts, practitioners, and scholars, the first comprehensive legal casebook aimed at integrating the study of neuroscience into the law school curriculum, *Law and Neuroscience*, was published in 2014.[40]

Within neurolaw, the most popular area of study centers on topics relevant to criminal law.[41] Neuroscience informs legal questions about criminal culpability and intentionality, for example, by revealing the degree of choice or free will a person executes over her or his intentional acts. It also informs work on criminal responsibility and punishment for adolescents by revealing how age influences brain development. Gert-Jan Lokhorst's work has explored how neuroscience implicates what we know about logical reasoning and the

---

[39] Graham v. Florida, 560 U.S. 48, 68–69 (2010) ("No recent data provide reason to reconsider the Court's observations in *Roper* about the nature of juveniles. As petitioner's *amici* point out, developments in psychology and brain science continue to show fundamental differences between juvenile and adult minds. For example, parts of the brain involved in behavior control continue to mature through late adolescence . . . Juveniles are more capable of change than are adults, and their actions are less likely to be evidence of 'irretrievably depraved character' than are the actions of adults. *Roper*, 543 U. S., at 570. It remains true that '[f]rom a moral standpoint it would be misguided to equate the failings of a minor with those of an adult, for a greater possibility exists that a minor's character deficiencies will be reformed.' *Ibid.* These matters relate to the status of the offenders in question; and it is relevant to consider next the nature of the offenses to which this harsh penalty might apply."); *see also* Kayla Pope, Beatriz Luna & Christopher Thomas, *Developmental Neuroscience and the Courts: How Science Is Influencing the Disposition of Juvenile Offenders*, 41 J. Am. Acad. Child. & Adolescent Psychiatry 341–342 (2012).

[40] Jones et al., *supra* note 10.

[41] For legal scholarship discussing the intersection of criminal law and neuroscience, see Pablo A. Ormachea et al., *The Role of Neuroscience in Drug Policy: Promises and Prospects*, 2 J. Sci. L. 1, 1 (2016) ("Neuroscience has begun to reveal the circuitry involved in drug addiction, and many experimental methods are being developed to help individuals combat cocaine use disorders."); A. C. Pustilnik, *Pain as Fact and Heuristic: How Pain Neuroimaging Illuminates Moral Dimensions of Law*, 97 Cornell L. Rev. 801, 804 (2012) (suggesting that neuroimaging will assist in achieving reliable quantification in cases); Terry A. Maroney, *Adolescent Brain Science After Graham v. Florida*, 86 Notre Dame L. Rev. 765 (2011) (arguing the influence of neuroscience at the Supreme Court decision); Teneille Brown & Emily Murphy, *Through a Scanner Darkly: Functional Neuroimaging as Evidence of a Criminal Defendant's Past Mental States*, 62 Stan. L. Rev. 1119, 1129 (2010) (arguing against the use of fMRI evidence in criminal trials); S. K. Erickson, *Blaming the Brain*, 11 Minn. J.L. Sci. & Tech. 27, 28–29 (2010) (describing the shift toward biological sciences in issues of criminal responsibility); Owen D. Jones et al., *Brain Imaging for Legal Thinkers: A Guide for the Perplexed*, 5 Stan. Tech. L. Rev. 5, 5–6 (2009) (discussing the various uses of brain images in legal proceedings); O. Carter Snead, *Neuroimaging and the "Complexity" of Capital Punishment*, 82 N.Y.U. L. Rev. 1265, 1269 (2007) (noting that cognitive neuroscientists seek to invoke brain imaging research on the neurobiological roots of criminal violence).

implications of such for legal concepts such as mens rea.[42] Walter Glannon
identifies several limitations in applying neuroscience to matters of criminal
intent, arguing, for example, that "[e]ven in cases where imaging displaying
brain dysfunction might be used to support the claim that an individual lacked
the capacity to intend to kill and thereby change a conviction from first degree
murder to second degree murder or manslaughter, behavioural evidence
would be needed to confirm the neuroscientific findings."[43] He finds that
neuroscience may play a stronger role in criminal matters involving questions
of impulse control as "the correlations between images of brain dysfunction
and behavior are stronger."[44] Michael Pardo and Dennis Patterson call for
caution in applying inferences derived from brain imaging studies to criminal
responsibility.[45]

The depth of study at the intersection of criminal law and neuroscience has
spurred the development of early frameworks for how the two fields can inform
one another in a methodologically responsible way.[46] A central example of this
is the MacArthur Foundation Research Network on Law and Neuroscience's
comprehensive guideline on the application of neuroscience in criminal law,
directed by Vanderbilt Professor Owen D. Jones.[47] Areas of focus include
research on mental states, adolescent brain development, and evidence, areas

[42]   Gert-Jan Lokhorst, Mens Rea, *Logic, and the Brain, in* 13 LAW AND NEUROSCIENCE:
       CURRENT LEGAL ISSUES 29 (M. Freeman ed., 2011) [hereinafter LAW AND
       NEUROSCIENCE].
[43]   Walter Glannon, *What Neuroscience Can (and Cannot) Tell Us About Criminal
       Responsibility, in* LAW AND NEUROSCIENCE, *supra* note 42, at 13, 17.
[44]   *Id.* at 21 ("A functional brain scan showing an underactive prefrontal cortex or overactive
       amygdala by itself will not be diagnostic of a loss of impulse control or cognitive control of
       one's behaviour.").
[45]   PARDO & PATTERSON, *supra* note 11, at 231–248 (critiquing neurolaw approaches by distin-
       guishing between behavior and brain activity associated with rule-following, interpretation,
       knowledge, and criminal responsibility); Michael S. Pardo & Dennis Patterson, *Neuroscience,
       Normativity, and Retributivism, in* THE FUTURE OF PUNISHMENT 133 (Thomas
       A. Nadelhoffer ed., 2013) (taking a cautious view of the influence of neurolaw in undermining
       criminal law).
[46]   Stephen J. Morse, *Lost in Translation?: An Essay on Law and Neuroscience, in* LAW AND
       NEUROSCIENCE, *supra* note 42, at 530, 541–543 (offering several ways neuroscience contri-
       butes to criminal law scholarship, including (1) confirming or challenging a central view that
       doctrine or practices relies upon; (2) indicating the need for new doctrine or practices; (3)
       using neural data as evidence in a trial or proceeding; and (4) enhancing accuracy of
       predictions that inform policy).
[47]   THE MACARTHUR FOUND. RES. NETWORK L. & NEUROSCI., http://www.lawneuro.org/n
       etworkoverview.pdf [hereinafter MACARTHUR FOUND.]. *See also* Iris Vilares et al., *Predicting
       the Knowledge-Recklessness Distinction in the Human Brain,* 114 PROC. NAT'L ACAD. SCI.
       3222 (2017); Matthew R. Ginther et al., *Parsing the Behavioral and Brain Mechanisms of
       Third-Party Punishment,* 36 J. NEUROSCI. 9420 (2016).

with high relevance to criminal legal scholarship. It poses useful questions, identifies limitations and aims to reduce misuse. Some questions include:[48]

- Can neuroscience help us assess the probability that a person in a certain situation knew a fact or circumstance existed, or was aware of a risk that it existed?
- Can neural activity distinguish awareness that one is committing an illicit act from awareness that one will be punished if caught?
- What influence do memory and emotion have on cognition?
- Can brain activity tell us whether an individual accurately recognizes a person whose face she has seen or an event she has witnessed?
- Can neuroscience be helpful in predicting an individual's future behavior, particularly the risk of violence?
- How can we design neuroscientific studies to answer these questions?

Although less common, scholars have also applied neuroscience to a variety of other doctrinal legal areas.[49] In tort law, for example, whether or not a person formed the requisite intent when committing a tort is of vital importance. New research on human cognition may alter the way certain doctrines, such as fraud, battery, or the concept of the reasonable person, are understood.[50] Jean Eggen and Eric Laury's recent work has advanced understanding of how neuroscience may affect these and other doctrines in tort law.[51] Additional work at the intersection of neuroscience and law is occurring in negotiation and mediation, as scholars seek to use neuroscience research on fear and bias to inform the practice of dispute resolution and decision-making.[52] Other

---

[48] These questions are taken from the MacArthur Foundation Research Network on Law and Neuroscience. For the complete overview, see MACARTHUR FOUND., *supra* note 47.

[49] Jay Sterling Silver, *Intent Reconceived*, 101 IOWA L. REV. 371, 379 (2015) (describing the effect of intent in tort cases); Edwin S. Fruehwald, *Reciprocal Altruism as the Basis for Contract*, 47 LOUISVILLE L. REV. 489 (2009).

[50] RESTATEMENT (SECOND) OF TORTS § 290 (AM. LAW INST. 1965) (The Second Restatement states that the reasonable person is required to know the following community standards: "[T]he qualities and habits of human beings and animals and the qualities, characteristics, and capacities of things and forces in so far as they are matters of common knowledge at the time and in the community.").

[51] Jean M. Eggen & Eric J. Laury, *Toward a Neuroscience Model of Tort Law: How Functional Neuroimaging Will Transform Tort Doctrine*, 12 COLUM. SCI. TECH. L.J. 235 (2012).

[52] Elizabeth E. Bader, *The Psychology and Neurobiology of Mediation*, 17 CARDOZO J. CONFLICT RESOL. 363, 364 (2016) (exploring the connection "between psychological and neurobiological dimensions" in mediation); Robert J. Condlin, *The "Nature" of Legal Dispute Bargaining*, 17 CARDOZO J. CONFLICT RESOL. 393, 394–395 (2016) (noting the social phenomenon of legal dispute bargaining); Richard Birke, *Neuroscience and Settlement: An Examination of Scientific Innovations and Practical Applications*, 25 OHIO ST. J. DISP. RESOL. 477–478 (2011) (discussing the effect of neuroscience in negotiations and mediations).

areas of neurolaw consider the use of fMRI and other brain imaging tests as
evidence in disputes before a court and broader questions about whether the
use of neuroscience in law is ethical.[53] These and related investigations pose
important questions about the appropriate use of neuroscience to advance
legal claims and theories and the limits of such use. To date, there is
a proliferation of ideas but little consensus.

There are important challenges and limitations that can arise in legal
scholarship that uses neuroscientific research. First, neuroscience provides
ways to understand human behavior by revealing the brain-based mechanisms
that can explain observed behavior.[54] Thus, where a behavioral science
approach to explaining behavior may be based on observational studies that
reveal, for example, that individuals are prone to confirmation bias,
a neuroscience study might use brain imaging techniques that map neural
activity associated with that behavior.[55] In this way, neuroscience is capable of
providing causal knowledge that enhances the veracity and accuracy of behavioral observations. The danger, however, is that legal scholars may seek to use
such data in ways that neuroscientists would not sanction. For example,
though an fMRI may show that a person suffers from a brain tumor affecting
judgment, such a neuroscientific causal explanation of a person's behavior is
not intended to provide a legal excuse for offending actions.

Second, such complexities make it risky to apply neuroscience data to legal
questions and write about them in a compelling and responsible way. Legal
scholarship frequently aims to describe a phenomenon and then prescribe

[53] Joshua D. Greene, *Beyond Point-and-Shoot Morality: Why Cognitive (Neuro)Science Matters for Ethics*, 124 ETHICS 695, 695–696 (2014) (describing the implications cognitive science can have on ethics).

[54] Morse, *supra* note 46, at 534 ("Neuroscience is simply the most recent mechanistic causal science that appears deterministically to explain behavior. It thus joins social structural variables, behaviorism, genetics and other scientific explanations that have also been deter-ministic explanations for behavior.").

[55] For behavioral approaches to decision making, see RICHARD H. THALER & CASS R. SUNSTEIN, NUDGE: IMPROVING DECISIONS ABOUT HEALTH, WEALTH, AND HAPPINESS 66 (2008) (claiming that desirable behavior can be increased by drawing public attention to what others are doing); Cass R. Sunstein, *Introduction* to BEHAVIORAL LAW AND ECONOMICS 1, 5–6 (Cass R. Sunstein ed., 2000) (presenting various rational choice models and explaining that people are displeased with losses); Russell B. Korobkin & Thomas S. Ulen, *Law and Behavioral Science: Removing the Rationality Assumption from Law and Economics*, 88 CALIF. L. REV. 1051, 1074–1075 (2000) (exploring how scholars in law and behavioral science seek to understand why individuals sometimes behave irrationally in their decision making); Christine Jolls, Cass R. Sunstein & Richard H. Thaler, *A Behavioral Approach to Law and Economics*, 50 STAN. L. REV. 1471, 1473–1475 (1998) (explaining that the field of economics may be undermined because humans do not always make rational economic choices).

what should change to solve the problem or fix the gap in understanding. Claims are often precise and bold. Research in neuroscience is more cautious, as it intends to study what a brain does under certain conditions.[56] For this reason, one particular study cannot claim to represent the workings of all brains in general. Where enough studies, or meta-analyses, confirm similar findings, the specific inferences gain strength in views about many or most brains.[57] Responsible use of the data requires seeking multiple verifications that confirm a central insight. Even where such an insight enjoys strong support, legal scholars must be careful not to advance claims about all people and their brains but, instead, provide insights about why a person may behave a certain way based on understandings about how a brain can react to certain stimuli.

Third, legal scholars must take care to understand what the limitations on using neuroscience research are and why they exist. For example, advancing new therapies or doctrines based on neuroscientific findings about mirror neurons is problematic when such claims fail to acknowledge that the existence of mirror neurons and how they operate remains unconfirmed and under study.[58] A second area of caution in neurolaw is to avoid conflating limitations in behavioral science research with those in neuroscience, as the two areas are distinct fields of study with distinct assumptions and methodologies. For example, legal scholars in the behavioral science arena have raised concerns about whether findings from a study of how lab participants make decisions apply to specialized groups of decision-makers such as judges, jurors, or lawyers. Dan Kahan, in introducing models of decision-making such as the Story-Telling Model and Coherence-Based Reasoning, argues against applying inferences from these lab studies to judges, noting that "[t]he study of cognition establishes that professional judgment is special."[59] He further notes that observational studies on the impact of judges' ideologies on their judicial

---

[56] *See, e.g.,* Oshin Vartanian & David R. Mandel, *Introduction* to NEUROSCIENCE OF DECISION MAKING, *supra* note 16, at 1, 3 ("We endeavor to show that current behavioral and neural evidence supports the assertion that the field has entered a stage in which context-dependence of choice must be seen as central to decision theory and as something that cannot be ignored without incurring a severe loss of explanatory completeness.").

[57] Armony & Vuilleumier, *supra* note 27, at 1 (providing "a comprehensive, up-to-date, and authoritative survey of knowledge and topics investigated" in the field of affective neuroscience or the cognitive neuroscience of human emotion).

[58] For example, Professor Iacaboni's work on mirror neurons is not unchallenged in the field, yet scholarship exists basing radical changes on his work. *See, e.g.,* Ti-Fei Yuan & Robert Hoff, *Mirror Neuron System Based Therapy for Emotional Disorders,* 71 MED. HYPOTHESIS 722 (2008).

[59] Daniel M. Kahan, *Laws of Cognition and the Cognition of Law,* 135 COGNITION 59 (2015).

decision-making can be fraught with methodological flaws such as selection bias.[60] By contrast, an fMRI-based study of decision-making leads to findings about the brain activity of those tested under particular conditions. Therefore, it would be inaccurate to say that any and all people will exhibit the same brain behavior. But it is also inaccurate to assume that certain groups of people, such as judges, would categorically be exempt from such inferences. In other words, we ought not apply the same reservation Kahan takes in the behavioral arena, that cognitive studies may not transfer to people with professional legal training, to neuroscience without further specificity and study. Instead, legal scholars should identify limitations in neuroscience from recognized discourses in that field. As neuroscience research in these areas develops, the field may introduce more specific guidance for the scope of this research, but until it does, legal scholars should remain cautious.

For international legal scholars, these earlier works in neurolaw provide important points of reference for understanding what advancements neuroscience has made in the study of law generally and what challenges have been revealed.[61] Legal scholarship employing such studies has the potential to reveal novel insights about the intersection of law, neuroscience, and decision-making. Gaining a better understanding of brain-based human behavior may necessitate rethinking relationships between law and human behavior. There is every indication that the field of neurolaw will continue to grow and, as it grows, to strengthen.

8.3 TOWARD NEURO-INTERNATIONAL LAW

The turn to neurolaw in legal scholarship has advanced legal understandings about human cognition, mental states, decision-making, and behavior and has motivated scholars to reevaluate many areas of law including tort, contract, and criminal law. However, scholarship integrating neuroscience into

---

[60] *Id.* at 60; Harry T. Edwards & Michael A. Livermore, *Pitfalls of Empirical Studies That Attempt to Understand the Factors Affecting Appellate Decision Making*, 58 DUKE L.J. 1895, 1895–1989 (2009).

[61] MICHAEL S. PARDO & DENNIS PATTERSON, PHILOSOPHICAL FOUNDATIONS OF LAW AND NEUROSCIENCE (2016) (describing implications of using neuroscience in law); Adam J. Kolber, *Will There Be a Neurolaw Revolution?*, 89 IND. L.J. 807, 808 (2014) (stating that there will be a neurolaw revolution due to new brain technologies); Oliver R. Goodenough & Micaela Tucker, *Law and Cognition Neuroscience*, 6 ANN. REV. L. SOC. SCI. 61, 63 (2010) (discussing the usefulness of intersections between law and neuroscience); Morse, *supra* note 46, at 529, 562 ("The relation between neuroscience and legal doctrine and practice is conceptually fraught. Neuroscience has the potential to make internal contributions to legal doctrine and practice if the relations is properly understood.").

international law is nascent.[62] Legal scholars using behavioral approaches recognize this and point out that neuroscience is needed and is next. For example, even as it highlights the behavioral turn in international law, a recent study by Hafner-Burton, Haggard, Lake, and Victor recognized the "new . . . efforts to anchor behavioral observations in a stronger neurological foundation through advances in brain science."[63] Several contributors to the recently published *Oxford Handbook on US Judicial Behavior* make similar findings.[64] For example, Eileen Braman identifies the need for "a unified understanding of legal decision-making in terms of several 'cognitively informed' theories developed by researchers doing experimental work."[65] Perhaps the enthusiasm for neuroscience work is motivated by the potential

[62] The few examples of international law scholarship involving neuroscience include Anna Spain Bradley, *The Disruptive Neuroscience of Judicial Choice*, 9 U. Cal. Irvine L. Rev. 1 (2018); Anna Spain Bradley, *Cognitive Competence in Executive Branch Decision Making*, 49 Conn. L. Rev. 713 (2017); John Mikhail, *Moral Grammar and Human Rights: Some Reflections on Cognitive Science and Enlightenment Rationalism, in* Understanding Social Action Promoting Human Rights 160 (Ryan Goodman, Derek Jinks & Andrew K. Woods eds., 2012) [hereinafter Understanding Social Action]; Adam B. Shniderman, *The Devil's Advocate: Using Neuroscientific Evidence in International Criminal Trials?*, 38 Brook. J. Int'l L. 655 (2012).

[63] Hafner-Burton et al., *supra* note 5, at S3 ("Also new are the efforts to anchor behavioral observations in a stronger neurological foundation through advances in brain science."). For international legal scholarship in this area, see Tomer Broude, *Behavioral International Law*, 163 U. Penn. L. Rev. 1099 (2015); Ganesh Sitaraman & David Zionts, *Behavioral War Powers*, 90 N.Y.U. L. Rev. 516, 521–523 (2015) (applying insights from behavioral psychology to the legal debate on presidential war powers); Anne van Aaken, *Behavioral International Law and Economics*, Harv. Int'l L.J. 421 (2014); Jean Galbraith, *Treaty Options: Towards a Behavioral Understanding of Treaty Design*, 53 Va. J. Int'l L. 309–310, 312, 356 (2013) (discussing the link between individual cognitive errors and state-decision errors in consenting to treaties and arguing that international legal actors should incorporate insights from choice architecture into their decision-making); Ryan Goodman, Derek Jinks & Andrew K. Woods, *Introduction* to Understanding Social Action, *supra* note 62, at 1, 6–17 (describing the new research in empirical economics and social psychology); Andrew K. Woods, *A Behavioral Approach to Human Rights*, 51 Harv. Int'l L.J. 51 (2010) (investigating the implications of recent behavioral insights, including behavioral economics, on the international human rights regime today); Anne van Aaken, *Towards Behavioral International Law and Economics*, 2008 U. Ill. L. Rev. 47 (2008) (describing the influence of the Law and Economics movements on international law).

[64] Doron Teichman & Eyal Zamir, *Judicial Decision-Making: A Behavioral Perspective, in* The Oxford Handbook of Behavioral Economics and the Law 1, 2 (Doron Teichman & Eyal Zamir eds., 2014) ("[T]hese camps share some basic assumptions, including the belief that judges' decisions are drive only by their goals, the primary goal being to make good legal policy . . . These theories hardly take into account insights from cognitive and social psychology that cast doubt on these assumptions.").

[65] Eileen Braman, *Cognition in the Courts: Analyzing the Use of Experiments to Study Legal Decision-Making, in* The Oxford Handbook of U.S. Judicial Behavior 483, 484 (Lee Epstein & Stefanie A. Lindquist eds., 2017).

for rich collaboration between neuroscience and behavioral science in ways that can mutually confirm key findings about the ways in which we decide, choose, judge, and behave.

In that spirit, this section advances the conversation about the promise and perils of integrating neuroscience into the realm of international law, in what we might term "neuro-international law." To do so, it first describes models for how to construct a conceptual framework for the study of neuro-international law. One critical feature of a future framework will be to determine how limitations in neuroscientific research mitigate the use of findings in the realm of international law. This section then outlines three potential areas of study in neuro-international law: international criminal law, individual decision-making in international law (e.g., international courts, international dispute resolution, national security, and more), and international law and new technology (e.g., brain-computer interfaces and artificial intelligence). In mapping the potential for scholarly development that does not yet exist, the discussion here is limited to creative exploration of how areas of significant study in neuroscience (e.g., mental states, emotion and pain, and executive functioning) may be relevant to topics that international legal scholars already study while recognizing the need for further study and refinement.

8.3.1 *Developing a Conceptual Framework for Neuro-International Law*

Neuro-international law does not yet exist as a field of study. In the international law arena, some scholars have employed various behavioral sciences in their scholarship, as this book and earlier work illustrates. Research integrating international law and neuroscience, however, is still emergent and lacks an organizing framework. This section takes the foundational step forward by framing three approaches for conceptualizing neuro-international law.

First, we might conceive of neuro-international law by starting with areas of study in international law. If understanding intent to commit a crime is a key issue in international criminal law, then the neuroscience on mental states can contribute. If scholars of international courts are concerned about judicial behavior, neuroscientific research on decision-making may provide useful insights. This way of thinking about a framework is organic. It would place decision-making control within each area of international legal study. Such an approach would follow the evolution of neurolaw, which emerged largely out of a criminal law framework wherein certain topics hold particular relevance. International legal scholars will need to assess if such a path of development is appropriate or desirable in our field.

A second approach would be to identify the most promising areas of research within neuroscience that might offer insights for and contribute to the study of international law. In neurolaw more generally this sort of organizing principle can be seen, in part, in the *Law and Neuroscience* casebook, which uses the brain as the unit of organization for its chapters. Herein, central themes of neurolaw study include (1) the injured brain and pain; (2) higher cognitive brain functions, including emotion, memory, logical reasoning, and judging; (3) brain research associated with adolescents and with addiction; and (4) brain-technology applications covering cognitive enhancement and neuroprosthetics.[66] Letting neuroscience take the lead in setting agendas in international law would ensure that the intersection between the two fields is consistent with what neuroscience can offer international law. It would be the responsibility of international legal scholars to then determine which areas of research are relevant to their work. However, neuroscientists have no particular motivation to pursue an international law research agenda absent institutional collaboration and financial support.

The third approach is to develop a conceptual framework for neuro-international law by bringing neuroscientists and international legal scholars together with the explicit aim of doing so. Similar approaches exist, where people gather from different fields at workshops and conferences to collect interdisciplinary views on what the framework of an emerging field ought to look like. For example, the outcome of the Delft University Philosophy Department's February 2010 conference on neurolaw and other topics provides a third example of a framework.[67] Conference participants from psychology, neuroscience, philosophy, psychiatry, law and more identified a five-part framework for themes relevant to law that neuroscience can inform: (1) conceptualization regarding responsibility ("what is neuroscience able to reveal that might assist in defining and determining criminal responsibility?"); (2) brain interventions and brain-machine interfaces, prediction and risk assessment ("what does neuroscience add to methods of behavioral prediction and treatment, and what are the implications for privacy?"); (3) memory ("what kinds of memories are reliant in the law, and how can neuroscience help us to identify them?"); and (4) impact of neuroscience in different legal systems.[68]

The purpose of providing such varied examples of conceptual frameworks for neurolaw as a field of study is to highlight the variety and, therefore, the

---

[66] JONES ET AL., *supra* note 10, at ix–xxii.

[67] Nicole Vincent, Pim Haslager, & Gert-Jan Lokhorst, *"The Neuroscience of Responsibility"* – Workshop Report, 4 NEUROETHICS 175 (2011).

[68] *Id.*

range of possibilities that exist. Scholars of international law readily recognize that because international law is a distinct field of study, work in other fields does not always transfer to international law. Here we might begin to think about the foundations, assumptions, and norms that make neuro-international law distinct from neurolaw. This chapter aims to start a discussion that will necessarily require a broader discourse to develop answers and direct further inquiry. The following questions may provide a useful starting point:

- Should neuro-international law follow a neurolaw framework? Why or why not?
- Based on neurolaw, what areas of study might be relevant in neuro-international law?
- How might the neuro-international law agenda differ from neurolaw given the distinctions between the two fields?
- How might neuroscience implicate theoretical discourses in international law?
- What are the parameters of using neuroscience responsibly in application to international legal questions?
- How should international legal scholars integrate findings from neurolaw with findings from behavioral science, empirical science and other methodologies currently employed in international legal scholarship? What areas of tension or cohesion will result?

8.3.2 Potential Areas of Study in Neuro-International Law

It is possible to conceive of a neuroscientific application for every subarea of international law, across private, public, and transnational legal divides and within various areas of international legal theory. To start, though, it is necessary to recognize a central difference between the two fields. The primary unit of study in neuroscience is the individual (and her or his brain). Based on the limitations that have been identified in neurolaw, it is clear that neuroscientific insights are most directly and safely applied to the study of individuals. However, the primary actor in international law has, historically, been the state. For now, neuroscience can help international law scholars better understand the brain-based mechanisms behind certain individual behaviors with the following limitation. Neuroscience offers insights about people in an individual capacity. From a neuroscience perspective, brain size, shape, and structure can and do differ in individuals. Neuroscientists are still working to determine the range of normal variation among human brains.[69] Not all brains are the same and most brains are likely distinct. Legal scholars seeking to say more – to extrapolate how individual choices might reshape a discourse on judicial behavior or on human rights more broadly – will have complexities to navigate in doing so. The challenge that lies ahead for neuro-international law will be in determining how to translate findings about individual decision-making to the study of collective decision-making, or about individual behavior to the study of state behavior. In this regard, the challenge facing neuro-international law is not unique, as scholars working in the areas of law and economics and behavioral law face similar challenges.[70]

These preliminaries and limitations aside, this section explores the application of neuroscience to three subject areas of international law – international criminal law, international law and decision-making, and international law and technology – in order to illustrate how neuroscience research may be useful to the study of international law. The selection of these legal topics is opportunistic, as each area concerns questions about human behavior and cognition that are ripe for exploration in neuroscience. Beyond that, this list does not intend to prioritize subjects for study in neuro-international law.

8.3.2.1 International Criminal Law

A central aim of international criminal law is to create legal frameworks for holding accountable those individuals who commit international crimes. The Rome Statute, which entered into force on July 1, 2002, provides a modern-day codification of the four international crimes recognized under international law and accepted by most nations in the world: genocide, crimes against humanity, war crimes, and acts of aggression.[71] Scholars study the meaning and development of these crimes along with the practice of international

---

[69] Belcher & Roskies, *supra* note 12, at 33 ("However, it is currently unknown exactly what the range of normal variation is. Moreover, because of brain *plasticity* during development, people with brains that look clearly abnormal structurally may have no clear functional deficits. These facts make it difficult to determine, purely on the basis of brain data of an individual, whether a brain that looks abnormal structurally will also operate abnormally, or whether a having a brain with abnormal-looking patterns of function necessarily implies that the person whose brain it is will be functionally impaired. Individual differences in brain structure and function thus complicate the interpretation of brain-imaging data in a number of ways (these will be elucidated more fully in the next chapter).").

[70] *See generally* Broude, *supra* note 63.

[71] For definitions of the four international crimes, see Rome Statute of the International Criminal Court, July 17, 1998, 2187 U.N.T.S. 900. For a useful overview of international criminal law and its applications, see ROUTLEDGE HANDBOOK OF INTERNATIONAL CRIMINAL LAW (William A. Chabas & Nadia Bernaz eds., 2011).

criminal law in various courts, tribunals, truth and reconciliation commissions, and hybrid institutions. Central to all of these areas of study are the individuals who commit said crimes and those who prosecute, defend, or adjudicate them. This makes international criminal law well suited for engagement with neuroscience because studies about an individual's brain-based behavior have implications for studies about individual criminal behavior. Of course, there are important differences between criminal law in domestic context of the US or other countries and criminal law in international law. As a legal matter, the standard of proof for genocide differs widely from that of first-degree murder, and for important reasons. But all crimes, to some extent, necessitate a discussion about the mental state of a person alleged to have committed a horrific act and related questions about intent, capacity, and awareness. Here, knowledge about the brain and how youth, addiction, disease, and other factors can change neurobiology and cognition are germane.

The task that lies ahead for international criminal law scholars is to identify areas of study in the field where data from neuroscience may be relevant. As in criminal law, one area where neuroscience may inform international criminal law concerns the relationship between the brain and criminal responsibility. If a person has a brain tumor, addiction, or other factors that change her capacity for empathy, judgment, or risk assessment, should this information serve as evidence for mitigating criminal responsibility? Another area of potential relevance concerns "the neural correlates of third-party punishment."[72] These examples provide a starting point for international criminal law scholars while raising vital questions about how to account for the important distinctions between criminal law and international criminal law.[73]

In international criminal law, questions about mental states and the defense of diminished mental responsibility were raised in the trial of Mr. Landzo, a prison guard at the Čelebići prison camp in Bosnia and Herzegovina during the war.[74] He, along with three other defendants, was charged with various crimes including willful killing and murder, torture and cruel treatment, and inhumane treatment. In hearing evidence by mental health experts on how his

[72]   Joshua Buckholtz et al., *The Neural Correlates of Third-Party Punishment*, in LAW AND NEUROSCIENCE, *supra* note 42, at 115.

[73]   Kevin Jon Heller, *The Cognitive Psychology of* Mens Rea, 99 J. CRIM. L. & CRIMINOLOGY 317 (2009); Henry T. Greely, *Neuroscience and Criminal Justice: Not Responsibility but Treatment*, 56 U. KAN. L. REV. 1103–1138 (2008).

[74]   Prosecutor v. Delalic et al., Case No. IT-96-21-T, Judgment (Int'l Crim. Trib. for the Former Yugoslavia Nov. 16, 1998); Prosecutor v. Delalic et al., Case No. IT-96-21-T, Appeals Judgment (Int'l Crim. Trib. for the Former Yugoslavia Feb. 20, 2001).

youth, inexperience, and other factors influenced his mental state, the Trial Chamber became the first body to consider mental capacity in international criminal law.[75] Landzo was found guilty of many of the charges against him.

This example raises complex questions for international criminal law about if and how neural data should be used to assess criminal responsibility, guilt, and punishment. If the Court had access to data derived from brain imaging technologies, should it choose to admit such evidence? While some people who commit violent crimes do have brain abnormalities, not all individuals with brain abnormalities commit crimes. If permitted, evidence derived from neural data may inform affirmative psychological defenses, such as diminished responsibility and whether treatment for mental disorders should replace incarceration.[76] Advancements in neuroscientific research will continue to inform our understanding of human cognition and mental states in ways that have implications for the study and practice of international criminal law. The International Criminal Court, and other courts and tribunals, will also need to determine whether or not to reform their practices to account for such emerging understandings of human behavior.

In addition to mapping the existing work at the intersection of criminal law and neuroscience onto international criminal law, there are numerous topics unique to international criminal law that are ripe for further study through a neuroscience lens. For example, mass atrocity crimes, which include genocide, war crimes, crimes against humanity, aggression, and ethnic cleansing, are horrid in their own right and also because the harms are caused to such a large number of people.[77] Here, we might ask if and why people are more influenced to commit murder or rape when everyone they know is also doing the same? Or if truth and reconciliation measures are effective, in part, because they occur en masse? A research project could be designed in consultation with neuroscientists to determine how what a person sees and hears influences her own choices concerning violence or forgiveness and whether the concept of mirror neurons, which remain unproven, has any value in this

---

[75] Ian Freckelton & Magda Karagiannakis, *Mental State Defences Before the International Criminal Tribunal for the Former Yugoslavia*, 12 PSYCHIATRY PSYCHOL. & L. 249, 251 (2005); Landy F. Sparr, *Mental Incapacity Defenses at the War Crimes Tribunal: Questions and Controversy*, 33 J. AM. ACAD. PSYCHIATRY & L. 59 (2005).

[76] Adam B. Shniderman & Charles A. Smith, *Toward Justice: Neuroscience and Affirmative Defenses at the ICC*, 66 STUD. L. POL. & SOC'Y 20 (2015); Heller, *supra* note 73, at 317; Greely, *supra* note 73, at 1103–1138.

[77] G.A. Res. 60/1, 2005 World Summit Outcome (Sept. 16, 2005) (listing ethnic cleansing alongside the international crimes). *See also* Saira Mohamed, *Deviance, Aspiration, and the Stories We Tell: Reconciling Mass Atrocity and the Criminal Law*, 124 YALE L.J. 1628 (2015) (describing the complexity of mass atrocity crimes).

context. At present, there are more questions than answers, but there is potential for valuable interdisciplinary interaction in the future.

8.3.2.2 Individual Decision-Making in International Law

Decision-making is a fundamental aspect of the study of international law, as legal rules are produced by people who create, interpret, and shape them. Neuroscience provides valuable insights for studying biological brain activity associated with decision-making. Thus, the study of decision-making in neuro-international law is ripe for exploration. Such findings will be relevant for the places and spaces in international law where the decisions of individuals take legal meaning and effect. These include the study of international courts and tribunals, international dispute resolution, treaty-making, and other forms of negotiation and national security decision-making.[78] To illustrate the potential for cross-fertilization between these areas and neuroscience, this section first describes topics of study in neuroscience generally that scholars may find relevant to decision-making in international law. It then describes specific areas of decision-making in international law where neuroscience may prove useful: crisis-based decision-making in the national security context and adjudicative decision-making in international courts and international arbitration.

Many areas of study in neuroscience promise rich starting points for the development of neuro-international law and decision-making. Research in this area focuses on understanding how biological data informs cognitive functions implicated in decision-making.[79] In this context, decision-making is understood to be the cognitive mechanisms that work to help a person select good from bad options.[80] Certain topics are considered to be theoretically

---

[78] *See* SUSAN D. FRANCK, ARBITRATION COSTS: MYTHS AND REALITIES IN INVESTMENT TREATY ARBITRATION 25–66 (2019) (discussing the use of insights from cognitive psychology, including cognitive illusions and biases, on international treaty arbitration); Dan M. Kahan, *Laws of Cognition and the Cognition of Law*, 135 J. COGNITION 56, 56 (2015) ("Law and particularly adjudication have historically been a vibrant site for the study of cognition ... [as] adjudication furnishes a consequential, real-world decision-making system, the relative simplicity of which supports experimental designs that isolate mechanisms of interest from confounds without (it is hoped) compromising external validity.").

[79] *See generally* ALEXANDER, *supra* note 6, at 8 (stating how neuroscience helps to learn more about the modern brain as well as helping heal people); DOIDGE, *supra* note 6, at vxi (discussing how the neuroplastic revolution has implications on different aspects of human life); KAKU, *supra* note 6, at 4 (noting the movement to understand how the human brain functions); SWART ET AL., *supra* note 6, at 2 (describing how the brain and decision-making processes work together).

[80] Bechara, *supra* note 16, at 76.

relevant to decision-making and enjoy a significant body of knowledge in neuroscience.[81] These include trust, cooperation, uncertainty, reward, and loss.[82] For example, certain hormones (e.g., oxytocin) stimulate certain neural functions (e.g., trust) due to this neural connection.[83] This can result in a person having a strong affiliation with their group, leading to altruism toward those within it and, notably, an increased harm for out-group members.[84] Memory is another area of study in neuroscience with relevance to decision-making.[85]

Another area of neuroscience relevant to international law concerns the study of brain activity associated with higher-level cognition, such as choice, judgment, and assessment of information and risk.[86] Neuroscientists are beginning to study the timeline of cognitive processes associated with decision-making activity in the brain given newly available techniques.[87] Directing oneself to think about solving a problem can involve a timeline of stages. For example, one fMRI study, where participants were trying to solve a math problem, identified four stages of cognitive processes: encoding, planning, solving, and responding.[88] But a brain engaged in assessing information and thinking about how valid the facts are might engage in a different order of cognitive processes. The ability to study decision-making activity in the brain in stages reveals that the brain can invoke distinct centers and pathways that may differ depending on whether a person is trying to assess information or solve a problem. Recognizing the various types of thought from a neurological perspective allows for a deeper appreciation of how memory, emotion, motivation, and other factors work in varying and complex ways to influence decision-making.

---

[81] Vartanian & Mandel, *supra* note 56, at 2.

[82] *See, e.g.*, Michael Kosfeld et al., *Oxytocin Increases Trust in Humans*, 435 NATURE 673, 673 (2005)

[83] *Id.*

[84] Interview with R. McKell Carter, *supra* note 19 ("[T]he exact mechanism of action on a broad functional level is not known.").

[85] Leslie Fellows, *The Neuroscience of Human Decision-Making Through the Lens of Learning and Memory*, 37 CURRENT TOPICS BEHAV. NEUROSCI. 231 (2018).

[86] Joshua Greene & Jonathan Cohen, *For the Law, Neuroscience Changes Nothing and Everything*, 359 PHIL. TRANSACTIONS ROYAL SOC'Y 1775 (2004) ("We argue that neuroscience will probably have a transformative effect on the law, despite the fact that existing legal doctrine can, in principle, accommodate whatever neuroscience will tell us. New neuroscience will change the law, not by undermining its current assumptions, but by transforming people's moral intuitions about free will and responsibility.").

[87] John R. Anderson, Aryn A. Pyke & Jon M. Fincham, *Hidden Stages of Cognition Revealed in Patterns of Brain Activation*, 27 PSYCHOL. SCI. 1215 (2016).

[88] *Id.*

A third, related area of important research comes from affective neu-roscience work on emotion-cognition interactions and, most recently, empa-thy. For example, an fMRI study revealed that when a brain faces a conflict between a belief and logic, it may change its reasoning process and recruit the right prefrontal cortex, which affords emotions – notably anger, fear, and empathy – a stronger role in decision-making.[89] The experience of fear can also stimulate more careful deliberative processes than normal because it links decision-making with our working memory and emotion systems.[90] Such research on how emotion may disrupt or enhance access to memory could have important implications for judicial behavior or national security deci-sion-making.[91]

Neuroscience research on decision-making has relevance for areas in inter-national law concerned with decisions taken during times of crises. Paramount among these is the literature on law and national security. After the attacks on September 11, 2001, President Bush's administration and the executive branch, for example, made a number of decisions that impacted the legality of torture, national security, and more.[92] The concerns about decision-making appear throughout the more traditional legal discourses on national

---

[89] George F. Loewenstein et al., *Risk as Feelings*, 127 PSYCHOL. BULL. 267, 267 (2001).

[90] For early groundbreaking work in this area, see ANTONIO DAMASIO, DESCARTES' ERROR: EMOTION, REASON, AND THE HUMAN BRAIN (1994) (demonstrating that emotions play a significant role in social cognition and in decision-making). For more recent work on the topic, see Antonio Damasio & Gil B. Carvalho, *The Nature of Feelings: Evolutionary and Neurobiological Origins*, 14 NATURE REV. NEUROSCI. 143, 143 (2013) (examining the evolu-tionary and neurobiological origins of feelings).

[91] For emergent scholarship taking such an approach, see Bradley, *supra* note 62; Paul S. Davies & Peter A. Alces, *Neuroscience Changes More Than You Can Think*, 1 J.L. TECH. & POL'Y 141 (2017). For work on neuroscience, law and decision making, see, for example, LAW AND NEUROSCIENCE, *supra* note 42; Goodenough, *supra* note 37, at 431 (discussing how to conceptualize law in response to insights from neuroscience).

[92] For recent work on national security decision making in the post 9/11 world, see, for example, MICHAEL GLENNON, NATIONAL SECURITY AND DOUBLE GOVERNMENT (2015) (arguing that U.S. national security policy is controlled more by a concealed "Trumanite network" and less by the President and describing the threats this form of double government poses for American democracy and legitimacy); Rebecca Ingber, *Interpretation Catalysts and Executive Branch Legal Decisionmaking*, 38 YALE J. INT'L L. 359 (2013) (identifying three triggers – defensive litigation, treaty body reporting, and speechmaking – that act as interpretation catalysts in executive branch decision-making on national security and international law); Jack Goldsmith, POWER AND CONSTRAINT: THE ACCOUNTABLE PRESIDENCY AFTER 9/11 (2012); Gillian Metzger, *The Interdependent Relationship Between Internal and External Separation of Powers*, 59 EMORY L.J. 423 (2009) (analyzing how administrative design and structure influences executive branch decision-making and the relationship between internal and external constraints); Neal Katyal, *Internal Separation of Powers: Checking Today's Most Dangerous Branch from Within*, 115 YALE L.J. 2314 (2006) (identifying proposals for realistic checks and balances on the executive branch).

security, such as striking the right balance between national security and human rights and civil liberties;[93] or the proper scope of Constitutional authority between the Executive and Congress;[94] or in external checks and internal design constraints on Executive authority;[95] or the tensions between US law and international law.[96] But allocating decision-making authority necessitates understanding not only who is making a decision but how she or he decides. Typically, the public is not privy to details about exactly how a specific Attorney General, Director of National Intelligence, or CIA operative made a particular choice, but neuroscience can help scholars better understand how brains operate at the neural level to produce various decision outcomes such as risk assessment, choice, or judgment.

Consider the example of the killing of Osama bin Laden. On the afternoon of May 1, 2011, President Obama was in the White House Situation Room with his national security team watching a live video feed (with audio narrated by CIA Director Leon Panetta) showing an aerial view of the operation carried out by US Navy SEALs in the killing of Osama bin Laden near Abbottabad, Pakistan.[97] The President, acting as Commander-in-Chief, is believed to have given final authorization for the operation that afternoon.[98] His decision was likely influenced by a number of factors, including a determination that the operation was possible given existing weather conditions and that it was

[93] *See, e.g.*, Jennifer Daskal, *The Geography of the Battlefield: A Framework for Detention and Targeting Outside the 'Hot' Conflict Zone*, 161 U. PENN. L. REV. 1165 (2013) (reconceptualizing the law of war to allow a balancing between a state's need to respond to enemies and limitations on the use of targeting killing and detention practices); Matthew C. Waxman, *Police and National Security: American Local Law Enforcement and Counterterrorism After 9/11*, 3 J. NAT'L SEC. L. & POL'Y 377 (2009) (discussing tensions between counterterrorism and local policing); Rosa Ehrenreich Brooks, *War Everywhere: Rights, National Security Law, and the Law of Armed Conflict in the Age of Terror*, 153 U. PENN. L. REV. 675, 745 (2004) (discussing how legal decisions about war have created a framework for understanding that war can be ongoing).
[94] JOHN YOO, THE POWERS OF WAR AND PEACE 142–181 (2005); GOLDSMITH, *supra* note 92, at xvi ("Consensus and legitimate power are happy consequences of constraint.").
[95] *See, e.g.*, GOLDSMITH, *supra* note 92; ERIC A. POSNER & ADRIAN VERMEULE, THE EXECUTIVE UNBOUND (2010).
[96] *See* JENS DAVID OHLIN, THE ASSAULT ON INTERNATIONAL LAW (2015) (arguing how a small group of scholars and government officials have ignited a new skepticism about the idea of international law).
[97] The CNN Wire Staff, *How U.S. Forces Killed Osama bin Laden*, CNN (May 3, 2011, 7:59 AM), http://www.cnn.com/2011/WORLD/asiapcf/05/02/bin.laden.raid/index.html; Jamie Crawford, *The bin Laden Situation Room Revisited – One Year Later*, CNN: SEC. CLEARANCE (May 1, 2012, 2:00 AM) http://security.blogs.cnn.com/2012/05/01/the-bin-laden-situation-room-revisited-one-year-later/.
[98] Julie Marks, *How SEAL Team Six Took Out Osama bin Laden*, HISTORY CHANNEL (May 24, 2018), https://www.history.com/news/osama-bin-laden-death-seal-team-six.

permissible under US and international law.[99] However, his own internal cognitive processes, which could have involved neural activity associated with fear, bias, empathy, and more, were also influential over his ultimate choice. Did the President, for example, make the choice to avoid bombing the compound because women and children were known to be inside? We will likely never know, but the example raises the question about how choices during crises are made and what neuroscience can contribute to such understandings.

Because of insights from research in neuroscience, we now know that the behavior that we commonly understand as decision-making involves a variety of cognitive functions in our brains.[100] These functions arise through multiple neural systems operating concurrently or in sequence.[101] This nonlinear system allows for parallel processing of various cognitive activity in the brain whereby a person can engage in perceiving and choosing at the same time.[102]

---

[99]   The Obama Administration relied upon the authority provided by Congress in the Authorization for Use of Military Force Against Terrorists Act, 50 U.S.C. § 1541 (2001).

[100] Cognitive functioning in decision-making has been tested through a variety of means. *See, e.g.*, Vartanian & Mandel, *supra* note 56, at 2 (describing the means of testing as including "behavioral experiments, brain imaging, neuropsychology, electrophysiology, computational modeling, and investigations of neurotransmitter systems.").

[101] *Id.* (describing why cognition is not easily defined as automatic vs. non-automatic as many processes feature some aspects of both). *See also* Jan De Houwer & Dirk Hermans, *Do Feelings Have a Mind of Their Own?, in* COGNITION AND EMOTION: REVIEWS OF CURRENT RESEARCH AND THEORIES 38, 44 (Jan De Houwer & Dirk Hermans eds., 2010) ("Evidence from Stroop studies, for instance, suggests that the processing of word meaning is automatic in that it does not depend on intention, resources or time, but at the same time occurs only when attention is directed toward the word ... An important implication of this conclusion is that one cannot simply characterise a process as automatic or non-automatic.").

[102] Houwer & Hermans, *supra* note 101, at 7 ("[A]ffective reactions can occur independently of controlled cognition."); Joo-Hyun Song & Ken Nakayama, *Hidden Cognitive States Revealed in Choice Reaching Tasks*, 13 TRENDS COGNITIVE SCI. 360 (2009). For studies investigating parallel cognitive processes, see Michael J. Spivey et al., *Do Curved Reaching Movements Emerge From Competing Perception? A Reply to Van Der Wal et al.*, 36 J. EXPER. PSYCHOL: HUM. PERCEP. & PERFORM. 251 (2009) ("[E]xistence proof that a discrete-processing speech perception system can feed into a continuous- processing motor movement system to produce reach trajectories."); Song & Nakayama, *supra*, at 360 ("[T]his line of research provides new opportunities to integrate information across different disciplines such as perception, cognition and action, which have usually been studied in isolation."); Alon Fishback & Ferdinando A. Mussa-Ivaldi, *Seeing vs. Believing: Conflicting Immediate and Predicted Feedback Lead to Sub-Optimal Motor Performance*, 28 J. NEUROSCI. 14140, 14140 (2008) ("Under normal conditions, perceptual and motor criteria for movement optimization coincide. However, when vision is perturbed adapted trajectories can be used to uncover the influence of perceptual criteria on movement planning."); Hongbao Li et al., *Prior Knowledge of Target Direction and Intended Movement Selection Improves Indirect Reaching Movement Decoding*, 2017 BEHAV. NEUROLOGY 1 (2017) ("Recruiting prior knowledge about target direction and

For example, if you are reaching for a hamburger but a yellow-jacket lands on top of it, your brain now has to redirect its thought to account for action (reaching) and perception (seeing a threat) at the same time. This data revises the earlier view that the brain processed information sequentially and demonstrates the complexity of cognitive processes involved in decision-making.[103] One inference that arises from this type of research is evidence that shows that neural activity resulting in our decision-making can interact with neural activity associated with empathy and with emotion.[104] For example, a 2013 study found that emotions generated from observing a film increase activation in the medial prefrontal cortex, the thalamus, and other emotion centers of the brain.[105] But, instead of triggering the brain's pain center, the observation would trigger the brain's center for processing the emotional content.[106]

What does all of this mean for President Obama in the Situation Room that day? We cannot know for sure. We can, however, imagine the following possibilities. If President Obama saw on the video feed that women and children were present in the compound (which they reportedly were) and if he empathized with them, that may have influenced his decision not to bomb the compound. Research on neuroscience and empathy helps us understand why, by showing how the brain processes empathy in ways that implicate decision-making. Of course, determining how to interpret this sort of information in the realm of national security law remains an ongoing aim of this project, but the first step is to acknowledge that the availability of the information bears importance for the field.

A second area of research in international law that considers decision-making concerns judicial behavior in international courts and international arbitration. The question of how judges (or arbitrators) decide is well-studied by legal scholars, both in the context of international law and more generally. Much of the literature focusing on judges in the US takes a positivist

---

intended movement selection extracted from the Dorsal Pre-Motor Cortex could enhance the decoding performance of hand trajectory in indirect reaching movement.").

[103] Through these varied methodologies, scientists can measure neural networks and systems in addition to neural functions. *See, e.g.,* John P. O'Doherty & Peter Bossaerts, *Toward a Mechanistic Understanding of Human Decision Making: Contributions of Functional Neuroimaging,* 17 CURRENT DIR. PSYCHOL. SCI. 119 (2008); Brian Knutson et al., *Distributed Neural Representation of Expected Value,* 25 J. NEUROSCI. 4806 (2005).

[104] *See, e.g.,* Antoine Bechara et al., *Different Contributions of the Human Amygdala and Ventromedial Prefrontal Cortex to Decision-Making,* 19 J. NEUROSCI. 5473 (1999) (discussing how the ventromedial prefrontal cortex and the amygdala affect different processes); Valeria Gazzola, Lisa Aziz-Zade & Christian Keysers, *Empathy and the Somatotopic Auditory Mirror System in Humans,* 16 CURRENT BIOLOGY 1824 (2006).

[105] Jeanne C. Watson & Leslie S. Greenberg, *Empathetic Resonance, in* THE SOCIAL NEUROSCIENCE OF EMPATHY 125, 128 (Jean Decety & William Ickes eds., 2013).

[106] *Id.* at 127–128.

approach – seeking to describe and define the behavior of judges, arbitrators, and other adjudicators.[107] Are judges biased?[108] Do apologies influence judges?[109] What role does reputation play?[110] How do arbitrators approach legal decision-making?[111] Scholars also advance our theoretical and normative understandings about judges and emotions. Martha Nussbaum's work, for example, describes emotion as an internally embedded influence in law. Susan Bandes has argued why emotion is central to the study of law.[112] Terry Mahoney's work has deepened theoretical understandings about emotional regulation and judging.[113] Another vital area of scholarly discourse concerns bias and representation on courts and tribunals.[114] Scholars have aimed to

[107] Susan D. Franck et al., *Inside the Arbitrator's Mind*, 66 EMORY L.J. 1117 (2017) (applying empirical research tools to asses decision making by international arbitrators); Richard A. Posner, *Judicial Behavior and Performance: An Economic Approach*, 32 FLA. ST. L. REV. 1259, 1261 (2005) ("We can expect, therefore, a tendency for arbitrators to 'split the difference' in their awards.").
[108] Andrea Bianchi, *Choice and (the Awareness of) Its Consequences: The ICJ's Structural Bias Strikes Again in the Marshall Islands Case*, 111 AJIL UNBOUND 81, 84 (2017); Jefferey J. Rachlinski, Chris Guthrie & Andrew Wistrich, *Inside the Bankruptcy Judge's Mind*, 86 B.U. L. REV. 1227 (2006).
[109] Jennifer K. Robbennolt, *The Effects of Negotiated and Delegated Apologies in Settlement Negotiation*, 37 LAW & HUM. BEHAV. 128 (2013); Jeffrey J. Rachlinski, *Contrition in the Courtroom: Do Apologies Affect Adjudication?*, 98 CORNELL L. REV. 1189 (2013); Jennifer K. Robbennolt, *Apologies and Legal Settlement: An Empirical Examination*, 102 MICH. L. REV. 460 (2003).
[110] NUNO GAROUPA & TOM GINSBURG, JUDICIAL REPUTATION: A COMPARATIVE THEORY (2015).
[111] Tom Ginsburg, *The Arbitrator as Agent: Why Deferential Review Is Not Always Pro-Arbitration*, 77 U. CHI. L. REV. 1013, 1014 (2010) ("[A]rbitrators might deliver poor quality decisions that undermine the attractiveness of arbitration as a whole . . ."); Sergio Puig, *Social Capital in the Arbitration Marketplace*, 25 EUR. J. INT'L L. 388 (2014); Joshua B. Simmons, *Valuation in Investor-State Arbitration: Toward a More Exact Science*, 30 BERKELEY J. INT'L L. 196, 200 (2012) (identifying "perceptions that arbitrators merely 'split the baby' between the parties' proposed valuations, particularly when awards are poorly explained.").
[112] MARTHA NUSSBAUM, HIDING FROM HUMANITY: DISGUST, SHAME, AND THE LAW (2004) (analyzing the role of emotion in criminal law, political liberalism, and more); MARTHA NUSSBAUM, POLITICAL EMOTIONS: WHY LOVE MATTERS FOR JUSTICE 6 (2013) (describing "the ways in which emotions can support the basic principles of an aspiring yet imperfect society."); MARTHA NUSSBAUM, UPHEAVALS OF THOUGHT: THE INTELLIGENCE OF EMOTIONS (2001); Susan Bandes, *Emotion and Deliberation: The Autonomous Citizen in the Social World*, in NOMOS LIII, PASSIONS AND EMOTIONS 189 (James E. Fleming ed., 2013); THE PASSIONS OF LAW (Susan A. Bandes ed., 2000).
[113] Terry A. Mahoney, *Emotional Regulation and Judicial Behavior*, 99 CALIF. L. REV. 1481 (2011). *See also* Terry A. Mahoney, *Angry Judges*, 65 VAND. L. REV. 1207 (2012) (providing a theoretical model for how to evaluate anger in judicial decision-making).
[114] WON KIDANE, THE CULTURE OF INTERNATIONAL ARBITRATION (2016); Nienke Grossman, *Achieving Sex Representative International Court Benches*, 110 AM. J. INT'L L. 82 (2016); Mirèze Philippe, *Speeding Up the Path for Gender Equality*, 1

provide evidence beyond theory that explains how judges decide. Using empirical analysis, scholars survey judges and arbitrators and conduct interviews, which may reveal quantitative and qualitative data, often self-reported, about judicial behavior.[115] Behavioral psychology-based approaches help establish that judges (and people in general) are prone to error, mistake, bias, and other decision-making pathologies.[116]

Neuroscience-based scholarship in this area reveals insights directly relevant to the behavioral law discourse on judicial behavior. From a neuroscientific view, emotion, whether good or bad, is integral to decision-making in the brain.[117] Emotion has the capacity to change what we think by changing the way we process thought at the neural level. Bechara's work, for example, suggests that emotion related to what you are deciding can

TRANSNAT'L DISP. MGMT. (2017); Lucy Greenwood & C. Mark Baker, *Is the Balance Getting Better? An Update on the Issue of Gender Diversity in International Arbitration*, 28 ARB. INT'L 413 (2015); Amy Farrell, Geoff Ward & Danielle Rousseau, *Intersections of Gender and Race in Federal Sentencing: Examining Court Contexts and the Effects of Representative Court Authorities*, 14 J. GENDER RACE & JUST. 1, 24 (2010) ("That is, women receive less-severe sentences because criminal justice system authorities view them as less dangerous, in addition to believing that they possess a generally greater potential for reform than men."); Ilene H. Nagel & Barry L. Johnson, *The Role of Gender in a Structured Sentencing System: Equal Treatment, Policy Choices, and the Sentencing of Female Offenders Under the United States Sentencing Guidelines*, 85 J. CRIM. L. & CRIMINOLOGY 181, 186 (1994) ("Women are more likely than similarly situated men to receive suspended sentences or probation."). For recent work on racial bias, see Braman, *supra* note 65, at 493 (describing "recent experimental work on racial bias among judges."); Jeffrey J. Rachlinski et al., *Does Unconscious Racial Bias Affect Trial Judges?*, 84 NOTRE DAME L. REV. 1195 (2009) (finding evidence that suggests both white and black judges demonstrated implicit bias with regard to racial preference).

[115] For empirical approaches to studying judicial and arbitrator behavior (some of which also employ a behavioral approach), see generally Rebecca Helm, Andrew J. Wistrich & Jeffrey J. Rachlinski, *Are Arbitrators Human?*, 13 J. EMPIRICAL LEGAL STUD. 666 (2016) (suggesting that "arbitrators lack an inherent advantage over judges when it comes to making high-quality decision."); Jeffrey J. Rachlinski, Andrew J. Wistrich & Chris Guthrie, *Can Judges Make Reliable Numeric Judgments? Distorted Damages and Skewed Sentences*, 90 IND. L.J. 695 (2015); Linda A. Berger, *A Revised View of the Judicial Hunch*, 10 LEGAL COMM. & RHETORIC 1, 17–18 (2013); Chris Guthrie, Jeffrey J. Rachlinski & Andrew J. Wistrich, *The "Hidden Judiciary": An Empirical Examination of Executive Branch Justice*, 58 DUKE L.J. 1477 (2009); Chris Guthrie, Jeffrey J. Rachlinski & Andrew J. Wistrich, *Blinking on the Bench: How Judges Decide Cases*, 93 CORNELL L. REV. 1 (2007); Andrew J. Wistrich, Chris Guthrie & Jeffrey J. Rachlinski, *Can Judges Ignore Inadmissible Information? The Difficulty of Deliberately Disregarding*, 153 U. PENN. L. REV. 1251 (2005); Chris Guthrie, Jeffrey J. Rachlinski & Andrew J. Wistrich, *Inside the Judicial Mind*, 86 CORNELL L. REV. 777 (2001).

[116] Amos Tversky & Daniel Kahneman, *Judgment Under Uncertainty: Heuristics and Biases*, 185 SCI. 1124 (1974) (explaining how the cognitive processes people use in making decisions are prone to errors).

[117] Bechara, *supra* note 16, at 76.

enhance your capacity to engage in decision-making.[118] Emotion that is unrelated can become a distraction.[119] Neuroscientific studies do not yet confirm, with a high degree of confidence, the various and important questions that follow this central claim, such as whether emotion is helpful or harmful in judicial decision-making. There are limitations we must acknowledge. The key is to recognize why, at the mechanism level, different outcomes are possible and to appreciate the importance of the complexities in our brains that allow for different outcomes. These important nuances aside, there is no basis at this time to suggest that judges or other adjudicators are cognitively exceptional and are therefore exempt from emotional influence in decision-making. This finding supports reevaluating how judges consider emotion in their judicial function, procedures a court adopts for judicial deliberation, and broader scholarship on judicial behavior.[120]

These two examples of how insights from neuroscience may inform areas of research in international criminal law and international judicial decision-making aim to illustrate the potential ways the two fields intersect. Because neuroscience studies brain activity, structure, and functions of individuals, its insights are most relevant for focusing on the individual person as the unit of study. Therefore, a neuro-international law agenda in this area should aim to study individual actors who make decisions important to international law. Future work might include evaluating decision-making by international judges and arbitrators, by political delegates at the United Nations Security Council, of CEO's of transnational corporations who inform international economic decisions, or heads-of-state who make important military and foreign policy decisions implicating international law. We might also consider using neuro-international law of individual decision-making to develop insights about how law will act upon people who are necessary for compliance. For example, international treaties that aim to address climate change and domestic regulations that aim to reduce carbon dioxide emissions may benefit from understanding how people decide whether to drive their cars or take public transportation and what factors shape such decisions.[121]

---

[118] *Id.* at 76–77.

[119] *Id. See also* Baba Shiv et al., *The Dark Side of Emotion in Decision-Making: When Individuals with Decreased Emotional Reactions Make More Advantageous Decisions*, 23 COGNITIVE BRAIN RES. 85 (2005).

[120] Spain Bradley, *supra* note 62.

[121] *See, e.g.*, Anna Spain, *Who's Going to Copenhagen?: The Rise of Civil Society in International Treaty-Making*, 13 ASIL INSIGHT (2009).

8.3.2.3 International Law and New Technology

8.3.2.3.1 BRAIN-COMPUTER INTERFACES AND MILITARY APPLICATIONS[122] New technology creates new circumstances that existing legal rules do not, yet, govern. In international law, regulating the behavior of how individuals and nations engage in the use of force remains a foundational aim. The advancement of military technologies in their capacity to perform functions previously performed by humans has raised important and complex questions for international lawyers. For example, even though the legality of the use of unmanned aerial vehicles, or drones, has been questioned, absent binding treaties, militaries continue to engage in these new ways of waging war.[123]

Today, brain-computer interfaces (BCI) exist that can translate the neural activity in our brains into technological inputs that machines and computers can process. The aspiration of such technologies is to enhance a person's cognitive abilities, such as memory, judgment, and risk assessment. Organizations, including the Defense Advanced Research Projects Agency (DARPA), are engaged in advanced technology development for military application, which may include BCI aspects.[124] For example, DARPA has funded research to link soldiers' brains to computers to enhance military capacity.[125] International legal scholars must develop the capacity to determine the legal and ethical implications of equipping military personnel with BCI binoculars, for example, capable of determining threats detected subconsciously. The future is open to such possibilities that may allow for neurocognitive advancements to be used in war and in illegal acts of

---

[122] Science, Technology, and Weaponization: Preliminary Observations, ARTICLE 36 (Nov. 2017), http://www.article36.org/wp-content/uploads/2017/11/Science-tech-and-weaponisation-preliminary-observations-FINAL-Nov17.pdf; NATIONAL RESEARCH COUNCIL, EMERGING COGNITIVE NEUROSCIENCE AND RELATED TECHNOLOGIES (2008); Ivan S. Kotchetkov et al., *Brain-Computer Interfaces: Military, Neurosurgical, and Ethical Perspective,* NEUROLOGICAL FOCUS E25 (2010); Michael N. Tennison & Jonathan D. Moreno, *Neuroscience, Ethics, and National Security: The State of the Art,* 10 PLOS BIOLOGY (2012); Patrick Lin, Maxwell J. Mehlman & Keith Abney, *Enhanced Warfighters: Risk, Ethics, and Policy,* 2013 CASE LEGAL STUD. RES. PAPER SERIES (2015).

[123] Rosa Ehrenreich Brooks, *Drones and the International Rule of Law,* 28 J. ETHICS & INT'L AFF. 83, 83 (2014) ("U.S. drone strikes represent a significant challenge to the international rule of law.").

[124] DEF. ADVANCED RES. PROJECTS AGENCY (DARPA), https://www.darpa.mil.

[125] Dr. Al Emondi, *Next-Generation Nonsurgical Neurotechnology,* DARPA, https://www.darpa.mil/program/next-generation-nonsurgical-neurotechnology ("To enable future non-invasive brain-machine interfaces, N3 researchers are working to develop solutions . . ."); Edd Gent, *The Government Is Serious About Creating Mind-Controlled Weapons,* LIVE SCI. (May 23, 2019), https://www.livescience.com/65546-darpa-mind-controlled-weapons.html.

aggression and terrorism. Neuroscience has advanced understandings of how our brains work making such a technology possible. Attempts to regulate brain-computer interfaces will require legal actors to be fully conversant in neuroscience in order to achieve their aims. As advancements are made on how to adapt nonhuman and partially human technology for use in war, neuroscience remains a key tool central to understanding human behavior.

8.3.2.3.2 ARTIFICIAL INTELLIGENCE AND ROBOTICS[126] Artificial intelligence (AI), when computers and other machines perform tasks that imitate human behavior, is a new area of technology that presents complexities for international law. We see AI running algorithms on Facebook that allow advertisers to target potential consumers based on preferences. AI also makes possible such advancements as Siri on our iPhones, Alexa on our Amazon Dots, and self-driving cars.[127] Due to the myriad ways AI does and will impact society, law and policy in this area are fast-developing.[128]

For legal scholars, one of the central questions in this area concerns how to assign liability to decisions and subsequent actions and harms caused by AI. These questions relate to the discussion above about the ways that legal doctrines in tort, contract, and criminal law approach mental states. A second area of interaction involves AI that create something entitled to intellectual property protections as a patent or copyrighted work.[129] These two examples have domestic and cross-border implications.

In the area of international law, additional questions about territoriality and jurisdiction will arise if an AI based in one nation can operate and cause legal harms in another nation. Awareness that AI can become weaponized or used as a tool to wage cyberwar, interfere in national elections, or hack into

[126] Rebecca Crootof, *The Killer Robots Are Here: Legal and Policy Implications*, 36 CARDOZO L. REV. 1837 (2015); Kenneth Anderson & Matthew Waxman, *Debating Autonomous Weapons Systems, Their Ethics, and Their Regulations Under International Law*, in THE OXFORD HANDBOOK OF LAW, REGULATION AND TECHNOLOGY 1097 (Roger Brownsword, Eloise Scotford & Karen Yeung eds., 2017); INT'L ASS'N ARTIFICIAL INTELLIGENCE & L., http://www.iaail.org.
[127] Robert L. Adams, *10 Powerful Examples of Artificial Intelligence in Use Today*, FORBES (Jan. 10, 2017), https://www.forbes.com/sites/robertadams/2017/01/10/10-powerful-examples-of-artificial-intelligence-in-use-today/%231c3cf940420d.
[128] INNOVATIVE GOVERNANCE MODELS FOR EMERGING TECHNOLOGIES (Gary E. Marchant, Kenneth W. Abbott & Braden Allenby eds., 2014).
[129] IEEE-USA, *Artificial Intelligence Research, Development and Regulation*, IEEE: GLOB. POL'Y (Feb. 10, 2017), http://globalpolicy.ieee.org/wp-content/uploads/2017/10/IEEE17003.pdf.

financial records is developing.[130] As with other new technologies, international law lacks an appropriate framework for dealing with illegal activity based on the use of AI because existing legal frameworks were established prior to the existence of AI. For example, Article 48 of the Additional Protocol to the 1949 Geneva Conventions, states that its international humanitarian law governs "the Parties to the conflict," which has generally been interpreted as applying only to humans.[131]

International law is only beginning to develop ideas about how to regulate and constrain nonhuman behavior that violates core legal rules, obligations, and norms. But understanding how AI is similar to and different from human intelligence will assist lawmakers in their task to regulate its use.[132] Thus, the more we know about our own cognitive capacities the better we can understand how AI operates. Advancing neuro-international law may prove useful in getting out ahead of the those employing such knowledge to the advancements of AI and robotic technology. In order to determine if and how an AI thinks, we must become expert at the possibilities of our own cognitive potential. This is where neuroscience holds both promise and peril. As we deepen our knowledge of how our brains operate, we can translate that knowledge to AI and robotics technologies in order to improve their capacities. What they might do with such expanded cognition, we can only imagine.

8.4 NORMATIVE DISCOURSES AND DIRECTIONS

International law's purpose and use is shifting in the twenty-first century. The world faces new threats to peace and security that the law has yet to adapt to, such as climate change, terrorism, cyberwarfare, and continued humanitarian crises that follow natural disasters and war. New actors beyond nations seek to have a role in shaping, applying, and interpreting the legal rules of the international order. Rising voices critique and expand the discourse about

---

[130] For a description of how AI can be hacked and used, see George Dvorsky, *Hackers Have Already Started to Weaponize Artificial Intelligence*, GIZMODO (Sept. 11, 2017), https://gizmodo.com/hackers-have-already-started-to-weaponize-artificial-in-1797688425.

[131] Protocol Additional to the Geneva Conventions of 12 August 1949 art. 48, Aug. 6, 1977, 1125 U. N.T.S. 3.

[132] JOHN P. HOLDREN & MEGHAN SMITH, NAT'L SCI. & TECH. COUNCIL, PREPARING FOR THE FUTURE OF ARTIFICIAL INTELLIGENCE, OBAMA WHITE HOUSE ARCHIVES (Oct. 12, 2016), https://obamawhitehouse.archives.gov/sites/default/files/whitehouse_files/microsites/ostp/NSTC/preparing_for_the_future_of_ai.pdf.; PETER STONE ET AL., ARTIFICIAL INTELLIGENCE AND LIFE IN 2030: ONE HUNDRED YEAR STUDY ON ARTIFICIAL INTELLIGENCE, STAN. U. (September 2016), http://ai100.stanford.edu/2016-report.

how international law works and who it should serve.[133] The common thread within international law amid such paradigmatic change is us – the human actors that create the rules and run the institutions that comprise the international legal system. Neuroscience helps explain human behavior in novel and groundbreaking ways in its capacity to explain what other research methodologies observe – the brain-based mechanisms behind reported human behavior.[134] Thus, just as neuroscience merged with law to produce neurolaw, a similar path is open for international law. But how might neuroscientific discoveries challenge or advance understandings not only about what international law is descriptively but what it ought to be normatively? This section considers two possibilities.

8.4.1 *Advancing Theory: Neuro-International Law and Individual Actors in International Law*

Some aspects of the international legal order remain as they have always been. Nations are still the dominant actors, using the tools of diplomacy, adjudication, and negotiation to conduct international affairs. But one significant change in the twenty-first century has been the rise of nonstate actors and their role in international law. Within this broadly defined group are the approximately 7.4 billion people who share our planet, who have increased capacity to communicate across borders due to new technology and who are demanding to be a part of international discourses that affect humanity.[135] This call for inclusion in international law can be seen in discrete moments, such as the United Nations Security Council's Landmark Resolution 1325 on Women, Peace and Security on the central role of women leadership in promoting peace; in broader movements, such as the proliferation of transitional justice in international criminal law; and in scholarly discourses about both.[136] Central to the inclusion of individuals in the international legal order

---

[133] *See infra* note 137. *See also* Makau Mutua & Antony Anghie, *What is TWAIL?* 94 PROC. ANN. MEETING (AM. SOC'Y INT'L L.) 31 (2000); Hillary Charlesworth Chinkin & Shelley Wright, *Feminist Approaches to International Law,* 85 AM. J. INT'L L. 613–645 (1991).

[134] Hafner-Burton, *supra* note 5.

[135] RUTI TEITEL, HUMANITY'S LAW 196 (2011) (calling for the "re-centering" of people and persons as the international subject).

[136] S.C. Res. 1325 (Oct. 31, 2000). *See also* Anne Marie Slaughter, *A Liberal Theory of International Law, in* FOUNDATIONS, *supra* note 2, at 95. *But see* Jose E. Alvarez, *Do Liberal States Behave Better? A Critique of Slaughter's Liberal Theory,* 12 EUR. J. INT'L L. 183 (2000); Jose E. Alvarez, *International Law: Comment, in* FOUNDATIONS, *supra* note 2, at 103 (advocating for more inclusive legal theories and identifying four assumptions about liberal theory that are divisive and may impede peace).

is a descriptively accurate understanding of them and their place in the broader framework of the field. In this light, advancements in the study of human behavior through neuroscience ought to inform theoretical and normative discourses about the future of international law. A starting point is to consider how existing theoretical frameworks in international law might account for individuals and where they don't.

Several areas of international legal theory hold particular salience for the integration of insights from neuro-international law because they concern how individuals think, feel, and behave. Critical international legal theory – from feminist theory, Third World Approaches to International Law, and New Approaches to International Law – are all rooted in a common mission to make international law more inclusive of diverse views and interests by dismantling the structural and endemic biases in the field.[137] International Legal Process theory, adapted from Henry Hart and Albert Sacks' American Legal Process theory, considers the behavior of people and how they make decisions as a vital component of a methodology about how to understand law and its purpose.[138] The project is to understand international law in relation to the decisions that shape it and the people who make such decisions.[139] The New Haven School defines law as a process of decision-making with the aim of human dignity.[140] Because this approach was designed to apply tools from social sciences, such as anthropology, to the study of who makes legal decisions and rules, it is well-suited to integrate insights from neuroscience. These theories and approaches concern not just what international law is but what it

[137] MAKAU W. MUTUA, HUMAN RIGHTS STANDARDS: HEGEMONY, LAW, AND POLITICS (2016); Adrien K. Wing, *Critical Race Feminism, in* THEORIES OF RACE AND ETHNICITY: CONTEMPORARY DEBATES AND PERSPECTIVES 162 (Karim Murji & John Solomos eds., 2015); David Kennedy, *The International Human Rights Regime: Still Part of the Problem?, in* EXAMINING CRITICAL PERSPECTIVES ON HUMAN RIGHTS 19 (Rob Dickinson et al. eds., 2012); JENNY S. MARTINEZ, THE SLADE TRADE AND THE ORIGINS OF INTERNATIONAL HUMAN RIGHTS LAW (2012); HENRY RICHARDSON III, THE ORIGINS OF AFRICAN AMERICAN INTERESTS IN INTERNATIONAL LAW (2008); ANTONY ANGHIE, IMPERIALISM, SOVEREIGNTY, AND THE MAKING OF INTERNATIONAL LAW (2005); BALAKRISHNAN RAJAGOPAL, INTERNATIONAL LAW FROM BELOW: DEVELOPMENT, SOCIAL MOVEMENTS AND THIRD WORLD RESISTANCE (2003); HILLARY CHARLESWORTH & CHRISTINE CHINKIN, THE BOUNDARIES OF INTERNATIONAL LAW: A FEMINIST ANALYSIS (2000).
[138] HENRY MELVIN HART ET AL., THE LEGAL PROCESS: BASIC PROBLEMS IN THE MAKING AND APPLICATION OF LAW (1995); Mary Ellen O'Connell, *New International Legal Process, in* FOUNDATIONS, *supra* note 2, at 191.
[139] ABRAM CHAYES, THOMAS EHRLICH & ANDREAS F. LOWENFELD, INTERNATIONAL LEGAL PROCESS: MATERIALS FOR AN INTRODUCTORY COURSE (1968).
[140] W. Michael Reisman, Siegfried Wiessner & Andrew R. Willard, *The New Haven School: A Brief Introduction*, 959 FAC. SCHOL. SERIES (2007).

should be and whom it serves. In doing this important work, international legal theorists ought to consider where and how their approaches reach individual behavior and how neuroscientific-based knowledge of such behavior might challenge or advance their theoretical perspectives.

8.4.2 *Challenging Assumptions: Discourses on Rationality*

A second area of normative discourse concerns how neuroscience may challenge core assumptions embedded in the foundations of the theory and practice of international law. One such assumption throughout legal history has been the view that humans are capable of behaving rationally. English philosopher John Locke espoused that humans are endowed by God with a "faculty of reason."[141] In Locke's view, people are both aware of their self-interests and are motivated by such in decision-making. This foundational concept prevailed in economic rational-choice theory that, in turn, influenced theories about government decision-making.[142] Max Weber declared that the modern state is the "rational state" based on "rational law."[143] Work by international relations scholars like Thomas Schelling, among others, solidified this view in understanding international strategy.[144] The classic example is the Prisoner's Dilemma in game theory, which provides a paradigm for predicting the future behavior of two actors based on self-interest, cooperation, and failure to cooperate.[145] This framework assumes that humans operate as rational actors motivated by reason and self-interest.

In international legal scholarship, some scholars believe that rational choice theory is the best methodological tool for understanding and predicting

---

[141] John Locke, Second Treatise of Government (C. B. McPherson ed., 1980) (1689).
[142] Jack L. Goldsmith & Eric A. Posner, The Limits of International Law (2005); Joel P. Trachtman, The Economic Structure of International Law (2008); Andrew Guzman, How International Law Works: A Rational Choice Theory (2008); Graham Allison & Philip Zelikow, Essence of Decision: Explaining the Cuban Missile Crisis 28–29 (2d ed. 1971) (identifying the "anthropomorphic fallacy" in policy analysis that assumes the government produces decisions as a unitary, rational thinker).
[143] Max Weber, Wirtschaftsgeschichte 289–290 (1923).
[144] *See* Thomas C. Schelling, The Strategy of Conflict 3–5 (1980) (discussing how the theory of strategy assumes rationality when analyzing government actions); Kenneth W. Abbott, *Modern International Relations Theory: A Prospectus for International Lawyers*, 14 Yale J. Int'l L. 355, 405–406 (1989) (using rational choice theory to explain state behavior in international relations).
[145] William Poundstone, Prisoner's Dilemma 8–9 (1992) (describing the Prisoner's Dilemma).

state behavior.[146] Posner and Goldsmith, for example, argue that "[i]nterna-
tional law emerges from states acting rationally to maximize their interests,
given their perceptions of the interests of other states and the distribution of
state power."[147] Interest-based theories of state behavior, such as realism,
institutionalism, and liberal theory, have helped perpetuate the assumption
that nations and the people that act for them are guided by rational, self-
interested behavior.[148] The rational-actor view of the world has had significant
and long-standing influence over law, economics, international relations, and
other fields.[149]

These theories of international law are built upon assumptions about how
people behave as a descriptive matter. Such description rests on views about
what kinds of human behavior are possible. For example, if international legal
theory treats the decisions made by people acting on behalf of states as being
devoid of emotion, that theory rests on an assumed truth that people are
capable of putting their emotions aside when making choices.

Yet findings in neuroscience are challenging this view by providing evidence to the contrary. Humans have complex neurological processes that

[146] *See, e.g.,* TRACHTMAN, *supra* note 142, at 128 (acknowledging that a rational state would
abandon a treaty if its benefit from doing so was greater than its benefit from adherence);
Anne van Aaken, *Making International Human Rights Protection More Effective: A Rational-
Choice Approach to the Effectiveness of Ius Standi Provisions,* MPI COLLECTIVE GOODS
PREPRINT (2005) (applying the "rational-choice approach" to analyze the effectiveness
behind individual complain mechanisms in international human rights bodies); Edward
T. Swaine, *Rational Custom,* 52 DUKE L.J. 559 (2002) (arguing why rational choice analysis is
helpful in analyzing state behavior regarding customary international law); GUZMAN, *supra*
note 142 (providing a comprehensive treatment of rational choice theory in international law
and in international relations). For an apt description of what rational choice theory means in
the context of international law, see Robert O. Keohane, *Rational Choice Theory and
International Law: Insights and Limitations,* 31 J. LEGAL STUD. S307 (2002).
[147] GOLDSMITH & POSNER, *supra* note 142, at 3.
[148] FOUNDATIONS, *supra* note 2, at 26.
[149] Scholarship on government decision-making is heavily influenced by rational choice theory.
See PAUL BREST & LINDA H. KRIEGER, PROBLEM SOLVING, DECISION MAKING, AND
PROFESSIONAL JUDGMENT: A GUIDE FOR LAWYERS AND POLICYMAKERS 366 (2010)
("People are in principle capable of pursuing their ends – whatever they may be – in
a rational manner."); ALEX MINTZ & CARLY WAYNE, THE POLYTHINK SYNDROME:
U.S. FOREIGN POLICY DECISIONS ON 9/11, at 3 (2016) (describing ways in which "rational
decision makers engage in flawed decision making process that deeply affect the security and
welfare of a country"). *But see* Gregory M. Herek, Irving L. Janis & Paul Huth, *Decision
Making During International Crises: Is Quality of Process Related to Outcome?,* 31
J. CONFLICT RESOL. 203–204 (1987) (explaining why rational choice theory is descriptively
and normatively inadequate for improving the quality of decisions); Jide O. Nzelibe &
John Yoo, *Rational War and Constitutional Design,* 115 YALE L.J. 2512 (2006). *But see* Paul
F. Diehl & Tom Ginsburg, *Irrational War and Constitutional Design: A Reply to Professors
Nzelibe and Yoo,* 27 MICH. J. INT'L L. 1239 (2006).

produce a result we might deem choice, judgment, or decision-making. The processes in our brains that operate to engage in logical reasoning can interact with those that process emotion in ways that influence each other and impact our choices.[150] Emotion influences capacities for reasoning and logic in both positive and negative ways, likely due to the interplay between neural areas involved with working memory and deductive reasoning.[151] Emotion that is related to what you are deciding can benefit your decision-making cognition, whereas emotion that is unrelated can become a distraction.[152] The central insight from research in affective neuroscience is that emotion is integral to decision-making.[153]

These important insights help to explain the basis behind some of the recognized problems with using rationality as a descriptive model of human behavior.[154] By showing that neural processes for logical reasoning and emotion intersect and interact in our brains, neuroscience provides evidence that refutes the rationality premise upon which many international legal theories stand.[155]

---

[150] *See* Antonio Damasio & Gil B. Carvalho, *The Nature of Feelings: Evolutionary and Neurobiological Origins*, 14 NATURE REV. NEUROSCI. 14 (2013) (arguing that emotions are the foundation for the evolution of human consciousness); Antoine Bechara et al., *Different Contributions of the Human Amygdala and Ventromedial Prefrontal Cortex to Decision-Making*, 19 J. NEUROSCI. 5473 (1999) (discussing how the ventromedial prefrontal cortex and the amygdala affect different processes).

[151] Isabelle Blanchette & Anne Richards, *Anxiety and the Interpretation of Ambiguous Information: Beyond the Emotion-Congruent Effect*, 132 J. EXPERIMENTAL PSYCHOL. 294, 301, 303 (2003) ("[A]nxiety leads to task irrelevant processing of affective information that depletes resources available for primary task"); *id.* at 301 ("Emotion (heighted affect) seems to negatively impair logical reasoning (affective state, trait and contents) with anxiety and depression negatively affecting verbal reasoning").

[152] *Id.* at 304–308 (concluding that "[e]motion can both enhance and impair normatively correct responses" and may improve ability to adapt responses.").

[153] Bechara, *supra* note 16, at 76.

[154] *See* Cass R. Sunstein & Richard H. Thaler, *Libertarian Paternalism Is Not an Oxymoron*, 70 U. CHI. L. REV. 1159, 1167–1170 (2003) (providing evidence that humans will commonly make decisions contrary to their own interests); OREN BAR-GILL, SEDUCTION BY CONTRACT: LAW, ECONOMICS, AND PSYCHOLOGY IN CONSUMER MARKETS 2 (2012); GEORGE A. AKERLOF & ROBERT J. SHILLER, PHISHING FOR PHOOLS: THE ECONOMICS OF MANIPULATION AND DECEPTION 6–7 (2015) (explaining how marketers use well known psychological principles to encourage customers to make purchases contrary to their best interests).

[155] Herek, Janis & Huth, *supra* note 149, at 204 (explaining why rational choice theory is descriptively and normatively inadequate for improving the quality of decisions); Amos Tversky & Daniel Kahneman, *Judgment Under Uncertainty: Heuristics and Biases, in* JUDGMENT UNDER UNCERTAINTY: HEURISTICS AND BIASES 3 (Daniel Kahneman, Paul Slovic & Amos Tversky eds., 1982) (explaining that the processes that individuals use to make decisions can sometimes lead to "severe and systematic errors").

8.5 CONCLUSION

In the twenty-first century, the challenges that international law will have to address demand that law motivates and constrains not just nations, but also people. The project of understanding international law as human behavior plays a vital part in this initiative. Neuroscience can and should play a central role therein. In pursuit of that aim, this chapter has presented the first comprehensive treatment of considering if and how to advance the study of neuro-international law. It also acknowledges that much work remains. Neuroscience reveals knowledge about brain-based mechanisms for human behavior that contribute to the rich, existing work in behavioral and social sciences as well as offer new insights. Beyond neuroscience, international legal scholars should investigate how findings in evolutionary biology and genetics also contribute to understanding human behavior in essential ways. Reconciling these different realms of knowledge will require integrating the people who hold such knowledge.[156] Interdisciplinary work can be fraught with institutional and interpersonal challenges but it is necessary for the comprehensive study of human behavior. Ultimately, such knowledge will enrich all who seek to understand humanity's place in the world.

---

[156] *See, e.g.*, White House Nat'l Sci. & Tech. Council Interagency Working Grp. Neurosci., *Priorities for Accelerating Neuroscience Research Through Enhanced Communication, Coordination, and Collaboration*, OBAMA WHITE HOUSE ARCHIVES (Feb. 21, 2014) http s://obamawhitehouse.archives.gov/sites/default/files/microsites/ostp/NSTC/accelerating_neuroscience_research_-_feb_2014.pdf.

9

The Missing Persons of International Law Scholarship

A Roadmap for Future Research

Tamar Megiddo[1]

"The society of states . . . is the most comprehensive form of society among men, but it is among men that it exists. States are its immediate, men its ultimate members. The duties and rights of States are only the duties and rights of the men that compose them."[2]

***

Interdisciplinary research of international law has been on the rise in the past two and half decades. As the collection of chapters encased in this volume indicate, scholars have adopted widely varying disciplines, methodologies, and theoretical frameworks to investigate international legal behavior. This chapter argues, however, that a lion's share of the literature on international legal behavior has understated the role of individual people in international law.

Although probably any scholar working in the field of international law would agree that international law is made, implemented, changed, or broken by people, this ontological insight has not found its way into influential paradigmatic views of international law. Consequently, it has not been adequately embedded in methodologies, theoretical accounts, and research agendas.

This may seem like a sweeping claim. One might be tempted to challenge it with examples of academic writing speaking particularly about individual people – activists in nongovernmental organizations (NGOs), domestic

[1] I thank Harlan Cohen for welcoming my unsolicited intrusion into the book workshop at Tillar House and for enlightening conversations since. I am also grateful to Tim Meyer for excellent comments on an early draft and to Eyal Benvenisti, Tomer Broude, Robert Howse, Yael Lifshitz, Mor Mitrani and Jeremy Waldron for their comments on previous versions of this paper. All errors are mine.
[2] JOHN WESTLAKE, THE COLLECTED PAPERS OF JOHN WESTLAKE ON PUBLIC INTERNATIONAL LAW 78 (1914).

judges, central bankers – who work to impact their states to comply with international legal obligations. One might be tempted, further, to point to approaches to international law research which view domestic politics as influential in shaping a state's international behavior. I recognize these works and endorse their importance, but argue that in this literature, too, there is still implicit the same paradigmatic vision that dominates the field. This vision is sometimes made explicit, but is often just assumed. According to this vision, states are the sole, or the primary actors of importance in the international legal system. Against this background, those disaggregationist theories which study individuals often study these individuals *as a means* for studying states. And those theories which place their trust with domestic politics still do so *as a means* for understanding state behavior. Both, thus, endorse, rather than challenge the paradigmatic statist view. Statism is thus more, not less prevalent in the literature than commonly considered.

This chapter's argument is therefore that future interdisciplinary work of international law would benefit from ridding itself of the dominance of paradigmatic statism. Instead, we must recognize the central role of individuals in the everyday practice of international law: not only their impact on their state's behavior, but also their engagement with international law and their potential influence outside and irrespective of their state.

The chapter does not develop a full theory about the role of individuals in international law. Rather, it offers a review of the scholarship, aiming to substantiate its critical claim while also pointing to some implications of the literature's entrenched statism, and thus to benefits likely to arise from forsaking it. Since the literature is extremely vast, the survey aims to be illustrative rather than comprehensive. The review lays the ground for further work developing a new paradigm more attentive to individuals.[3]

One corollary of the literature's statism is that the dialogical nature of the international legal system has not been adequately recognized. Some approaches to international law stress its hierarchical, top-down nature while others emphasize a bottom-up reading of it, but few recognize a reciprocal relationship of influence between international law and its community of practice. As I discuss in the chapter, much constructivist analysis, which would have been expected to do so, has not so far delivered on this potential. This, too, is a result of the statism that limits influential constructivists' definition of international law's community of practice to states.

---

[3]   *See* Tamar Megiddo, *The Everyday Life of International Law: How International Law Is Practiced Within States* (2016) (unpublished JSD dissertation, New York University).

State centricity has several implications. Chief amongst which are the literature's excessive occupation with questions of compliance with international law, and its discounting of how law might serve as a potential explanatory paradigm for international legal behavior. Both, I argue, could be corrected if the literature abandoned its paradigmatic statism.

I recognize that this proposed reading of the literature is not the common reading. I submit that this is part of the problem. Widely recognized works are often filed in collective memory as making claims that they do not actually make or as reflecting views that are unsupported by their texts. If my criticism seems unfair at first blush, I urge the reader to suspend the intuitive objection and consider the following: I recognize that many of the authors whose work I review below might agree with the plea of this chapter, and, if asked, would endorse the importance of recognizing the role of individuals in the practice of international law. My argument is not that existing literature is wrong. It is further not that (all of) the existing literature is in contradiction with the proposal that we should recenter our focus to individual people. My critique is that the literature has not embraced these views; that it has not anchored the role of people in paradigmatic outlooks about international law; that it, perhaps unknowingly and often only implicitly, continues to maintain a commitment to statism. And my argument is that relieving the literature of this commitment would be enlightening and helpful, and might reveal new and promising research agendas. In that, the chapter hopes to add to the existing literature on international law, rather than detract from it.

Section 9.1 of the chapter presents a critical review of the scholarship's statism. Section 9.2 discusses its implications. Section 9.3 then uses the United States case of the Torture Memos as a means to demonstrate the pitfalls of the literature's present limitations and the potential benefits of stirring away from them and toward greater recognition of the role of individuals in the life of international law. Section 9.4 concludes.

9.1 WHERE'S WALDO? THE MISSING PERSONS OF INTERNATIONAL LAW SCHOLARSHIP

Interdisciplinary scholarship about international law and behavior in its context has been on the rise in the past few decades. This literature borrows extensively, and increasingly, from the social sciences. Much of the time, such borrowed theories, originally constructed to apply to natural persons living in a social context made up by other people, are applied wholesale to international relations and to the international legal system, with states replacing people as the researcher's unit of analysis. In this sense, international law scholarship is still dominated by a vision which champions states as international law's sole, or principal actors. A possible, I would argue a necessary, alternative would be to apply insights from the study of people in (domestic) society to the study of people in global society.

For many scholars, statism is a methodological choice rather than a genuine blind spot. As I now show, however, this choice is more common than regularly thought and characterizes scholars with widely differing theoretical approaches. While some scholars make explicit their methodological choice to focus exclusively on states, the choice of others is implicit in their choice to confine their research to the international level of analysis, where they study states as primary, if not exclusive actors. There are, of course, scholars whose primary object of research are individuals and their actions in the context of international law. However, as this review shows, many of these still limit their exploration to particular kinds of individual actors, or study individuals primarily as a means to understand state action in the context of international law. In the latter case, individuals are studied as proxies for states rather than as actors in their own right. In the former, only some individual actors are taken into account while others are overlooked. In both, the greater point, that individuals – broadly speaking – participate in the everyday practice of international law, is missed.

The oft-referenced "two-level game" metaphor[4] entails scholars' division of the international social and legal system into two separate spheres: national and international. One problem with such compartmentalizing is the consequent disregard of the fluidity and interconnectedness between the levels. A silencing of the role of individual people in the international level naturally follows. Granted, states are a crucially important locus for human interaction, and state actions are the product of domestic processes of negotiation and deliberation between individuals and groups. But individuals and groups also operate transnationally, in different states, as well as in the international legal system independently of their states. Failing to recognize this activity leads to an unsatisfactory understanding of the phenomenon of international law. Further, substate actors and nonstate actors, generally, are influenced by norms, ideas, and practices that derive from the international level and from interstate dynamics. A denial of the relevance of international law to domestic dynamics and vice versa creates a myopic scholarship blind to crucial occurrences that embody the everyday practice, interpretation, implementation, or breaking of international law by people.

---

[4]   Robert D. Putnam, *Diplomacy and Domestic Politics: The Logic of Two-Level Games*, 42 INT'L ORG. 427 (1988).

Another problem with compartmentalization is that law is essentially a human business; law interacts with people, rather than states, and international law must similarly be understood as interacting with and as constructed by people.[5] Discounting the influence of individual people on and in international law limits our understanding of international law's reach and scope, possible meanings and consequences, and how it actually operates.

The scholarship's statism and prevalent compartmentalization could be attributed, at least in part, to a general phenomenon characteristic of interdisciplinary research of international law. While lawyers have, for the past two and a half decades, joined hands with scholars from many different fields in the study of international law, for the most part these collaborations have adopted the perspectives and methodologies of extralegal disciplines.[6] The academic research of international law as a sociopolitical phenomenon has been particularly dominated by the perspective of International Relations (IR) scholars and IR, by definition, studies the relations between states. One could, perhaps justifiably, protest that IR scholars could hardly be blamed for disregarding substate dynamics or for underplaying the role of law: they make no presumption to account for these. Their premise is that states are identified as composing the particular society in which international law operates and as the relevant units of analysis. It is thus not unreasonable for IR scholars to focus on the relations between states and dedicate less attention to intrastate politics or to nonstate actors. IR is further a science of politics and its disinterest or underappreciation of law is likewise understandable.

Yet, as Jeffrey Dunoff and Mark Pollack argue, academic research of international law will benefit from a greater intellectual balance between the disciplines.[7] Another core theme of this chapter is therefore to urge a return to law as both an object of study and an explanatory paradigm. Its point, however, is not to show that multidisciplinary research into international law is wrong or a bad choice; quite the contrary. Instead, the chapter shines a light on angles that interdisciplinary work has neglected in order to identify those pitfalls it should avoid and set out a roadmap for a future interdisciplinary

---

[5]   *See, e.g.,* JULIUS STONE, VISIONS OF WORLD ORDER 10 (1984) (arguing that "international law is homocentric law, to be studied as such.").

[6]   *See, e.g.,* Jeffrey L. Dunoff & Mark A. Pollack, *International Law and International Relations, in* INTERDISCIPLINARY PERSPECTIVES ON INTERNATIONAL LAW AND INTERNATIONAL RELATIONS 3, 10 (Jeffrey L. Dunoff & Mark A. Pollack eds., 2013) [hereinafter INTERDISCIPLINARY PERSPECTIVES] ("[T]he intellectual terms of trade have been highly unequal, consisting primarily of the application of the theories and methods of political theory as a discipline to the study of international law as a subject.").

[7]   Jeffrey L. Dunoff & Mark A. Pollack, *Reviewing Two Decades of IL/IR Scholarship, in* INTERDISCIPLINARY PERSPECTIVES, *supra* note 6, at 626, 627, 649–653.

research of international law that is more attentive to people, to processes and to law.

***

For scholars working with a realist approach, a focus on states is a core tenet and a central assumption.[8] States are further assumed to be unitary actors, their internal dynamics irrelevant for the study of their behavior internationally.[9] This does not mean that scholars deny, for instance, that people act on behalf of states. Even Hans Morgenthau, a prominent realist, speaks of statesmen as those navigating states,[10] and acknowledges that they may have freestanding motives or ideological preferences, and that they may act irrationally. But he thinks that researching those is "futile and deceptive" for they are illusive and easily distorted, and cannot be shown to correlate with foreign policies.[11] He presumes, instead, that statesmen will distinguish between their "'official duty', which is to think and act in terms of the national interest, and their 'personal wish', which is to see their own moral values and political principles realized throughout the world."[12] Kenneth Waltz stresses that a theory should be evaluated in terms of what it claims to explain. While he is willing to "freely admit" that states are not in fact unitary, purposive actors, he defends the assumption that they are as useful in explaining international politics, and in particular, his theory of balance-of-power.[13]

These assumptions extend to realist-flavored accounts dealing more specifically with international law. Jack Goldsmith and Eric Posner, for instance, define the state as the lead actor in their theory of international law and assume that it acts rationally to maximize its interests. While they do take

---

[8]   Richard H. Steinberg, *Wanted – Dead or Alive: Realism in International Law*, in INTERDISCIPLINARY PERSPECTIVES, *supra* note 6, at 146, 148; *see also* EDWARD HALLETT CARR, THE TWENTY YEARS' CRISIS, 1919–1939, at 290–293 (1964); HANS J. MORGENTHAU, POLITICS AMONG NATIONS 4–12 (Kenneth W. Thompson ed., 1985); KENNETH WALTZ, THEORY OF INTERNATIONAL RELATIONS 88, 94 (1979); John J. Mearsheimer, *The False Promise of International Institutions*, 19 INT'L SEC. 5, 10–13 (1994); JACK L. GOLDSMITH & ERIC A. POSNER, THE LIMITS OF INTERNATIONAL LAW 4 (2005).
[9]   WALTZ, *supra* note 8, at 118.
[10] *See* GOLDSMITH & POSNER, *supra* note 8, at 7.
[11] MORGENTHAU, *supra* note 8, at 5–6.
[12] *Id.* at 7 (Morgenthau insists that "a theory of foreign policy which aims at rationality must … abstract from these irrational elements and seek to paint a picture of foreign policy which presents the rational essence to be found in experience, without the contingent deviations from rationality which are also found in experience."); *see also id.* at 10 ("Political realism presents the theoretical construct of a rational foreign policy which experience can never completely achieve.").
[13] WALTZ, *supra* note 8, at 118–119.

the interests of certain individuals into account – political leaders – they
equate them with those interests of the state and use them as proxies to explain
state action.[14] Again, this is explained to be a methodological choice aimed
at achieving nuanced explanations of state behavior related to international
law.[15]

Richard Steinberg similarly defends the realist assumption of the state as
a central actor. Steinberg acknowledges that one limitation of realism is that
it offers no explanation for how state interests are defined or why they are
changed.[16] While he recognizes that individuals interact with international
law, including, for instance, judges interpreting and applying international
norms, he denies that they are able to make a significant impact on international law and politics.[17] Furthermore, Steinberg claims that efforts to construct meta-theories that will encompass all levels of analysis have been
unsuccessful.[18] He is willing to entertain the merits of hybrid models where
realism serves to explain state behavior and other theories, such as liberalism,
explain the formulation of its preferences. However, he argues that they are
useful only providing that the state remains the central actor; in other words,
that they maintain realist theoretical commitments – statism and a two-level
game paradigm.[19]

Statism is by no means limited to realists. As Barbara Koremenos explains,
authors working with institutionalist assumptions also identify states as central
actors and are agnostic to domestic dynamics and to how or why states
formulate their preferences.[20] While institutionalism is not at odds with the
liberal theories that do study the domestic arena, she explains, institutionalists
consider some of liberalism's assumptions to be "irrelevant."[21] The two
approaches are deemed to address "two distinct sets of questions," with

[14] GOLDSMITH & POSNER, *supra* note 8, at 4–6.
[15] *Id.* at 6–7.
[16] Steinberg, *supra* note 8, at 166; *see also* ANDREW T. GUZMAN, HOW INTERNATIONAL LAW WORKS: A RATIONAL CHOICE THEORY 17 (2008).
[17] Steinberg, *supra* note 8, at 162 ("Realists do not believe that judicial interpretation of international law can fundamentally shift the balance of rights and responsibilities established
through the law-making process because judicial interpretation of international legal commitments is constrained and determined by international politics … interpretation replicates
power.").
[18] *Id.* at 155.
[19] *Id.* at 158, 160.
[20] Barbara Koremenos, *Institutionalism and International Law, in* INTERDISCIPLINARY
PERSPECTIVES, *supra* note 6, at 59, 69, 74; *see also* ROBERT O. KEOHANE, AFTER
HEGEMONY 245 (1984); ABRAM CHAYES & ANTONIA HANDLER CHAYES, THE NEW
SOVEREIGNTY 27 (1995).
[21] Koremenos, *supra* note 20, at 69.

liberalism exploring states' formation of preferences while institutionalism assumes that states have "a set of given preferences, taking these as the starting point."[22]

What is perhaps more surprising is that prominent constructivist theorists also share this statism.[23] Constructivists "focus attention upon the role that culture, ideas, institutions, discourse, and social norms play in shaping identity and influencing behavior."[24] When applied to individuals in society, constructivism explains how one is shaped by her surrounding social context. Even if applied to states as primary actors, one would expect that in addition to investigating states' construction by international society and their peers at the international level, such theories would also bring into the mix those processes that occur within states, since these can also potentially contribute to constructing both states and international reality.

However, influential constructivist accounts too choose to maintain a theoretical commitment to viewing states as the sole appropriate actor of interest. Alexander Wendt explicitly states that he shares the realist assumptions, including a "commitment to states as units of analysis."[25] John Ruggie seeks to "problematize the identities and interests of states and to show how they have been socially constructed,"[26] but rejects the neoliberal turn to domestic politics for doing so, and instead emphasizes the role of international (namely, interstate) interaction in generating state identity.[27] Hedley Bull, too, centered on states as the central units of interest in his vision of *The Anarchical Society*.[28]

This choice of limiting one's attention to states is not the sole purview of constructivist IR scholars. It is also found in accounts proposed by lawyers or by interdisciplinary coauthors inspired by constructivism. Ryan Goodman and Derek Jinks,[29] for instance, make clear that states are their primary target of interest.[30]

---

[22]   *Id.* at 69.

[23]   Alexander Wendt, *Constructing International Politics*, 20 INT'L SEC. 71, 72 (1995); John Gerard Ruggie, *What Makes the World Hang Together? Neo-Utilitarianism and the Social Constructivist Challenge*, 52 INT'L ORG. 855, 879 (1998).

[24]   Jutta Brunnée & Stephen J. Toope, *Constructivism and International Law*, in INTERDISCIPLINARY PERSPECTIVES, *supra* note 6, at 119, 121.

[25]   Wendt, *supra* note 23, at 72.

[26]   Ruggie, *supra* note 23, at 879.

[27]   *Id.* at 879. *But see, e.g.*, MARGARET E. KECK & KATHRYN SIKKINK, ACTIVISTS BEYOND BORDERS 2–3, 29–32 (1998); Martha Finnemore & Kathryn Sikkink, *International Norm Dynamics and Political Change*, 52 INT'L ORG. 887, 896 (1998) (discussing "norm entrepreneurs").

[28]   HEDLEY BULL, THE ANARCHICAL SOCIETY 44–49 (2002).

[29]   RYAN GOODMAN & DEREK JINKS, SOCIALIZING STATES (2013).

[30]   *Id.* at 39.

Although they express their appreciation of the importance of the substate level,[31] the theoretical account they propose nevertheless allocates little theoretical weight to individuals or to substate dynamics. On their account, individuals are merely agents of states, and moreover they are mere receptors of exogenous input.[32] Individuals' influence is limited in this model to serving as the axis through which international law influences states.

There are exceptions to this statist streak in the literature: accounts that have theorized the role of sub- and nonstate actors in shaping their own states' policies and even the international legal system more generally. These theories are some-times collectively referred to as "disaggregationist."[33] They explore the actions of groups, organizations, and individuals, or coalitions of such actors in international law and in international politics.[34] Disaggregationist scholars normally work with liberal or constructivist theoretical approaches. They may emphasize, for instance, as Charles Kegley does, that state motives and interests may change;[35] or study, like Anne-Marie Slaughter, Beth Simmons, or Martha Finnemore and Kathryn Sikkink, the various courses of actions taken by government officials and NGO activists in order to apply pressure on governments to change their policies and comply with international norms.[36] These scholars have also investigated transna-tional epistemic communities in which officials and nonofficials liaise and collaborate with peers in other countries to further compliance with international norms.[37] Further, it has been argued that these actors consequently generate effects not only in their own states,[38] but also transnationally and internationally.[39]

---

[31]   *Id.* at 9 (proclaiming the authors' intention to ultimately develop a theory that "takes both social structure and agency seriously," and that leaves room for what they call the micro-level, *id.* at 13, 40).

[32]   *Id.* at 40–41.

[33]   José E. Alvarez, International Organizations as Law-Makers 32 (2005).

[34]   Anne-Marie Slaughter, *International Law in a World of Liberal States*, 6 Eur. J. Int'l L. 503, 508 (1995); Andrew Moravcsik, *Liberal Theories of International Law*, *in* Interdisciplinary Perspectives, *supra* note 6, at 83, 83, 87–88; Keck & Sikkink, *supra* note 27; Finnemore & Sikkink, *supra* note 27, at 896–898.

[35]   Charles W. Kegley Jr., *The Neoidealist Moment in International Studies?*, 37 Int'l Stud. Q. 131, 137 (1993).

[36]   Slaughter, *supra* note 34, at 518–528; Beth A. Simmons, Mobilizing for Human Rights 126–148 (2009); Finnemore & Sikkink, *supra* note 27, at 896–898.

[37]   *See, e.g.*, Harold K. Jacobson & Edith Brown Weiss, *Strengthening Compliance with International Environmental Accords*, 1 Glob. Gov. 119, 142–143 (1995); Slaughter, *supra* note 34, at 518–528; Emanuel Adler, *Constructivism and International Relations*, *in* Handbook of International Relations, 104, 109–10 (Walter Carlsnaes, Thomas Risse & Beth Simmons eds., 2002); Keck & Sikkink, *supra* note 27, at 2–3, 16–25, 29, 209–214; Simmons, *supra* note 36, at 128, 131; Moravcsik, *supra* note 34, at 86.

[38]   Simmons, *supra* note 36, at 126–148.

[39]   Moravcsik, *supra* note 34, at 83, 86.

One could argue (and some have)[40] that statism and disaggregationism complement each other; that each deals with a distinct set of questions; that no one theory can do the entire explanatory work of accounting for the whole of international law's life both domestically and internationally; that it makes sense to make different methodological choices for different kinds of actors, practices, and dynamics. This is the argument which supports endorsing a "two-level game" paradigm.

This chapter challenges this argument. It challenges it because such compartmentalization is statism in disguise. Its upshot is the acceptance of having two sets of approaches for two separate fora. But accepting as a premise that there exists such separation between the domestic and the international levels blinds us to realities that defy it. Erecting an imaginary wall between the domestic sphere and the international sphere has a price. It restricts and decontextualizes our understanding of occurrences in each space. It limits our theoretical imagination and our ability to identify, theorize, and conceptualize action that is unencumbered by this alleged barrier. It hampers our ability to recognize the constant dialogue between the domestic, the transnational, and the international.

As Andrew Moravcsik explains, "the critical quality of liberal theories is . . . that they are 'bottom-up'":[41] states and international law are perceived to be influenced and shaped by actions of domestic and transnational actors. However, as Moravcsik concedes, liberal theories can only serve as a "first stage," explaining only the distribution of states' underlying preferences but not their choice of specific legal norms or international law's compliance pull, tasks that such scholars hand off to other theories.[42]

Constructivist scholars, however, place primary emphasis on dialogue and two-way interactions: bottom-up as well as top-down.[43] Such theories explore the reciprocity and mutual construction that occur in the international legal

---

[40]   Koremenos, *supra* note 20, at 69.

[41]   Moravcsik, *supra* note 34, at 87.

[42]   *Id.* at 91. Moravcsik qualifies this statement by claiming that liberal theory does address international law's normativity to the extent that they relate to the influence of individuals and groups on state preferences, given that international norms often directly regulate or empower such actors or are internalized and enforced domestically. *Id.* at 92–96. This echoes Goodman and Jinks's vision of people serving as an axis through which international law influences states and is compatible with liberals' ultimate interest in explaining state action, as seen in GOODMAN & JINKS, *supra* note 29, at 40–41.

[43]   Excluding some constructivist accounts that seem to assume that law is largely hierarchical and "authority" based (that is, top-down), see Brunnée & Toope, *supra* note 24, at 127, for Brunnée & Toope's analysis of Onuf and Kartochwil.

system in interaction with and among its community members.[44] Nonetheless, the promise of this scholarship is constrained by the persistent statism of influential accounts.

A new paradigm is past due for the research of international law. One that not only accounts for both levels of the game, but which denies the division of our world into such separate compartments. One that collapses the wall between the levels and replaces it with a new attention for interaction between the multiple, overlapping spheres of human action: the domestic, the transnational, the international, the global. One that acknowledges the role that people, generally speaking, play in making, interpreting, challenging, implementing, and breaking international law. One that realizes that the ordinary actions of ordinary people operating in these various spheres are the building blocks of the everyday life of international law and should be reflected in academic writing. The time is ripe to topple the paradigmatic wall between the so-called domestic and international levels and recognize that there is only one game, and that it consists not of two, but of one complex, multilayered universe which individuals and other nonstate actors cohabit alongside states and which international law permeates.

Such a paradigmatic outlook would encourage widening the focus of scholarly research to include more than only certain kinds of actors. In this respect, scholars working with a disaggregationist approach have too often confined their work to a limited cache of individual actors – state officials, such as judges[45] or central bankers,[46] or NGO activists[47] – and have refrained from meaningfully evaluating the role of individuals outside those few recognized influential elites. Only a handful of scholars have, in various ways, directed attention to individuals outside such "immediate suspects." Simmons as well as Jutta Brunnée and Stephen Toope have discussed political mobilization and the role of "ordinary" citizens in generating state behavior.[48]

---

[44]   *Id.* at 123–127, 132–134. *See also* Keck and Sikkink, *supra* note 27, at 1–3, 7, 213.

[45]   For example, Eyal Benvenisti & George W. Downs, *National Courts, Domestic Democracy, and the Evolution of International Law*, 9 Eur. J. Int'l L. 59 (2009).

[46]   Michael S. Barr & Geoffrey P. Miller, *Global Administrative Law: The View from Basel*, 17 Eur. J. Int'l L. 15 (2006).

[47]   Keck & Sikkink, *supra* note 27.

[48]   *See* Simmons, *supra* note 36, at 136–148 (discussing political mobilization as one mechanism by which state behavior may be influenced by domestic processes); Sally Engle Merry, Human Rights and Gender Violence: Translating International Law into Local Justice 192–217 (2009) (describing local activists' efforts to mobilize individuals by offering human rights consciousness as a tool for remedying grievances); Jutta Brunnée & Stephen J. Toope, Legitimacy and Legality in International Law: An Interactional Account 5 (2010) (identifying relevant actors as including "elites, the

George Downs and David Rocke have explored the influence exerted by pressure groups on domestic formulation of state preferences as well as their consequent impact on international relations and international institutions.[49] It is this vision of the engagement with international law by the person on the street that I think it is imperative to embrace in order to generate a new generation of international law research: one which accounts for individuals not as proxies of states but as actors in their own right, proactively influencing their reality both in their states and beyond their borders and independently of them.

The scholarship has often focused, further, on the irregular; on the exceptional actions of actors operating outside a certain national comfort zone. It has studied, for instance, central bankers not in their day-to-day work, but in conferencing with their peers from other countries; or activists when they choose to operate transnationally, perhaps after despairing of the domestic arena. A new paradigm should account for these but it should also account for the boring, ordinary, everyday engagement of each of us with international law. It should divert attention to the rule, rather than the exception, of the practice of international law by individual people.

In addition to being unsatisfactory in and of itself, state centricity has several negative implications for academic scholarship. I now review two of these: a strong emphasis on questions of compliance and an insufficient engagement with law as an explanatory paradigm.

9.2 IMPLICATIONS OF STATE-CENTRICITY

9.2.1 *Compliance As a Central Object of Research*

As the previous discussion establishes, much of the scholarship on behavior in the framework of international law is interested in explaining state behavior. This flows naturally from the fact that most international law obligations explicitly identify states as their subjects, and norms clearly directed at non-state actors are more often the exception. Moreover, scholars have focused heavily on state *compliance* with international law.

media, NGOs and 'ordinary' citizens"); *see also* Galit A. Sarfaty, *Why Culture Matters in International Institutions: The Marginality of Human Rights at the World Bank*, 103 Am. J. Int'l L. 647, 672–673 (2009) (an anthropological study of World Bank culture and bureaucrats. Sarfaty says that the most influential factor impacting staff behavior was their professional affiliation (economists, lawyers, etc.), a factor that could not have been identified without her focus on individual actors).

[49] George W. Downs & David M. Rocke, Optimal Imperfection? 3, 130–131 (1995).

Louis Henkin famously observed that almost all nations observe almost all of their obligations almost all of the time.[50] Against this background, theorists and, more recently, empirical researchers have strived to conceptualize, explain, and measure state compliance with international law.[51] Scholars offer various explanations for state compliance. Those working with a rationalist set of assumptions explain states' behavior, generally, as rational, self-interested and preference-maximizing.[52] As realists from John Mearsheimer to Goldsmith and Posner explain, it follows that if states comply with international law, this is only because doing so serves their interests. This could be due to temporary convergence between the rule's guidance and a state's preferred course of action, or due to coercion exerted on a state by other, more powerful states. But it would not be due to any innate preference for law-abidance.[53]

Nevertheless, rationalist scholars working with an institutionalist outlook have stressed that institutions and long-term relationships may change state behavior even when holding constant states' characterization as rational, interest-maximizing agents.[54] For instance, Robert Keohane explains that institutions shape interests of states by providing information to parties; lengthening the shadow of the future and linking issues, and thus raising the importance of reputation, and particularly that of fulfilling commitments.[55] Andrew Guzman speaks of the three Rs: Reputation, Reciprocal noncompliance, and Retaliation. Reputation figures most heavily as states struggle to maintain their image as promise-keepers in order to be able to make credible commitments, necessary to facilitate future international cooperation.[56] In other words, when considering their long-term interests, states may rationally choose to comply with international law.

[50] LOUIS HENKIN, HOW NATIONS BEHAVE 47 (1979).
[51] See Gregory Shaffer & Tom Ginsburg, *The Empirical Turn in International Legal Scholarship*, 106 AM. J. INT'L L. 1, 1–11 (2012), for a review, as well as Emilie M. Hafner-Burton, David G. Victor & Yonatan Lupu, *Political Science Research on International Law: The State of the Field*, 106 AM. J. INT'L L. 47 (2012).
[52] GUZMAN, *supra* note 16, at 17; Niels Petersen, *How Rational Is International Law?*, 20 EUR. J. INT'L L. 1247, 1248 (2009).
[53] MORGENTHAU, *supra* note 8, at 296, 312–313; WALTZ, *supra* note 8, at 113, 117; Mearsheimer, *supra* note 8, at 13; GOLDSMITH & POSNER, *supra* note 8, at 9–15. *But see* Andrew T. Guzman, *A Compliance-Based Theory of International Law*, 90 CALIF. L. REV. 1823, 1827 (2002); GUZMAN, *supra* note 16, at 17.
[54] WALTZ, *supra* note 8, at 11, 197–198; Kegley, *supra* note 35, at 142; Robert O. Keohane, *International Relations and International Law: Two Optics*, 38 HARV. INT'L L.J. 487, 500–501 (1997); Guzman, *supra* note 53, at 1841; Koremenos, *supra* note 20, at 59–62, 73–75; CHAYES & CHAYES, *supra* note 20, at 22; *but see* Guzman, *supra* note 53, at 1846–1847.
[55] Keohane, *supra* note 54, at 500.
[56] Guzman, *supra* note 53, at 211.

For scholars working with liberal premises, domestic and transnational politics explain the patterns of state behavior, including with respect to international law. In this vein Slaughter suggests, for instance, that liberal states that hold rule of law as a value would be more disposed to follow international law.[57] Scholars, including Harold Jacobson and Edith Brown Weiss, as well as Finnemore and Sikkink, have worked to show, among others, how coalitions of state officials and NGO activists and the transnational communities in which they are members have joined forces in order to induce state action in compliance of a legal rule.[58] At the same time, as Downs and Rocke argue, noncompliance too can be explained by the domestic impact of nonofficials.[59] Finally, scholars adopting a constructivist outlook, from Ruggie to Goodman and Jinks, have explained state compliance as a result of social learning processes that states undergo and peer pressure to which they are subject.[60]

In a 2012 survey article Gregory Shaffer and Tom Ginsburg identify an empirical turn in international law scholarship.[61] They review the empirical literature and conclude that it is focused on "midrange theorizing concerning the *conditions* under which international law (IL) is formed and those under which it had effects in different contexts, aiming to explain variation."[62] The literature, they say, "helps to explain how the effectiveness of international law is linked to the characteristics of states and their institutions and social contexts."[63] Interestingly, they claim that scholars "sometimes focus on states, but even when they do, they also tend *to disaggregate the state and study the role of networks, firms and civil society as actors* that affect state compliance."[64]

Another important survey article published in the same 2012 volume of the American Journal of International Law by Emilie Hafner-Burton, David Victor and Yonatan Lupu also identifies increasing attention to domestic politics and to nonstate actors.[65] This has been expressed on three fronts: arguing that the organization of domestic politics affects international

---

[57] Slaughter, *supra* note 34, at 508, 532–534.

[58] *Id.* at 518–28.; Jacobson & Brown Weiss, *supra* note 37, at 142–143; *see also* Moravcsik, *supra* note 34, at 84, 87–88; Thomas Risse & Stephen C. Ropp, *Introduction and Overview, in* THE PERSISTENT POWER OF HUMAN RIGHTS 3, 5 (Thomas Risse, Stephen C. Ropp & Kathryn Sikkink eds., 2013); Finnemore & Sikkink, *supra* note 27, at 902; Benvenisti & Downs, *supra* note 45.

[59] DOWNS & ROCKE, *supra* note 49.

[60] For example, Ruggie, *supra* note 23, at 879; GOODMAN & JINKS, *supra* note 29, at 38; Risse & Ropp, *supra* note 58, at 13–21; Finnemore & Sikkink, *supra* note 27, at 902–903.

[61] Shaffer & Ginsburg, *supra* note 51, at 7.

[62] *Id.* at 1 (emphasis in the original).

[63] *Id.* at 43.

[64] *Id.* at 44 (emphasis in the original).

[65] Hafner-Burton, Victor & Lupu, *supra* note 51, at 51, 69–72.

cooperation; studying how domestic politics affect the credibility of states' commitments; and linking the type of states' regimes (democratic, authoritarian, etc.) to their perception of their international commitments.[66] As these coauthors explain, the recent years' advance has been generated, in large part, through two moves.[67] The first emphasizes the study of social processes and nonstate actors that influence norms and behavior.[68] Among others, they have studied the particular individuals who craft, interpret, and spread norms.[69] The second move has been the coupling of theories addressing domestic politics with those addressing international politics and thus accounting for each of the levels in the "two-level game."

Nonetheless, as both articles show, the study of individual action as a proxy for state action, or as an explanatory aid for state behavior, maintains a central place even in this scholarship. It remains a rarer occasion when individuals are studied independently of states as agents in their own right interacting with, making, breaking, and following international law. Further, to the extent that this scholarship maintains a commitment to the "two-level game" paradigmatic outlook, it suffers, like its predecessors, from the statist undercurrents that this outlook embodies.

The literature's focus on compliance could again be attributed to the domination of IR perspectives in the interdisciplinary scholarship on international law. Due to the lack of an entity that orders the international system, IR considers interstate relations anarchic and international law is therefore viewed as an anomaly that warrants explanation. The assumption of anarchy explains the scholarship's tilt toward compliance in the study of international law, trying to understand why, despite the lack of a coercing agent, states do comply with it.

The difficulty with the scholarship's infatuation with compliance is twofold: First, the focus on compliance simultaneously reflects and reinforces the literature's already persistent statism. Since most international norms facially identify states as their addressees, compliance studies naturally turn to state action to consider whether it is in line with such norms. Second, and relatedly, the concept of compliance obscures more than it reveals. International law's effectiveness is not limited to a binary test of state compliance or noncompliance. Studying compliance alone limits our understanding of the ways and extent to which international law shapes the lives of individuals across the world.

---

[66]   *Id.* at 70–71.
[67]   *Id.* at 69.
[68]   *Id.* at 54.
[69]   *Id.* at 55.

As Robert Howse and Ruti Teitel convincingly argue, international law's impact is not exclusively captured by a binary determination of whether a state complied.[70] Arguably, even where a state has not eventually complied, international law may have been instrumental in internal deliberation processes preceding the final outcome. Some actors within the state may have advocated for an international law-compliant action and lost in this battle but may now be more likely to win the next. Moreover, international law might serve to shape views, attitudes, and actions of various actors within the state, set a standard of behavior, serve to impact the interpretation of domestic law and much else.[71]

Further, states' de facto and de jure policies should both be of significance for the study of international law's effectiveness, but they may serve as conflicting indicators for compliance. For instance, if a certain arm of the military consistently violates the rules of international humanitarian law, even in the face of a de jure policy of the executive branch to uphold it, its actions may constitute a de facto policy of the state in violation of international norms. The state can therefore be seen as maintaining two contradicting policies, one de jure and one de facto: the former in compliance with international norms, and the latter in breach of them.

Categorizing this situation as one reflecting either compliance or noncompliance would be unsatisfactory and fail to capture the complexity of the situation. Further, if the military then succeeds in eradicating this phenomenon, for instance by punishing and removing rogue officers, the de jure and de facto policies of the state may fall back in line with each other as well as with international humanitarian law. The fact that the situation could now be characterized as one of compliance contributes only minimally to understanding the sequence of events; the identity of the actors whose action constituted either the state's noncompliance or its compliance; the reasons for their actions or their capacity to influence international law and international relations.

Furthermore, the arbitrariness of selecting either of these moments for classification as compliant or noncompliant state action exemplifies an additional problem with compliance studies: an inherent selection problem. By exploring state actions, many compliance studies are calibrated to overlook intrastate dynamics and focus on what are deemed their final outcomes, actions of the state. Doing so, they – by definition – overlook an important part of international law's effectiveness.

---

[70]   Robert Howse & Ruti Teitel, *Beyond Compliance*, 1 GLOB. POL'Y 127, 127 (2010).
[71]   *Id. See also* Tamar Megiddo, *The Domestic Standing of International Law: A Non-State Account*, 57 COLUM. J. TRANSNAT'L L. 494 (2019)

Moreover, by imposing a binary benchmark on international life, compliance scholarship disregards a complex reality in which compliance constantly cohabits with noncompliance, and a whole scale of gray in between. Consider a scenario where a formal policy criminalizing homosexual sex exists alongside a decision by the chief prosecutor to never prosecute for such conduct. The former policy amounts to a breach of international human rights obligations on the part of the state and this will persist as long as the de jure policy continues to exist. But the latter is a contradictory policy that, at least to some extent, mitigates the severity of the breach caused by the former policy.

Howse and Teitel therefore rightly submit that compliance alone is much too narrow an angle to comprehend international law's effects.[72] One additional illuminating angle is to study noncompliance. Monica Hakimi suggests that retaliatory noncompliance, which she calls "unfriendly unilateralism," can play an important role not only in international law enforcement but also in making international law. This may be good for international law, she argues, even when the conduct itself is unlawful, and not excused as legitimate enforcement measures. It may "help develop new norms, prevent existing norms from eroding, reconcile competing objectives, and strengthen or recalibrate regimes."[73] In a separate piece she stresses that conflict is the bread and butter of the international legal system and that viewing international law's core purpose as being that of fostering cooperation between states is seriously flawed.[74] Cooperation is thus not the right metric for assessing international law and international law should not be viewed as lacking when it does not satisfy it.[75]

Timothy Meyer highlights the expressive function of noncompliance and suggests a shift of focus from compliance to effectiveness. As he explains, states may use noncompliance as a tool for negotiating the appropriate interpretation of legal rules. Also, tribunals' determinations of noncompliance are attentive to their role in shaping expectations for all states, beyond the immediate parties to the dispute. Meyer differentiates compliance from effectiveness and submits that only the latter seeks to answer whether a rule of international law has changed state behavior when compared to its absence.[76] Taking his argument to its limit, one could argue that compliance studies do not even address the deep question they presume to answer: whether international law has made a difference. They merely show correlations

---

[72] *Id.* at 128.
[73] Monica Hakimi, *Unfriendly Unilateralism*, 55 Harv. Int'l L.J. 105, 107 (2014).
[74] Monica Hakimi, *The Work of International Law*, 58 Harv. Int'l L.J. 1, 5–6 (2017).
[75] *Id.* at 5.
[76] Timothy L. Meyer, *How Compliance Understates Effectiveness*, AJIL Unbound (Jun. 18, 2014), https://www.asil.org/blogs/how-compliance-understates-effectiveness.

between rules and state behavior at arbitrarily selected moments. Note, however, that Meyer's proposed pivot from compliance to effectiveness maintains a commitment to study the behavior of states.

The upshot of this critique is not that studying compliance is useless, but that compliance has been elevated to the primary metric through which the effectiveness of international law is judged, and this is misleading. As Benedict Kingsbury has pointed out, compliance is a deeply contested concept and its relation to law, behavior, objectives, and justice must be theorized before any true theory of "compliance" could emerge.[77] Furthermore, as Peter Spiro has pointed out, there exists a "compliance fallacy" in the debate. "No system of law achieves perfect compliance: why should international law be any different?" – he asks.[78] I argue that instead of focusing on compliance, we should be studying the everyday practice of international law and the processes to which it contributes within, across, and among states.

Further, compliance has been conceptualized primarily at the level of state behavior. International law's impact in producing gradual and incremental effects and influencing behavior, perceptions, and ideas of nonstate actors has thus not been accounted for. Shaffer and Ginsburg's findings suggest that empirical research could serve as helpful groundwork for theorizing the role of individual people in the everyday practice of international law. As their review indicates, a host of studies show that "nonstate actors and subdivisions within the state play key roles, both in producing international legal norms and in communicating and implementing them within states, including by reframing them in light of local social contexts."[79] But, as they explain, these studies have confined themselves on midrange theorizing. As the anecdotal evidence regarding international law's effectiveness beyond states continues to build, the challenge for interdisciplinary scholarship remains to rearrange our paradigmatic premises in light of this evidence, and to produce big picture theoretical accounts that reflect it.

9.2.2 *The Role of Law*

Our thinking about law and law-following is commonly intrinsically tied up with human traits. In the paradigmatic vision we have of law, the human

---

[77] Benedict Kingsbury, *The Concept of Compliance as a Function of Competing Conceptions of International Law*, 19 Mich. J. Int'l L. 345, 346 (1997).

[78] Peter J. Spiro, *Ukraine, International Law, and the Perfect Compliance Fallacy*, Opinio Juris (Mar. 2, 2014), http://opiniojuris.org/2014/03/02/ukraine-international-law-perfect-compliance-fallacy.

[79] Shaffer & Ginsburg, *supra* note 51, at 44.

person figures as the central actor to whom law speaks and who is expected to follow its call. When we try to answer why people would follow law, the kinds of answers we give are also intrinsically tied up to humans living in a human society: fear of sanctions;[80] an internal acceptance of legal rules;[81] the authority that law represents to us;[82] respect for law out of respect or attachment to one's community;[83] the respect for human dignity that is inherent in law,[84] and more. When the discussion turns to international law, however, theories that explain human behavior in human society are often replicated unto an international background where the person is replaced by a state and the society and (domestic) legal system are replaced by the international society of states and international law. The human person is thus eliminated from view.

[80] According to John Austin, law, properly so called, is defined as commands backed by the threat of sanctions. JOHN AUSTIN, THE PROVINCE OF JURISPRUDENCE DETERMINED 8, 11 (David Campbell & Philip Thomas eds., 1998) (1832). Commands are issued by a political superior whom the bulk of society habitually obeys, but who himself obeys no other human superior. *Id.* at 147.

[81] According to H. L. A. Hart, rules are distinguished from mere habits by the fact that individuals in the community hold a reflective, critical attitude which views certain patterns of behavior required by a rule as a common standard to be followed by the group as a whole. This "acceptance" of the rule is manifested not only in willingness to act as instructed, but also by demanding conformity of others and criticizing oneself as well as others for failing to perform the required conduct, viewing such criticism as legitimate, and describing the need for such conduct using evaluative language such as "ought" or "should." *See* HERBERT LIONEL ADOLPHUS HART, THE CONCEPT OF LAW 56–57 (2d ed. 1994).

[82] Joseph Raz explains that subjects are bound to obey a rule that is issued by someone who has authority, or a right to rule. It would be morally justified for a person to subject her will to that of another when (1) she would better conform to reasons that apply to her anyway if she would allow herself to be guided by the directives of authority, and (2) the matter is not such where to decide for oneself is to be preferred over better conforming to reason. Legitimate authority in this picture is a device for people to achieve the goal of their capacity for rational action. *See* Joseph Raz, *The Problem of Authority: Revisiting the Service Conception*, 90 MINN. L. REV. 1003, 1012–1014 (2006).

[83] In a separate account, Raz suggests that a developing sense of belonging to, and identifying with a community may give rise to a semi-voluntary obligation to obey the law. He calls it "respect for law." *See* JOSEPH RAZ, THE AUTHORITY OF LAW 250–261 (2009); Joseph Raz, *The Obligation to Obey*, 1 NOTRE DAME J.L. ETHICS & PUB. POL'Y 139, 153–154 (1984).

[84] By presenting law for the self-application of people, the legal system operates on a certain set of assumptions regarding its subject. As Lon Fuller puts it, "To embark on the enterprise of subjecting human conduct to the governance of rules involves of necessity a commitment to the view that man is, or can become, a responsible agent, capable of understanding and following rules, and answerable for his defaults. Every departure from the principles of the law's inner morality is an affront to man's dignity as a responsible agent." LON L. FULLER, THE MORALITY OF LAW 162 (rev. ed. 1969); Lon L. Fuller, *Human Interaction and the Law*, 14 AM. J. JURIS. 1, 24 (1969); Gerald J. Postema, *Implicit Law*, 13 LAW & PHIL. 361, 363–371 (1994).

In this part of the chapter I outline two arguments which I develop in separate work.[85] I argue, first, that the move of replication described above is not at all as natural or as neutral as regularly perceived. Second, I argue that, possibly as a result of this move and its resultant elimination of humans, the literature aiming to explain whether and how international law – *qua* law – works has only rarely produced theoretical accounts that could be deemed to derive from an explanatory theory that is legal, as opposed to stemming from other branches of the social sciences.

Let me start by stating the obvious: individuals are those who make law and apply it, change it and break it – and this is true for any law, international as well as domestic. If so much is taken for granted, why waste any more ink? Because the fact is that despite its intuitiveness, this proposition has not found its way into the paradigmatic conceptions, theories, and methodologies of the academic scholarship on international law. It may be used as an ontological premise of various accounts, but this premise has not been translated into epistemic and methodological frameworks and research programs. Rather, much of the scholarship has assumed, rather than established, that the central actor interacting with international law is the state and that the relationship between the state and the international system (social and legal) could be equated with that between a person and a (domestic) social or legal system. Both parts of this assumption are unsound.

I propose an alternative to this assumption and to the common move of replication: to hold constant the individual human person, and to recognize that her context – social, legal, political – has expanded over the past centuries. This context now includes not only the local or the national but also the international or global. Rather than apply insights originally obtained by observing the person in a domestic social context to state behavior in an international social context, this alternative move would have us apply them to the person in an international context. Hence, although the domestic system may be replaced by an international system, the person is not replaced by a state. This alternative move, I argue, is not only warranted by contemporary realities, but also better preserves the scientific integrity and intuitive bite of theories developed through observations of natural persons in human society.

The move of replication does not eliminate only the person. It also eliminates law. Why people follow the law is a topic with a long history of inquiry in legal philosophy. Although economic, psychological and sociological

---

[85] Megiddo, *supra* note 3; Tamar Megiddo, *Methodological Individualism*, 60 HARV. INT'L L.J. 219 (2019).

explanations have always been part and parcel of this discussion and they are hard to separate out, thinkers have strived to isolate what was special about law – as law – in generating behavior. Such endeavors have presumed that there is a point to this chase after the illusive particularity of law; that law does, or at least can make a difference that is distinct from other types of social ordering; that law is unique in its interaction with people and that this uniqueness can be conceptualized and studied. Scholars have consequently strived to produce explanations which capture law's uniqueness. With some exceptions that I discuss below, this presumption has not been carried over to research of the international legal system. I understand this neglect of the legal angle to be strongly connected to the scholarship's commitment to states as primary actors of interest. While it may be intuitive that law may serve as a reason for people's actions, it is a more difficult task to argue that it may serve as a reason for state action.

As earlier discussions in the chapter show, the scholarship on international law has provided a variety of explanations for state behavior in the framework of international law. Economic, behavioral-economic, sociological, and other insights, originally developed with respect to individual people in their human social context, have been translated into "internationalese" and applied to states' behavior. Power-seeking, rational choice, social pressure, and the like have been championed as explanatory staples. Yet, although many academic publications have framed their exploration as addressing "why international law matters" or "how international law works," the explanatory theories proposed in response have only rarely offered law itself as an explanatory paradigm for behavior in the context of international law.[86]

Moreover, many theorists have considered and have rejected law as a plausible explanation for behavior in international law. Scholars with rationalist commitments – both realist and institutionalist – who have championed power or interests more broadly construed as explanations for state action outright reject the possibility that law serves as a distinct reason for such action.[87] It is, moreover, a core assumption for them that states have no innate

---

[86] For similar critiques, see Dunoff & Pollack, *supra* note 6, at 19, and Brunnée & Toope, *supra* note 24, at 120–121.

[87] *See* WALTZ, *supra* note 8, at 113, 117; MORGENTHAU, *supra* note 8, at 296, 312–313; Mearsheimer, *supra* note 8, at 13; GOLDSMITH & POSNER, *supra* note 8, at 9–15; Guzman, *supra* note 53; Harlan Grant Cohen, *Can International Law Work? A Constructivist Expansion*, 27 BERKELEY J. INT'L L. 636, 657–661 (2009); Koremenos, *supra* note 20, at 73–75. *But see also* Steinberg, *supra* note 8, at 165 (arguing that realism's explanatory power simply does not extend to "identifying what 'work' law is doing – how and why it affects behavior and outcomes, and the contexts in which it does so.").

preferences for complying with international law.[88] Therefore, to them, if states act in a manner compatible with international law, this could only be explained as a result of a temporary (whether long- or short-term) overlap between law's guidance and their freestanding interests.[89]

As already mentioned, however, other theories have acknowledged that factors additional to power and interest may explain action in international law. Scholars working with liberal or constructivist outlooks suggest that ideas, norms, material assets, or domestic and international social and political structures may produce conceptions, beliefs, or identities conducive to international law-following.[90] They detail how these factors generate,[91] or at least "constrain, enable and constitute"[92] action in international law. For the most part, these theories describe processes undergone by states.[93] States are those motivated by their ideals or identities. States are those subjected to and those who respond to various processes of socialization and peer pressure. Only exceptionally, as discussed below, has law been proposed as a mechanism that drives or explains international legal action.

Therefore, despite offering a menu of possible political, economic, social, and even psychological explanations for behavior in international law, for the most part, the scholarship has not been able to explain how law plays into the mix: whether it makes a difference for actors that an international norm is a legal, as distinct from a social norm; whether it makes any difference for the actors participating in the everyday practice of international law that it is a legal system with which they interact.[94] Rather, law's unique normativity is dismissed.[95]

---

[88] GOLDSMITH & POSNER, *supra* note 8, at 9; GUZMAN, *supra* note 53, at 1827; *see also* Cohen, *supra* note 87, at 642 (discussing Guzman).

[89] CARR, *supra* note 8, at 194, 245; WALTZ, *supra* note 8, at 93–114, 197–198; MORGENTHAU, *supra* note 8, at 12, 296; Mearsheimer, *supra* note 8, at 5, 7–13; GOLDSMITH & POSNER, *supra* note 8, at 11–15; Kegley, *supra* note 35, at 141–143; HENKIN, *supra* note 50, at 49–51, 54–67.

[90] Moravcsik, *supra* note 34, at 85–86; Brunnée & Toope, *supra* note 24, at 121.

[91] Moravcsik, *supra* note 34, at 84.

[92] Brunnée & Toope, *supra* note 24, at 123.

[93] Kegley, *supra* note 35, at 141–143; KEOHANE, *supra* note 20, at 245. *But see also* Harold Hongju Koh, *Why Do Nations Obey International Law?*, 106 YALE L.J. 2599, 2636, 2655 (1997); Wendt, *supra* note 23, at 80.

[94] For similar critiques of the literature, see also, for example, Brunnée & Toope, *supra* note 24, at 120–121, 135–136; Jutta Brunnée & Stephen J. Toope, *Interactional International Law: An Introduction*, 3 INT'L THEORY 307, 308 (2011); Dunoff & Pollack, *supra* note 7, at 627, 649–653.

[95] *See, e.g.,* Martha Finnemore, *Are Legal Norms Distinctive?*, 32 N.Y.U. J. INT'L L. & POL'Y 699 (1999).

The "soft law" debate could be understood as trying to figure out law's special role when parsing out a state's regard for nonbinding soft law from their regard for "hard law's" binding rules.[96] As some scholars have noted, soft law norms sometimes succeed in attracting significant state following,[97] despite not being legally binding. But the background for such state following of soft law is not necessarily any disposition to comply with law or fidelity to it. Arguably, adherence to soft norms may be well accounted for by the explanations proposed by existing compliance scholarship with respect to state action (even if applied to individuals and other substate actors as well). In other words, it seems plausible that adherence to soft law is a result of power relations, self-interest, reputation concerns in the context of interdependence, peer pressure, and so on. Granted, these factors may also explain many instances of hard law-following. But they do not explain all such instances, nor do they capture, I argue, all aspects of the phenomenology of compliance. Arguably, legality adds to hard law an additional source of compliance pull that soft norms do not enjoy.[98]

Several theories do offer specifically *legal* accounts of behavior in international law, and consider law an independent mechanism that may contribute to shaping behavior. The most noteworthy is Brunnée and Toope's 2010 book, *Legitimacy and Legality in International Law*.[99] Brunnée and Toope try to understand how international law influences the behavior of key actors, which

[96] Multiple definitions have been offered for the concept of "soft law." Some view international legality as a continuum. For example, Kenneth W. Abbott & Duncan Snidal, *Hard and Soft Law in International Governance*, 54 INT'L ORG. 421, 424 (2000); Gregory Shaffer & Mark A. Pollack, *Hard vs. Soft Law*, 94 MINN. L. REV. 706, 716 (2010); Andrew T. Guzman & Timothy L. Meyer, *International Soft Law*, 2 J. LEGAL ANALYSIS 171, 173 (2010). However, others such as Jan Klabbers draw a binary distinction between hard law and soft law and a bright line between the legal and nonlegal, binding and nonbinding. For example, Jan Klabbers, *The Undesirability of Soft Law*, 67 NORDIC J. INT.'L L. 381, 381 (1998). I understand soft law to refer to norms that do not purport to be legally binding and are not perceived to be legally binding by those whose action they nonetheless seek to guide. This definition seems to fall within what scholars writing on the subject would accept. For example, Guzman & Meyer, *supra* at 172 (defining soft law norms as those that "fall short of" binding rules); Shaffer & Pollack, *supra* at 714–715, 717; Abbott & Snidal, *supra* at 421–422. According to this understanding, instruments such as recommendations of international organizations, standards, declarations, and possibly advisory opinions, among others, would be classified as soft law.

[97] ALVAREZ, *supra* note 33, at 257–268.

[98] As Jeremy Waldron puts it, it adds another "layer" of allegiance, on top of others. *See* Jeremy Waldron, *Why Law – Efficacy, Freedom, or Fidelity?*, 13 LAW & PHIL. 259, 257 (1994). However, for this to be translated to a significant advantage in outcome when compared to soft norms, the international legal system must be successful in generating a robust compliance pull, and this requires substantial adherence to principles of legality on which the international legal system often falters.

[99] BRUNNÉE & TOOPE, *supra* note 48.

they identify as including not only states, but also elites, the media, NGOs, and "ordinary" citizens. They set out to understand what is unique about the role of law in constructing and shaping the global society.[100] They propose an "interactional" account of international law that is essentially premised on a process of mutual social construction but follows legal philosopher Lon Fuller in claiming that this reciprocity is embedded in the very nature of law, properly understood.[101]

Simmons' work is another notable exception. Simmons argues that states' ratification of human rights conventions can influence the behavior of governmental as well as other actors in ways that accord with the contents of these agreements.[102] She stresses the importance of exploring international law, rather than more broadly defined norms, explaining that "[t]he key here is commitment: the making of an explicit, public, and lawlike promise by public authorities to act within particular boundaries in their relationship with individual persons."[103] She explains how international treaties alter domestic politics, empower local actors, assist them in viewing themselves as right-bearers, and influence their values, identities, and interests. Consequently, treaties enhance the strategies as well as the intangible resources at the disposal of such actors to mobilize and pressure governments to comply with their international commitments.[104]

Simmons has confined her theoretical claims, however, to the domestic sphere, in dialogue with existing scholarship emphasizing, for instance, transnational processes.[105] Her theory is further confined to the momentum that succeeds the ratification of human rights treaties and to studying how state compliance is generated and it is from this standpoint that her theory is developed.

Harold Koh's model of a "transnational legal process" is also relevant. Koh studies states' internalization of an international legal norm into domestic law. He argues that internalization occurs as a result of transnational interaction around possible interpretations of a norm.[106] Koh views norm internalization by a state as a "critical moment"[107] which leads the state to obey it "as part of

---

[100] *Id.* at 4–5, 15.
[101] *Id.* at 7, 20–21.
[102] SIMMONS, *supra* note 36, at 12.
[103] *Id.* at 7.
[104] *Id.* at 4–5, 126–148.
[105] *Id.* at 126.
[106] Koh, *supra* note 93, at 2646.
[107] Harold Hongju Koh, *Jefferson Memorial Lecture-Transnational Legal Process After September 11th*, 22 BERKELEY J. INT'L L. 337, 343 (2004).

its internal value set."[108] Internalized international law thus explains state action. Nonetheless, transnational legal processes are initiated and conducted by a variety of nonstate actors, in addition to states.[109] Yet, the model's recognition of individuals' role seems to end at the moment of the domestic adoption of the norm.[110]

Finally, Thomas Franck's work also warrants reflection. Franck argues that a state's voluntarist social obligation to comply with an international rule is dependent on two elements: the rule's perceived legitimacy and its perceived fairness.[111] For Franck, legitimacy is a matter of form. When formed according to generally agreed principles, rules and rulemaking institutions are perceived as legitimate, and thus create in their target audiences a "pull" toward compliance, even without coercion, and even with regard to those who cannot be coerced.[112] Legitimacy depends on communally accepted symbols or rituals which define what the "right" process is.[113] Nevertheless, Franck differentiates legitimacy from legality.[114] The fairness or justness of rules has to do with their substance. In order to be fair, international law must take into account its consequences and effects; it must reflect elements of distributive justice.[115]

Franck applies legal philosophical ideas to international law. His application, however, is to state actors, rather than to individuals. He thus repeats the move of replication that I criticize above. Further, although Franck appears to take direct issue with the role of law, in fact, at least in his early work, Franck assumes that international law is not "law" in the sense that the term is used domestically since law is premised on the possibility of coercive enforcement by the state.[116] But this does not mean, for him, that international law creates no obligation. It may still do so, as a result of its legitimacy.[117] Franck's

---

[108]   Koh, *supra* note 93, at 2646, 2651.

[109]   Koh, *supra* note 107, at 339.

[110]   Koh, *supra* note 93, at 2646 (although his analysis of examples is more nuanced). For a more in-depth engagement with Koh's model, see Megiddo, *supra* note 71, at 501–504.

[111]   THOMAS M. FRANCK, THE POWER OF LEGITIMACY AMONG NATIONS 37–38 (1990).

[112]   *Id.* at 24.

[113]   THOMAS M. FRANCK, FAIRNESS IN INTERNATIONAL LAW AND INSTITUTIONS 30–41 (1995). This includes requirements of textual clarity (determinacy), symbolic validation, coherence (referring to the rule's generality and equal, principled application), and adherence to secondary rules of the creation, interpretation and application of norms accepted in the community.

[114]   FRANCK, *supra* note 111, at 36.

[115]   FRANCK, *supra* note 113, at 7–8.

[116]   FRANCK, *supra* note 111, at 35.

[117]   *Id.* at 37; *see also id.* at 39 (further explaining that "[o]bedience to law is a recognition of the power of the organized state; obedience to international rules is a recognition of the existence of an organized international community, but one that loosely resembles the modern state

exploration of international law is therefore not actually an exploration of the role of law, but rather of international law's success in enticing compliance despite not being law. Nevertheless, in later work, Franck seems to depart from this position, declaring instead that international law has matured and has reached its "post-ontological era."[118]

Although these are important contributions, law's distinct role in contributing to behavior in international law has not been addressed sufficiently by the scholarship. Although it is merely one item on our menu of explanations for international legal behavior, its neglect impoverishes our understanding of the international legal system.

In the following and last part of this chapter, I use the US Torture Memos as case study for illustrating the implications of the previous discussion. The main goal of this engagement is to illuminate what we have been missing and might gain by adjusting our focus as proposed by this chapter: from states to people, from compliance to process, from social science theories generally, to law. After briefly recalling the main facts of the case, I turn to discuss how it has been analyzed by international law scholarship and what this analysis has overlooked.

9.3 THE TORTURE MEMOS

A series of legal memoranda drafted in 2002 by members of the Office of Legal Counsel (OLC) at the US Department of Justice have remained at the center of widespread attention ever since their existence became public knowledge in summer 2004.[119] On January 22, 2002 a memo[120] signed by Assistant Attorney General and OLC head Jay Bybee declared that the conflicts between the US and Al-Qaeda and between the US and the Taliban are not, or could be determined by the President not to be governed by the Third Geneva

---

and does not issue or enforce sovereign commands . . . International 'law' is thus not of a legal order of obligation.").

[118] FRANCK, *supra* note 113, at 6.

[119] Jess Bravin, *Pentagon Report Set Framework For Use of Torture*, WALL ST. J., June 7, 2004, at A1; Dana Priest & Jeffrey R. Smith, *Memo Offered Justification for Use of Torture*, WASH. POST, June 8, 2004, at A1.

[120] Jay S. Bybee, Memorandum for Alberto R. Gonzales, Counsel to the President, and William J. Haynes II, General Counsel of the Department of Defense, Re: Application of Treaties and Laws to al Qaeda and Taliban Detainees (Jan. 22, 2002), *reprinted in* THE TORTURE PAPERS 81 (Karen J. Greenberg & Joshua L. Dratel eds., 2005). The memo follows a January 9 draft, John Yoo & Robert Delahunty, Memorandum for William J, Haynes II, General Counsel, Department of Defense, Re: Application of Treaties and Laws to al Qaeda and Taliban Detainees (Jan. 9, 2002), *reprinted in* THE TORTURE PAPERS, *supra* at 39 .

Convention.[121] The consequence is that the US is not bound by Common
Article 3 of the Geneva Conventions,[122] which lays down rules for the treatment of detained combatants. The memo also stated that detainees are not
entitled to Prisoner of War status.[123]

This legal opinion was adopted by President George W. Bush in
February 2002.[124] This paved the way for a series of additional memos drafted
later in the course of that year, known today as the "Torture Memos." These
memos, signed by Bybee and his deputy, John Yoo, held that only treatment
that intentionally generates organ failure or permanent impairment of a bodily
function, or causes long-lasting psychological harm amounts to torture and is
therefore prohibited in all circumstances under US and international law.
Treatment that does not quite reach that high bar does not violate the
prohibition on torture and it is not similarly banned.[125]

These and other memos produced by the OLC between 2002 and 2003 are
deemed by many to be the manifestation of ultimate lawlessness and disdain

---

[121]   Geneva Convention Relative to the Treatment of Prisoners of War, Aug. 12, 1949, 75 U.N.T.
       S. 135; Bybee, *supra* note 120, at 9 ("We conclude that Geneva III does not apply to the al
       Qaeda terrorist organization. Therefore, neither the detention nor trial of al Qaeda fighters is
       subject to Geneva III"); *id.* at 11 ("[W]e conclude that the President has more than ample
       grounds to find that our treaty obligations under Geneva III towards Afghanistan were
       suspended during the period of the conflict ... [T]here appears to be developing evidence
       that the Taliban leadership had become closely intertwined with, if not utterly dependent
       upon, al Qaeda. This would have rendered the Taliban more akin to a terrorist organization
       that used force not to administer a government, but for terrorist purposes. The President could
       decide that no treaty obligations were owed to such a force.").
[122]   Common Article 3, so named for its appearance in all four 1949 Geneva Conventions,
       requires, among others, that in armed conflict not of an international character occurring
       in the territory of one of the Parties, states treat detained combatants humanely, and that they
       at all times refrain from "violence to life and person, in particular murder of all kinds,
       mutilation, cruel treatment and torture" and from "outrages upon personal dignity, in
       particular, humiliating and degrading treatment." It is seen as providing a minimum yardstick
       for the protection of human rights. Military and Paramilitary Activities in and Against
       Nicaragua (Nicar. v. U.S.), 1986 I.C.J. Rep. 14, ¶ 218–220 (June 27).
[123]   Bybee, *supra* note 120, at 28.
[124]   George W. Bush, Memorandum for the Vice President and Others, Humane Treatment of Al
       Qaeda and Taliban Detainees (Feb. 7, 2002), *reprinted in* THE TORTURE PAPERS, *supra* note
       120, at 134, 134–135. Bush accepted the OLC's legal opinion when declaring, on February 7,
       that combatants detained in either conflict are not entitled to treatment in accordance with
       Common Article 3 and that they do not qualify as prisoners of war. Bush declared that as
       a matter of policy (rather than law) the US armed forces shall treat detainees "humanely and,
       to the extent appropriate and consistent with military necessity, in a manner consistent with
       the principles of [the third Geneva Convention]".
[125]   Jay S. Bybee, Memorandum for Alberto R. Gonzales Counsel to the President, Re: Standards
       of Conduct for Interrogation under 18 U.S.C. §§2340–2340A (Aug. 1, 2002), *reprinted in* THE
       TORTURE PAPERS, *supra* note 120, at 172; John Yoo, Letter to Alberto R. Gonzales, Counsel to
       the President (Aug. 1, 2002), *reprinted in* THE TORTURE PAPERS, *supra* note 120, at 218.

for international law.[126] Their authors have been described as acting with "bad intentions";[127] as "torturing" the rule of law and international law for policy ends,[128] as misconstruing or ignoring international law;[129] and said to "knowingly overstep legal doctrine."[130] The memos have been said to "reveal a carefully orchestrated legal rationale, but one without valid legal or moral foundation."[131]

Let me state for the sake of clarity that I endorse the criticism of the memos as presenting a poor, unconvincing analysis of international law. Nevertheless, I think that it is important to notice that Bybee and Yoo and others at the OLC have compiled hundreds of pages of legal argumentation in the attempt to make a case *in international law* to support their conclusions. They did not, as it were, completely ignore international law. Quite the contrary: they found it necessary to engage with international legal doctrine and sought to portray their decisions as an application of it. That they failed to produce a valid, convincing argument is a separate point. It would be more accurate, therefore, to say that, in some way, international law did figure in Bybee's and Yoo's deliberations on a course of action for the US. They took it seriously at least to the extent that they apparently felt obliged to address it.

International law's role in shaping behavior in the Torture Memos saga is not satisfactorily captured by existing scholarship on international legal behavior. Surely, state interests on the one hand and state ideology or socialization on the other hand likely played a role in shaping the outcome. But so did international law, and particularly, how it was regarded by individual people. Without bringing international law and its interaction with people into the field of exploration and identifying it both as an object of research and as an explanatory paradigm, we would be able to give only partial explanation to behavior in the context of international law in this and other instances.

It remains a question whether Bybee and Yoo and others produced a purposefully distorted interpretation of international law to suit their ends, or whether they genuinely believed in the soundness of their legal

---

[126] *See, e.g.,* PHILIPPE SANDS, TORTURE TEAM 225 (2008) (characterizing the lawyers' role in legitimizing torture as "a conscious decision to set aside international rules constraining interrogations . . . motivated by a combination of factors, including fear and ideology and an almost visceral disdain for international obligations.").

[127] Joshua L. Dratel, *The Legal Narrative, in* THE TORTURE PAPERS, *supra* note 120, at xxi.

[128] José E. Alvarez, *Torturing the Law*, 37 CASE W. RES. J. INT'L L. 175, 222–223 (2005).

[129] *Id.* at 179.

[130] Karen J. Greenberg, *From Fear to Torture, in* THE TORTURE PAPERS, *supra* note 120, at xvii, xix.

[131] Dratel, *supra* note 127, at xxii.

arguments.[132] If the second account is correct, their action seems to have indeed been guided, at least in part, by international law as they understood it – although their understanding of the content of international law was then clearly different from that of their critics. On this account, Bybee and Yoo honestly believed that, consistently with international law doctrine, torture could be construed as narrowly as they suggested, and not include the types of interrogation techniques their memos and consequent advice legitimized.

But even if it is the first account that is correct, and Bybee and Yoo had little, if any, respect for international law and coldly distorted it to suit the policy ends they wanted to legitimize, then it is still very interesting that they felt compelled to find a way to argue through international law. They could just plainly ignore it or limit themselves to denying its applicability, but did neither. Without defending Bybee or Yoo, and without presuming to determine which of these accounts is more accurate, what I am trying to bring out here is the fact that even in the worst case scenario, there is something to be learned from their choice to address international law at all. On both accounts, therefore, international law figured in Bybee and Yoo's calculations when they carried out their part in the national policymaking process in the US at the time. To some extent, international law seems to have mattered.

The fact that Bybee and Yoo took the trouble to research and write hundreds of pages of international legal analysis to support their position is illuminating. It is an indication, if not of their own position that international law is applicable and contains guidance which is relevant to the situation at hand, then at least that they believed that their superiors, their interlocutors, or the community to which they belong care about international law's applicability and guidance that they need to make an international law argument in order to be convincing or meet some standard, even if perfunctorily.

Further, Bybee and Yoo's use of international law has entrenched the need to consider it when contemplating similar national policy decisions of this magnitude or in this issue-area; it has signaled an agreed-upon common language to discuss the issue; and – importantly – it has largely ceded the argument on the grounds for evaluating national policy of this sort. Nonetheless, even if all of international law's impact on the final result of their work was in having the authors stop to consider their proposal's compatibility with international law, this is not insignificant.

---

[132] *See* JOHN YOO, WAR BY OTHER MEANS 24–36, 43, 169–172 (2006). In his memoir published after having left office, Yoo continues to defend these positions as legally sound, and he relies once more on interpretation of international law to make his point. He further stresses that the memos reflect a position on law, rather than policy, the latter being the prerogative of the President, and not his call to make.

Note that critics were not content to direct their blows merely at the OLC or at the Department of Justice or even at the Bush Administration. Much of the criticism leveled against these memos was personally directed at named individuals: Bybee and Yoo and others,[133] who are characterized in the scholarship as personally responsible for subverting international law to suit the ends of the Bush Administration. Jack Goldsmith, who replaced Bybee as head of the OLC, argued that he sought to correct the errors of Bybee's and Yoo's ways by, among others, withdrawing (some of)[134] the Torture Memos in the summer of 2004.[135] His and others' criticism seems to imply that had someone else occupied the leading OLC positions in 2002, the results may also have been different: perhaps those memos would never have been written and perhaps such gross mistreatment of detainees would never have been officially sanctioned.[136] The underlying premise of such criticism indicates the importance we attach to people, not only to organizations or to formal roles. We think that it matters who it is that holds a position because we think that people make a difference.

This intuitive understanding of the importance of people operates as a kind of ontological premise which surfaces in many academic writings about the Torture Memos. It is probably particularly acute for international lawyers because this episode hit particularly close to home. As José Alvarez, himself a former OLC lawyer, put it:

> [t]he torturer is now us – distinguished, accomplished, highly credentialed public servants and high government officials, current or former professors of law at famous law schools, civil servants in the White House Counsel's Office, the US Department of Defense, or the Office of Legal Counsel ("OLC") within the US Department of Justice, even one who has since become a federal judge.[137]

But the theoretical literature on who it is who might matter in international law does not conceptualize each of "us" – now referring to each and every

---

[133] *See, e.g.,* MICHAEL P. SCHARF & PAUL R. WILLIAMS, SHAPING FOREIGN POLICY IN TIMES OF CRISIS: THE ROLE OF INTERNATIONAL LAW AND THE STATE DEPARTMENT LEGAL ADVISER 129–130 (2010) (where William Taft, the Legal Adviser at the Department of State during the Bush Presidency, recounts his and his staff's grave differences with lawyers at Department of Justice at the time); *see also* Alvarez, *supra* note 128, at 198–208 (noting Alvarez's harsh criticism of Jack Goldsmith, who replaced Bybee).

[134] Michael P. Scharf, *International Law and the Torture Memos Accountability for the Torture Memos*, 42 CASE W. RES. J. INT'L L. 321, 349–350 (2009) (detailing also the memos not withdrawn and their implications).

[135] JACK GOLDSMITH, THE TERROR PRESIDENCY 149–152 (2007).

[136] *But see* Scharf, *supra* note 134, at 349 (describing Goldsmith as endorsing the legality of "extraordinary interrogation techniques" in certain circumstances).

[137] Alvarez, *supra* note 128, at 176.

person – as a potential practitioner of international law. It does not account for the impact that people, all people, have, in principle, simply by virtue of being members in the community to which international law applies. It does not even account for Professor Goldsmith as opposed to OLC Head Goldsmith. This intuitive understanding – in other words – has not been embedded in paradigmatic and theoretical accounts of international law.

So far I have discussed the story of the Torture Memos, as opposed to the more general story of the US policy of "enhanced interrogation." One might justly point out that the two are not the same, and that policymakers may ignore legal guidance and are not obligated to follow it. The fact remains, however, that Bush Administration government lawyers were hard pressed to provide legal analysis supportive of the contemplated policy[138] and that policy decisions, as far as I am aware, were not made absent such legal vetting. Further, note that my analysis here seeks to shine a light, particularly, on how the academic debate on the Torture Memos and the US torture program has been attentive to the contribution of individual persons, and to argue that this is indicative of a more general ontological premise we carry with respect to international law but which is not adequately represented in our paradigmatic outlooks, methodological assumptions, and theoretical accounts.

As I understand it, at least part of the urgency of the scholarly criticism on the Torture Memos was related to a fear that the US legal position might jeopardize not only US compliance with international law but also the integrity of the international legal prohibition on torture.[139] One major concern was thus the memos' potential destructive capacity with respect to the international legal taboo. A potential, direct harm to international law was believed to flow simply from the fact that the US Department of Justice adopts a position that denies the validity or scope of the prohibition against torture. Responding to this concern, critics hastened to offer counterarguments, disprove Bybee and Yoo's memos, and condemn them personally for their role in

---

[138] *See, e.g.,* GOLDSMITH, *supra* note 135, at 146–147 ("[T]he administration's aim was to go right up to the edge of what the torture law prohibited, to exploit every conceivable loophole in order to do everything legally possible to uncover information that might stop an attack ... Was it right for the administration to go right up to the line? ... Ultimately, my role as the head of the OLC was not to decide whether these policies were wise. It was to make sure that the policies were implemented lawfully.").

[139] *See* BRUNNÉE & TOOPE, *supra* note 48, at 237 (arguing that the worldwide process of the weakening of the shared understanding supporting an absolute prohibition on torture could be traced to the US process of justifying any means in the fight against terrorism, including the Torture Memos).

offering false international legal arguments in support of a practice whose prohibition amounts to *jus cogens*.[140]

This concern presumes – I think, rightly – an international legal system which is a reciprocal, constantly evolving endeavor. It reflects an image of international law which, on the one hand, flows into domestic deliberation on policy and is endorsed, challenged or applied and, at the same time, is liable to be influenced and reshaped by such practice. This echoes what I have referred to above as the dialogical nature of the relationship between the practice of international law by both states and nonstate actors and the law itself.

This image stands in contradiction to the prevalent "two-level game" paradigm. As argued above, a breakup of the international legal system into a domestic sphere and an international sphere and the erection of a barrier between them obscures the constant multilateral flows of interaction in the system. Statism props up this barrier. Incomplete disaggregationism, which disaggregates the state but is still willing to accept the separation between the national and the international spheres, also supports it.

Nevertheless, as evident in the academic discussion of the Torture Memos, the fact is that we are able to see beyond this wall, and that when we scrutinize real-world scenarios we often are able to see how interaction is unencumbered by it. Regrettably, this ontological – intuitive – understanding is not then translated into epistemology, and does not impact influential, paradigmatic outlooks of international law, which thereafter educate and inform scholarly analysis as well practical imagination. One might even venture to suggest that the content of the views pronounced by Bybee and Yoo is not itself unrelated to the paradigmatic separation thesis between the domestic and the international,[141] and that their uncompromising insistence on the broad powers of the President to revoke international law's applicability, evident in the memos, are the extreme manifestation of this view.[142]

Of course, lawyers were not the only relevant agents identified in the scholarly discussion of the US torture program. The scholarship casts several villains as well as several insurgents who spoke out against the program. On both sides, many are identified by name and their stories repeated, with the latter including Secretary of State Colin Powell and State Department Legal

---

[140] Prosecutor v. Furundžija, Case No. IT-95-17/1-T, Judgment, ¶ 144 (Int'l Crim. Trib. for the Former Yugoslavia Dec. 10, 1998).

[141] For example, JULIAN KU & JOHN YOO, TAMING GLOBALIZATION (2012).

[142] *See* Peter J. Spiro, *Sovereigntism's Twilight*, 31 BERKELEY J. INT'L L. 307 (2013) (commenting that Yoo and Ku "favor presidential power except when exercised to advance the incorporation of international law.").

Advisor William Taft,[143] as well as Guantanamo Bay Staff Judge Advocate Diane Beaver,[144] and others celebrated anonymously.[145]

The ranks of the villains include psychologists "Bruce" Jessen and James Mitchell who devised the torture program for the Central Intelligence Agency (CIA) and who have taken a significant role in implementing their techniques in interrogations. They have recently been dragged into the limelight by a lawsuit brought against them by torture survivors and their families.[146] Their involvement led to a statement from the American Psychological Association which stresses that psychologists "shall not knowingly engage in, assist, tolerate, direct, support, advise, facilitate, plan, design, or offer training in torture or other cruel, inhuman, or degrading treatment or punishment" and "affirms the prerogative of psychologists to refuse to work" in "settings in which detainees are deprived of adequate protection of their human rights."[147] Implicit here again is the weight attached to the actions of named individual people, who perhaps should have refused to cooperate with the CIA's requests to devise "enhanced interrogation techniques," and the recognition of their contribution to the consequent violation of the human rights of detainees.

The media has also been said to have a substantial effect on public opinion and national policy. This is not limited to news media. The TV series "24," for instance, has been claimed to shore up public support for torture after 9/11.[148] Conversely, news coverage of the Abu Ghraib scandal and later of the Torture Memos themselves, set the stage for Goldsmith's withdrawal of some of the Bybee-Yoo memos in summer 2004.[149] The public debate in the US as well as globally on the issue of torture is further indicated to have made an impact.[150]

---

[143]   Scharf, *supra* note 134, at 343; Alvarez, *supra* note 128, at 178, ¶ 12.

[144]   Greenberg, *supra* note 130, at xix.

[145]   Dratel, *supra* note 127, at xxiii.

[146]   Sheri Fink, 2 *Psychologists in C.I.A. Interrogations Can Face Trial, Judge Rules*, N.Y. TIMES, July 29, 2017, at A18; Sheri Fink & James Risen, *Psychologists Open a Window on Brutal C.I.A. Interrogations*, N.Y. TIMES (June 21, 2017), https://www.nytimes.com/interactive/2017/06/20/us/cia-torture.html.

[147]   Policy Related to Psychologists' Work in National Security Settings and Reaffirmation of the APA Position Against Torture and Other Cruel, Inhuman, or Degrading Treatment or Punishment, AM. PSYCHOL. ASS'N, http://www.apa.org/about/policy/national-security.aspx (last updated Aug. 2015).

[148]   BRUNNÉE & TOOPE, *supra* note 48, at 233–235, 244–245; SANDS, *supra* note 126, at 54–55 (blaming the TV series "24" as well as Harvard Law School Professor Alan Darshowitz for effectively changing the environment in the US to such that condones the use of torture in interrogation of terrorist suspects).

[149]   GOLDSMITH, *supra* note 135, at 157–160.

[150]   *Id.* at 156–158.

If we were only to consider the US through its policies or actions at the international level, we might not have been able to explain the dramatic difference in its position regarding torture during a single Presidential term and in a little under two years. Only if we also take into account the actions of individuals operating within the state – within as well as outside government bureaucracy – and explore the public deliberation (local and global) on the issue of torture could we begin to comprehend the sequence of events and the catalysts that led to the revocation of the memos.

Further, restricting the research merely to questions of compliance would have made it difficult to recognize how international law played on all sides of the US debate on torture, and how it often set the terms for the debate. Focusing on a binary compliance/noncompliance bottom line has made it difficult for commentators to notice that there is a significance to the memos' insistence to use international law in the first place.

This case further shows the problematic and arbitrary nature of selection in compliance studies. Arguably, the degree of US compliance with international law fluctuated between 2002 and 2004 and between then and January 22, 2009, when President Barack Obama prohibited the use of previously authorized interrogation methods.[151] The complexity and various shades of conduct by US actors over time would have been lost if compliance had been the only metric according to which conduct could be assessed. It would have hindered in-depth analysis of actors, structures, processes, community perceptions, and incremental change.

9.4 CONCLUSION

When commenting on international events, we often instinctively notice that people matter. But we have refrained from embedding this recognition into our working paradigms, adequately addressing it in theoretical accounts and building it into our methodologies.

Interdisciplinary research of international law is gaining popularity, and for good reason. It offers the promise of rising above disciplinary limitations to produce ever-more comprehensive, complex, and nuanced scientific accounts of the international legal system. But if this literature is to deliver on its promise, it must avoid the pitfalls of its first-generation predecessor.

This chapter outlines some of these pitfalls in the hope of drawing a road-map for a more successful future interdisciplinary research of international

---

[151] Exec. Order 13,491, 74 Fed. Reg. 4,893 (Jan. 22, 2009) (prohibiting interrogation methods not authorized by and listed in the Army Field Manual).

law. It suggests that scholars recalibrate their paradigmatic approaches to take notice of the central role of individual people in the everyday life of international law. It submits that this requires not only noticing the actions of particular elites, but also conceptualizing the potential role of each and every one of us in contributing to shaping our states as well as international law itself through a dialogical interaction with that law.

The upshots of undertaking these steps are significant. They include a more sophisticated understanding of international law's effectiveness, shifting away from binary compliance studies. They include, furthermore, the promise of a renewed exploration into the uniqueness of international law's normativity. As scholars of international law have always acknowledged when pressed, individual people are the ultimate members of international law's community of practice. We ought to recalibrate our paradigms to appropriately account for their role.

10

The Wrong Way to Weigh Rights

Andrew Keane Woods[*]

Consider the following puzzle: just as human rights appear to have won wide-spread acceptance, legal scholars suggest they have very little effect.[1] For evidence of human rights' ascendance, we can look to any number of things. Levels of personal violence appear to be trending downward worldwide.[2] Just as importantly, the rhetoric of rights has saturated our political discourse.[3] Politicians speak in rights terms; courts aim to protect basic rights; and companies issue corporate social responsibility reports to show their commitment to rights. Rights are everywhere.

Yet despite this seeming success, legal scholars ask whether human rights law makes a difference.[4] Indeed, there is little evidence to suggest that international human rights treaties have significant impact on state behavior.[5] How can this be? How can human rights be thriving if the legal instruments that implement them have little measurable effect on state behavior?

[*] This chapter is adapted from and builds upon my essay, *Discounting Rights*, 50 N.Y.U. J. INT'L L. & POL. 509 (2018).

[1] I will refer interchangeably to "basic rights," "human rights," and "fundamental rights" – any basic set of rights guaranteed by the state to the individual. For the purposes of this chapter, the exact terminology – and the substantive rights involved with any particular set of rights – are not as important as the relationship between those rights and the legal instruments that implement them.

[2] *See* STEVEN PINKER, THE BETTER ANGELS OF OUR NATURE (2011) (summarizing existing data about violence and indicators of violence around the world and concluding that violence is on the decline).

[3] MARY ANNE GLENDON, RIGHTS TALK: THE IMPOVERISHMENT OF POLITICAL DISCOURSE (1991) (using the phrase "rights talk" to characterize claims on behalf of civil and human rights to the exclusion of more inclusive moral values and community norms).

[4] *See, e.g.,* Oona A. Hathaway, *Do Human Rights Treaties Make a Difference?*, 111 YALE L.J. 1935, 1938–1939 (2002) (using an original dataset to ask whether "human rights treaties [are] complied with [and whether] they [are] effective in changing states' behavior for the better.").

[5] *See* Adam Chilton & Eric Posner, *An Introduction to the Empirical Evidence on the Effectiveness of International Human Rights Treaties* (draft on file with author).

The explanation for this disconnect is likely that scholars are measuring rights with the wrong tools. While of course it matters how rights "work," so to speak, quantitative tools are not, as deployed, up to the task of answering the question.[6] A number of recent large-N quantitative studies purport to answer capacious questions – such as, "does human rights law matter?" – by measuring whether states deviate from the commitments they make in their constitutions and international agreements.[7] This scholarship largely consists of comparing two things: (1) states' legal commitments to human rights, typically in an international treaty, with (2) conditions on the ground, typically by relying on numeric scores given to the country.[8]

While this sort of inquiry is useful for identifying trends and testing hypotheses about treaty effects, it is unlikely to answer deeper questions about the overall health of the human rights regime, or even the efficacy of rights. Rights are subtler and more complex than these studies presume. This chapter seeks to explain why.

This is not, I should clarify, a critique of quantitative efforts in human rights scholarship. In fact, quantitative research of the kind addressed here is part of a larger – and very welcome – trend toward empirical legal research. Nor is this chapter a defense of the current human rights regime. Indeed, one of the reasons that I find quantitative rights scholarship to fall short of its promise is precisely the fact that it fails to diagnose – and in a certain sense perpetuates – the regime's worst tendencies toward fetishizing consistency with

---

[6] When I say large-N, I am referring to surveys of larger datasets – typically anything larger than twenty is considered "large-N." *See* David Collier, Jason Seawright & Henry E. Brady, *Qualitative v. Quantitative: What Might This Distinction Mean?*, QUALITATIVE METHODS 1 (Am. Pol. Sci. Ass'n, Washington D.C.) Spring 2003, at 1; David Collier, *The Comparative Method*, *in* POLITICAL SCIENCE: THE STATE OF THE DISCIPLINE II (Ada Finifter ed., 1993).

[7] Adam S. Chilton & Mila Versteeg, *Do Constitutional Rights Make a Difference?* 60 AM. J. POL. SCI. 575 (2016) (arguing that rights make a difference if and only if they impact government behavior); Adam S. Chilton & Mila Versteeg, *The Failure of Constitutional Torture Prohibitions*, 44 J.L. STUD. 417 (2015) (concluding that constitutional rights against torture have failed insofar as they have not had measurable impact on levels of state torture); David S. Law & Mila Versteeg, *Sham Constitutions*, 101 CALIF. L. REV. 863, 896 (2013) (surveying most of the world constitutions and grading them as more or less of a "sham" if there is a large gap between rights enumerated in the constitution and conditions on the ground, as measured by indicators); Tom Ginsburg, Zachary Elkins & Justin Blount, *Does the Process of Constitution-Making Matter?*, 5 ANN. REV. L. & SOC. SCI. 5 (2009) (relying on large-N cross-country databases to draw conclusions about the link between constitutions and outcomes). *But see* Bill Rubenstein, *Do Gay Rights Laws Matter?*, 75 S. CAL. L. REV. 65, 68 (2001) (arguing that measures of state behavior are not the only or even best indicator of whether rights matter).

[8] For a survey of indicators in the rights context, see SALLY ENGLE MERRY, THE SEDUCTIONS OF QUANTIFICATION: MEASURING HUMAN RIGHTS, GENDER VIOLENCE, AND SEX TRAFFICKING 13–16 (2016) (describing the different types of indicators, including "counts" which do just that).

commitments. This is true both for quantitative rights scholarship arguing that the human rights regime is effective and scholarship arguing that it is not.[9]

Part of the problem is the focus on states as the primary – or even the best – units of analysis for measuring the impact of basic rights. Many empirical rights studies do not show that rights are ineffective, do not matter, or have failed. Rather, they show something much narrower: that there is insufficient evidence, at the moment, to suggest a clear and direct causal link between (1) some commitments to civil and political rights and (2) the committing state's behavior toward its citizens.

The other problem with this focus on what can be quantified is that it hides potentially much more worrisome aspects of today's rights regimes. As I have written elsewhere, the human rights regime is plagued by a number of unfortunate features, such as: the fetish for compliance with commitments; the privileging of rights violations over rights promotions; the outsized role that moral outrage plays in regime design; and the way that rights talk emboldens political rivals, making compromise difficult.[10] To the extent that any of these features are hard to quantify, they will be missed by quantitative evaluations of a rights regime.

This chapter proceeds as follows. The first part examines some of the drawbacks of the current empirical rights scholarship. The second part surveys some of the features of the human rights regime that are deeply problematic yet not captured by standard empirical accounts. The final part of the chapter sketches a few different paths that basic rights enforcement might take – paths that would represent a radical departure from the regime in place today.

10.1 MEASUREMENT PROBLEMS

A considerable number of legal scholars and social scientists ask whether rights matter.[11] Much of this scholarship asks if states behave differently after making

---

[9] Beth Simmons, Ryan Goodman, and Derek Jinks are some of the staunchest defenders of the existing human rights regime. They seek proof of human rights law in state behavior. *See* BETH SIMMONS, MOBILIZING FOR HUMAN RIGHTS (2009); Ryan Goodman & Derek Jinks, *How to Influence States: Socialization and International Human Rights Law*, 54 DUKE L.J. 621 (2004). Posner and Hathaway draw the opposite conclusion, but they too look to state behavior for answers. *See* ERIC A. POSNER, THE TWILIGHT OF HUMAN RIGHTS LAW (2014); Hathaway, *supra* note 4.

[10] Andrew K. Woods, *Moral Judgments and International Crimes: The Disutility of Desert*, 52 VA. J. INT'L L. 633 (2012).

[11] *See, e.g.*, SIMMONS, *supra* note 9 (evaluating state compliance with treaty commitments to protect civil and political rights and finding modest gains); Yonatan Lupu, *Best Evidence: The Role of Information in Domestic Judicial Enforcement of International Human Rights*

commitments to basic rights – typically only civil and political rights.[12] The results are both clear and relatively unsurprising: there is little evidence that states are strongly influenced by their rights commitments.[13]

10.1.1 *Asking the Wrong Questions*

There is a long line of international relations and international law scholarship about whether rights matter, and this scholarship took a particular turn toward state compliance with rights commitments. As Larry Helfer noted over a decade ago, "[q]uestions of compliance dominate international human rights law."[14] Kal Raustiala and Anne-Marie Slaughter, writing the same year, noted that compliance is a near-central feature of the scholarship at the intersection of international relations international law.[15] Writing before this scholarship really took off, Chayes and Chayes warned that "[t]he general level of compliance with international agreements cannot be empirically verified" and that perfect compliance is not the goal.[16]

But this warning was not heeded. Today, there is more of a focus on compliance than ever before – and many scholars seek to answer these compliance questions with quantitative tools. Some of the quantitative rights scholarship seeks to answer exceedingly broad questions, such as, "do rights matter?" or, "have rights failed?"[17] For example, Chilton and Versteeg ask whether constitutional rights against torture have "failed," and conclude that

  Agreements, 67 INT'L ORG. 469 (2013) (finding that state commitments to the ICCPR have not significantly improved state practices); Hathaway, *supra* note 4.

[12] These include the International Covenant on Civil and Political Rights (ICCPR), the Convention on the Elimination of All Forms of Discrimination Against Women (CEDAW), and the Convention Against Torture and Other Cruel, Inhuman or Degrading Treatment or Punishment (CAT). Few studies included the International Convention on the Elimination of All Forms of Racial Discrimination (CERD), the Convention on the Rights of the Child (CRC), or the International Covenant on Economic, Social and Cultural Rights (ICESCR).

[13] One of the features that international law and constitutional law share is the lack of strong enforcement mechanisms. There are many other striking similarities. For a summary, see Daryl J. Levinson & Jack L. Goldsmith, *Law for States: International Law, Constitutional Law, Public Law*, 122 HARV. L. REV. 1791 (2009).

[14] Lawrence R. Helfer, *Overlegalizing Human Rights: International Relations Theory and the Commonwealth Caribbean Backlash Against Human Rights Regimes*, 102 COLUM. L. REV. 1832, 1834 (2002).

[15] Kal Raustiala & Anne-Marie Slaughter, *International Law, International Relations and Compliance*, *in* HANDBOOK OF INTERNATIONAL RELATIONS 538 (Walter Carlsnaes, Thomas Risse & Beth Simmons eds., 2002).

[16] Abram Chayes & Antonia Handler Chayes, *On Compliance*, 47 INT'L ORG. 175 (1993).

[17] *See* sources cited *supra* note 7.

they have because torture persists, even in states that have committed to a right against torture – either in the form of a constitutional commitment or international treaty.[18] At some level, of course, asking this question makes sense: surely the point of a right against torture is to eradicate it, so if torture persists then we might wonder what use the right serves. But in a very significant sense, this is very much the wrong question to ask.

This approach to state commitments to human rights is exceedingly narrow. Rather than treat rights as a vehicle for airing political grievances, or a language for motivating social movements, the quantitative rights scholars treat rights as a simple promise by the state not to behave a certain way. This is convenient for quantitative scholarship, of course, because we can measure how states behave and whether that behavior is consistent with their stated commitments. But this narrow conception of rights paints an extremely shallow picture of the politics of rights.

Rights are not just a promise from the state. They can also be: a language for articulating grievances; a tool for building a social movement; a mast-tying device for leaders of a country; a general aspirational goal; and more. If people articulate their grievances in terms of rights, and build social movements out of those rights, and politicians are elected or not based on their views about those rights, it would hardly be fair to conclude that the rights themselves do not make a difference, only because the state's behavior is not reflective of its commitments.

10.1.2 *Seeking Answers in the Wrong Place*

10.1.2.1 Restrictive Independent Variable

To measure whether rights work, many scholars focus narrowly on what Beth Simmons calls "lawlike commitment[s]."[19] The independent variable for quantitative study, then, is a commitment that has the hallmarks of legalization – meaning a commitment that may be binding and or may delegate authority for interpretation and enforcement to a third party.[20] Focusing on lawlike commitments makes sense from the perspective of empirical research design. It is far simpler to look at state commitments and ask how they influence state behavior than to attempt to explain how norms

---

[18] Chilton & Versteeg, *The Failure of Constitutional Torture Prohibitions, supra* note 7.

[19] *See* SIMMONS, *supra* note 9, at 7.

[20] *See* Kenneth W. Abbott et al., *The Concept of Legalization*, 54 INT'L ORG. 401, 404–08 (2000) (describing international legalization as a feature that can be modulated along three axes: precision, obligation, and delegation).

influence state action. But one wonders how much is gained from such a study if common sense already tells us that a state's commitments are unlikely, in the short term, to be a significant direct influence on that state's behavior toward its citizens.

The mechanism presumed by quantitative rights scholars is as follows: states make a commitment to treat their citizens a certain way and then observers measure the state's actions against their commitments and shame them to encourage better behavior.[21] This is how the advocacy tactic known as "shame-and-blame" works.[22] Yet this is only one possible mechanism for how rights might have meaning, and it is hardly the only or even the dominant way that human rights are likely to influence state behavior.

For example, this model does little to explain why states comply with international laws to which they have not committed and to which they are not bound. For example, the US government voluntarily grants certain humanitarian protections to armed combatants, even though it is not compelled to under the laws of armed conflict.[23] There are many possible explanations for this behavior – explanations that have to do with epistemic communities, audience costs, and the influence of legal norms – but they do not have much to do with the state's legal commitments. Focusing only on the state's commitment ignores other ways that law can influence state practice.

In the real world of human rights advocacy, for example, it appears not to matter much which human rights agreements are legally binding. Advocates will take a state to task for violating human rights regardless of whether the target state has made a commitment not to violate the rights in question. For example, China has not ratified the ICCPR, yet advocates are as critical of Chinese government efforts to limit free expression as they are of states that have made a "binding" commitment to freedom of expression; if anything, they are *more* critical of China's measures to control speech. If, say, China were to ratify the ICCPR next year, would we expect it to be suddenly easier for human rights organizations to influence the state? That seems doubtful. States are criticized for their human rights record independent of their treaty

---

[21] *See* SIMMONS, *supra* note 9, at 7 (noting that lawlike commitments "raise expectations of political actors in new ways").
[22] *See* Kenneth Roth, *Defending Economic, Social and Cultural Rights: Practical Issues Faced by an International Human Rights Organization*, 26 HUM. RTS. Q. 63, 67 (2004) (explaining the shame-and-blame methodology).
[23] For a recent example, see Marty Lederman, *Of So-Called "Folk" International Law and Not-So-Grey Zones*, LAWFARE BLOG (October 2, 2014), http://justsecurity.org/15830/folk-international-law-grey-zones/ (discussing the debate over the merits and effects of the White House's 2013 Presidential Policy Guidance, which purports to offer stricter humanitarian protections to combatants than required under international law).

obligations, and this suggests that human rights advocacy does not directly depend on a state's lawlike commitments.

Perhaps a better inquiry would be to interrogate the relationship between the "legalization" of human rights norms through these instruments and the spread of (and political use of) those norms. This is no easy thing to study; it would require a decent way to measure the spread of human rights norms – both the breadth and the depth of their adoption, something like a global saturation rate – as well as a more realistic mechanism to explain the relationship between norms and law.

10.1.2.2 Restrictive Dependent Variable

Quantitative rights scholars also tend examine a simplistic dependent variable: state practice toward its citizens. State practice, whatever it tells us, is far too narrow to answer the question of whether human rights law matters. This is so for at least three reasons. First, state practice only captures a part of the overall human rights picture. Second, most large indicators of human rights only capture civil and political rights, and even then only certain political rights. And third, country-level indicators of rights practices are notoriously flawed metrics. Let us consider each.

The first problem is that most quantitative rights studies rely on datasets that measure *state practice*, not overall human rights conditions. For example, the most highly regarded dataset used by scholars studying the efficacy of international human rights law is the CIRI dataset compiled by Cingranelli, Richards, and Clay.[24] This dataset is explicitly limited to government actions taken related to human rights, and it excludes the actions of NGOs, INGOs, corporations, and individuals to improve human rights.[25] One cannot get an accurate sense of whether human rights are thriving in a particular state only looking to how the state behaves. Not all human rights issues are a function of state behavior, so focusing exclusively on state practice will miss many important data points about the state of human rights in a given place.

---

[24] *See* Chilton & Posner, *supra* note 5.
[25] *See* David L. Cingranelli & David L. Richards, *The Cingranelli-Richards (CIRI) Human Rights Data Project Coding Manual*, CIRI HUMAN RIGHTS DATA PROJECT (May 20, 2014), http://www.humanrightsdata.com/p/data-documentation.html (last visited Sept. 23, 2014) ("A country's human rights conditions constitute the whole universe of human rights-related events happening in a country. The state of a country's human rights conditions can be caused by all kinds of things aside from that country's government: foreign companies, domestic non-state actors such as guerilla groups, and so forth. CIRI only codes the practices of the government, not the overall human rights conditions of a country.").

For example, the human right to health is not typically captured in quantitative metrics of state human rights practice. For example, handwashing with soap is largely a function of individual choices – not state treatment of its citizens – yet it has enormous implications for overall rates of health. Many countries struggle to contain communicable diseases that are easily eradicated when people regularly wash their hands with soap. This is true even where soap and clean water are widely available, and where public awareness about the utility of soap use is high.[26] So how to increase soap use? One study found that the most effective technique to encourage handwashing with soap was to link soap use with feelings of disgust, and to encourage that feeling after toilet use.[27] A pilot project in Ghana ran ads designed to make people have an urge to wash their hands after visiting the bathroom. (One of the ads showed a purple stain on someone's hands that would only go away after washing with soap.) The ads appear to have been effective: in the communities exposed to the advertisements, soap use after toilet use was up by 13 percent, and soap use before eating was up 41 percent.[28]

This kind of improvement – which would matter to anyone studying health and human rights in Ghana – would not register on a standard human rights indicator. The relevant change in these cases was individual behavior change, not state behavior change, and it was mediated by a partnership between a corporation and several academics. This sort of intervention is unlikely to be measured by a dependent variable that focuses on state practice toward its citizens. Moreover, interventions of this sort are unlikely to be directly tied to Ghana's signature on one of the international legal instruments guaranteeing a human right to health.

The second reason that human rights studies are too narrow is that they tend to focus exclusively on civil and political rights (CPRs), and they tend to ignore economic and social rights (ESCRs). This makes a certain amount of sense from the perspective of study design: CPR violations are easier to identify than violations of ESCRs, which may be more diffuse and harder to link to a particular cause. For example, it is relatively easy to show that a state has violated the right of freedom of expression when it censors newspapers and television broadcasts, whereas it is much harder to

[26] *See* Beth E. Scott, David W. Lawson & Val Curtis, *Hard to Handle: Understanding Mothers' Handwashing Behaviour in Ghana*, 22 HEALTH POL'Y & PLAN. 216 (2007).
[27] *See* Beth E. Scott et al., *Health in Our Hands, But Not in Our Heads: Understanding Hygiene Motivation in Ghana*, 22 HEALTH POL'Y & PLAN. 225 (2007).
[28] Charles Duhigg, *Warning: Habits May Be Good for You*, N.Y. TIMES, July 13, 2008, at B6.

show exactly how the state violated an individual's right to education or health.[29]

Better than a measure of state actions, perhaps, would be a measure of human flourishing along certain rights dimensions. Rather than attempt to tick through a series of binary qualities about a state – do the state's citizens have the right to vote? Do they have freedom of expression? – a better approach would attempt to capture overall human welfare in the state.

One of the starker absurdities of the modern human rights regime is the fact that China gets essentially no credit for its advances in human rights. If economic rights mean anything, they ought to mean improving the chances of finding work that pays a living wage. China has actively pursued state policies that benefit a fast-growing economy that has lifted hundreds of millions of people out of poverty – perhaps one of the bigger human rights accomplishments of the last century – and yet China is typically portrayed (exclusively) as a rogue state when it comes to human rights.[30]

This is reflected in human rights advocates' statements about China, but also in scholarship about China's human rights record. The CIRI dataset, for example, gives the impression that human rights in China have not improved much in the last thirty years. That is because the dataset only measures a tiny portion of the ESCRs – workers' rights and women's rights – and on these two measures of economic rights, the CIRI dataset gives China the same score for every year from 1981 to 2010.[31] Any measure of human rights that does not adequately reflect the advances of China's economy is too narrow to be meaningfully considered comprehensive.

Finally, even if one cared only about civil and political rights, the indicators used to evaluate a state's rights record are notoriously blunt instruments that often do not reflect important changes in society. Consider the example of speech and assembly rights in China – the enjoyment of which have changed over the years as state regulators have adapted to a maturing Internet. When a series of train crashes occurred in 2011, Chinese citizens banded together using microblogging services to demand safer public housing and transportation, and the government responded.[32] This kind of citizen speech, assembly,

[29] *See* MERRY, *supra* note 8, at 165 (noting that until very recently, the best indicators focused exclusively on civil and political rights).
[30] Search online for the term "China Human Rights" and you will not find websites celebrating China's economic growth. *See, e.g.,* https://www.google.com/search?q=china+human+rights.
[31] *See* David Cingranelli, David L. Richards & K. Chad Clay, *The CIRI Human Rights Dataset,* CIRI HUMAN RIGHTS DATA PROJECT (2014), http://www.humanrightsdata.com.
[32] *See* Ananth Krishnan, *China's Middle-Class Raises Its Voice on Train Crash,* HINDU (July 31, 2011), http://www.thehindu.com/news/international/chinas-middleclass-raises-its-voice-on-train-crash/article2311361.ece.

274 Andrew Keane Woods

and advocacy, represents an advancement in civil and political rights in China – something not much imaginable twenty or thirty years ago. Yet the CIRI dataset gives China a score of "0" on freedom of association for every year going back thirty years. Any metric that does not capture this shift in China's citizenry toward greater freedom to associate is not adequately measuring the extent to which people need the protections guaranteed them by international human rights law.

10.1.2.3 Short Time Horizons

How long after a state makes a commitment to a particular right should we expect to see change? In a year? In ten years? In a hundred years? The answer likely depends on what is being measured. If the measure is of a more powerful political rhetoric for advocacy, then we may see successful campaigns very soon after states make rights commitments.[33] But if the goal is narrowly defined as shaping state behavior, it may be too early to tell whether the law has failed or succeeded. It seems unreasonable to expect that state practice would change significantly five years after signing a treaty, and it seems even more unreasonable to say that the legal regime has failed outright if state practice has not changed in that time frame.

In fact, there is some evidence that longer time horizons change the results of quantitative rights studies. Chilton and Versteeg look at constitutional rights against torture on a ten-year time horizon.[34] But as they acknowledge, this may not be enough time to register any meaningful change in state behavior. As Elkins, Ginsburg, and Melton have shown, attempts to study state commitments to rights without very careful attention to time effects – both long time horizons and period effects – will have errors.[35]

The same is true in the domestic setting, where laws are considerably easier to enforce. Core civil rights like the right to vote have taken years to be implemented – and there is still a great deal of work – yet few would say that universal suffrage in the United States failed. In the early days of the United

---

[33] *See* Emilie M. Hafner-Burton & James Ron, *Human Rights Institutions, Rhetoric and Efficacy*, 44 J. PEACE RES. 379 (2007) (summarizing literature demonstrating that human rights rhetoric is more influential than ever).

[34] *See* Chilton & Versteeg, *The Failure of Constitutional Torture Prohibitions*, *supra* note 7, at 429.

[35] *See* Zachary Elkins, Tom Ginsburg & James Melton, *Response: Comments on Law and Versteeg's* The Declining Influence of the United States Constitution, 87 N.Y.U. L. REV. 2088, 2091 (2012) (showing that Law and Versteeg mistakenly draw conclusions based on a dataset that starts with WWII, but extending the dataset back another hundred years yields different results).

States, when many of the rights guaranteed in the Bill of Rights had little practical meaning, would it have been fair to say that the Constitution had failed? That would have been both premature and unrealistic in terms of what to expect from a constitution. It is similarly premature and too demanding of basic rights – especially those that have only recently been adopted – to point to state practice in light of state rights commitments and declare that the rights themselves have failed. Perhaps in a hundred years we will have a better answer to the question.[36] But if it really does take a hundred years to study the effects of rights commitments on state behavior, then we have a measurement problem because there is very little reliable data on country practices going back that far.

10.2 UNQUANTIFIABLE PROBLEMS

Some problems simply do not lend themselves to quantitative inquiries. For example, what can quantitative studies tell us about the fact that rights advocates are overly motivated by a concern with rights violations (a negative focus) rather than creative ways of engendering rights flourishing (a positive focus)? Or the fact that much of rights advocacy is built around an idea of moral outrage – and outrage is a dangerous, often unpredictable emotion? To some, these are the most pressing problems in the rights regime, and quantitative research does not seem to offer meaningful insights into these problems.

10.2.1 *The Commitment Fetish*

Human rights and civil rights advocates' primary mode of advocacy is to secure public commitments against which they can measure the state's behavior.[37] Compliance with commitments becomes a fetish on its own, independent of the promotion of the underlying norm. Worse, it seems, is that rights groups sometimes seek to secure commitments to basic rights, even where doing so could actually jeopardize the rights themselves from being fulfilled.

Consider an example. Facebook is widely assumed to be considering establishing an Internet presence in China.[38] Knowing that this is the case,

---

[36] Sally Merry suggests that in fact the longer that time passes, the more resistant indicators are to change. *See* MERRY, *supra* note 8, at 7–8 (describing the "temporal dimensions" of indicators, which are slow to develop and slow to change).

[37] Roth, *supra* note 22, at 63, 67 (describing the core rights advocacy method as name-and-shame).

[38] *See* Jessi Hempel, *Facebook's China Problem*, FORTUNE (Sept. 24, 2012), https://fortune.com /2012/09/10/facebooks-china-problem/.

human rights groups have been pressuring Facebook to abandon its "real name" policy – which prohibits user aliases – on the grounds that such policies are bad for human rights activists in repressive regimes.[39] Facebook has resisted these efforts, insisting it is a politically neutral platform for communication, rather than a human rights technology.[40] However, there is evidence that the firm has privately taken steps to create aliases for democracy activists in authoritarian states.[41] Such a situation may actually be optimal for the promotion of human rights: Facebook says it will not go out of its way to help human rights activists, thereby making it less likely that the online service will be blocked in repressive regimes, where the company can engage in foot-dragging and other steps to resist government requests for information that ultimately benefit activists. Assuming that Facebook and related services would be kicked out of the repressive regime if they announced their commitment to helping human rights activists, those activists should prefer that Facebook be either inexpressive or hypocritical about human rights. Not only is Facebook better situated to provide services if they are in a country, but the aliases that activists seek are worth more if no one knows they are aliases. In this scenario, Facebook's reticence about online activism gives it a measure of plausible deniability to tell the repressive state that it is not directly inciting activism there. Yet human rights activist organizations like Human Rights Watch still want Facebook to make a commitment to human rights, even though doing so would be suboptimal from the standpoint of maximizing the promotion of human rights in China.[42]

10.2.2 *Narrow Focus on Rights Violations*

One seeming problem with today's human rights regime is advocates' near-obsessive focus on rights violations, and in particular civil and political rights

---

[39] See Kenneth Roth, *Letter to Mr. Mark Zuckerberg, Chairman and CEO of Facebook, Regarding Human Rights Considerations Before Entering China Market*, HUM. RTS. WATCH (June 3, 2011, 4:30 PM), https://www.hrw.org/news/2011/06/03/letter-mr-mark-zuckerberg-chairman-and-ceo-facebook-regarding-human-rights (asking whether Facebook would alter its real name policy if the company were to enter China).

[40] Verne G. Kopytoff, *Sites Like Twitter Absent from Free Speech Pact*, N.Y. TIMES, Mar. 6, 2011, at B4.

[41] See Alexis Madrigal, *The Inside Story of How Facebook Responded to Tunisian Hacks*, ATLANTIC (Jan. 24, 2011), http://www.theatlantic.com/technology/archive/2011/01/the-inside-story-of-how-facebook-responded-to-tunisian-hacks/70044/.

[42] My conversations with both technology firms and human rights groups, including Human Rights Watch, suggest that this is not strategic behavior by both groups who are secretly "in" on the strategy to trick China.

violations committed by identifiable perpetrators. Rights advocates' backwards looking orientation is narrowly concerned with identifying rights violations to the detriment of other forms of rights promotion. This is partly a consequence of the nature of rights law, which can be difficult to legislate and administer but comparatively easy to judge.

One problem with a violations-centric approach to rights is that it takes the universe of potential human rights claims and reduces it down to an identifiable set of things that can be measured as violations. This means that rights promotion is seen through the political and legal lens of accountability and justice – backwards looking, often retributive – rather than a forward looking and consequentialist analysis of optimal policies. If a regulator has a fixed budget to spend on rights promotion, and she is given a choice between better training for police investigators and prosecuting past episodes of police brutality, the crime-and-justice approach is to take the latter course, even where it is unclear the prosecution will accomplish much in human rights terms.

This has a number of unfortunate effects on the promotion of human rights. First, it orients the human rights regime to ignore perpetrator-less rights abuses – those abuses that are difficult to pin on a single, identifiable perpetrator – a potential defendant in a human rights trial. Since ESCRs are harder to pin on an individual perpetrator than CPRs, they tend to get much less attention from rights advocates.[43] Using the same hypothetical $100 and giving a human rights bureaucrat the choice between buying and distributing rice to those in need and punishing bad actors, the standard approach is to take the latter path – even where there is no evidence that doing so will mean fewer human rights violations.

This focus also leads to a reliance on courts rather than other, perhaps better-situated institutions. Courts are good at resolving disputes between two parties; they are bad tools for untangling complex social phenomena and crafting sweeping social policy. Yet in the international human rights context, they are asked to do just that. Because calls for accountability must not only make a claim about a violation and a violator, but also that actor's role in creating the violation, they tend to focus on individual bad actors and ignore social situations that are on the whole harmful to the promotion of human rights.

Why does the modern rights regime exhibit these worrying features? Part of the explanation lies in the very nature of rights. Rights call to mind both bright moral lines and entitlements against the state – two things that

---

[43] Roth, *supra* note 22, at 67.

exacerbate these tendencies.[44] But today's basic rights regime seems to exhibit these features to a greater degree than one might have predicted. The best explanation for this is that human rights law – the regime, its courts, its advocates – appears to be modeled on domestic criminal law. It looks at human rights violations and asks: Who is the victim? Who is the defendant? Where and when do we go to trial? It was not always inevitable that human rights violations would be criminalized. As international criminal scholar Cherif Bassiouni notes, "The three major Allies, Great Britain, the US, and the USSR ... did not start out with the clear intention of establishing international judicial bodies to prosecute accused offenders, whether at Nuremberg or Tokyo."[45] Yet today, these bodies are central institutions for regulating the worst rights abuses – specifically, crimes against humanity, war crimes, and genocide.[46]

10.2.3 Moral Outrage

Another problematic aspect of rights advocacy – one largely ignored by quantitative inquiries – is the outsized role given to moral outrage. Through fact-finding missions, press releases, shaming campaigns, and criminal trials, rights activists incite and stoke outrage among the public for rights violations. This makes good sense, of course. Advocates hope to arouse strong retributive impulses to gather the political will to prosecute international human rights abuses.[47] For the most part, this use of moral outrage is celebrated in the literature. The conventional wisdom suggests that because moral intuitions can be harnessed for political power, human rights advocates and policy-makers should embrace them.[48]

---

[44] For an account of how rights cause people to think in nonconsequentialist ways, see Joshua D. Greene, The Terrible, Horrible, No Good, Very Bad Truth About Morality and What to Do About It (2002) (unpublished Ph.D. dissertation, Princeton University), available at http://www.wjh.harvard.edu/~jgreene/GreeneWJH/Greene-Dissertation.pdf.

[45] CHERIF BASSIOUNI, CRIMES AGAINST HUMANITY: HISTORICAL EVOLUTION AND CONTEMPORARY APPLICATION 113 (2011).

[46] I focus in particular on these three "international crimes" and do not address transnational crimes. These are the crimes laid out in the Rome Statute, which created the International Criminal Court. See Rome Statute of the International Criminal Court art. 5, July 17, 1998, 2187 U.N.T.S. 900 [hereinafter Rome Statute]. I do not discuss here the crime of aggression, which is not yet an actionable offense in the International Criminal Court.

[47] See generally STANLEY COHEN, STATES OF DENIAL: KNOWING ABOUT ATROCITIES AND SUFFERING (2001) (describing the tactics that human rights advocates use to arouse sympathy for victims of faraway suffering, a particularly difficult task given that audiences are bombarded daily with images of suffering in the news).

[48] See, e.g., Richard Rorty, Human Rights, Rationality and Sentimentality, in ON HUMAN RIGHTS 111 (Stephen Shute & Susan Hurley eds., 1993).

But a significant body of knowledge shows that moral outrage can crowd out more deliberative thinking, leading people to make suboptimal policy decisions – policy decisions they would not defend under cooler conditions.[49] Psychologists elegantly demonstrated this with an experiment about a hypothetical set of damages awards.[50] Subjects were given a fact pattern detailing the evidence of a tort and asked to determine damage awards – the experimental group received a fact pattern that was designed to evoke strong feelings of moral outrage while the treatment group received a similar but more neutrally worded fact pattern.[51] After reading charged fact patterns that evoked strong intuitions like moral outrage and indignation, respondents set very high damage awards – both when they were told the high damages would have no effect on the company's behavior and, separately, when they were told the high damages would have *harmful* effects, such as forcing the company to stop manufacturing its other socially beneficial products.[52] In this scenario, subjects who were outraged were *willing to create a net social harm* in order to satisfy their deep retributive impulses.

Human rights advocates rarely tell stories of human flourishing. To the contrary, they traffic in stories of rights violations. These stories encourage sympathy for the victim and they encourage outrage against the identifiable perpetrator.[53] It would be easy to dismiss this as advocacy strategy with no real impact on real-world policy, but legal institutions respond to and foment this outrage. This is not just a feature of advocacy. International criminal courts are tasked with identifying the individuals who bear the greatest responsibility for otherwise diffuse but terrible group crimes.[54] From the standpoint of moral outrage, that individuation is not ideal. Studies have shown that, just as people are more sympathetic and generous toward identifiable victims, they are more punitive with identifiable wrongdoers, even when the identity of the

---

[49] *See generally* Cass Sunstein, *Some Effects of Moral Indignation on Law*, 33 Vt. L. Rev. 405 (2009) (surveying the literature on moral outrage and its implications for law and policy).

[50] This description is taken from Andrew K. Woods, *The Limits of Moral Intuitions for Human Rights Advocacy*, 9 Law & Ethics Hum. Rts. 91 (2015).

[51] *See* Jonathan Baron & Ilana Ritov, *Intuitions about Penalties and Compensation in the Context of Tort Law*, 7 J. Risk & Uncertainty 17 (1993) [hereinafter Baron & Ritov, *Intuitions*]; Ilana Ritov & Jonathan Baron, *Reluctance to Vaccinate: Omission Bias and Ambiguity*, 3 J. Behav. Decision Making 263, 275 (1993) [hereinafter Ritov & Baron, *Reluctance to Vaccinate*].

[52] Baron & Ritov, *Intuitions, supra* note 51; Ritov & Baron, *Reluctance to Vaccinate, supra* note 51.

[53] *See* Makau Mutua, *Savages, Victims, and Saviors: The Metaphor of Human Rights*, 42 Harv. Int'l L.J. 201 (2001).

[54] *See* Mark A. Drumbl, *Collective Guilt and Individual Punishment: The Criminality of Mass Atrocity*, 99 Nw. U. L. Rev. 539, 581 (2005).

wrongdoer is irrelevant to the wrongness of the act.[55] The international criminal regime, in its effort to individuate justice, is in fact creating special distortion effects – unique opportunities for moral outrage to crowd out deliberative thinking.

10.2.4 *Naïve Realism*

One of the costs of the language of human rights is that it encourages simplistic thinking about right and wrong. Naïve realism, a term coined by psychologist Lee Ross, is the idea that people tend to think the world can only be the way they see it, and to dismiss competing explanations or competing values as wrong or insincere.[56] When people take a naïve realist view about a subject, they are much less likely to compromise with someone (whose view they see as either stupid or biased).

   This is well supported in the social psychological literature.[57] One experiment by Ross showed that both pro-Arab audiences and pro-Israeli audiences watching the same news coverage of the Israeli invasion of Lebanon in 1982 thought the coverage was biased against them. Similar results were found with Dartmouth and Princeton fans watching the same football game and judging the fairness of the game. A related study showed that when Palestinians and Israelis were given policy proposals, both sides preferred the others' proposals – but only when they thought it was in fact being proposed by their side.[58] The policy choices were less salient than the *source* of the policies. The naïve realist scholarship teaches us that we tend to see our own way of looking at the world as objective, and this mindset makes it harder to negotiate compromise.[59] When we see an issue in moral realist terms – black and white, right and wrong – we become emboldened and less willing to negotiate.

   This is the sort of bias that human rights advocacy amplifies. Rights stories take complex situations of harm and attempt to sort out the good from the bad. As admirable as that may be from a corrective justice perspective, it also introduces costs in the form of emboldening political rivals to see their conflict

---

[55]   *See* Deborah Small & George Loewenstein, *The Devil You Know: The Effects of Identifiability on Punishment*, 18 J. BEHAV. DECISION MAKING 311 (2005).
[56]   *See* Lee Ross & Andrew Ward, *Naïve Realism: Implications for Social Conflict and Misunderstanding, in* VALUES AND KNOWLEDGE (Edward S. Reed, Elliot Turiel & Terrence Brown eds., 1996) (describing how naïve realist thinking emboldens rivals and inhibits meaningful negotiation).
[57]   This description is taken from Woods, *supra* note 50.
[58]   Susan Hackley et al., *Psychological Dimensions of the Israeli Settlements Issue: Endowments and Identities*, 21 NEGOT. J. 209 (2005).
[59]   *See* Ross & Ward, *supra* note 56.

in naïve realist terms. When an armed conflict breaks out, an international human rights monitor will visit the conflict zone and produce a thoughtful report detailing all of the wrongs committed by each side. What happens with this report? It is immediately used by the public affairs officers on each side of the conflict to say, "see how horrible our enemies are?" and to recruit support for their efforts in the conflict. This may not be ideal from the perspective of maximizing human rights protections: it may lead to worse atrocities, a larger conflict, and a longer conflict.

10.3 TOWARD A NEW WAY TO PROMOTE WELLBEING

If quantitative scholars and rights advocates are both overly concerned with state commitments to individual civil and political rights violations – and this focus misses some of the bigger problems with the rights regime today – what is the alternative? What might a different model look like? Let us consider a few radical (and briefly sketched) ideas.

10.3.1 *Rights Violations As Accidents*

If today's rights advocacy suffers from being overly moralistic, perhaps a more neutral approach would be better. One model is the way the tort system addresses the costs of accidents. Moral wrongs are present in torts, of course, but the dominant approach in the regime is one of harm reduction. This presents a number of benefits over the existing, largely criminal model of rights advocacy. First, such an approach would be forward looking in a way that criminal law often is not. Rather than treat rights violations as opportunities for shaming, a torts approach might treat rights violations as costly accidents to avoid going forward. Second, a torts approach would encourage negotiated settlements, rather than binary, up-or-down determinations of guilt or innocence. And such an approach may also place less emphasis on identifying winners and losers. One potential benefit of focusing so explicitly on deterrence is that it may paper over clashes of cultural values, where a retributive approach would likely exacerbate it.[60] There are many obvious objections to such an approach. For one, we may fear that pricing human rights abuses would crowd out normative objections.[61] And this approach still depends to an enormous degree on courts to implement human rights policy.

---

[60] *See* Woods, *supra* note 10, at 646 (applying Kahan's idea of the secret ambition of deterrence in the context of international criminal law).
[61] *See* Uri Gneezy & Aldo Rustichini, *A Fine is a Price*, 22 J. LEGAL STUD. 1 (2000).

10.3.2 *Rights As a Development Challenge*

Another option would be to borrow from the literature on economic development. There are several advantages to such an approach. Rather than focus on individuals – individual perpetrators or individual victims – development economists tend to evaluate policies in terms of total welfare maximization across a swath of society. This approach would naturally focus on structural features that lead to human rights abuses – things like poverty, food scarcity, and political instability – and less on particular instances of rights violations. Accordingly, the development approach would likely emphasize economic rights as much or more than civil political rights.

To implement such an approach would require sweeping and politically impractical changes to the existing human rights regime. For example, courts would likely play a much smaller role than they currently play in human rights policymaking. In fact, the only crimes that one might imagine being systematically addressed under a development model to human rights promotion might be incitement and related crimes where an individual is responsible for changing an entire social situation rather than directly violating another person's human rights.

There are costs associated with this approach, to be sure. Just as international human rights are criticized for being a western imposition, development aid from the north to the south suffers similar neocolonialist critiques. And with good reason; the track record of development aid is hardly confidence inspiring.[62] The argument for adopting a development-based approach to human rights is not that development aid "works"; rather, the argument is that we are getting better at determining what works and what does not. More importantly, we are learning this faster in the development context than in the human rights context. There is simply more experimentation in development – both entrepreneurship and experimental social science – than in international law for obvious reasons. Because it would be difficult to randomly assign treatment and experimental groups in law – and people would likely object to randomizing policies explicitly promising to deliver justice – it is difficult to gain convincing empirical data about, for example, amnesties as compared to prosecutions after mass atrocity. In development, rather than controlling for countless variables and attempting to draw a causal pathway back to some policy, scholars working in development can simply run an experiment.

---

[62] *See, e.g.,* WILLIAM EASTERLY, THE WHITE MAN'S BURDEN: WHY THE WEST'S EFFORTS TO AID THE REST HAVE DONE SO MUCH ILL AND SO LITTLE GOOD (2006).

10.3.3 *Rights As Humanitarianism*

A third model for human rights comes from humanitarian law. One actor in particular, the International Committee for the Red Cross (ICRC), has adopted a method of legal compliance that is radically at odds with the backwards-facing approach adopted by most human rights groups. Where human rights advocates uses public shaming to enforce international and constitutional legal commitments, the ICRC rarely names and shames the actors it seeks to influence, choosing instead to arrange private meetings, offering confidentiality and even secrecy.[63] This enables the ICRC to engage with and influence the practices of armed groups that otherwise might never agree to meet. Not only does the ICRC guarantee confidentiality, but it also remains purposefully ambiguous about its own legal interpretations of a particular armed conflict.[64] This runs contrary to the "shame and blame" model of advocacy pursued by many NGOs, and is "a compelling counter-narrative to international law's emphasis on inducing compliance through identification of violations via detailed interpretation of rules, followed by procedures for correction of them."[65] On this account, the ICRC's secrecy and ambiguity are crucial to the organization's success.[66] The ICRC fights – sometimes quite hard – to preserve this confidentiality, including refusing to disclose to courts of law the sources and details of ICRC investigations.[67]

For the human rights regime to adopt this approach, it would have to embrace unprincipled action – that is, celebrate (or tolerate) the times that states and corporations promote human rights *for the wrong reasons*.

---

[63] For a detailed overview of the role of secrecy in ICRC communications with combatants, see Steven R. Ratner, *Law Promotion Beyond Law Talk: The Red Cross, Persuasion, and the Laws of War*, 22 Eur. J. Int'l L. 459, 460 (2011) (noting that while human rights groups publicize and shame rights violations, the ICRC "rarely identifies any party, state or non-state, by name as violating international humanitarian law, including by keeping its application of the law secret; it leaves its legal position on many key issues ambiguous, sometimes even from the target of its discussions.").

[64] *Id.* at 474 (noting that ICRC "sometimes deliberately keeps its position on legal matters ambiguous").

[65] *Id.* at 505.

[66] *Id.* at 489–490 (noting the difficulty of measuring the success of particular ICRC strategies, partly because of the secrecy with which they are implemented, but that the identity of the organization is bound together with its embrace of secrecy and ambiguity).

[67] *See* Gabor Rona, *The ICRC Privilege Not to Testify: Confidentiality in Action*, 845 Int'l Rev. Red Cross 207 (2002); *see also* Jane Sutton, *ICRC Says Opening Its Guantanamo Files Would Set Dangerous Precedent*, Reuters (June 18, 2013), http://reut.rs/17wwALG.

10.4 CONCLUSION

I have tried, in this very brief chapter, to do three things. First, I tried to show
that existing quantitative approaches to studying human rights have significant
design flaws. Second, I tried to show that the biggest challenges for today's
rights regimes are qualitative in nature, and not easily evaluated by quantitative metrics. Finally, I gestured in the direction of new avenues for thinking
about the things that human rights seek to attain – improving human capabilities, welfare, and flourishing. Rather than count states' rights commitments and measure them against crude indicators of state conditions, a more
fruitful line of inquiry would be to ask whether law at all is the best tool for
improving human welfare.[68] This is the ultimate goal, after all, and it is largely
absent from inquiries about state commitments to international legal instruments. Those commitments are as much a symptom as they are a cause. They
relate to a movement that has growing political power at a time when some are
asking hard questions about the utility of the movement's rhetoric and tactics.

---

[68]   *See* Eric A. Posner, *Human Welfare, Not Human Rights*, 108 COLUM. L. REV. 1758 (2008)
      (arguing for a welfare treaty rather than one focused on individual rights).

Index

CPSIA information can be obtained
at www.ICGtesting.com
Printed in the USA
LVHW082004250321
682478LV00002B/209